The
READING
TEACHER'S
Survival Kit

Wilma H. Miller, Ed.D.

 JOSSEY-BASS
A Wiley Imprint
www.josseybass.com

Published by Jossey-Bass
A Wiley Imprint
989 Market Street, San Francisco, CA 94103-1741   www.josseybass.com

Jossey-Bass books and products are available through most bookstores. To contact Jossey-Bass directly call our Customer Care Department within the U.S. at 800-956-7739, outside the U.S. at 317-572-3986 or fax 317-572-4002.

Jossey-Bass also publishes its books in a variety of electronic formats. Some content that appears in print may not be available in electronic books.

Library of Congress Cataloging-in-Publication Data

Miller, Wilma H.
      The reading teacher's survival kit/Wilma H. Miller
          p. cm.
      Includes bibliographical references.
      ISBN 0-13-026202-1
      ISBN 0-13-042593-1 (layflat)
        1. Reading.   2. Teaching—Aids and devices.   I. Title.

LB1050.M553   2001
372.4—dc21   00-059000

Printed in the United States of America
FIRST EDITION
PB Printing 10 9 8 7 6 5 4 3 2

Dedication

Dedicated to the memory of my beloved parents,
William and Ruth Miller,
and
to my professional advisor and dear friend for nearly thirty years,
Win Huppuch, Vice President,
The Center for Applied Research in Education.

Acknowledgments

I would like to gratefully acknowledge a number of people who have made it possible for me to write this teacher resource. I first would like to acknowledge the memory of my mother, Ruth K. Miller, who worked with me on all my writing projects until the age of eighty. She remains an inspiration to me in all my writing projects.

I also would like to thank my former undergraduate and graduate students at Illinois State University for being a source of information and motivation for me for thirty years.

I would like to express my special gratitude to Susan Kolwicz, my editor at The Center for Applied Research in Education who has so competently worked with me on many writing projects. I would also like to take this opportunity to express my appreciation to Eileen Ciavarella for her illustrations used throughout the book, and to Diane Turso and Mariann Hutlak for their editorial and production expertise.

ABOUT THE AUTHOR

A former classroom teacher, Wilma H. Miller, Ed.D. has taught at the college level for thirty-three years. She completed her doctorate in reading at the University of Arizona under the direction of the late Dr. Ruth Strang, a nationally known reading authority.

Dr. Miller has contributed numerous articles to professional journals and is the author of more than twenty other works in the field of reading education. Among the latter are *Identifying and Correcting Reading Difficulties in Children* (1972), *Diagnosis and Correction of Reading Difficulties in Secondary School Students* (1973), *Reading Diagnosis Kit* (1975, 1978, 1986), "*Corrective Reading Skills Activity File*" (1977), *Reading Teacher's Complete Diagnosis & Correction Manual* (1988), *Reading Comprehension Activities Kit* (1990), *Complete Reading Disabilities Handbook* (1993), *Alternative Assessment Techniques for Reading & Writing* (1995), and *Ready-to-Use Activities and Materials for Improving Content Reading Skills* (1999) all published by The Center for Applied Research in Education.

She also is the author of an inservice aid for teachers entitled *Reading Activities Handbook* (1980); several textbooks for developmental reading, *The First R: Elementary Reading Today* (1977) and *Teaching Elementary Reading Today* (1983), published by Holt, Rinehart & Winston, Inc.; a guide to secondary reading instruction, *Teaching Reading in the Secondary School* (1974), published by Charles C. Thomas; and *Strategies for Developing Emergent Literacy* (2000) published by McGraw-Hill College Publishers.

THE PRACTICAL HELP
THAT THIS BOOK PROVIDES

I have been writing books about reading education for more than thirty years. During that time I often have emphasized that too many children are not learning to read so well as they should. In addition, many children do not value reading either for pleasure or information. This is still the case today as it was thirty years ago. Why are so many children failing to become good readers? The answer to that question is complex.

Many reasons can be given for the lack of good reading skills. Some of them are as follows: a home environment that does not stress reading, inadequate or improper reading instruction in school, learning disabilities, physical disabilities such as visual or hearing impairments, and emotional maladjustment, among many others. In a number of cases, the child's reading disability probably is the result of a combination of factors. However, with some exceptions, determining an exact cause may not be so important as providing reading instruction that will help the child learn to read better. Providing appropriate strategies, materials, games, and reproducibles for children with reading problems may be more important than determining the precise cause.

Providing such help for reading teachers and tutors is the primary focus of *The Reading Teacher's Survival Kit*. This teacher's resource contains many classroom-tested reading strategies, materials, games, and reproducibles that should help reading teachers and tutors most effectively meet the unique reading needs and interests of the children with whom they are working.

Because there are so many children in the United States who do not read well today, the federal government sponsors the *America Reads* program in which tutors work with children in the public schools who have reading difficulties. Such tutors often are not professionally trained, so they can benefit greatly from easy-to-understand and use resource books such as *The Reading Teacher's Survival Kit* which contains a wealth of ready-to-use materials. Other target populations for this teacher's resource are Title I reading teachers, special education teachers, teachers of culturally or linguistically diverse children, classroom reading teachers, paid or unpaid reading tutors, and family members and friends. All of these people should find the *Survival Kit* to be a reader-friendly book that contains countless practical ideas and materials.

The Reading Teacher's Survival Kit presents strategies and materials for implementing a *balanced reading program* that uses the unique strengths of whole language instruction and skills instruction, particularly phonics. In addition, the *Survival Kit* emphasizes the philosophy that virtually all children can learn to read adequately or effectively with appropriate properly paced instruction. This also is true of most children with special needs—they also should be able to learn to read adequately or very well. The philosophy of balanced reading instruction and reading success for all children permeates this entire book.

The first chapter of this resource provides an introduction, stressing the need for this book and its philosophy. It also presents some important principles for the reading teacher. Chapter 2 discusses assessing reading strengths and weaknesses, and provides important information about both standardized and informal (authentic) assessment. The first part of the chapter explains standardized reading tests of various types, while the major portion of the chapter presents many authentic ways of determining a child's reading competencies and weaknesses. It contains seven reproducible checklists for "kid-watching" or teacher observation, and enables the reader to use the running record and miscue analysis. In addition, the chapter contains a complete Individual Reading Inventory with reproducible graded word lists and passages from the preprimer level through the twelfth-grade reading level. Also included are reproducible copies of the San Diego Quick Assessment List, the Quick Survey Word List, and the El Paso Phonics Survey. In closing, the chapter also briefly discusses using portfolio assessment in any reading program.

The third chapter is devoted to improving ability in letter–name knowledge and sight word knowledge. It discusses both of these important reading skills in detail, providing many classroom-tested strategies for improving ability in each of them. For example, the chapter explains tracing strategies and describes the language-experience approach—both of which can be used to help children learn either letter names or sight words. It also contains games and reproducible activity sheets for improving ability in both of these reading skills. In addition, the chapter provides reproducible copies of the *Dolch Basic Sight Word List* and *The Instant Words*. Reading teachers and tutors will find this to be a very useful chapter especially for beginning readers.

Chapter 4 is devoted to improving ability in phonics, the reading skill that is currently receiving the greatest amount of emphasis. It briefly describes the importance of teaching phonics and explains the most common phonetic elements and rules. The chapter describes three commonly used phonic programs—*The Benchmark Word Identification Program, Hooked on Phonics—Learning to Read*, and *The Phonics Game*. The chapter presents numerous strategies and materials for improving ability in phonics, including the word wall, cross-checking word identification techniques, Elkonin boxes, Hinks Pinks, and a phonic strategy for children with learning disabilities. The chapter also contains games and reproducible activity sheets for reviewing phonics skills.

The fifth chapter explains how to improve ability in word structure and context. It provides classroom-tested strategies and materials for improving word structure, such as using the analogy strategy and rimes; teaching syllabication using the pattern approach; and using word roots, prefixes, and suffixes to create new words. It also includes a number of games and reproducibles for improving ability in word structure. This chapter also briefly describes context clues and presents a number of strategies and materials for improving ability in them. Some of these are wide reading, self-monitoring reading, variations of the cloze procedure, and using cryptology and mutilated messages. The chapter also includes four reproducible activity sheets that will improve context clue usage.

Chapter 6 is a very important chapter that describes how to improve vocabulary and comprehension skills. It first describes the "Cone of Experiences" for vocabulary development and then suggests a number of ways for improving ability in meaning vocabulary, including direct and second-hand experiences, wide reading of relevant materials, semantic mapping (webbing), scaffolding, a semantic features analysis grid, and word derivation. The chapter also includes several games and reproducibles for improving meaning vocabulary knowledge. This chapter then explains the different levels of reading comprehension in detail and suggests numerous strategies and materials that can be used to improve ability in the various elements of comprehension, including prediction strategies, story impressions, K-W-L and K-W-H-L, visual imagery, questioning strategies (QARs), and the herringbone technique. The chapter includes specific directions for constructing the following kinds of puppets which are effective in improving comprehension: sock puppets, paper bag puppets, stick puppets, and papier-mâché head puppets. The chapter concludes with a number of games and ready-to-use activity sheets for improving ability in comprehension.

The seventh chapter is a very important one designed to help the reader most effectively teach reading to students with special needs of various types. The chapter concisely describes the characteristics of children with learning disabilities (LD), attention deficit disorders (ADD), and attention deficit/hyperactivity disorders (ADHD). It also discusses English as a Second Language (ESL), Limited English Proficiency (LEP) and bilingual students, mildly mentally handicapped students, and students with visual and hearing impairments. The chapter then explains the inclusion philosophy, Individual Educational Plans (IEPs), and the least restrictive environment. Next, the chapter presents a number of useful guidelines for teaching reading to children with special needs of various kinds. A very important part of this chapter is the comprehensive list of trade books for diverse learners which readers will find especially helpful. The chapter also suggests strategies for teaching reading to culturally or linguistically diverse students, including whole language programs, the language-experience approach, cooperative learning groups, the Rosetta Stone technique, choral reading, and providing authentic experiences. The chapter concludes by presenting strategies for teaching reading to students with other special needs. It discusses mnemonic devices, multisensory approaches, using technology, the Carbo Approach, and Reading Recovery strategies, among others. Readers will find this chapter to be of special value because meeting children's unique needs is of great importance.

The last chapter of *The Reading Teacher's Survival Kit* is devoted to enlisting the support of family members and friends in helping students with reading. Thus, it is designed both for reading teachers, tutors, and the family members and friends of schoolchildren. First, it provides a number of suggestions for family members and friends that they can use in supporting the school reading program. Several are reading to the child, encouraging the child to read for pleasure and information, and seven steps to creating a literate home environment. Next, the chapter describes a number of activities that the reading teacher or tutor can do to help family members or friends participate in the reading program, including family literacy programs, reading workshops, parent–teacher conferences, teacher-made brochures, and a home–school library exchange. The chapter concludes with several reproducibles that can be used in supporting the school reading program including reading checklists for family members and friends at different grade levels, and a sample newsletter for family members and friends.

Readers will find the following to be unique about *The Reading Teacher's Survival Kit:*

➡ Published in a spiral-bound format that makes reproducing the material very easy.

➡ Focus on balanced reading instruction that capitalizes on the unique strengths of whole language instruction and skills approaches (especially the very important skill of phonics).

➡ Emphasis on the belief that almost all children can learn to read effectively with appropriate well-paced instruction.

➡ Discusses both standardized and informal (authentic) assessment, and provides many reproducible authentic assessment devices that include checklists, the running record, miscue analysis, a complete Individual Reading Inventory with graded word lists and passages, the San Diego Quick Assessment List, and the El Paso Phonics Survey.

➡ Suggestions on numerous interesting ways of improving ability in letter–name knowledge including games and reproducibles.

➡ Emphasis on the importance of sight word knowledge. Includes the reproducibles *Dolch Basic Sight Word List* and *The Instant Words.* Also suggested are numerous strategies for improving ability in that very important reading skill as well as games and reproducibles that can be used for this purpose.

➡ An entire chapter about how to teach phonics, an important and sometimes neglected reading skill. Important phonic elements and rules are explained in an easy-to-understand manner. The chapter also contains games and reproducibles which can be used to improve ability in this reading skill.

➡ Interesting suggestions for improving ability in both word structure and context. Numerous strategies, games, and materials will enable the reading teacher or tutor to teach these two reading skills successfully.

➡ Concise explanations of meaning vocabulary and reading comprehension. Suggests meaningful, interesting ways of improving both meaning vocabulary and comprehension. Effective comprehension is the cornerstone of the reading process, so this is a very important chapter.

➡ A very relevant chapter that is devoted to teaching reading to children with special needs of various kinds. Such a chapter is much needed by reading teachers and tutors today. This chapter includes many useful suggestions and materials for effectively teaching reading to children with unique needs. The comprehensive list of trade books included in this chapter should be especially helpful to reading teachers and tutors.

➡ A final chapter about how to enlist the support of family members and friends in the child's reading program. With the increased emphasis on effective home–school relationships, this chapter will be especially helpful to reading teachers and tutors.

After teaching and writing about reading for more than thirty years, I still remain optimistic that <u>all children can learn to read</u>. Competent reading skills are very important to the professional and personal lives of all children and adults. Certainly no one book can solve all of the reading problems that exist today. However, if *The Reading Teacher's Survival Kit* can be of significant help, it will have served its purpose well. It is my sincere hope that this *Kit* can be of very beneficial help to reading teachers and tutors as well as family members and friends.

Wilma H. Miller

CONTENTS

Chapter 1

INTRODUCTION

Do you know any adults who do not read so well as they might? Most of us do, and they seem to have great difficulty with tasks that are simple for people who read well. For example, such adults may have difficulty reading recipes, prescription labels, directions for assembling various items, and even survival words that may be necessary for their health and safety. Think of how different their lives might have been if they had learned to read effectively as children or even now as adults. In the past our schools have graduated far too many students who did not know *how to read effectively and who did not value reading for information and pleasure*. This should not have been the case, and it certainly should not be the case in the future.

Because there are far too many children today who do not read well, the federal government is now sponsoring the *America Reads* program, in which tutors work with children in the public schools who have reading difficulties. Such tutors often are not professionally trained and can greatly benefit from easy-to-understand and -implement resource books such as *The Reading Teacher's Survival Kit*, which contains a wealth of practical classroom-tested materials.

In addition, North American schools consistently are becoming more culturally diverse. For example, shortly after the year 2000, pupils who are African American, Latino, Asian, or Native American will constitute *one-third or more* of the entire school population. In a number of schools today such children already make up the majority of the school population. In addition, many more pupils currently are being designated as either learning disabled (LD), attention deficit disordered (ADD), or attention deficit/hyperactivity disordered (ADHD). Contemporary school administrators are not certain if the population of such children actually is increasing or if they are merely being identified more often than before. In any case, it is vital that each reading teacher be prepared to meet all of the diverse needs of children in contemporary schools as effectively as possible.

Teachers, family members, friends and the larger community should be more successful in teaching children both *how to read and to value reading for information and pleasure*. In the future everyone must have a good command of the higher-level reading skills in order to live successfully in the technological society that is now emerging. How will students and adults exist with only inadequate reading skills and no true motivation to read unless they are required to do so? No one teacher's resource book can include all of the strategies and materials that will accomplish this monumental task. However, the material that is contained in this book is a start toward helping children to learn the basic reading skills and to value reading both for information and pleasure.

THE TARGET POPULATION FOR
THE READING TEACHER'S SURVIVAL KIT

The Reading Teacher's Survival Kit is written in an easy-to-understand, reader-friendly manner. Therefore, it should be very easy to understand and to implement. One of its major target populations are Title I reading teachers. Special reading teachers often are called upon to work with children with various kinds of reading problems and many diverse types of cultural and linguistic backgrounds. Title I reading teachers need simple-to-understand and -implement reading strategies and materials that they can use to assess and correct reading disabilities. Title I reading teachers as well as reading specialists will find such materials in this resource book. The practical material contained in this book will save such teachers much time and effort and will be effective with the vast majority of children.

Special education teachers also will find the *Survival Kit* very helpful for a number of reasons. It contains concise but valuable descriptions of the various types of children with special needs. These are children with learning disabilities, attention deficit disorders, attention deficit/hyperactivity disorders, mild mental handicaps, visual impairments, hearing impairments, and speech and language impairments. In addition to the comprehensive descriptions of the various types of special needs, special education teachers will find many practical and effective teaching strategies and materials for teaching reading to these children. These materials should help special education teachers provide the best possible reading program for such children—a challenging but important task.

Teachers of children with other special needs, such as those who are culturally or linguistically diverse, also will find much material in the *Survival Kit* that will be beneficial to them. Such children are commonly found in contemporary classrooms, and their unique needs must be provided for. To give them less than the optimum reading instruction is to cheat both them and society. Chapter 7 contains a myriad of teaching strategies and materials that will help such teachers provide an effective reading program for culturally or linguistically diverse children. The chapter, for example, includes a comprehensive *list of multicultural literature* that is motivating and useful with such students.

Classroom reading teachers also will find the *Survival Kit* very helpful. Especially since the *inclusion movement*, classroom teachers are now being expected to teach reading to many children with diverse special needs. In a number of instances, they do not have the expertise that this difficult task requires. Classroom reading teachers may not have received the specialized training that would enable them to teach children with special needs. This *Survival Kit* provides such teachers with many strategies and materials that should enable them to provide effective instruction for all the children in their classes.

One important element of the target population of the *Survival Kit* are paid and volunteer reading tutors. Even well-trained and motivated professional reading teachers often need the assistance of both paid and unpaid volunteers to teach reading successfully to all children, especially those with various types of reading disabilities, learning disabilities, and other special needs. The federal government has acknowledged the importance of reading tutors in the *America Reads* program, in which a million reading tutors are being recruited to work with children who have various types of reading needs. A number of these novice reading tutors have minimal or no training in the teaching of reading, and they desperately need access to accurate and easy-to-read materials that will enable them to tutor effectively the children to whom they are assigned. Even without expertise or access to useful materials, a supportive and caring reading tutor often can help a child improve his or her reading skills dramatically. How much more effective then can such tutors be when they have access to reading strategies and materials that have been especially designed for children with different types of special needs. This *Survival Kit* provides a wealth of such material, much of which is reproducible and ready to use.

Often family members and friends do not know how to help children improve their reading skills. They would make the time to help them if they had access to proven strategies and materials. They may instead choose to do nothing or, perhaps even worse, they may spend their hard-earned money on a reading program (typically a phonics program) that research and experience has not shown to be beneficial for most children. Such programs are commonly advertised on television and radio and in newspapers and magazines. This *Survival Kit* contains simple-to-understand materials that family members and friends can use to help children with their reading.

NEED FOR *THE READING TEACHER'S SURVIVAL KIT*

Of course, many hundreds of thousands of children in North America are learning to read very well. In fact, some of them probably would learn to read adequately with mediocre instruction. However, thousands of children are not learning to read up to the limits of their capability. This includes children with average or above average intelligence, no real emotional maladjustment, and a good home environment. In addition, there are many children with special needs of various types who are not learning to read adequately. These may be children with special needs such as learning disabilities, physical disabilities, or cultural or linguistic diversity. The percentage of children who are reading below their potential grade level probably has remained stable over recent years. An average of about *15%* to *25%* of the children in rural, small-town, or suburban North America are said to be disabled in reading, while *50%* to *100%* of the children in inner cities may be disabled in reading.

There are many reasons for these troubling statistics. Because reading is a very complex process, it is difficult to arrive at a single cause for any child's reading problems. However, some of the causes may be one or more of the following: a home environment that did not provide many emergent literacy experiences (especially reading to the young child), inadequate or improper reading instruction (especially in first grade), family members who do not value and model reading for pleasure and information, learning disabilities of various kinds, physical disabilities such as visual or hearing impairments, or cultural or linguistic diversity. Most often, there are several causes for a child's difficulties in reading. Each of these causes reinforces the other(s) and adds to the child's problems.

In any case, there are far too many children in North American schools who are not reading so well as they should. This *Survival Kit* has been designed to help teachers, tutors, and family members help these children learn to read both for information and pleasure and to value reading as a worthwhile activity.

Unfortunately, there also is a need for the information contained in this *Survival Kit* since reading scores recently have been falling in a number of states. Perhaps the most well-publicized of these states is California, which now mandates that all children learn phonic elements and rules and that all instruction in school must be in standard English, the official language of the state.

It is obvious that there probably are a number of reasons for the reading test score decline in various states. Because reading is a complex process, it is simplistic to suggest that there is only one cause for the declining test scores. However, a number of reading specialists, school administrators, boards of education, and, most commonly, parents have stated that the widespread use of whole language programs with the corresponding deemphasis on phonics probably is the major culprit in declining test scores. Therefore, this *Survival Kit* places *appropriate emphasis* on phonic elements and rules as a very important, but not the only important, word identification technique. In addition to the material found in the *Kit* itself, there are two phonics workbooks containing reproducibles that the teacher can use to provide reinforcement in this important word identification strategy.

This *Survival Kit* emphasizes *balanced reading instruction,* in which the reading program uses the unique strengths of whole language instruction and skills instruction, particularly phonics instruction. *This is the type of reading program that is the most effective and appropriate for most children.* However, balanced reading instruction is especially useful with children who have special needs of various types. When such children use either *only* a whole language or phonics program, they are much less likely to be successful in reading and may become a disabled reader.

PHILOSOPHY BEHIND
THE READING TEACHER'S SURVIVAL KIT

The philosophy behind the *Survival Kit* is that virtually all children can learn to read adequately or even effectively with appropriate, properly paced instruction. However, administrators, teachers, family members, and the children themselves must believe that they can learn to read. Because that is not always the case, children may be a victim of the self-fulfilling prophecy that states children achieve just about as well in school as they are expected to achieve.

My doctoral advisor, the late Ruth Strang, told me many years ago that it was her experience after working with thousands of children at the Reading Clinics at Columbia

University and the University of Arizona that almost all children can learn to read. She said that she had met only a few children who seemed unable to learn to read adequately. After tutoring children myself and supervising the tutoring of thousands of children at Illinois State University, I would make the same statement.

Therefore, the most important underlying philosophy behind this *Survival Kit* is that almost all children can learn to read with appropriate instruction and support.

My belief that nearly all children can learn to read also applies to the vast majority of children with special needs. With well-trained, motivated teachers and appropriate, well-paced, individualized instruction, children with LD, ADD, ADHD, mild mental handicaps, visual impairments, hearing impairments, and speech and language disorders should be able to learn to read adequately or very well.

Children who are culturally or linguistically diverse also should be able to learn to read with instruction that best capitalizes on their prior knowledge, oral language, abilities, and interests. These children may be members of a minority group, may be non–English speaking, may have limited English, or may be bilingual. Some of them may be proficient in a nonstandard dialect, such as the black or Latino dialect. However, these children should be able to learn to read adequately or well with proper instruction and teacher support.

A balanced reading program that emphasizes trade books (real reading materials) of various kinds along with appropriate skills instruction both in and out of context is the best program for most children. While it is true that many children have learned to read with either a totally whole language or skills-based reading program, normally such a program is not the ideal program for most children. A total whole language program may be effective with children who are linguistically adept or come from a home environment that provided many emergent literacy experiences. In addition, a few children who seemed to need structure in their reading instruction have achieved very well with only a systematic phonics program.

However, it seems logical to use the major strengths of whole language: It uses real reading materials and creates an interest in reading along with structured skills instruction, which presents phonics in a structured, developmental way. Although such a balanced reading program is effective with the vast majority of children, it usually is especially effective with children who have special needs of various types. For example, many children with learning disabilities do not find enough structure in a total whole language program to be successful. They need the structure and explicit teaching of phonics.

In addition, a wide variety of reading strategies, materials, reproducibles, and games is the most effective with most children. Although a few children simply will read because they enjoy it, a number of others must have the motivation that comes with using innovative, interesting materials, reproducibles, and games. Although I acknowledge that *reading motivating materials is the best way to improve reading skills,* a number of children, especially those with special needs, benefit greatly from using motivating reproducibles and games. Most children also learn phonic elements (especially the short vowel sounds) most effectively when they are presented and practiced in isolation. True whole language proponents believe that phonic elements and structural elements are best learned in the context of actual reading materials. However, many children with special needs, such as learning disabilities or visual or hearing impairments, are simply unable to hear the phonic elements (especially the short vowel sounds) in isolation and need considerable instruction and practice with these elements in isolation, such as provided by interesting reproducibles and games. That is why this *Survival Kit* contains many classroom-tested and creative reproducibles and games. Although these may be the most effective with children who have special needs of various types, almost all children should enjoy using them.

Reading assessment and instruction should be ongoing processes. For example, a child's corrective reading program may begin with a very brief period of meaningful assessment to determine his or her approximate reading level and reading strengths and weaknesses. However, appropriate reading instruction should quickly follow that is based on the hypotheses (hunches) made by the reading teacher as a result of this preliminary assessment. The assessment can be either formal (standardized) or informal (see Chapter 2). However, informal (authentic) assessment usually is the most worthwhile for most children.

Assessment should be continuous during instruction with the teacher using mainly informal assessment devices, such as teacher observation of reading strengths and weaknesses, the running record, miscue analysis, an Individual Reading Inventory, or possibly an appropriate standardized test. However, additional assessment should point the way for additional corrective reading instruction. There is no valid reason to assess a child's reading performance if the results of that assessment are not acted on. Far too many tests simply are scored, and the results are placed in the child's cumulative folder or in the school district office, never to be used in improving reading instruction. It is true that some standardized test scores may be necessary as part of a school district's "report card" for the state or another outside source. However, the vast majority of assessment, whether it is authentic or standardized, should result in altered reading instruction for the child and in his or her reading improvement.

In the past North American schools have done a fairly good job of teaching many children the basic reading skills. However, schools have not been successful in motivating children to *value reading for pleasure and information*. In fact, schools generally have failed in this important task with many children. It has been reported that one-half of all college graduates holding a Bachelor's degree never read a book for pleasure after college graduation. That is a disappointing statistic. Unless children value reading for pleasure *and* information, reading instruction has not been fully successful.

One important reason that children do not find reading motivating is because it has always "seemed like work" to them. Many elementary school children have spent their entire school career reading materials on their frustration reading level (i.e., materials that are too difficult for them). They rarely, if ever, have had the opportunity to read an easy book just "because they wanted to." Therefore, they have never learned that reading can be a pleasurable and rewarding activity. The old-fashioned book report may have turned more children off reading than any other single factor. Children must learn in the elementary school that reading is a worthwhile and rewarding activity. Only then can their reading instruction be considered successful.

The *Survival Kit* also stresses that a combination of whole class, small group, partner, and individual instruction will result in the most effective reading program. Each of these grouping practices has unique advantages and limitations. Therefore, an overreliance on only one or two of them is usually not effective. Some children do well with whole group instruction, while others do not. Although most children benefit from individualized instruction, often it is not practical to use this approach as the only grouping practice. However, some of the benefits of one-on-one instruction can be found in the careful use of small group and partner (buddy) reading groups. Individual or partner reading instruction is especially helpful to children who have unique needs, such as learning disabilities or cultural or linguistic diversity. Such children may not perform so well in reading with whole class instruction as they will with more personal attention and support.

Reading instruction should be integrated with writing and spelling instruction as much as possible. Because listening, reading, writing, spelling, and the visual arts all comprise the *language arts*, improvement in one of them may result in improvement in one or more of the others. In the past each language art usually was taught and practiced in isolation, with little opportunity for children to notice the interrelationships among them. Reading has always been the primary focus in the language arts curriculum. Although reading certainly is the capstone of the curriculum, the remainder of the language arts are important also. For example, "for every $3000 spent on children's ability to receive information, $1.00 was spent on their power to send it in writing" (Graves, 1980). Therefore, the *Survival Kit* provides strategies, materials, and reproducibles that stress the interrelationships among reading and the other language arts.

IMPORTANT PRINCIPLES FOR THE READING TEACHER

The following principles are pivotal for reading teachers and for the *Survival Kit*:

➡ *Assessment should always drive instruction.* A child's reading program always should be based on his or her reading strengths and weaknesses as determined by thoughtful assessment and analysis. Normally, authentic or informal assessment is the more accurate way of determining a child's unique reading needs, although standardized or formal assessment also may be of some use.

➡ *Begin the reading instruction at the child's present level and move forward from there.* It is important to present and practice reading skills at the child's independent (easy) or high instructional (fairly easy with limited teacher support) levels so that he or she can experience as much success as possible. Since "nothing succeeds like observed success," it is important for any child, especially a child with reading problems, to have material that is easy enough to ensure success. There is no point in "covering the book" if the child has great difficulty identifying the words that are contained in it or if he or she cannot understand the material. As the child progresses, he or she can read more difficult material. A major cause of reading problems is that children are required to read materials in school that are too difficult for them.

➡ *Use a variety of motivating reading strategies, materials, reproducibles, and games.* Many whole language proponents accurately state that the best way to improve reading skills is to read. I agree with this *if the child will read for information and pleasure.* Unfortunately, it is often difficult to motivate disabled readers and children with special needs. Such children often use a variety of avoidance techniques so that they do not have to read either at school or at home.

Motivating reading material at the independent (easy) or high instructional (with teacher support) levels along with a variety of interesting reading strategies, reproducibles, and games constitutes the best reading program for most children, including children with special needs. Interesting strategies such as the visual imagery, prediction strategies, the Anticipation Guide, story impressions, the herringbone technique, semantic mapping, K-W-L (What I know—What I want to know—What I have learned), and K-W-H-L (What I know—What I want to know—How I can find out—What I have learned), among many others, can be both motivating and helpful to children. Descriptions and examples of all of these useful strategies are contained in Chapter 6 of the *Survival Kit*. Although reproducibles and games reinforce word identification and comprehension skills in isolation, which is contrary to the whole language philosophy, they are useful with many children, especially children with special needs. For example, I interviewed 212 first-grade pupils in 1997 and found that most of them enjoyed completing worksheets, contrary to the beliefs of whole language proponents (Miller, 1998). Games also are extremely motivating to most children even though they encourage competition and practice reading skills in isolation. Research has shown that children demonstrate 53% greater gain in knowledge when they participate in *active games* in comparison with practice in only using worksheets. Even passive games result in a 30% better game than does the use of just worksheets (Dickerson, 1982).

➡ *Emphasize both "real reading" materials and reading skills instruction both in and out of context.* I believe that "real reading" materials, such as trade books of all types (including informational books, children's magazines, children's newspapers, and materials found on the Internet, among others), are preferable to the excerpts found in basal readers, phonic workbooks, or worksheets. However, the use of excerpted material to present or practice a specific reading skill may be helpful at times with some children.

Reading skills instruction, including word identification and comprehension skills, is effective for most children when it is taught and practiced both in context and isolation. For example, some children are unable to discriminate between the short vowel sounds unless they are isolated from the rest of the word. Of course, all of the skills that are presented or reinforced in isolation should be placed in the context of real reading materials as quickly as possible. Reading is a contextual activity, not a matter of pronouncing words in isolation. Therefore, for most children (with the possible exception of superior readers with good linguistic aptitude) teaching in context and isolation results in the best achievement.

➡ *Use extrinsic rewards and behavior modification when appropriate.* Reading for information and pleasure should be its own reward, as it is for most good readers who need no extrinsic rewards or behavior modification. However, many disabled readers and children with special needs find no rewards in reading because it is too difficult for them and they have never been shown that it can be enjoyable. Although extrinsic rewards and behavior modification are not ideal, they may be necessary until reading itself provides the necessary rewards. This is the ultimate goal, and rewards are just stop-gap measures.

Some of the extrinsic rewards and behavior modification strategies that teachers have used are as follows: a written and signed contract specifying certain behavior on the part of the child that will lead to an ultimate reward. For example, at the completion of three successful tutoring sessions, the child will receive a token gift. Some of the extrinsic rewards that teachers have used are stickers, creative graphs of progresses, small erasers in the shape of various animals, or some special privilege in school.

➡ *All children, including those with special needs, should be able to learn adequately with appropriate materials and strategies.* As stated earlier, the basic philosophy behind the *Survival Kit* is that almost every child should be able to read adequately or even well with appropriate, properly paced instruction. However, the reading teacher must believe this and convey this belief to the child. The *Survival Kit* contains a wealth of classroom-tested strategies, materials, reproducibles, and games that should enable the teacher to reach this important goal.

➡ *The most effective motivation for a child is observed success.* As stated previously, "nothing succeeds like observed success," so the child must know that he or she is making progress in reading improvement. Well-deserved praise and extrinsic rewards of various types are a good indication of progress, but only if they are really earned and merited.

➡ *Provide children with challenging and motivating, but achievable, goals.* The child must be given reading goals and tasks that are not too difficult but not so simple that they are not challenging. The goals must be attainable but enable the child to learn additional reading skills, not merely review the skills that he or she already knows. However, many children with reading disabilities and other special needs spend their entire school career reading materials that are on their frustration reading level—much too difficult for them. This is a major cause of continued reading difficulties. How can a child make reading progress when he or she is consistently reading material that is too difficult? He or she never has the opportunity to read with fluency or rapidly identify the words in the material. If such children are given the opportunity to read easier materials, their word identification and comprehension skills, silent and oral reading fluency, and self-confidence will all improve.

➡ *Learning to read should be pleasurable for the most part.* Learning to read should be fun for children. Many disabled readers and children with special needs do not understand that reading can be anything but work. Is it any wonder that they dread reading both at school and at home? Reading can be made pleasurable by allowing children to select the material they are going to read at least part of the time. It also can be made fun by providing children with reading materials that are not too hard for them. In addition, motivating, innovative reproducibles and games help many children learn that reading can be an enjoyable activity.

➡ *Children must want to read for pleasure and information if reading instruction is to be considered successful.* As stated earlier, North American schools have done a fairly good job of teaching reading skills but a rather inadequate job of motivating children to want to read for pleasure and information. Without this component, reading instruction cannot be considered successful. This goal can be accomplished by giving children a variety of materials to read that are not too difficult and by providing many other interesting ways of practicing their reading skills, such as reproducibles, games, computer software, and the Internet.

➠ *No one reading approach or type of reading material is effective with all children. Most children learn to read most effectively with a balanced reading program.* A balanced reading program that capitalizes on the strengths of several different reading approaches while overcoming limitations is the best reading program for most children. Although it is true that children with good linguistic aptitude and prior knowledge usually can learn to read by any method, it is especially important that a combination of approaches, strategies, and materials be used with children who have special needs. The *Survival Kit* uses the best features of whole language, the language-experience approach, the basal reader approach, and phonics to comprise a balanced reading program.

➠ *Teach to the child's present reading strengths while correcting his or her weaknesses.* It is important to present reading instruction and practice on the child's present reading level and to present only those reading skills in which the child has been weak. There is no point in having a child read material that is too difficult or learning or practicing reading skills that he or she already knows. Teaching to the child's present strengths also will enhance his or her self-esteem, thus adding to the likelihood that reading improvement will take place.

➠ *Use one-on-one instruction and interviews with children and family members when applicable.* One-on-one instruction usually is helpful with children who have reading difficulties. The reading instruction and practice can be tailored to their specific reading level and difficulties. In addition, in one-on-one instruction classmates are not listening to the child read and thus the child feels less self-conscious. Children with reading problems usually thrive in a one-to-one or one-to-two teacher–pupil relationship when the teacher is supportive, caring, well organized, and knowledgeable. One-to-one meetings also can be helpful in informing family members about the child's reading progress and about what they can do to aid in the reading improvement program. Most family members are willing to help if they know what to do.

WORKS CITED IN CHAPTER 1

Dickerson, D. (1982). A study of the use of games to reinforce sight word recognition. *The Reading Teacher, 36*, 46–49.

Graves, D. (1980). A new look at writing research. *Language Arts, 57*, 914–918.

Miller, W. (1998). First-grade children's perceptions of reading. *Arizona Reading Journal, 25*, 7–12.

Chapter 2

ASSESSING READING STRENGTHS AND WEAKNESSES

I have presented a speech entitled "Alternative Assessment Techniques in Reading and Writing" at several reading conventions. I always read aloud the children's book entitled *First Grade Takes a Test* by Miriam Cohen (New York: Greenwillow Books, 1980) at the beginning of this presentation. Briefly, the book describes how a first-grade class took a standardized reading achievement test. It clearly shows how the children found both the tests and the results disturbing and how invalid those results were. It also shows how the test taking was not connected in any substantive way with classroom reading instruction and how many of the questions were subject to misinterpretation. I recommend reading Cohen's book; you will learn a great deal about standardized tests and test taking in doing so.

This chapter discusses the following aspects of assessment:

➦ Guidelines for reading assessment

➦ Standardized reading tests

➦ Advantages and limitations of standardized reading tests

➦ Authentic (informal) assessment

➦ The running record with reproducible examples

➦ Miscue analysis with reproducible examples

➦ A variation of the Individual Reading Inventory with reproducible examples

➦ Reproducible copy of the San Diego Quick Assessment Test

➦ Reproducible copy of the El Paso Phonics Survey

➦ Benchmarks and rubrics for authentic assessment

➦ Literacy portfolios

After you have completed this chapter, you will understand both standardized reading tests and authentic reading assessment and will have access to many useful reproducible examples of authentic assessment devices. These reproducibles are helpful in determining a child's reading levels as well as his or her reading strengths and weaknesses. You will understand that a reading teacher or tutor should primarily use authentic assessment devices because they are effective in directing instruction. However, standardized devices usually are required for accountability.

GUIDELINES FOR READING ASSESSMENT

Here are some important guidelines on which the *Survival Kit* is based:

➡ *Teach reading skills in which the child is weak.* Assessment, whether standardized or informal, should drive instruction. Therefore, a child should learn and practice only those reading skills that he or she needs. There is no point in presenting or reinforcing word identification or comprehension skills that a child already knows. A number of basal reading approaches and phonics systems teach all skills to all children whether or not they already know them. However, this is not the case with whole language.

➡ *Present and reinforce reading skills on the child's high instructional and independent levels.* Most disabled readers and children with special reading needs spend their entire school career reading on their frustration reading level. It is important that all children, but especially those with reading difficulties and special needs, have the opportunity to read motivating, easy materials. These materials often should be self-selected to enhance the child's motivation and should be on the child's independent or high instructional levels. Try to imagine if you were a college student who had to read calculus material that was much too difficult for several hours five days a week for an entire school year. How motivated do you think you would be to read or to improve your reading skills? That is the case with children who are constantly required to read materials that are too difficult for them. Thus, they do not improve their reading skills, and their teacher and family members wonder why. *Give them easy and interesting materials to read and you may be surprised at how much progress they make quickly.*

➡ *Children should not learn or practice skills that are too difficult for them.* Children should have reading tasks that are challenging and rewarding but not overly difficult. This is especially true for children with reading or learning disabilities or other special needs. Such children are used to failing in reading in school, and they must be shown in a concrete way that they can be successful. Easy, motivating reading materials, concrete (extrinsic) rewards, well-deserved praise, and rereading of materials that they have already read to ensure fluency are helpful for such children.

➡ *Assessment scores should not be used merely for accountability but mainly to direct reading instruction.* It is true that school administrators, boards of education, and states need standardized test scores for a variety of reasons. They need to ensure that the children in a school district are making acceptable reading progress, to compare reading achievement in various school districts, and to evaluate a particular reading curriculum, such as whole language, basal reader, or phonics programs. However, most assessment should be *authentic*, meaning that it should be used to assess accurately a child's reading levels, competencies, and weaknesses so that appropriate changes can be made in the child's reading curriculum. It also can be used to determine a child's progress over time and how well he or she is responding to particular reading strategies or programs. If assessment does not change reading curriculum in a positive way, it is of no value, and the time, effort, and expense of the assessment cannot be justified.

➠ *Children learn to read most effectively with a program that is specifically designed for them as a direct result of assessment.* Most children learn to read the most effectively with a program that has been specifically designed for them, taking into account their reading levels, strengths, and weaknesses. While it is true that a few children with good linguistic aptitude can learn to read adequately or even well with any program, this is not true with disabled readers or children with special needs.

➠ *Assessment should be continuous.* At the beginning of a school year or the beginning of the tutoring sessions, the teacher should assess each child's independent and instructional reading levels and his or her specific reading skill strengths and weaknesses. Then the reading improvement program should begin. During a classroom or special reading program, the teacher (tutor) should continually assess the child's reading progress in a mainly authentic manner using teacher observation with or without structured checklists, running records, miscue analysis, or possibly an Individual Reading Inventory, among others. All of these devices are described in detail later in this chapter with reproducible examples. Continuous assessment should direct the reading program of the classroom or a child.

➠ *Assessment should be collaborative and reflective.* Assessment should be a collaboration among any teachers who are involved with the child and with the child himself or herself. If two teachers are working with the child in a reading improvement program, they should collaboratively use the results of both authentic and standardized assessment to arrive at a reading program for a child that is prescribed in terms of the child's reading levels, competencies, and limitations. The child also should be helped to do effective self-assessment of his or her reading performance in terms of word identification and comprehension skills. Self-assessment checklists may be of help in this case. In addition, the child should be encouraged to self-assess his or her reading performance while compiling a portfolio. Every reading teacher and child should learn how to do reflective assessment of the child's performance and learn what to do about the results of this reflective self-assessment.

➠ *Assessment should be multidimensional.* Effective assessment should involve many standardized and authentic devices, including reading achievement tests, teacher observation with or without a structured checklist, running records, miscue analysis, perhaps an Individual Reading Inventory, and self-assessment, among others. It also can involve large group assessment, small group assessment, and individual assessment. In general, authentic individual assessment techniques are the most effective.

➡ *Assessment should be developmentally and culturally appropriate.* Young children often do not perform well on standardized tests. They generally demonstrate their actual reading skills more accurately in authentic assessments such as teacher observation, a running record, or miscue analysis. Often the test is more difficult for them than actual reading. For example, many young children can read the material on a standardized reading test but are not able to translate their answers to test bubbles, especially if the answer sheet is on a different page. Some children who are already reading well do not perform well on a reading readiness test that measures such nonreading behaviors such as matching pictures or isolated letters or groups of letters. In addition, many children who are culturally or linguistically diverse do not perform well on a standardized test simply because these tests usually evaluate prior knowledge and experiences that are uncommon to them. Virtually no standardized test is free of cultural references, and most of them underestimate the actual reading level of a culturally or linguistically diverse child.

➡ *Assessment should identify children's strengths as well as their weaknesses.* Because reading improvement in a classroom or in another setting always should build on a child's strengths while correcting his or her weaknesses, it is important that the reading teacher identify the weaknesses. Because most children with reading or learning disabilities have a low self-image with regard to reading, it is important to show them that they have reading strengths. Too often their reading weaknesses were stressed in the classroom or another setting and they were never shown that they possessed reading strengths as well. Usually both their reading skills and their self-esteem will improve greatly if they are shown that they have many reading skills.

In summary, if all of these assessment guidelines are followed both in classrooms and in special reading programs, the likelihood that children will improve their reading skills will be enhanced.

CHARACTERISTICS OF READING ASSESSMENT

To make it easier to understand the concepts presented in this chapter, the terms *evaluation*, *assessment*, and *authentic assessment* are defined.

FORMATIVE AND SUMMATIVE EVALUATION

Evaluation is judging the information that is obtained by assessment. It is evaluating the answers that a child gives, and it usually is more formal than is assessment. For example, standardized tests are an example of evaluating a child for the purpose of making a diagnosis of his or her reading level and reading skills. Having a child respond to a criterion-referenced test with *benchmarks* (discussed later in this chapter) is another example of evaluation.

   Formative evaluation is continuous and is used to improve instruction (Bertrand, 1991). However, *summative evaluation*, which takes place near the end of a predetermined period of time, evaluates the effectiveness of instruction. The final exam that a high school student takes at the end of a semester is an example of summative evaluation. Almost all of the evaluation that is done with students in the elementary school, including all children with special needs, should be formative so that it can direct instruction.

Evaluation has three main parts: those of the *self*, *collaborative others*, and *society* (Short, 1990). The self is the child himself or herself, and the collaborative others include those who work with the child, such as teacher(s), reading buddies, and members of a cooperative learning group. Society includes family members, the community, and the school district and board of education. Each group probably has a different purpose for evaluation and therefore requires a different type of information. For example, a school board may be interested in the results of a standardized reading achievement test so that it can compare the results obtained in its school district with similar districts in the state and nation. However, a teacher may need to know that a particular child does not have mastery of the difference between the short /e/ phoneme (sound) and the short /i/ phoneme (sound). Because children, teacher, family members, and school boards all have different perspectives, they all need different types of information.

Since school boards and family members usually want objective evaluation measures, standardized devices will continue to be mandated in the future.

ASSESSMENT AND AUTHENTIC ASSESSMENT

Assessment can be defined as gathering information to meet the particular needs of a child. It involves looking at children's strengths and weaknesses. Although assessment is usually informal, it is often more useful than are standardized tests, and because it is usually informal, it is often called *authentic assessment*. The word *authentic* is used because these type of assessment procedures normally reflect the actual instructional activities of the classroom. For example, in authentic assessment, children can retell a story or write a summary of a content assignment. This is in direct contrast to objective tests, in which children must answer multiple-choice questions about short, unrelated paragraphs. Authentic assessment also can include "kid watching," teacher observation using structured checklists, and anecdotal records. Although authentic assessment currently is most closely identified with whole language, it is useful in all reading improvement programs.

Authentic assessment programs strongly stress the *process* of reading, while standardized reading tests mainly evaluate the *product (end result)* of reading. Assessment always should resemble real reading activities as much as possible. The main purposes of authentic assessment are as follows:

➡ To document stages in children's development as readers

➡ To identify children's strengths and weaknesses in order to plan for instruction

➡ To record children's reading activities

➡ To determine grades and materials for the reading portfolio

➡ To help teachers learn more about children's reading strategies

Assessment is more than testing—it is an important part of teaching. The main purpose of assessment should be to direct classroom instruction. Through authentic assessment, teachers learn about their students, about themselves as teachers, and about the success of the reading program. In addition, when children reflect about their reading, they learn about themselves as readers.

STANDARDIZED SURVEY/READING ACHIEVEMENT TESTS

Every elementary school child has taken standardized reading tests during his or her school career. A few children enjoy them and perform very well, while many others dread taking them or consider them a waste of time. In any case, these tests are likely here to stay. For example, according to Airaisan (1994), Bauman (1988), Nitko (1996), and Stiggins (1994), standardized tests will stay around because they are cheap, efficient, and they give "scientific" results. According to Neill and Medina (1989), an estimated 105 million standardized tests of all kinds are given during every school year—an average of $2\frac{1}{2}$ tests per pupil per year, and this probably is a conservative estimate. In addition, the amount of testing that is done in schools seems to be increasing (Haney & Madaus, 1989). Schools have a heavy philosophical and financial investment in formal testing especially of reading.

Of all the curriculum areas, standardized testing seems to affect reading most. Because success in reading is so important to success in all school activities, everyone seems to be interested in reading tests. Reports about local performance on reading achievement tests usually make the front page of the newspaper even in fairly large cities. According to Valencia and Pearson (1987, p. 727), "the influence of [reading] testing is greater now than at any time in our history." I agree with this statement based on my observations of schools throughout the United States.

Standardized tests are formal tests with standard directions and scoring. A reading teacher or tutor cannot vary from the procedures that are contained in the test if the results are going to be considered accurate. Contemporary standardized reading tests are somewhat different from those of the past in that they may contain original stories by children's authors, have somewhat longer reading, and contain multiple-choice questions with more than one possible correct answer. However, they are the same as they were in the past because they have rigid directions and time limits.

Most standardized reading tests are *norm-referenced.* A norm-referenced test enables a teacher to compare his or her pupils with a standardization sample that is similar in age, grade level, gender, geographic location, and socioeconomic status. These norms are typically reported in all of the following ways:

- *Raw score*—The total number of correct answers. This score has no meaning until it is changed into a percentile rank, stanine, or some other type of score.
- *Percentile rank*—The point on a scale of 1 to 99 that indicates what percentage of pupils obtained an equal or lower score. For example, a percentile rank of 48 means that 48% of those who took the test received an equal or lower score.
- *Grade equivalent score*—This score characterizes a child's performance as being equivalent to that of other students in a particular grade. For example, a grade equivalent score of 4.8 indicates that the child answered the same number of items correctly as the average fourth grader in the eighth month. The grade equivalent

does not tell on what level the child is performing (i.e., a score of 4.8 does not mean that the child is reading at the end of the fourth-grade level).

➡ *Stanine*—The point on a nine-point scale, with 5 being the average stanine. The word *stanine* is a combination of the words *standard* and *nine*. The stanines 4, 5, and 6 are average points, with 1, 2, and 3 being below average and 7, 8, and 9 above average. Stanines are useful when comparing subtests of norm-referenced tests.

➡ *Scaled scores*—A continuous ranking from 000 to 999 of a series of norm-referenced tests from the lowest to the highest. These tests may be useful for tracking long-term reading development through the grades. They are useful for comparing scores from several different tests as they are the only scores that can be averaged.

Children are often given a *standardized survey reading* or *achievement test* to determine their reading progress. Such a test can be a reading test only with the subtests of vocabulary (word meaning) and sentence or paragraph comprehension (perhaps word-study or reading-study skills) or just the reading subtests of an achievement test battery, which also evaluate achievement in the various content areas. In either case, these types of tests are screening devices that evaluate a child's word meaning (vocabulary), sentence comprehension or paragraph comprehension, and sometimes word-study or reading-study skills. They are usually given to locate those children who need additional testing in reading, typically in September to determine a child's current overall reading level or in April or May to determine how much reading progress the child has made during the school year. Such tests are usually simple to give and to score. They are often evaluated by computer; the school district is given a computer printout of the complete results. These tests are often mandated by the school districts. *The results from such a test should always be interpreted cautiously especially when the test is given to a very good or below average reader, a child with special needs such as learning disabilities, or a child who is culturally or linguistically diverse.*

The following are the most common contemporary standardized survey/reading achievement tests. They are all available in a variety of equivalent forms and on various grade levels from beginning reading through the middle-upper level.

California Achievement Test—California Test Bureau
Comprehensive Test of Basic Skills—California Test Bureau
Iowa Test of Basic Skills—Riverside
Metropolitan Achievement Test—Psychological Corporation
Stanford Achievement Test—Psychological Corporation

STANDARDIZED DIAGNOSTIC READING TESTS

Some children in a reading improvement program may be given a *standardized diagnostic reading test*. These tests can be given either on a group or an individual basis to children with special reading needs. Such a test is usually given to a child who achieved significantly below grade level on the survey reading or reading achievement test.

This type of test attempts to evaluate a child's reading in terms of his or her exact weaknesses in sight word identification, phonics, word structure, explicit (literal or factual) comprehension, implicit (interpretive) comprehension, and study skills. This kind of test does not locate the causes for a child's reading difficulties, but it does attempt to locate the exact difficulties. The results usually are reported by norms of various kinds, such as percentile ranks, stanines, or scaled scores.

The most common and useful group diagnostic reading test is the *Stanford Diagnostic Reading Test* (SDRT), Fourth Edition (Psychological Corporation, 1995). The test provides six levels for assessing reading competency with a single form for the first three levels and two parallel forms for the three upper levels. The six levels are designated by color: red level for grades 1.5–2.5; orange level for grades 2.5–3.5; green level for grades 3.5–4.5; purple level for grades 4.5–6.5; brown level for grades 6.5–9.0; and blue level for grades 9.0–12.0 and entering college freshmen. In addition, the SDRT has three optional assessment devices: *Reading Strategies Survey*, for determining which reading strategies students understand and use; *Reading Questionnaire*, for assessing attitudes, interests, and factors that influence comprehension; and *Story Retelling*, which has a scoring rubric for assessing either oral or written story retelling.

The two most common individual diagnostic reading tests are as follows:

Diagnostic Reading Scales—California Test Bureau

Durrell Analysis of Reading Difficulty—Psychological Corporation

Although both of these tests can be useful, they are best given and evaluated only by a well-trained, experienced reading specialist.

CRITERION-REFERENCED ASSESSMENT

Criterion-referenced assessment is another way of assessing the reading progress of children. In some cases this is a type of authentic assessment. The results of such a test are reported in terms of a *standard* or *criterion*. For example, after reading a passage silently, the child must answer 80% of the comprehension questions correctly. Criterion-referenced tests are formal measures designed to focus on a child's mastery of a specific reading skill or skills. Therefore, they are often called *mastery tests* since a child has to receive a certain score on the test to have mastery of it. They are not norm referenced since they do not compare a student's performance with that of other children. They are *not* identified with whole language since they measure whether or not a child has mastered a specific reading skill(s) rather than his or her understanding of the entire global reading process. Therefore, they are more compatible with a skills-based reading program.

Criterion-referenced tests may be criticized since the criterion level that is set is arbitrary. For example, because such tests evaluate only a small portion of a child's actual knowledge, the difference between passing and not passing may be very small. In addition, some children can learn reading skills very well but still not read whole stories or books effectively.

Two types of standards that are often identified with criterion-referenced assessment are *benchmarks* and *rubrics*. A *benchmark* is a written description of a key task that children are expected to perform. As an example, a benchmark for explicit (literal) comprehension might be "Is able to retell a story in correct sequence." Benchmarks are useful because they provide a concrete description of what children are expected to do. Therefore, they provide children, teachers, family members, and administrators with an observable way of assessing reading accomplishments and needs. When a reading teacher or tutor uses benchmarks, he or she can assess when a child has mastered important skill strategies and is ready to move ahead.

Ways of observing benchmark behaviors can include standardized criterion-referenced tests, observing reading skills during reading groups, retelling, drama, and teacher–pupil conferences. Allowing children a variety of ways to demonstrate benchmark behaviors seems more natural and is preferred by some teachers. However, other teachers want to use standard tasks and standard materials so that the tasks are the same for all children. Weaver (1992) has established a series of tasks and observational guidelines that can be used to assess children's reading progress. Her benchmarks include activities such as "Can write a simple story with an awareness of story structure" (p. 55). For most benchmarks the teacher uses a series of books that gradually get more difficult. For example, on the primary reading level, the teacher can use the trade book *Cat on the Mat* (Wildsmith, 1982) and suggestions contained in Weaver's *Benchmark Assessment Guide* (1992) to assess children's performance. The advantages of using designated books for assessing benchmark behaviors is that they provide material at the appropriate level of difficulty. If children are given materials that are too difficult, they cannot demonstrate their reading strategies effectively.

A *basal reader series* may be accompanied by an extensive assessment and placement system. Basal reader tests are one type of criterion-referenced test. Such a test stresses a pupil's ability to reach a certain level of performance in areas that the test is designed to measure. Usually this is the 80% level of competency. Both group and individual inventories usually are available in basal reader assessment. Assessment devices may include periodic tests (which may be criterion referenced) to be given at the end of a unit, a section, or a book. Contemporary basal reader series may feature holistic tests in which children read a fairly long passage and write essay-type answers. Checklists, observation guides, and portfolios also may be an important part of the basal assessment system.

Another type of standard is the *rubric*. A rubric is a written description of what is expected in order to meet a certain level of performance and is accompanied by samples of typical performance. Although rubrics usually are used in assessing writing tasks, they can also be used to assess reading tasks and portfolios. The main advantage of a rubric is that it provides criteria or standards for task assessment.

THE NATIONAL ASSESSMENT OF EDUCATIONAL PROGRESS

The *National Assessment of Educational Progress (NAEP)* is the only ongoing assessment of what students in the United States know and can do within subject areas. The NAEP regularly reports to the public on the academic progress of students in grades 4, 8, and 12.

In 1998 the NAEP conducted a national reading assessment of fourth-, eighth-, and twelfth-grade students and a state-by-state assessment of fourth- and eighth-grade students. Results in 1998 were compared with those in 1994 and 1992. Students' performance on the assessment is described in terms of their average score on a 0 to 500 scale and in terms of the percentage of students reaching three achievement levels: *Basic, Proficient,* and *Advanced.* The achievement levels and performance standards are collective judgments of what students should know and be able to do for each grade tested.

Here are the results of the 1998 NAEP reading tests for the United States:

➠ Average reading scores increased for grades 4, 8, and 12. At the fourth and twelfth grades, the national average score was higher in 1998 than in 1994. At eighth grade, the national average score was higher in 1998 than in 1994 and 1992.

➠ While the average reading score increased at all three grade levels in 1998, increased scores were not found for all students. At grade 4, score increases were only found among lower-performing students. At grade 8, score increases were found among lower- and middle-performing students. At grade 12, score increases were found among middle- and upper-performing students. However, the score for lower-performing twelfth graders was not so high in 1998 as it was in 1992.

➠ Across the three grades (4, 8, and 12) the percentages of students performing at or above the Basic level of reading achievement were 62%, 74%, and 77%. The percentages who performed at the highest achievement level, Advanced, were 7%, 3%, and 6%.

➠ At grade 4, no significant changes since 1994 or 1992 were observed in the percentages of students attaining any of the achievement levels.

➠ At grade 8, there was a greater percentage of students at or above the Basic level and the Proficient level of reading achievement in 1998 compared with 1994 and 1992.

➠ At grade 12, a greater percentage of students performed at or above the Proficient level and the Advanced level of reading achievement in 1998 compared with 1994. The percentage of students at Advanced was also greater in 1998 than in 1992. Although the 1998 percentage at or above Basic was greater than in 1994, it remained lower than the 1992 percentage.

Although the NAEP may be of value in allowing the federal government to determine how well U.S. students are reading, it has many of the limitations of standardized tests (summarized later in this chapter). Therefore, the results from this test should be viewed with the same degree of caution as those of any other standardized test. Complete results of the 1998 NAEP are found on the Web site: http://nces.ed.gov/nationsreportcard/pubs/main1998/.

STANDARDIZED TESTS THAT ARE DESIGNED TO SATISFY STATE STANDARDS

Most, if not all, states now administer some type of state-mandated reading test. The results from such a test are generally used in a "state report card," in which the scores of school districts and, in some cases, individual children and classes are reported. Most of these tests are somewhat different from the typical standardized survey reading or achievement test.

The typical state-mandated test uses full-length materials, in constrast to the paragraphs that are used in a survey reading or achievement test. Typically, an entire narrative or content selection is printed in the test booklet, and the children must read it silently and then respond to a number of comprehension questions. This provides them with both narrative and content material (social studies or science) that is similar to that found in ordinary reading. It is intended to give children a better chance to demonstrate their actual reading skills and comprehension ability than using short passages, which are not typical of everyday reading.

Most of these tests also assess a child's prior knowledge before he or she begins reading. Since prior knowledge is important in determining how well a child will understand what is read, it is important for a reading teacher to know how much prior knowledge a child has and how well he or she uses it while reading. Children answer a number of prior knowledge questions before they actually read a passage. Each of these questions usually has several possible answers.

State-mandated tests usually include a number of multiple-choice questions with several different correct answers for each one. This is unlike a traditional reading test that contains only one correct answer for each question. Having more than one correct answer to a question is more nearly like the children's actual reading requirements and should stimulate their interpretive and critical thinking. The typical traditional reading test does not evaluate critical comprehension well. The answers to the multiple-choice questions on these nontraditional tests are weighted so that the child receives credit for all of the answers that he or she has given that are correct.

Many of these tests also try to learn about a child's use of various reading strategies by having the child answer questions about the reading strategies that he or she would use in certain reading situations. For example, the test tries to determine if a child would use skimming, rereading only a very short part, rereading an entire paragraph or passage, phonic analysis, context, or word structure in various reading situations. These tests also may attempt to determine a child's use of self-assessment while reading, and a reading survey of home reading habits may also be included.

State-mandated tests have many of the same limitations of standardized reading tests although they are more effective at evaluating a child's higher-level comprehension skills than traditional reading tests. The main problem comes when individual children's scores are reported and school districts are judged as being above or below average in reading achievement only on the basis of this one test.

ADVANTAGES AND LIMITATIONS OF USING STANDARDIZED TESTS FOR ASSESSING READING

Standardized reading tests have a number of advantages and limitations. The following are some of the advantages:

⇒ They are relatively easy for teachers and tutors, including those who are untrained, both to give and to evaluate.

➡ They usually do not take much time for children to take.

➡ Many are norm referenced, which means that the teacher can compare the results achieved by his or her class with those of a standardization group of children who are similar in age, gender, grade level, geographic location, and socioeconomic class, among others. However, criterion-referenced tests are not norm referenced.

➡ They are both reliable and valid. *Test reliability* means that a test provides consistent results in that a child who takes equivalent forms of the test usually receives about the same results. *Test validity* means that the test measures what it is supposed to measure or is truthful or accurate.

➡ They have been formulated by test experts, which theoretically makes them both reliable and valid.

The major limitations of standardized reading tests are as follows:

➡ Although they are theoretically objective, they may not be completely objective in reality.

➡ Many overestimate a child's actual instructional reading level (with teacher support) due to the guessing factor. For example, I had a child named Marty in my second-grade class during my first year of teaching. Although Marty was a nonreader near the end of the school year, he received a score of 2.5 on the reading subtests of the Stanford Achievement Test. This means that he scored about as well as an average child at the fifth month of second grade. He received this inaccurate score because he went through the entire test guessing at all of the items, while none of the children who actually read the test were able to finish it. This example indicates how misleading standardized test scores can be especially when they are used as the only way of evaluating children's reading achievement.

➡ The *actual taking of the test* may be much more difficult than the material that is included on the test, especially with young children or children with special needs, such as learning disabilities or cultural or linguistic diversity. For example, a child may know the answer to a test item but be unable to find the proper space on which to make the answer. Filling in the answer bubbles can be a difficult task for young children or for children who have special needs. They are unable to fill in the test bubbles even though they can easily understand the material on the test.

➡ Standardized tests are not culture fair. This means that such tests evaluate a child's prior knowledge and experiences. Usually these are middle-class experiences and culture. Therefore, a child who does not have this cultural background is discriminated against. The score that the child earns on such a test is likely to be significantly lower than his or her actual reading level.

➡ Many of the test items are on the lower levels of comprehension, such as explicit (literal) comprehension items. Although lower-level (literal) questions are simple to construct and to answer, they usually are not so relevant as are questions at the higher levels of comprehension.

➡ The reading teacher or tutor must be sure that the items on a test are passage dependent. Some test items can be answered only on the basis of the reader's prior knowledge (experience) without reading the material. Sometimes students can answer most, if not all, of the items on a test only on the basis of their prior knowledge.

➡ The grade equivalent score is subject to much misunderstanding although it is commonly used in reporting the results of standardized tests. *The grade equivalent score represents the grade level for which a raw score is the median (middle) score.* For example, if the median raw score of all the students in the norming group who were in the second month of fourth grade was 52, any child getting 52 correct answers has earned a grade equivalent score of 4.2.

   Bauman and Stevenson (1982), in an article on how standardized reading test scores are used by test publishers in determining grade equivalent scores, stated that the processes of interpolation and extrapolation (estimating) involve some guess-work and may result in scores that can be misunderstood. According to the authors, this is particularly the case with the use of extrapolated (estimated) scores that are very high or very low. Therefore, grade equivalents are usually the most accurate with average readers and the least accurate with very good or very poor readers.

   It is important to understand that a child cannot be expected to read material on the grade level that is indicated by a grade equivalent score. This score usually represents the child's frustration reading level rather than the instructional reading level. Usually a child does not have the prior knowledge, interests, or vocabulary to read up to the grade equivalent level found on a standardized reading test.

➡ The teacher or tutor must be sure that the child is given the proper level of the test. This concept is called *out-of-level testing.* For example, if a child with reading disabilities is given a test that is too hard, the score is likely to be incorrect. Therefore, a standardized reading test is likely to be the most accurate with average readers and less accurate with above average or below average readers.

➡ Standardized tests often focus on isolated reading skills instead of evaluating reading as a global language-based process. This limitation especially affects children who are in whole language classrooms, which emphasize skills in the context of whole language.

➡ Since most of these tests are timed, they penalize the slow, but careful, reader who cannot complete the reading test during the rigid time limit. Such children may have good word identification and comprehension skills, but they just read slowly and carefully.

➡ Some children are poor test takers and have a high degree of test anxiety. Thus, a standardized test underestimates their actual instructional reading level.

➡ Most standardized tests do not measure problem-solving skills, which are required in many real-life reading situations.

In summary, standardized reading tests have both advantages and limitations. The limitations far outweigh the advantages. Early (1992–1993), for example, states that "the need to know how children are doing persists—with teachers, with parents, with the children themselves—but recently gained knowledge of the reading process convinces us that standardized tests fail to measure those processes accurately, wholly, or diagnostically" (p. 306).

However, a reading teacher or tutor often must give such tests due to the requirements of administrators, school boards, and family members. It is important that these tests make up only a small part of evaluating a child's reading skills because there are many other ways in which an assessment is done more accurately. *Standardized reading tests always should be thought of as only a tentative indicator of a child's actual instructional reading level and his or her reading needs. Their use always should be supplemented by using many of the authentic (informal) assessment devices that are discussed later in this chapter.*

AUTHENTIC ASSESSMENT AND "KID WATCHING"

It is important for all reading teachers and tutors to be continuous and knowledgeable observers of children's reading behaviors. If reading teachers and tutors observed reading behaviors on a regular basis and acted on those observations in planning a reading improvement program, many cases of reading disabilities could be prevented. In addition, children would enjoy reading for information and pleasure.

"Kid watching" is an important aspect of authentic assessment. The term "kid watching" was coined by Yetta Goodman (1987), a well-known proponent of whole language philosophy who teaches at the University of Arizona. She called "kid watching" direct or informal observation of a child during different regular classroom activities. It is based on the idea that reading is a natural process that is part of every child's normal literacy development. "Kid watching" allows teachers and tutors to think about these two questions:

➡ What evidence can be found that reading development is taking place?

➡ What does a child's unexpected production of reading behaviors tell the teacher or tutor about the child's knowledge of reading?

"Kid watching" or informal teacher observation includes these three aspects:

➡ *Observation*—Carefully observing a single child's activities, a group's activities, or the whole class's use of reading and social behaviors.

➡ *Interaction*—This takes place when the teacher or tutor asks questions, responds to journal writing, and conferences with children in order to stimulate further reading and cognitive development.

➡ *Analysis*—The teacher or tutor obtains information by listening to a child read and discuss and by looking at a child's written work. The teacher or tutor then applies knowledge of learning principles to evaluating reading abilities.

Expert "kid watchers," whether they are reading teachers or tutors, demonstrate the following characteristics:

➡ They understand the reading process and have knowledge of children's behavioral characteristics at various stages of development.

➡ They have a good command of children's and adolescent literature so that they know what narrative and informational trade books to recommend to children.

➡ They listen attentively and perceptively to children.

➡ They understand important patterns of behavior differences in reading abilities demonstrated by different children. This is especially important when working with children who have special needs or who are culturally or linguistically diverse.

➡ They constantly evaluate while teaching or tutoring.

➡ They accept responsibility for curriculum development and are careful not to place undue emphasis on standardized test scores but rely more on techniques of authentic assessment.

➡ They keep detailed records of a child's reading strengths and weaknesses and reading progress. Running records and simple miscue analysis, which are important in authentic assessment, are explained and illustrated later in this chapter. Some teachers or tutors keep records by writing dated notes on self-stick tags while meeting with children and later placing them in the child's files. In addition, teachers or tutors can use sheets with a square for each name, as in the form of a calendar. Other teachers or tutors carry clipboards on which they have children's names listed with a space for important comments. These comments later are placed in the child's file but first must be transcribed or cut apart and glued to each child's record sheet. Figure 2.1 shows an example of this kind of recordkeeping.

Anecdotal records and teacher-completed observational checklists of various kinds are important to the success of any reading improvement program. However, for the reasons explained earlier, standardized test scores give little help to "kid watching," which involves minute-to-minute decision making in teaching reading or tutoring. Based on effective "kid watching" (informal observation and hunches), reading teachers and tutors can select and/or modify various teaching strategies, provide additional explanations and scaffolding (support), give extra help to children who seem to need it, and provide the appropriate review to children who need it. This review can be in the form of teacher-made and commercial activity sheets, teacher-made and commercial reading games, supplementary reading materials, and appropriate reading software among many others.

Effective "kid watching" or teacher observation is essential to a child's success in any reading improvement program, whether it is done by a reading teacher or tutor. It is especially important that children with learning disabilities, reading disabilities, and children with other special needs (including cultural or linguistic diversity) be carefully observed by reading teachers or tutors on a regular, if not daily, basis. This is crucial to their improvement in the various reading skills and in valuing reading both for information and pleasure. Although "kid watching" is

---

FIGURE 2.1
OBSERVATION CHECKLIST FOR CLASS OR READING GROUP

Activity _____ Date _____

Name

Casey Harrington   _____

Gilbert Chapman   _____

Diana Contreras   _____

Rich Enzenbacher   _____

Becky Ichniowski   _____

Pat Walen   _____

Gary Rice   _____

---

demanding, it can be made easier by using reproducible checklists such as those found in this chapter.

SEVEN REPRODUCIBLE CHECKLISTS TO FACILITATE "KID WATCHING" OR TEACHER OBSERVATION

You can duplicate and use in their present form or modify in any way the following checklists:

➡ Concepts about Print Checklist

➡ Phonemic Awareness Checklist

➡ Phonics Skills Checklist

➡ Structural Skills Checklist

➡ Comprehension Skills Checklist

➡ Retelling Ability Checklist

➡ Assessing Your Classroom or Tutoring Reading Program Checklist

These checklists will help you assess children's reading strengths and weaknesses effectively and save time.

CONCEPTS ABOUT PRINT CHECKLIST
(Kindergarten and First-Grade Level)

Name _____ Grade _____

	USUALLY	SOMETIMES	NOT YET
1. Is able to identify environmental print such as *STOP, Wal-Mart, K-Mart, Crest™, corn*, etc.	❑	❑	❑
2. Knows what a *letter* is and can point to it on a page.	❑	❑	❑
3. Knows what a *word* is and can point to it on a page.	❑	❑	❑
4. Understands that there are white spaces (word boundaries) between words.	❑	❑	❑
5. Understands that print is written from left to right.	❑	❑	❑
6. Knows the purpose of a period.	❑	❑	❑
7. Knows the purpose of a comma.	❑	❑	❑
8. Understands that oral language (talk) can be written down and then read by someone.	❑	❑	❑
9. Can identify simple sight words such as *father, mother, dog, cat, rat, pig,* and *school*.	❑	❑	❑
10. Is able to use picture clues as a word identification technique.	❑	❑	❑
11. Can identify all of the capital letter names.	❑	❑	❑
12. Can identify all of the lower-case letter names.	❑	❑	❑
13. Can provide a rhyming word to a word that is given (*bell, fell, tell, sell, well*).	❑	❑	❑
14. Associates consonant blends with their sounds (*br, cr, dr, fr, gr, pr, tr*).	❑	❑	❑
15. Associates vowels with their matching long and short vowel sounds (*/a/—ate, apple; /e/—eat, Eskimo; /i/—ice, igloo; /o/—open, octopus; /u/—use, umbrella*).	❑	❑	❑
16. Can blend phonemes (sounds) into words.	❑	❑	❑
17. Can divide (segment) phonemes (sounds) in words.	❑	❑	❑
18. Uses semantic (context) clues to identify unknown words.	❑	❑	❑
19. Uses word placement or grammar clues to identify unknown words.	❑	❑	❑
20. Can predict unknown words by using context clues along with phonics (letter–sound relationships).	❑	❑	❑

PHONEMIC AWARENESS CHECKLIST*
(Kindergarten or First-Grade Level)

Name _____ Grade _____

	USUALLY	SOMETIMES	NOT YET
1. Listens attentively to nursery rhymes and tries to repeat them.	❑	❑	❑
2. Listens attentively to Dr. Seuss books and enjoys experimenting with the words in them.	❑	❑	❑
3. Listens to predictable books such as *Brown Bear, Brown Bear, What Do You See?* (B. Martin, Holt, 1983) and then tries to make up his or her own version of the book such as the following: Yellow dog, yellow dog, what do you see? I see a black cat looking at me. Black cat, black cat, what do you see? I see a white duck looking at me (etc.).	❑	❑	❑
4. Is able to differentiate between pairs of words that are alike and different (*bell—bill, tub—tug, sat—sit, bump—dump, bet—bit, fry—try*).	❑	❑	❑
5. Is able to point to the one of two pictures whose name is pronounced (*cat—rat, man—pan, house—mouse, boy—toy, baby—lady, frog—dog, pail—tail, moose—goose, star—car*).	❑	❑	❑
6. Is able to give a rhyming word for a pronounced word even if it is a nonsense word (**bump**—*dump, fump, hump, lump, mump, sump, tump, wump*).	❑	❑	❑

---

*Phonemic awareness is defined as the consciousness of the sounds in words. It includes the ability to notice rhyme, separate (segment) the sounds in words, and hear consonant and vowel sounds.

PHONEMIC AWARENESS CHECKLIST* *(Cont'd)*

	USUALLY	SOMETIMES	NOT YET
7. Is able to provide the final rhyming word for a couplet: *It is a warm and sunny day* *So I can go out and _____.* *I hope that my big black cat* *Can catch that big fat _____.*	❏	❏	❏
8. Is able to blend three separate phonemes into a recognizable word. (*/s/-/u/-/n/ sun*).	❏	❏	❏
9. Is able to stretch out the sounds of words. (*/t t t/-/o o o/-/p p p/ top*).	❏	❏	❏
10. Is able to use consonant substitution (onsets and rimes) as a word identification technique (*b-all, c-all, f-all, h-all, sm-all, t-all, w-all*).	❏	❏	❏
11. Is able to divide words using the *Elkonon technique.* (Give the child a drawing of a short word, below which are blocks that correspond to the number of sounds in the word. Below a drawing of the word *man* there are three blocks. A token is placed in each block to represent the sounds in *man.*)	❏	❏	❏
12. Is able to point out the one object in a group that begins with a different sound (*phoneme /d/—duck, dog, dish, bell, doll*) (*phoneme /m/—mouse, man, newspaper, mitten*) (*phoneme /t/—toy, towel, dog, tub*).	❏	❏	❏

PHONICS SKILLS CHECKLIST
(Primary-Grade Level)

Name _____ Grade _____

	USUALLY	SOMETIMES	NOT YET
1. Is able to give the sounds of each of these consonants and can give a word that begins with each of them: *b, hard c (/k/), soft c (/s/), d, f, hard g (/g/), soft g (/j/), h, j, k, l, m, n, r, s, t, v, w, y,* and *z.*	❏	❏	❏
2. Is able to pronounce the consonant *x* correctly when it is found at the end of a word, such as *box,* and is able to supply a rhyming word to *box.*	❏	❏	❏
3. Is able to pronounce each of the following consonant blends and can give a word that begins with that blend: *bl, cl, cr, dr, fl, fr, gl, gr, pl, pr, qu, sc, scr, shr, sk, sm, sn, spl, str, squ, thr,* and *tw.*	❏	❏	❏
4. Is able to pronounce each of the following consonant digraphs and give a word that begins with that digraph: */ch/, /ng/, /ph/, /sh/, voiceless /th/, voiced /th/,* and */wh/.*	❏	❏	❏
5. Is able to give a word that ends with each of these consonant clusters: *ck, ld, mp, nd,* and *st.*	❏	❏	❏
6. Understands that *w* is silent in *wr, g* is silent in *gn,* and *b* is silent in *mb.*	❏	❏	❏
7. Is able to pronounce each of these vowel digraphs and give a word containing that vowel digraph: *ai, ea (reach), ea (bread), ae, ee, oa, ay, ow (bowl), oo (look), oo (goose), ie.*	❏	❏	❏
8. Is able to pronounce each of these *r*-controlled vowel combinations and give a word containing the *r*-controlled vowel combination: *ar, air, er, ear, ir, or, ur.*	❏	❏	❏
9. Is able to pronounce each of these vowel diphthongs and give a word containing that diphthong: *oi, oy, ou, ow (cow),* and *ew.*	❏	❏	❏
10. Is able to pronounce each of these special vowel combinations and give a word that contains that special vowel combination: *au* and *aw.*	❏	❏	❏
11. Understands that the *gh* is silent in *ght (night).*	❏	❏	❏

PHONICS SKILLS CHECKLIST *(Cont'd)*

	USUALLY	SOMETIMES	NOT YET
12. Is able to give a word that contains each of these rimes (phonograms or word families): *-ace, -ade, -amp, -arm, -each, -eap, -edge, -eep, -eld, -elp, -ew, -idge, -ile, -ince, -inch, -ive, -oak, -oast, -ol -ool, -ore, -ork, -ought, -ouse, -out, -uck,* and *-ust.*	❏	❏	❏
13. Understands and can use the *schwa (ə) sound* (the vowel in an unaccented syllable in a word of more than one syllable).	❏	❏	❏
14. Is able to apply these two rules for *y: y* at the end of a word of more than one syllable records (takes) the long */e/ sound (lady); y* at the end of a word of only one syllable records (takes) the long */i/ sound (why).*	❏	❏	❏
15. Is able to apply the following phonic rules:			
• A single vowel in a closed syllable is usually short (a closed syllable has one vowel between two consonants, such as *bat, led, lip, top,* and *hut*).	❏	❏	❏
• A single vowel at the end of a word is usually long, such as *go.*	❏	❏	❏
• When there are two vowels side by side, the long sound of the first vowel *may be* heard, such as *rain, tie, goat,* and *juice,* while the second *may be* silent.	❏	❏	❏
• When the same two consonants are found side by side, only one consonant is heard, such as *butter, letter,* and *ladder.*	❏	❏	❏
• When a word contains two vowels, one of which is final *e,* the first vowel is long and the final *e* is silent, such as *bake, hope,* and *mane.*	❏	❏	❏
• *y* at the end of a single syllable word usually records (takes) the long */i/* sound, such as *fly, why,* and *try.*	❏	❏	❏
• *y* at the end of a word of two or more syllables usually records (takes) the long */e/* sound (except in some dialects it records [takes] the short */i/*sound), such as *baby, lady,* and *turkey.*	❏	❏	❏

STRUCTURAL SKILLS CHECKLIST
(Intermediate-Grade Level)

Name _____ Grade _____

	USUALLY	SOMETIMES	NOT YET
1. Is able to identify (recognize by sight) these contractions: *I'll, I'm, it's, wasn't, he'll, here's, let's, that's, she'll, there'll, there's, they'll, you'll, doesn't, don't, can't, they're, he's, I've, we're, you've, you're, I'd, he'd, she'd, we'd,* and *you'd.*	❑	❑	❑
2. Understands the use of the possessive, such as *mother's.*	❑	❑	❑
3. Understands the basic function of prefixes and can add the following prefixes to base words: *a-, re-, un-, be-, ex-, in-, dis-, pre-, ad-, anti-, com-, con-, de-, im-, inter-, mis-, pro-, post-, sub-, trans-, ante-, bene-, bi-, circum-, extra-,* and *micro-.*	❑	❑	❑
4. Understands the basic function of suffixes and can add the following suffixes to base words: *-s, -ed, -ing, -y, -ly, -en, -er, -es, -ful, -able, -less, -ment, -ness, -tion, -al, -ance, -ant, -ation, -ence, -hood, -ible, -ic, -ion, -ish, -ist, -ity, -ive, -or, -ous, -ship, -some, -ty, -ure,* and *-ward.*	❑	❑	❑
5. Understands the principle of doubling the final consonant in a short word before adding the suffix (*hop—hopping*).	❑	❑	❑
6. Understands and is able to apply the principle of changing *y* to *i* before adding the suffix *es* (*baby—babies*).	❑	❑	❑
7. Understands and is able to apply these syllabic principles:			
• When two *like* consonants are found between two vowels, the word is usually divided between the two consonants. *lad/der VC/CV*	❑	❑	❑
• When two *unlike* consonants are found between two vowels, the word is usuallydivided between the two consonants. *lis/ten VC/CV*	❑	❑	❑
• *Prefixes* and *suffixes* are usually separate syllables (*un/happy, wish/ful*).	❑	❑	❑

STRUCTURAL SKILLS CHECKLIST *(Cont'd)*

	USUALLY	SOMETIMES	NOT YET
• When a word ends in a consonant and *le*, the consonant usually begins the first syllable (*cir/cle, tur/tle*).	❑	❑	❑
• Compound words are divided between the two words that comprise them (*straw/berry, play/ground*).	❑	❑	❑
• Do *not* divide the letters in a consonant blend or consonant digraph (*kitch/en, bask/et*).	❑	❑	❑
8. Is able to syllabicate multisyllabic accent g (*2–4 syllables*) words.	❑	❑	❑
9. Understands and is able to apply these eneralizations:			
• In two-syllable words the first syllable is usually accented (*bas´ ket, mon´ key, ta´ ble, cor´ ner*).	❑	❑	❑
• In inflected or derived forms of a word, the primary accent usually falls on the root word (*around´, about´*).	❑	❑	❑
• If two vowels are together in the last syllable of a word, it is a clue to an accented final syllable (*im peach´*).	❑	❑	❑
• If there are two of the same consonant within a word, the syllable before the double consonant is usually accented (*let´ ter*).	❑	❑	❑
10. Is able to use primary and secondary accents and is able to apply accents to general and specialized vocabulary terms.	❑	❑	❑
11. Uses structural skills before using phonic skills in decoding an unknown word when this is applicable.	❑	❑	❑
12. Is able to use the meaning of prefixes, suffixes, or word roots to determine the approximate meaning of unknown vocabulary terms found in narrative or content reading.	❑	❑	❑
13. Uses good judgment about when to apply structural analysis skills as a word iden-tification technique.	❑	❑	❑
14. Uses structural analysis skills before phonic skills in decoding unknown words.	❑	❑	❑

COMPREHENSION SKILLS CHECKLIST
(Intermediate-Grade Level)

Name _____ Grade _____

	USUALLY	SOMETIMES	NOT YET
I. Prediction Skills			
1. Is able to formulate his or her own purposes for reading a narrative or content selection.	❑	❑	❑
2. Is able to predict the content of narrative or content material from its title.	❑	❑	❑
3. At appropriate stopping points in a narrative story is able to predict accurately what is going to happen next.	❑	❑	❑
4. Is able to use the Directed Reading-Thinking Activity (DR-TA) successfully with narrative and content material.	❑	❑	❑
5. Is able to formulate predictions that were determined to be accurate following reading.	❑	❑	❑
II. Use of Self-Monitoring Skills			
1. Has a positive attitude toward reading and a good self-image about his or her reading skills.	❑	❑	❑
2. Knows the purpose of reading.	❑	❑	❑
3. Is able to formulate his or her own questions while reading.	❑	❑	❑
4. Usually self-corrects his or her own word identification errors while reading.	❑	❑	❑
5. Is able to change reading strategies to fit his or her reading purposes.	❑	❑	❑
6. Is able to relate new information to what is already known.	❑	❑	❑
7. Knows which "fix-up" strategies to use when he or she does not understand the material.	❑	❑	❑
8. Is able to determine the important information in a reading selection.	❑	❑	❑
III. Other Important Comprehension Skills			
1. Understands the purpose of semantic maps or webs and is able to formulate a semantic map or web from narrative or content material at the appropriate level.	❑	❑	❑

COMPREHENSION SKILLS CHECKLIST *(Cont'd)*

	USUALLY	SOMETIMES	NOT YET
2. Is able to use visual imagery as a comprehension strategy while reading narrative or content material.	❑	❑	❑
3. Observes punctuation marks, such as periods, commas, exclamation points, semicolons, and colons, while reading.	❑	❑	❑
4. Is competent in using such guide words as *if, when, so, as, for, until, meanwhile, before, after, during, following,* and *always* while reading.	❑	❑	❑
5. Is able to understand and apply such elements of *story grammar* as the setting, characters, theme or plot, a few episodes in the plot, and the resolution of the problem that motivated the characters to action.	❑	❑	❑

IV. Explicit (Literal) Comprehension

	USUALLY	SOMETIMES	NOT YET
1. Is able to answer explicit (literal) comprehension questions from narrative material at the appropriate reading level.	❑	❑	❑
2. Is able to answer explicit (literal) comprehension questions from content material at the appropriate reading level.	❑	❑	❑
3. Is able to understand the purpose of *who, what, when, where,* and *why* questions at the appropriate reading level.	❑	❑	❑
4. Is able to competently retell narrative or content material.	❑	❑	❑
5. In narrative retelling includes these elements:			
• setting	❑	❑	❑
• characters	❑	❑	❑
• theme	❑	❑	❑
• plot episodes	❑	❑	❑
• resolution	❑	❑	❑
6. Is able to locate a directly stated main idea and/or topic sentence in a paragraph.	❑	❑	❑
7. Is able to write an accurate statement of the main idea of a trade book, basal reader story, or content selection.	❑	❑	❑
8. Is able to read and follow directions at the appropriate reading level.	❑	❑	❑

COMPREHENSION SKILLS CHECKLIST *(Cont'd)*

	USUALLY	SOMETIMES	NOT YET
9. Is able to locate the significant details in a paragraph at the appropriate reading level.	❑	❑	❑
10. Is able to locate the irrelevant details in a paragraph at the appropriate reading level.	❑	❑	❑

V. Implicit (Interpretive) Comprehension

	USUALLY	SOMETIMES	NOT YET
1. Is able to answer implicit (interpretive) comprehension questions from narrative material at the appropriate reading level. These questions require predicting outcomes, interpreting, inferring, drawing conclusions and generalizations, and summarizing.	❑	❑	❑
2. Is able to answer implicit (interpretive) comprehension questions from content material at the appropriate reading level. These questions require predicting outcomes, interpreting, inferring, drawing conclusions and generalizations, and summarizing.	❑	❑	❑
3. Is able to apply fairly complex cause–effect relationships.	❑	❑	❑
4. Is able to apply comparison–contrast relationships.	❑	❑	❑
5. Is able to determine an author's purposes for writing a narrative or content selection.	❑	❑	❑
6. Is able to verify in writing predictions about a selection that were made before reading it.	❑	❑	❑
7. Is able to locate an implied main idea in a paragraph.	❑	❑	❑

VI. Critical (Evaluative) Comprehension

	USUALLY	SOMETIMES	NOT YET
1. Is able to answer critical (evaluative) comprehension questions from reading narrative material at the appropriate reading level.	❑	❑	❑
2. Is able to answer critical (evaluative) comprehenison questions from reading content material at the appropriate reading level.	❑	❑	❑

COMPREHENSION SKILLS CHECKLIST *(Cont'd)*

	USUALLY	SOMETIMES	NOT YET
3. Is able to distinguish between real and make-believe (fact and fantasy).	❑	❑	❑
4. Is able to distinguish between fact and opinion.	❑	❑	❑
5. Is able to critically read parts of the newspaper, such as editorials, letters to the editor, and advertisements.	❑	❑	❑
6. Is able to recognize such common propaganda techniques as *testimonials*, *the bandwagon effect*, *the halo effect*, and *emotionally charged words*.	❑	❑	❑
7. Is able to compare material from several different sources, such as a content textbook and a trade book.	❑	❑	❑
8. Is able to evaluate an author's biases.	❑	❑	❑
9. Is able to evaluate the actions of book characters.	❑	❑	❑
10. Is able to estimate the answer to a verbal problem in arithmetic.	❑	❑	❑

VII. Creative (Applied) Comprehension

	USUALLY	SOMETIMES	NOT YET
1. Is able to combine his or her own prior knowledge with the printed material in understanding and applying what was read.	❑	❑	❑
2. Is able to relate what he or she has read in some way that contributes to his or her improvement.	❑	❑	❑
3. Is able to relate reading and writing in a creative way.	❑	❑	❑
4. Is able to follow up reading in a problem-solving way, such as by cooking or baking activities, art activities, construction activities, rhythm activities, dramatic play, creative dramatics, sociodrama, storytelling, pantomiming, and creative writing.	❑	❑	❑

RETELLING ABILITY CHECKLIST
(Third- or Fourth-Grade Level)

Name _____ Grade _____

	USUALLY	SOMETIMES	NOT YET
1. Is able to begin the retelling of a book (story) with some type of introduction.	❑	❑	❑
2. Is able to name the main character in a book (story) while retelling it.	❑	❑	❑
3. Is able to name the other characters in the book (story) while retelling it.	❑	❑	❑
4. Includes a statement about the time and place in the book (story) retelling.	❑	❑	❑
5. Mentions the goal of the main character or the problem to be solved in the book (story) while retelling it.	❑	❑	❑
6. Is able to recall all of the episodes or plot events in the book (story) while retelling it.	❑	❑	❑
7. Is able to remember all of the episodes or plot events in the book (story) in correct sequence while retelling it.	❑	❑	❑
8. Includes the solution to the problem while attaining the goal in the retelling.	❑	❑	❑
9. Is able to provide some type of ending to the book (story) retelling.	❑	❑	❑
10. Seems to enjoy retelling the books and stories that he or she has read.	❑	❑	❑

ASSESSING YOUR CLASSROOM
OR TUTORING READING PROGRAM CHECKLIST
(Reading Teacher or Tutor)

Name _____ Grade _____

	ALWAYS	SOMETIMES	NEVER
1. I provide my student(s) with a reading program that has a balance of whole language and skills-based instruction.	❑	❑	❑
2. My student(s) have an adequate or good sight vocabulary.	❑	❑	❑
3. My student(s) understand and apply the important phonic skills.	❑	❑	❑
4. My student(s) understand the purpose of semantic (context) clues and use them regularly when appropriate.	❑	❑	❑
5. My student(s) understand what they read.	❑	❑	❑
6. My student(s) seem to enjoy reading for information (the Internet, content textbooks, newspapers, magazines, and informational trade books).	❑	❑	❑
7. My student(s) seem to enjoy reading for pleasure (trade books, magazines, the Internet).	❑	❑	❑
8. I use a variety of authentic (informal) assessment tools (observation, running records, miscue analysis, the Individual Reading Inventory, and portfolio assessment).	❑	❑	❑
9. Although I give standardized reading tests, I understand their uses and limitations.	❑	❑	❑
10. I act upon the results of standardized and authentic (informal) assessment to appropriately modify my classroom or tutorial reading program.	❑	❑	❑
11. I use many different types of grouping in my classroom reading program, such as whole class instruction, small group instruction, cooperative learning groups, reading "buddies," and individualized reading.	❑	❑	❑

ASSESSING YOUR CLASSROOM OR TUTORING READING PROGRAM CHECKLIST *(Cont'd)*

	ALWAYS	SOMETIMES	NEVER
12. I try to provide students who have special needs, such as learning disabilities, physical impairments, or cultural and linguistic diversity, with a reading program that maximizes their unique strengths while compensating for their weaknesses.	❑	❑	❑
13. I try to capitalize on the unique cultural backgrounds of my student(s).	❑	❑	❑
14. I provide concrete reinforcement to those students who seem to benefit from it.	❑	❑	❑
15. My classroom or tutorial reading program is carefully planned and carried out.	❑	❑	❑
16. My classroom or tutorial reading program contains both structured and informal activities.	❑	❑	❑
17. I try to have positive teacher–pupil relationships in my teaching or tutoring of reading.	❑	❑	❑
18. I use technology in my teaching or tutoring of reading when appropriate.	❑	❑	❑
19. I use reading games, activity sheets, and computer software for practice in reading skills when needed.	❑	❑	❑
20. I have an extensive classroom library and regularly take my student(s) to the school library.	❑	❑	❑
21. I inform appropriate administrators and the parents of my student(s) about the purpose and content of the classroom reading or tutorial program.	❑	❑	❑
22. I believe that I am knowledgeable about the reading process and the teaching of reading.	❑	❑	❑
23. I try to keep up to date in the reading field by reading appropriate professional journals, attending reading conferences and conventions, and talking with my colleagues about how to improve the teaching of reading.	❑	❑	❑
24. I generally enjoy teaching reading in my classroom or tutoring sessions.	❑	❑	❑
25. I believe that I am a successful reading teacher or tutor.	❑	❑	❑

USING THE RUNNING RECORD FOR AUTHENTIC ASSESSMENT

Running records are a good way of assessing a student's reading progress. The running record is an individually administered assessment device that does not require any special materials except the child's own copy of the material that he or she is going to read aloud and a sheet of paper and a pencil or pen for the reading teacher or tutor. A pen is preferable because it makes less noise while the child is reading. Although an oral reading sample is obtained, comprehension is not evaluated in a running record. Therefore, many reading specialists believe that a running record always should be followed up by having the child briefly retell the material that he or she has read.

The running record has two main purposes: to determine whether a child's reading materials are on the correct level and to obtain information about the word identification processes that the child is using. Running records are most commonly used with first-grade children, although they also can be useful with older children, especially if those children seem to have word identification difficulties. They are useful in second and third grades and may be of use in the intermediate grades, especially with children who have special needs, such as learning or reading disabilities.

As used in the first-grade early intervention program Reading Recovery and described in Clay's book *An Observational Survey of Early Literacy Achievement* (1993), running records are given according to a standardized format in which a student's errors and self-corrections are recorded on a separate sheet of paper. Even so, they are thought of as authentic (informal) assessment devices. As adapted by reading teachers and tutors, running records may be recorded (as long as the fair-use provision of the copyright law is adhered to or permission is obtained from the publisher of Clay's book) on a photocopy of the reading material that the child is reading or on a blank sheet of paper (more common and preferable) (Learning Media, 1991).

To assess whether reading materials are on a suitable level of difficulty and to determine whether a child is making good use of cueing strategies (*meaning* [use of semantic or context cues], *visual* [sight word or phonic clues], or *syntactic* [grammar or word order clues]) that were learned previously, take a running record on a child's trade book or content textbook that he or she has read recently. To assess a child's ability to read more difficult materials and to apply cueing strategies independently, take a running record on material that the child has not read previously. If the book is fairly short, take a running record on the entire book. However, if the book is fairly long, take a running record from a sample of 100 to 200 words in length. As the student reads the material aloud, record his or her performance using symbols such as those shown in Figure 2.2. You will soon discover that it takes a great deal of practice to become adept at taking running records. Therefore, you probably will want to tape record the child's oral reading until you become adept at this assessment strategy even though true proponents of the running record do not recommend this. Instead of the running record symbols shown in Figure 2.2, you can use the traditional Individual Reading Inventory symbols if you feel more comfortable with them (found on page 66 of this chapter). After taking the running record, record the number of words in the entire selection, the number of errors that the child made, the error rate, the number of self-corrections made (a very desirable reading strategy), and the accuracy rate.

FIGURE 2.2
RUNNING RECORD SYMBOLS

Symbols	Text	Example
Each word read correctly is marked with a check mark.	A loon is a very good fisherman.	✓ ✓ ✓ ✓ ✓ ✓
Substitutions are written above the line.	Do you know what loons are?	✓ ✓ knew ✓ ✓ ✓ 　　know
Self-corrections are marked SC.	Do you know what loons are?	✓✓ knew/sc ✓✓✓ 　　know
A dash is used to indicate no response.	They are black with little white markings.	✓ ✓ ✓ ✓ ✓ — 　　　　markings
A dash is used to indicate an insertion of a word. The dash is placed below the inserted word.	They are black with white markings.	✓ ✓ ✓ ✓ little 　　✓　✓
A T is used to indicate that a child has been told a word.	Sometimes people in boats bother them.	✓T　✓✓✓✓ people
The letter A indicates that the child has asked for help.	Sometimes people in boats bother them.	✓A　✓✓✓✓ people
At times the child becomes so confused by a misreading that it is suggested that he or she "try that again" (coded TTA). Brackets are put around the section that has been misread, the whole misreading is counted as one error, and the student reads it again for a new score.	A person should never get too near a loon.	✓people ✓not　TTA person　never ✓ ✓ nice ✓ ✓ 　　near
A repetition is indicated with an R. Although not counted as errors, repetitions are often part of an attempt to puzzle out a difficult term. The point to which the student returns in the repetition is indicated by an arrow.	A loon has a sharp beak that helps it catch fish.	✓✓✓ short ✓✓✓✓✓ 　　sharp　　　R

Although Clay (1993) recommends 90% as an adequate accuracy rate, 95% probably is more desirable. Since word identification is emphasized in the running record, comprehension is not evaluated. After taking a running record, you can use retelling to assess comprehension skills.

It is important that you analyze a child's reading errors to determine what reading strategies he or she is using. Some children use such incorrect reading strategies that they are greatly hindered in making reading progress. These incorrect strategies must be corrected before children can make real reading improvement. As you examine a child's reading errors, you can consider the following questions:

➨ Do the student's errors usually make sense? Are they semantically acceptable? Does the child usually read for meaning?

➨ Is the child using visual or sound-symbol (phonic) cues? Are the child's errors similar in appearance and sound to the target word?

➨ Is the child using picture clues?

➨ Is the child using syntactic (word order or grammar) clues?

➨ Is the child integrating cues? Does he or she balance the use of meaning cues with sound-symbol cues? Does he or she avoid relying too heavily on just one type of word identification cue?

➨ Is the child self-correcting errors, especially those that interfere with the meaning of the sentence? Is the child aware when his or her errors do not make sense in the material?

➨ Based on the child's performance on a running record, what reading strategies does he or she need to master?

In addition, you can notice whether or not children read from left to right and from top to bottom and whether there is one-to-one correspondence (voice-print match). For more detailed information about analyzing and interpreting running records, consult Clay's book (1993).

HOW TO EVALUATE A RUNNING RECORD

The following is a passage on the second-grade reading level. It was given to a second-grade student named Rita, and her performance on a running record is included. A detailed analysis of Rita's performance on this running record and some recommendations for her classroom reading teacher or reading tutor are presented later in this chapter.

HOW DOGS ARE LIKE WOLVES

All dogs are descended from wolves whether the dogs are large or small. Studying the habits of wolves can help people understand the behaviors that we see in domesticated dogs.

Sociability is a wolf's most striking feature. A dog's history as a social animal explains why it barks, is protective, or wags its tail.

Since dogs are social animals, there can be problems when owners ignore their need for companionship. Since its human family is a dog's pack, the average dog does not like to be alone. The dog may bark and howl in an attempt to locate its missing pack members. Because a dog may be nervous when it is left alone, it may chew. Dogs usually chew things that have the owner's smell on them.

Since a dog feels that it must protect its territory, it usually barks when it sees or hears anything that it feels is invading its territory. Although this barking can be protective for the family, it also can be very annoying for the family and their neighbors.

To reduce a dog's nervousness about having to guard the whole house, an owner can give it a "minimum den" inside the house. This usually is a wire kennel crate like those used at dog shows.

The wolf pack always has an *alpha* or "top wolf." A dog that growls, bites, or refuses to obey may think that it is the alpha or "top dog" in its pack. The dog that thinks it is the alpha dog uses threats and intimidation to control its pack members or family. If a person has a dog that he or she can't control, that person must get help from a dog trainer right away.

BRIEF ANALYSIS OF RITA'S PERFORMANCE ON THE RUNNING RECORD

The passage "How Dogs Are Like Wolves" that Rita read contained 285 words. She made 29 miscues while reading this passage aloud. Since the passage contained 285 words, the reading teacher or tutor divides 29 by 285 to obtain a reading error percentage of about .10 or 10%. Rita read the passage at about the 90% level of accuracy. This passage is fairly difficult for her and is at her low instructional or high frustration (hard) reading level. She should have an error rate of 5% or less to be able to read it easily. Although Clay (1993) has written that a 90% accuracy rate is acceptable, I believe that a child should have an accuracy rate of 95% or better to be able to read a passage with fluency and ease.

It may be helpful to examine Rita's errors line by line on a copy of the passage.

HOW DOGS ARE LIKE WOLVES

All dogs are descended from wolves whether the dogs are large or

Two errors—One "teacher told the word" and one substitution

small. Studying the habits of wolves can help people understand the

No errors—The self-correction and the repetition are not counted as errors.

behaviors that we see in domesticated dogs.

Two errors—One substitution and one "teacher told the word"

Sociability is a wolf's most striking feature. A dog's history as a

Two errors—Two substitutions

social animal explains why it barks, is protective, or wags its tail.

One error—One substitution. The self-correction is not counted as an error.

Since dogs are social animals, there can be problems when owners

One error—One substitution

ignore their need for companionship. Since its human family is a dog's

Two errors—One "teacher told the word" and one substitution. The repetition is not counted as an error.

pack, the average dog does not like to be alone. The dog may bark and

One error—One "teacher told the word"

howl in an attempt to locate its missing pack members. Because a dog

Two errors—Two substitutions

may be nervous when it is left alone, it may chew. Dogs usually chew

One error—One substitution

things that have the owner's smell on them.

No errors

Since a dog feels that it must protect its territory, it usually barks

One error—One substitution

when it sees or hears anything that it feels is invading its territory.

Two errors—Two "teacher told the word." The self-correction is not counted as an error.

Although this barking can be protective for the family, it also can be very

One error—One substitution. The repetition is not counted as an error.

annoying for the family and their neighbors.

One error—One "teacher told the word"

To reduce a dog's nervousness about having to guard the whole

Two errors—One substitution and "one teacher told the word"

house, an owner can give it a "minimum den" inside the house. This

One error—One "teacher told the word"

usually is a wire kennel crate like those used at dog shows.

Two errors—One substitution and one try again (not scored in the preceding line)

The wolf pack always has an *alpha* or "top wolf." A dog that

One error—One "teacher told the word"

growls, bites, or refuses to obey may think that it is the alpha or "top dog"

Two errors—One substitution and one "teacher told the word. The repetition is not counted as an error.

in its pack. The dog that thinks it is the alpha dog uses threats and

No errors

intimidation to control its pack members or family. If a person has a dog

Two errors—One "teacher told the word" and one substitution

that he or she can't control, that person must get help from a dog trainer

No errors

right away.

No errors

Rita showed several strengths while reading the passage "How Dogs Are Like Wolves." She had a good sight vocabulary and could recognize the majority of the words found on a sight word list immediately. Some of her substitutions made fairly good sense in context, which was helpful. In addition, she made only three repetitions while reading, which was not excessive. Her reading teacher or tutor can build on these strengths while correcting her weaknesses. However, Rita demonstrated the following weaknesses in her oral reading of the passage:

➡ Because she made only two self-corrections, it is obvious that she did not monitor her reading comprehension effectively. A good reader is continually monitoring what he or she reads to make sure that it is understood. Rita was not particularly concerned whether or not her reading makes sense. This is a major reading problem, and self-monitoring must be stressed a great deal in her reading improvement program.

➡ Rita needs to learn to take more risks while she is reading. Rita's teacher had to supply eleven words for her while she was reading. That is entirely too many and shows that not only is the material too difficult for her but that she often did not even attempt to identify the words by using either semantic, syntactic, visual cues, or a combination of them.

➡ Rita needs to look more carefully at the words found in the printed material. Sometimes she looked at only the first letter or first several letters in a word and did not look at the rest of the word.

➡ Rita needs to have instruction and/or practice in using visual (sight word and phonic) cues and especially in *cross-checking cues* (semantic, syntactic, and visual). She needs to be sure to use visual and phonic cues along with semantic (meaning) and syntactic (grammar) cues

In summary, Rita's reading teacher or tutor should provide her with fairly easy, very motivating reading materials that are on her independent (easy) or high instructional (with some teacher support) level to improve her reading confidence and fluency. In addition, she should have practice in phonic analysis. She also should be given much practice in cross-checking cues (semantic, syntactic, and visual). Perhaps, most important, she needs to be more aware that reading always must make sense. She must have considerable practice in monitoring her own reading skills to be sure that it always makes sense. All of these goals can be accomplished in a good reading improvement program planned and carried out either by a reading teacher or tutor.

USING MISCUE ANALYSIS

Miscue analysis is another strategy that can be used to assess a student's reading skills. Although some reading teachers and tutors think that miscue analysis is not quite so helpful as a running record, you may find it useful. Therefore, this book provides a brief description of this strategy.

A useful, fairly simple system for coding reading miscues (errors) was developed by Argyle (1989). Simply, this coding system attempts to determine if the miscue (error) caused a meaning change, a graphic change, or was a self-correction. If the child's miscues resulted in few meaning changes, they usually are not significant because they probably would not interfere with comprehension. If the student made a number of visual (sight, phonic, or word structure) miscues, he or she may need additional instruction and/or practice in sight words, phonics, or word structure depending on the frequency of the miscues and whether or not they interfered significantly with comprehension. If the student made a number of self-corrections, he or she probably does not have a significant reading problem in comparison to a child who does not recognize his or her miscues and therefore does not attempt to correct them.

In general, Argyle recommends the following steps for using this system of miscue analysis:

1. Choose reading material that is not familiar to your students. This may be part of a narrative or informational trade book, a passage from a content textbook, or a basal reader story.

2. Copy the reading selection.

3. Tell the child that it is not a test, to reduce his or her anxiety about it.

4. Have the student read the selected passage without any preparation. Tape recording helps you to code all of the miscues but may not be practical in a noisy setting. Although it is possible to code the miscues while the student is reading, it is fairly difficult to do so.

5. Place the miscues on a summary sheet so that they can be analyzed. Here is a brief sample of how Argyle's system may work:

   ⟶ Omission   (orbit) around the sun
   ⟶ Addition   orbit around the ⌄sun   *bright*
   ⟶ Pause   orbit // around the sun

➡ Substitution	*orange* ~~orbit~~ around the sun
➡ Repetition	orbit <u>around the sun</u>
➡ Reversal	orbit around the sun
➡ Self-Correction	<u>orbit</u> around the sun
➡ Words Supplied by Teacher	orbit around the sun

EXAMPLE OF MISCUE ANALYSIS

An oral reading passage entitled "Saturn, the Planet with Rings" was written at about the fourth-grade level. It was given to Benny, a fourth-grade student who had exhibited reading problems. The passage was tape recorded, and Benny's reading tutor coded his oral reading miscues using the system just described. The coded copy of this reading passage in included on pages 51 and 52.

Benny's teacher then transferred his miscues to a brief summary sheet that she had constructed. For each miscue the correct word is written first. Then a representation of the student's response is written in each sentence. If the miscue resulted in a meaning change, the word *yes* is written, and if only partial meaning change occurred, the word *partial* is written. If no meaning change resulted from the miscue, the word *no* is written. Next, each miscue is analyzed in terms of a graphic (visual or phonic) change in the beginning, middle, or end of the word. In either case, an underscore (–) is written for a miscue in that part of the word, while a ✔ is written for a correct response in that part of the word. If a student self-corrects a miscue, a self-correction also is coded.

After coding Benny's responses on the summary sheet, his teacher should try to analyze some of his reading strengths and weaknesses in terms of the patterns that were found in the oral reading miscue analysis. You will find that it takes some time and effort to be adept at interpreting a student's oral reading miscues and to develop an in-depth understanding of the reading process.

You will notice that Benny made 21 miscues that interfered with comprehension and 11 miscues that only partially interfered with comprehension. In addition, he made 9 miscues that did not seem to interfere significantly with comprehension.

The percentages of graphic miscues that Benny made also were coded by his reading tutor. From this analysis Benny's tutor tried to determine if Benny seemed to be more competent in identifying beginnings, middles, or endings of the miscued words. His tutor noticed that he had the most difficulty with word endings and somewhat less difficulty with word middles. This is not the most typical pattern of graphic miscues for a student with reading problems. Most students are competent with word beginnings, which was the case with Benny, but have the most difficulty with word middles. Benny's tutor noticed that he made 4 self-corrections, also fairly common in a student with significant oral reading miscues who does not monitor his or her reading comprehension as well as should be done to ensure that reading always makes sense.

You will notice that Benny made a total of 41 oral reading miscues on this passage out of a total of 297 words. (The 4 self-corrections are not counted as errors.) This indicates that he mispronounced about 14% of the words and correctly pronounced about 86% of them. Therefore, this passage is somewhat too hard for Benny and is on his frustration reading level.

Because the slash marks in the coding of Benny's reading behavior indicate pauses in his oral reading, it appears as though he may not have so good an oral reading fluency as he should. Although the pauses that Benny made are fairly typical of a student with reading disabilities, they are not so significant as they are with more severely disabled readers. However, pauses while reading tend to hinder comprehension skills, especially in the upper primary grades and beyond. Benny had only a few repetitions and only one reversal. The repetitions are not counted as miscues, while the words that are reversed are counted as miscues. The self-corrections are not counted as miscues because a self-correction indicates that a student is reading for meaning.

In summary, here are some of Benny's reading strengths:

➡ He has a fairly good knowledge of word beginnings.

➡ He shows some willingness to make self-corrections while reading.

Here are some of Benny's reading weaknesses:

➡ He shows an unwillingness to try to analyze words that he does not know by sight. He allowed his reading tutor to supply twelve unknown words in this passage instead of trying to use semantic, syntactic, or visual cues to identify them.

➡ He makes reading changes that do not have semantic acceptability (do not make sense in sentence context).

➡ He lacks competence in identifying word endings.

Based on these observations, it is obvious that Benny's reading improvement program should have a number of different aspects to ensure his optimum reading growth. He must be given materials that he can read without great difficulty. These materials should be on his independent (easy) or high instructional (with some teacher support) reading level even if this is below the fourth-grade reading level. Additional analysis may be required to determine these levels with some degree of accuracy. The running record explained earlier may be helpful for this purpose as well as an Individual Reading Inventory. Benny should be given instruction and practice in using semantic, syntactic, and visual cues as well as a combination of them so that he can identify words independently instead of relying on his reading teacher or tutor to supply them.

In summary, the preceding is one example of how a variation of oral reading miscue analysis can be used to determine a student's reading strengths and weaknesses. Although this is a fairly simple system to use because it is informal, it does require considerable experience and expertise in the reading process. Therefore, this device should be used carefully by an inexperienced reading teacher or tutor. It may be helpful to practice giving it to another adult before giving it to a student to be sure that you know how it is given and evaluated. In many instances, you may want to use a running record and certainly teacher observation as a supplement to this system of miscue analysis.

The oral reading passage just described is presented next, as well as the completed summary sheet of oral reading miscues. In addition, a reproducible example of the summary sheet for this type of miscue analysis is included. You may duplicate and use the example if you want.

SATURN, THE PLANET WITH RINGS

Saturn is one of nine planets that travel around the sun. Their paths around the sun are called *orbits*. Since Saturn is far away from the sun, it is called an ~~outer~~ *planet.*
[out]

In 1610 the Italian ~~scientist~~ Galileo looked at Saturn ~~through~~ his
[science]   [though]
telescope and said that *"Saturn has <u>ears"</u>* because of the bulges on either side. Today scientists ~~know~~ that those "ears" are rings that circle the planet
[knew]
which make it very ~~beautiful.~~ Saturn is the second largest planet in the solar
[pretty]
system.

Saturn's atmosphere is mainly hydrogen and ~~helium,~~ gases that are
[held]
~~poisonous to~~ people. Since its atmosphere is very cold, the gases <u>in the</u>
[bad for]
<u>atmosphere</u> ~~freeze~~ into ~~crystals~~ that make up the swirling bands of clouds
[froze]   [crys]
that circle the planet. Saturn doesn't have a solid ~~surface~~ like the Earth.
[service]
Instead, liquid hydrogen forms its surface. At the very center of Saturn is a
~~rocky~~ core which is about the <u>same size as the Earth.</u>
[rock]

The farther a planet is from the sun, the longer is its <u>*year*</u>—or the time it takes to make its orbit around the sun. Saturn's ~~journey~~ around the sun
[trip]
takes 295 Earth years.

Saturn's rings are made up of particles of water ice but also may con-tain dust and rock. Each of Saturn's major rings is made up of thousands of

rings
~~ringlets~~ or thin rings. It has some of the ~~strongest~~ **strong** winds in the solar

equal
system. Near its ~~equator~~ the wind <u>roars</u> at 1,100 miles an hour. It has

more moons//than any other planet//in the solar system. There are at least

around
twenty moons ~~orbiting~~ Saturn.

The Cassini Orbiter blasted into space in 1997 and will reach Saturn

in 2004. Then it will orbit Saturn//and will send back (new) information

about this beautiful (ringed) planet.

SUMMARY SHEET OF ORAL READING MISCUES

TEXT	MISCUE	MEANING CHANGE	GRAPHIC B	M	E	SELF-CORRECTION
1. planet	_____	yes	—	—	—	
2. orbits	_____	yes	—	—	—	
3. outer	out	partial	✓	✓	—	
4. planet	_____	yes	—	—	—	
5. scientist	science	yes	✓	✓	—	
6. through	though	yes	✓	—	✓	
7. telescope	_____	yes	—	—	—	
8. ears			✓	✓	✓	*
9. bulges	_____	yes	—	—	—	
10. know	knew	partial	✓	—	✓	
11. circle	_____	yes	—	—	—	
12. very	_____	no	—	—	—	
13. beautiful	pretty	no	—	—	—	
14. second	_____	yes	—	—	—	
15. solar	_____	yes	—	—	—	
16. system			✓	✓	✓	*
17. atmosphere	_____	yes	—	—	—	
18. hydrogen	_____	yes	—	—	—	
19. helium	held	yes	✓	—	—	
20. poisonous	bad	no	—	—	—	
21. to	for	no	—	—	—	
22. atmosphere	_____	yes	—	—	—	
23. very	_____	partial	—	—	—	
24. freeze	froze	partial	✓	—	✓	
25. crystals	crys	yes	✓	—	—	

SUMMARY SHEET OF ORAL READING MISCUES *(Cont'd)*

TEXT	MISCUE	MEANING CHANGE	GRAPHIC B	M	E	SELF-CORRECTION
26. swirling	_____	partial	__	__	__	
27. surface	service	yes	✓	__	__	
28. liquid	_____	yes	__	__	__	
29. rocky	rock	no	✓	✓	__	
30. year			✓	✓	✓	*
31. orbit	_____	yes	__	__	__	
32. journey	trip	no	__	__	__	
33. particles	_____	partial	__	__	__	
34. of	_____	no	__	__	__	
35. dust	rock	no	__	__	__	
36. rock	dust	no	__	__	__	
37. major	_____	yes	__	__	__	
38. ringlets	rings	partial	✓	✓	__	
39. strongest	strong	partial	✓	✓	__	
40. solar	_____	yes	__	__	__	
41. equator	equal	yes	✓	__	__	
42. roars			✓	✓	✓	*
43. orbiting	around	partial	__	__	__	
44. new	_____	partial	__	__	__	
45. ringed	_____	partial	__	__	__	
			16/	9/	7/	

Total 100%/36% correct/20% correct/16% correct

Name _____ Date _____

SUMMARY SHEET OF ORAL READING MISCUES

TEXT	MISCUE	MEANING CHANGE	GRAPHIC B M E	SELF-CORRECTION

USING AN INDIVIDUAL READING INVENTORY

The *Individual Reading Inventory* (IRI) also can be called an *informal reading inventory*. It is an informal assessment device in contrast to a standardized assessment device. The IRI as it is known today probably began with the late Emmett A. Betts and his doctoral student Patsy A. Kilgallon (1942). Kilgallon established criteria for accuracy in word identification and comprehension that then were tested with 41 students. In the informal test the students read each passage silently and then orally, a different procedure from what is used today when giving an IRI. Although these criteria are not used in this book, they still are commonly used. Betts formulated his own definition of the independent (easy), instructional (with teacher support), and frustration (difficult) levels and the listening comprehension (1946).

An IRI is a fairly useful, classroom-oriented informal assessment device. Its main purposes are as follows:

→ Determine a student's prior knowledge and reading interests.

→ Determine a student's ability to predict reading content.

→ Determine a student's *approximate* independent (easy), instructional (with teacher support), and frustration (difficult) reading levels.

→ Estimate a student's listening comprehension level.

→ Place a student in the appropriate reading group.

→ Determine a student's progress in word identification (use of the three main cueing systems), oral reading fluency, and comprehension skills.

→ Permit the teacher to make close-up observations of children engaging in a variety of reading tasks.

→ Determine a student's skills in self-monitoring or metacognition.

The IRI differs somewhat in format depending on who is administering it. The version presented in this book can be used by a Title I reading teacher, a classroom reading teacher, a learning disability teacher, or a reading volunteer. If you are a Title I reading teacher, you probably will want to give an IRI to most of the students with whom you will be working near the beginning of the school year or the tutoring program. If you are a classroom reading teacher, you may want to give an IRI to a few disabled readers in your classroom early in the school year. If you are a teacher of students with learning disabilities, you can give an IRI near the beginning of the school year. If you are a reading volunteer, you can give an IRI near the beginning of the tutoring sessions.

I prefer using the running record instead of an IRI. However, a number of reading and learning disability teachers prefer to give an IRI. In any case, you should not use too many assessment devices near the beginning of a remedial reading program. To do so will likely overwhelm the child and contribute significantly to his or her dislike of all reading activities. Most reading specialists, including this author, believe that assessment and correction of reading difficulties always should be a continuous, interwoven process.

Here are the main parts of a typical IRI:

➡ *Establish rapport with the student.* It is necessary to establish rapport with the student before giving him or her an IRI, especially if you do not know the student well. Ask the child informal questions about his or her interests, hobbies, reading interests, and view of his or her reading skills. Ask the student questions about family only if this is pertinent to the assessment and can be done tactfully and sensitively.

➡ *Give a sight word test.* Give a student a sight word test, such as the *Dolch Basic Sight Word Test* or *Fry's Instant Words*, only if a student seems to be weak in sight word identification ability by teacher observation. *You usually do not give a sight word test and the graded word lists on an IRI because they are duplicative.*

➡ *Give the graded word lists.* The graded word lists of an IRI are lists of words that begin at the preprimer or primer level and usually end at the tenth- or twelfth-grade reading level. There usually are about 25 words on each graded word list. The child is to read each word aloud and continue until he or she misses about 5 words out of 25 words (20%) or reaches the obvious frustration reading level. The major purpose of the graded word lists is to determine how well a student can identify words in isolation in comparison to in (sentence) context, to observe which cues a student uses to identify words, and to determine at about what level to have the student begin reading the graded oral reading passages.

A student with learning disabilities may be able to pronounce words in isolation more effectively than in (sentence) context. However, a disabled reader may be able to use meaning (semantic) cues better and pronounce words better in context.

➡ *Give the graded oral (silent) reading passages.* The graded reading passages are a series of narrative and expository (content) passages that begin at the preprimer level and continue through the tenth- or twelfth-grade reading level. Some of the passages can be used for evaluation of silent reading or listening comprehension. Obviously, students do not read all of the passages either orally or silently. Students usually begin reading aloud a passage that is two or more grade levels below their estimated instructional (with teacher support) reading level. This estimation can be made from the word lists and from teacher observation of previous reading performance if possible.

ADVANTAGES AND LIMITATIONS OF USING AN IRI

The following are the main advantages of using an IRI for informal assessment of reading skills:

➡ The reading levels as determined from an IRI usually are considerably more accurate than are those from a group-administered standardized reading test. For example, if a student receives a reading score of 4.6 on a standardized reading test, his or her actual instructional (with teacher support) reading level may be about 3.5 or less. That may occur because group-administered standardized reading tests allow students to guess randomly at answers. I once taught a second-grade boy who was a nonreader yet was able to earn a grade equivalent score of 2.5 on the Stanford Achievement Test.

➡ An IRI allows a teacher to observe a student's reading behaviors while he or she is reading orally and to a lesser degree while reading silently. You can notice if the child makes good use of meaning cues, visual (graphophonic) cues, and structure cues and cross-checks the three different cueing systems. You also can notice other elements of his or her reading performance, such as one-to-one correspondence, answers to comprehension questions that are partially correct, comprehension questions that are answered correctly after teacher prompts, distractibility, oral reading fluency, and word-by-word reading. None of these behaviors can be observed while a student is taking a group-administered test.

➡ Most of the commercially available IRIs have been classroom tested at least to an extent and may have been evaluated for reliability and validity. Because they have been written by experienced reading specialists, they are well done in most cases.

➡ Most of the IRIs have comprehension questions at both the explicit (literal) and implicit (interpretive, critical, and applied) levels. In most cases the child is given credit for answers to the implicit questions which make sense even if they are not the answers provided by the inventory. Although some standardized reading tests try to allow students to give divergent answers to implicit comprehension questions, it is difficult for them to do so since the tests are typically computer scored.

➡ An IRI allows a reading teacher to observe a child's pattern of errors. It allows the teacher to notice if the child has made an excessive number of omissions, substitutions, repetitions, reversals, pauses, or words supplied by the teacher. Some commercial inventories also enable a reading teacher to determine if the student's miscues (errors) are typically major (interfering significantly with comprehension) or minor (not interfering significantly with comprehension). However, not all commercial IRIs do this. This is an important feature of a valid IRI and is provided for in the inventory included in this chapter.

➡ Some of the contemporary IRIs, such as the one contained in this chapter, use activation of prior knowledge and interests, which cannot be assessed in a group-administered standardized reading test. Since these are important elements of reading comprehension, they should be evaluated, and a few commercial IRIs do this.

➡ Some commercial IRIs reflect the actual narrative and content materials that a child is reading better than do many standardized reading tests.

The following are the main limitations of using an IRI:

➡ Because an IRI is given individually, it is fairly time-consuming to give and to evaluate. Although it might be helpful to give an IRI to most children in the elementary school, this usually is not practical because of the time involved in giving and evaluating it. This is why usually only moderately or severely disabled readers or children with learning disabilities are given an IRI. It usually takes less time to use the running record, which was described earlier.

➡ It is somewhat difficult to learn how to evaluate an IRI since each of them differs quite a bit on how to count and score miscues, and each has a different scoring system. A teacher or volunteer must spend considerable time learning how to evaluate an IRI before giving it, and usually this knowledge is not entirely transferable to different IRIs. Some IRIs do not penalize dialectal differences, errors that may not interfere with comprehension, and self-corrections. You must study each IRI to determine what that inventory stresses. It is important that dialect-based miscues and self-corrections *not* be counted as errors. For example, a self-correction usually indicates that a student is trying to read for meaning. In addition, miscues that interfere with comprehension should be weighted more heavily than those that do not.

➡ A student's performance may vary greatly because of his or her prior knowledge and interest in any specific passage. Although most commercial inventories attempt to have both narrative and content passages that should interest both boys and girls, in practice this does not always happen. Some IRIs contain much more interesting passages than do others. The teacher must examine all of the passages on an IRI carefully to determine how free from culture and gender bias they are and how interesting they would be to most students.

➡ A student's performance on an IRI does not always "stair-step" in the way in which a teacher may think that it should. For example, here is a way in which you might predict a student's performance on an IRI:

    Independent reading level—Fourth grade

    Instructional reading level—Fifth grade

    Frustration reading level—Sixth grade

However, here is an actual student's performance on an IRI:

    Independent reading level—Fourth grade

    Instructional reading level—None

    Frustration reading level—Fifth grade

➡ Some of the IRIs have passages in which the readability level is not accurate. Even if a passage does have the correct readability for that grade according to a readability formula, a student's prior knowledge and interest in a particular passage may not make it accurate for that particular child.

➡ Some IRIs have questions accompanying the passages that are not passage dependent. This means that a child might be able to answer some of the comprehension questions without reading a passage because he or she is able to answer them on the basis of prior knowledge.

➡ Reading specialists do not agree on the criteria for determining the independent, instructional, and frustration reading levels. Some of these standards are set much higher than others, and none of them have been verified by enough true research.

➥ According to a research study by Duffelmeyer and Duffelmeyer (1989), nearly 50% of the graded passages on the IRIs that they studied did not have explicitly stated main ideas. Therefore, you should be sure that any IRI that you plan to use has a clearly stated main idea in each passage.

In summary, an IRI is a fairly useful informal assessment device for determining a student's approximate reading levels and specific reading strengths and weaknesses. However, a running record often may be a more useful informal assessment technique because it can be used with any narrative or content material that the student is going to read. If you decide to use an IRI, you should always interpret the findings cautiously and not regard them as completely accurate. Such findings should always be regarded only as tentative indicators of a child's reading levels and skills and should be modified when necessary in a reading program. For example, if you have found on an IRI that a student has a fifth-grade instructional reading level but cannot seem to read material on that level without much difficulty, you should have the child read fourth-grade material.

Although most teachers will probably want to give a commercial IRI, any reading or learning disabilities teacher can construct his or her own version of an IRI. However, doing so is a time-consuming job. If you want detailed directions about how to do this, you can consult the following teacher's resource book: Miller, W. H. (1995). *Alternative Assessment Techniques for Reading & Writing*. West Nyack, NY: The Center for Applied Research in Education.

HOW TO ADMINISTER THE GRADED WORD LISTS AND READING PASSAGES OF AN IRI

When giving the graded word lists on an IRI, have the child begin pronouncing the words aloud on a word list that is *at least two reading levels* below his or her estimated instructional reading level. Then have the student continue pronouncing the words on the lists until he or she reaches the point at which he or she is able to pronounce fewer than 90% of the words on a list. Although this percentage is a widely used place at which to stop, there is logic to instead using an 80% accuracy level so that the student can begin reading an easier passage.

Before the student begins reading the first appropriate reading passage, ask him or her the questions to determine prior knowledge and interest in the material. Then have the student begin reading the graded oral reading passage that corresponds to the level at which 80 to 90% of the words on a list were recognized. The beginning passage is like the basal (easy or basic) passage on an oral reading test.

It is vital that a student begin reading at a low enough level so that he or she will not get discouraged at the beginning. If the student begins reading either a graded word list or a passage that is too difficult, it is almost impossible to motivate him or her to continue and to try to do his or her best.

As the student reads each of the passages aloud, mark his or her oral reading miscues on your copies of the passage. Here is one good system for marking oral reading miscues:

➠ *Omission*—Circle the entire word or letter sound.

$$\text{(deer)}$$

➠ *Addition*—Insert with a caret.

little
Λ

➠ *Substitution/mispronunciation*—Draw a line through a substitution or mispronunciation and write it in.

trees
~~woods~~

➠ *Reversal*—Use the transposition symbol.

| slowly | walking |

➠ *Repetition*—Use a wavy line to indicate a repetition of *two* or *more words*.

mother deer

➠ *Word aided*—If a student gives no response after about five seconds, give him or her the word and cross it out.

~~miss~~

When you first learn how to mark oral reading miscues, you will find it quite difficult to do. Because you must think so much about the marking system, you may fall behind in the marking of a student's miscues and may not be able to observe many other characteristics of the student's reading, such as excessive pauses or word-by-word reading. Therefore, it usually is helpful to tape record a student's reading of the passages. Then you can mark a student's miscues later when you play back the tape recording. You may have to replay some of the passages several times to locate all of the reading miscues. Even when you feel competent in the marking system, you may want to tape record a student's oral reading of the passages. A student often is more self-conscious about his or her oral reading if he or she sees you marking the miscues as he or she reads aloud. This probably is the most true with children who have reading or learning disabilities.

When a child has finished reading each passage aloud, ask him or her the comprehension questions that accompany the passage. Each of the answers can be scored at that time or during a later playback of the tape recording. After the child has answered the comprehension questions, you can ask him or her to assess how well he or she has done. (This is illustrated in the next section.) As an alternative to asking the comprehension questions, you can have the child retell the important points of the passage. You should not ask the comprehension questions and also use retelling.

Have the student stop reading the graded passages when he or she reaches the frustration (hard) reading level. The frustration reading level is similar to the *ceiling level* on an oral reading test. This is the point at which the student makes many miscues, has inadequate comprehension, appears tense and nervous, and wants to stop.

When a student reaches the frustration reading level, you can use the remaining reading passages as a *listening comprehension test* to establish his or her potential or capacity level. To do this, read several passages that follow the passage at which the student stopped reading and ask him or her the comprehension questions accompanying those passages. The level at which the student can answer approximately 75% of the questions correctly is called the *potential or capacity level*. This is the level to which a student *may be able to learn to read with very good individually prescribed corrective or reading instruction if he or she has the appropriate prior knowledge*. However, this level must be thought of as a *tentative indicator of reading potential* along with a number of other factors, such as intelligence, prior knowledge, and motivation.

HOW TO EVALUATE THE GRADED WORD LISTS AND READING PASSAGES OF AN **IRI**

The main purpose for giving the graded word lists and reading passages of an IRI is to determine the student's approximate reading levels, to determine his or her pattern of oral reading miscues, to observe his or her self-corrections, and to assess his or her strengths and weaknesses in reading.

As the child pronounces each of the words on a graded word list, mark his or her response by placing a + for each correct word and a – or 0 for each incorrect response. If a child pronounces a word phonetically, in addition to the – or 0 you can write the phonetic spelling of that word. If you have printed the words on a list on individual cards, put them into two different piles—one pile of correctly pronounced words and one pile of incorrectly pronounced words. If you want, the word lists can be scored from replaying the tape recording.

You can then determine the child's approximate reading level on each of the word lists. This indicates his or her ability to pronounce words in isolation. You can use the following *approximate percentages* to make this determination:

➠ 99% or more of the words on a list recognized—independent reading level

➠ 90%–98% of the words on a list recognized—instructional reading level

➠ fewer than about 89% of the words on a list recognized—frustration reading level

You can assess student's prior knowledge and interest in reading a passage in an informal manner by asking yourself questions such as these:

➡ Did the student have excellent, good, or poor prior knowledge for reading this passage?

➡ Was the student able to access (activate) his or her prior knowledge for reading this passage?

➡ Did the student probably have enough interest in reading the passage so that a lack of interest did not interfere significantly with his or her comprehension?

Because the IRI is an informal assessment device, these parts of an IRI are evaluated informally by the teacher or volunteer.

Here are the recommendations you should use when evaluating the IRI contained in this chapter.

1. Count any error that interferes significantly with comprehension as a *major oral reading miscue* and deduct one point.

2. Count any deviation from the printed text that does not seem to interfere significantly with comprehension and deduct one-half point.

3. Count an addition as half a miscue if it does not interfere significantly with the meaning of the material. Usually it does not.

4. Do not count a self-correction as an error if it occurs within a short period of time. Usually a self-correction indicates that a child is trying to read for meaning.

5. Count a repetition as half a miscue only if it occurs on *two or more words*.

6. Do not count more than one miscue on the same word within any passage.

7. Do not count a miscue on any *proper noun* found in a passage.

8. Deduct one point for any word that the student cannot pronounce after about five seconds *if that word interferes with comprehension*. Deduct one-half point for any word a student cannot pronounce after about five seconds *if that word does not interfere significantly with comprehension*.

9. Do not count miscues that seem to exemplify a student's cultural or regional dialect. However, to consider this point you should be fairly familiar with the student's basic speech patterns, such as the African American dialect, the Hispanic dialect, or the Native American dialect.

Then evaluate the student's answers to the comprehension questions. On the first line by each question under the word *Score*, write the number 1 for a correct answer and the number 0 for an incorrect answer. On the second line by each answer under the word *Appropriateness*, write a + for a detailed or thoughtful answer or a ✔ for a completely irrelevant answer. You do not have to place either of these marks if they are not relevant. If more than one-third of the child's answers have been marked with a ✔, the child probably does not have a true idea of the purpose of the passage and certainly does not understand it very well. If the child has a number of +'s, he or she has a good understanding of the material.

Then determine the student's comprehension score on each of the graded passages. If there are *six* comprehension questions accompanying a passage, the following scores are needed to reach the various reading levels:

➡ Independent reading level—6 questions correct

➡ Instructional reading level—4–5 questions correct

➡ Frustration reading level—3 or fewer questions correct

If there are *eight* comprehension questions accompanying a passage, the following scores are needed to reach the various reading levels:

➡ Independent reading level—8 questions correct

➡ Instructional reading level—5–7 questions correct

➡ Frustration reading level—4 or fewer questions correct

Instead of the comprehension questions that accompany each passage, you can use retelling to assess comprehension skills. If you use retelling instead of the comprehension questions to determine a student's reading levels, you will have to use quite a bit of judgment in determining his or her reading levels. This is acceptable for an experienced reading teacher because an IRI is an informal assessment device. However, this may be a difficult task for a novice reading teacher.

After you have evaluated a student's oral reading miscues and comprehension levels, you can determine his or her approximate independent (easy), instructional (with teacher support), and frustration (difficult) reading levels. There are a number of different classification schemes for determining these levels. Various IRIs use slightly different levels. The percentages used in this book were chosen after a careful examination of the fairly limited research in the area, logical analysis, and the reactions of thousands of reading teachers, undergraduate and graduate students, and children who have used the graded reading passages found in my previous publications.

The characteristics of the three main reading levels used in the IRI included in this book are as follows:

➡ **Independent (easy) level**—The point at which a student is about 99% accurate in word identification and has about 95% or better comprehension.

➡ **Instructional (with teacher support) level**—The point at which a student is about 90% accurate at word identification and has 75% or better comprehension.

➡ **Frustration (difficult) reading level**—The point at which a student is less than about 90% accurate in word identification and has less than about 50% accuracy in word identification.

From using the graded passages with hundreds of children over many years, adding several sublevels to the three basic levels can be useful in accurately placing children in reading materials. Therefore, this book also contains the following three subcategories:

➡ **Low independent level**

➡ **High instructional level**

➡ **Low instructional level**

This book uses these three subcategories of reading levels in addition to the three basic levels. Because any IRI is an informal assessment device, you must use your own judgment in arriving at these reading levels, and you should take into account a student's word identification miscues and comprehension score into account together. **I usually recommend weighting the student's performance on comprehension more highly than weighting his or her performance on word identification because comprehension is much more important.** Comprehension is the ultimate goal of the reading process. Using the three approximate reading levels is justified since the graded oral reading passages always must be thought of as *informal assessment devices and should not be thought of as infallible indicators of a child's reading levels.*

In addition, you can informally assess a student's self-monitoring of his or her comprehension by noticing his or her responses to the questions following the comprehension questions for each passage. For example,

How well do you think you answered these questions:

very well _____

all right _____

not so well _____

You then can make an informal comparison between each student's response on these questions to his or her actual score on the comprehension questions. It seems the following would be the most comparable responses:

Child's Response	Comprehension Score on the Passage	
	6 total questions	*8 total questions*
very well	6	8
all right	4–5	5–7
not so well	3 or fewer	4 or fewer

A significant deviation from this pattern of responses may indicate that the student does not monitor his or her comprehension so effectively as possible.

GRADED WORD LISTS AND READING PASSAGES FOR THE INDIVIDUAL READING INVENTORY

This section contains the graded word lists and reading passages for a sample IRI. They are designed to be used at the preprimer reading level through the tenth- or twelfth-grade reading level. One set of the word lists should be duplicated for the student to pronounce, and another set should be duplicated on which to record the scores. One set of graded reading passages at the appropriate level should be duplicated without the questions to assess prior knowledge and interest in the passage, the comprehension questions, and the self-monitoring questions. This is the set from which the student reads aloud. The other set contains the questions and the formula for scoring and is the set that you evaluate. The student's set (both the word lists and the reading passages) can be laminated for durability if you want.

The following code has been placed on each of the graded word lists and reading passages so that the student cannot determine the levels of the word lists and passages that he or she is going to read.

Preprimer Level (Jill's Dog Pat)

Primer Level (The Baby Deer)

First-Grade Reading Level (The Hungry Bear)

Second-Grade Reading Level (The Dog Who Rides in a Cart)

Third-Grade Reading Level (Jim Henson, "Father" of the Muppets)

Fourth-Grade Reading Level (Learning About the Objibwa Indians)

Fifth-Grade Reading Level (Caroline Quarles and the Underground Railroad)

Sixth-Grade Reading Level (Castles Built by the Normans)

Seventh-Grade Reading Level (The Vikings, A Fascinating People)

Eighth-Grade Reading Level (The Great Chicago Fire)

Ninth-Grade Reading Level (The Laser)

Tenth- to Twelfth-Grade Reading Level (Learning About Rocks)

Because it is difficult to discriminate between the Tenth Reader Level, Eleventh Reader Level, and the Twelfth Reader Level, these levels have been placed together in one word list and one passage.

The following sources contain additional sets of graded word lists and graded reading passages that you can use for pretesting and posttesting or for different kinds of administration, such as oral-silent-oral, silent-oral, oral-silent, and silent-oral-silent.

Miller, W. H. (1995). *Alternative Assessment Techniques for Reading & Writing.* West Nyack, NY: The Center for Applied Research in Education, 158–215.

———. (1993). *Complete Reading Disabilities Handbook.* West Nyack, NY: The Center for Applied Research in Education, 64–95.

———. (1986). *Reading Diagnosis Kit.* West Nyack, NY: The Center for Applied Research in Education, 198–259.

———. (1988). *Reading Teacher's Complete Diagnosis & Correction Manual.* West Nyack, NY: The Center for Applied Research in Education, 69–95.

WORD LISTS

1. black	1. mother	1. many
2. look	2. yellow	2. brown
3. play	3. two	3. snow
4. in	4. was	4. father
5. jump	5. cake	5. again
6. and	6. laugh	6. give
7. it	7. good	7. once
8. little	8. please	8. street
9. green	9. all	9. why
10. big	10. white	10. every
11. you	11. away	11. tell
12. ride	12. what	12. much
13. will	13. fly	13. men
14. red	14. your	14. paint
15. can	15. find	15. can't
16. see	16. one	16. found
17. I	17. thank	17. from
18. said	18. have	18. ask
19. make	19. now	19. may
20. up	20. out	20. walk
21. to	21. tree	21. open
22. me	22. that	22. call
23. an	23. hold	23. wish
24. back	24. children	24. love
25. funny	25. very	25. say

Independent reading level—24–25 correct on a word list
Instructional reading level—22–23 correct on a word list
Frustration reading level—21 or fewer correct on a word list

WORD LISTS

1. better	1. thought	1. parachute
2. should	2. mountain	2. weight
3. together	3. country	3. decorate
4. been	4. decide	4. protection
5. does	5. diamond	5. predict
6. friend	6. remember	6. critical
7. today	7. several	7. machine
8. write	8. wander	8. knowledge
9. breakfast	9. escape	9. island
10. surprise	10. enough	10. modern
11. those	11. close	11. coward
12. small	12. strange	12. experience
13. grow	13. magic	13. pollute
14. always	14. eight	14. exercise
15. save	15. special	15. balance
16. cupcake	16. travel	16. interrupt
17. beautiful	17. earth	17. theater
18. hurt	18. planet	18. original
19. upon	19. though	19. dignity
20. their	20. storm	20. ancient
21. finish	21. ocean	21. force
22. grandfather	22. vegetable	22. pavement
23. brave	23. impossible	23. scientific
24. squirrel	24. soup	24. pronounce
25. lazy	25. mystery	25. ability

Independent reading level—24–25 correct on a word list
Instructional reading level—22–23 correct on a word list
Frustration reading level—21 or fewer correct on a word list

WORD LISTS

—	7	7 (slash)
1. intense	1. applause	1. tolerate
2. photograph	2. helicopter	2. collapse
3. burden	3. transfusion	3. independent
4. horizon	4. technical	4. famine
5. image	5. moisture	5. exception
6. gentle	6. competition	6. horizontal
7. grief	7. associate	7. warden
8. responsible	8. depression	8. humidity
9. manager	9. symbol	9. notable
10. territory	10. coyote	10. perpetual
11. considerable	11. wreath	11. conceive
12. ceremony	12. request	12. boulevard
13. qualify	13. transparent	13. domestic
14. plateau	14. microphone	14. sculpture
15. argument	15. hearth	15. alliance
16. amount	16. antibiotic	16. implication
17. region	17. sensitive	17. scaffold
18. value	18. bail	18. neutral
19. organize	19. miniature	19. famine
20. international	20. vibration	20. merchandise
21. legend	21. structure	21. monarch
22. ambulance	22. resemble	22. personally
23. operation	23. representative	23. laden
24. physical	24. phase	24. vaguely
25. review	25. loathe	25. algebra

Independent reading level—24–25 correct on a word list
Instructional reading level—22–23 correct on a word list
Frustration reading level—21 or fewer correct on a word list

WORD LISTS

1. arrogant	1. aggressive	1. heirloom
2. politician	2. enviable	2. malign
3. juvenile	3. disposition	3. gregarious
4. oppressive	4. premature	4. fictitious
5. rehearsal	5. environment	5. fallacy
6. prescription	6. ventilator	6. memoir
7. quota	7. lucrative	7. proprietor
8. triumphant	8. malicious	8. contemplate
9. discipline	9. avalanche	9. prolific
10. competent	10. desolation	10. hypothesis
11. embankment	11. legitimate	11. kinetic
12. torture	12. brazen	12. callous
13. congregation	13. judicial	13. exhilarate
14. extension	14. priority	14. devastate
15. conservative	15. undergraduate	15. consecrate
16. yacht	16. regime	16. charlatan
17. rebuke	17. enviable	17. mediocre
18. custody	18. obsolete	18. eloquent
19. substantial	19. spouse	19. rhapsody
20. authentic	20. quadruple	20. amethyst
21. currency	21. memorable	21. phenomenal
22. wistful	22. fervently	22. spasm
23. dishonor	23. credential	23. eccentric
24. cavity	24. chariot	24. vigilant
25. curiosity	25. commute	25. philanthropy

Independent reading level—24–25 correct on a word list
Instructional reading level—22–23 correct on a word list
Frustration reading level—21 or fewer correct on a word list

Name _____ Grade _____ Teacher _____ Date _____

JILL'S DOG PAT*

Jill has a big dog.

The dog's name is Pat.

Pat is a big black dog.

Jill and Pat like to play.

Pat has a blue ball.

Pat likes to run after the ball.

Jill and Pat like to go for a walk.

Pat likes to eat dog food.

He likes to jump up on the bed.

Jill likes Pat.

Jill and Pat have fun.

*The readability level of this passage was computed by the Spache Readability Formula.

JILL'S DOG PAT

BEFORE READING

Assessing Prior Knowledge and Interest

1. What are some of the ways a child and a dog could have fun together?

2. Do you think you will like to read this story about a girl and her dog? Why? Why not?

AFTER READING

Number of words in this selection _____65_____

Number of word identification miscues _____

Word Identification Miscues

Independent reading level _____0–1_____

Low independent reading level approx. _____2_____

High instructional reading level approx. _____3–4_____

Instructional reading level approx. _____5–6_____

Low instructional reading level approx. _____7–8_____

Frustration reading level _____9+_____

Assessing Comprehension

Score 1 for a correct response and 0 for an incorrect response in the appropriate column. Score ✔ for any answers that are clearly illogical or + for any answers that are very good.

	Score	Appropriateness

Reading the Lines (Literal Comprehension)

1. What color is Pat's ball? **(blue)** _____ _____

2. What does Pat like to jump up on? **(the bed)** _____ _____

Reading Between the Lines (Interpretive Comprehension)

3. Why do you think Jill and Pat like to go for a walk together? **(it's fun; they like to be out of doors; it's good for them)** _____ _____

4. Why do you think Pat likes to jump up on the bed? **(he likes to sleep with Jill; it feels soft to him)** _____ _____

JILL'S DOG PAT *(Cont'd)*

Score   Appropriateness

Reading Beyond the Lines (Applied Comprehension)

5. If you had a dog, what could you do together for fun?
   (any logical answer—some examples: play ball; take a walk; play with a Frisbee; take it to "dog school")

    ____   ____

6. What would you do to take care of a dog?
   (any logical answer—some examples: feed it; give it water; take it outside to go to the bathroom; brush and comb it)

    ____   ____

Number of comprehension questions correct _____

Comprehension Score

    Independent reading level   6

    Instructional reading level   4–5

    Frustration reading level   3 or fewer

SELF-MONITORING OF COMPREHENSION

    How well do you think you answered these questions?

    very well _____

    all right _____

    not so well _____

Name _____ Grade _____ Teacher _____ Date _____

THE BABY DEER*

I saw a baby deer today. It was very little. It was brown with white spots.

The baby deer was walking slowly on the road. I'm happy that I didn't hit it with my car. I did miss it.

I saw the baby deer's mother. She was by the side of the road. She was waiting for her baby. Then the mother deer and baby deer went into the trees.

I am happy that the mother deer had her baby with her. She almost didn't.

*The readability level of this passage was computed by the Spache Readability Formula.

THE BABY DEER

BEFORE READING

Assessing Prior Knowledge and Interest

1. What do you think a baby deer looks like?

2. Do you think you will like to read a story about a baby deer? Why? Why not?

AFTER READING

Number of words in this selection _____85_____

Number of word identification miscues _____

Word Identification Miscues

Independent reading level ____0–1____

Low independent reading level approx. ____2____

High instructional reading level approx. ____3–4____

Instructional reading level approx. ____5–8____

Low instructional reading level approx. ____9____

Frustration reading level ____10+____

Assessing Comprehension

Score 1 for a correct response and 0 for an incorrect response in the appropriate column. Score ✔ for any answers that are clearly illogical or + for any answers that are very good, detailed, or insightful.

	Score	Appropriateness

Reading the Lines (Literal Comprehension)

1. Where was the baby deer walking? **(road; on the road)** _____ _____

2. Where was the mother deer waiting? **(by the side of the road)** _____ _____

Reading Between the Lines (Interpretive Comprehension)

3. Why was the person driving the car happy that she didn't hit the baby deer? **(any logical answer—some examples: she likes animals; she likes baby deer; she didn't want to hurt a baby deer)** _____ _____

4. Why do you think the mother deer and baby deer went into the trees? **(any logical answer—some examples: it was safe for them; they couldn't get hurt then)** _____ _____

THE BABY DEER *(Cont'd)*

Score   Appropriateness

Reading Beyond the Lines (Applied Comprehension)

5. If a person sees a baby deer by itself on the road,
   what should he or she do? **(any logical answer—
   some examples: slow down; stop the car; leave
   it alone; don't try to touch it)**   _____ _____

6. Why would you enjoy seeing a tiny baby deer?
   **(any logical answer—some examples: it is pretty; it
   would be exciting; it is cute)**   _____ _____

Number of comprehension questions correct _____

Comprehension Score

    Independent reading level _____6_____

    Instructional reading level _____4–5_____

    Frustration reading level _3 or fewer_

SELF-MONITORING OF COMPREHENSION

    How well do you think you answered these questions?

    very well _____

    all right _____

    not so well _____

© 2001 by John Wiley & Sons, Inc.

THE HUNGRY BEAR*

You may be surprised that black bears live in the big woods today. Yes, they do. This is the story of a hungry big black bear.

One night this hungry bear wanted to eat food from a bird feeder. First he went to a house where the dog Ben saw him. Ben barked, and the bear broke a bird feeder. Then he ran away.

Then the bear wanted to eat from another bird feeder. At that house a dog named Max barked. Then the bear ran away.

Later that night the black bear went to a big house. At that house a big black dog named Crow barked. The bear broke that bird feeder too. Then the bear ran away.

That night this hungry black bear went to three houses in the woods. He broke two bird feeders. He never did get any food to eat. Do you feel bad about that or not?

_____
*The readability level of this passage was computed by the Spache Readability Formula.

THE HUNGRY BEAR *(Cont'd)*

BEFORE READING

Assessing Prior Knowledge and Interest

1. What do you think bears like to eat?

2. Would you like to see a big black bear in the woods? Why? Why not?

AFTER READING

Number of words in this selection _____154_____

Number of word identification miscues _____

Word Identification Miscues

Independent reading level _____0–2_____

Low independent reading level approx. _____3–5_____

High instructional reading level approx. _____6–8_____

Instructional reading level approx. _____9–14_____

Low instructional reading level approx. _____15–17_____

Frustration reading level _____18+_____

Assessing Comprehension

Score 1 for a correct response and 0 for an incorrect response in the appropriate column. Score ✔ for any answers that are clearly illogical or + for answers that are very good, detailed, or insightful.

	Score	Appropriateness

Reading the Lines (Literal Comprehension)

1. What did the bear break? **(bird feeders)**   _____ _____

2. What was the name of the big black dog? **(Crow)**   _____ _____

Reading Between the Lines (Interpretive Comprehension)

3. Why do you think the bear broke the bird feeders? **(he wanted to get the food out of it; he got scared when he heard the dogs bark)**   _____ _____

4. Why do you think all of the dogs barked at the bear? **(they were trying to scare the bear away; they don't like bears; they wanted to protect their home)**   _____ _____

THE HUNGRY BEAR *(Cont'd)*

Score *Appropriateness*

Reading Beyond the Lines (Applied Comprehension)

5. What would you do if you saw a big black bear at your house? **(any logical answer—some examples: yell for him to go away; bang a pan to scare him; keep the door closed)**

   _____ _____

6. Do you think you should put out food for a bear to eat? **(any logical answer—some examples: yes, they may be very hungry; no, bears shouldn't be too near people's houses; no, bears should find their own food)**

   _____ _____

Number of comprehension questions correct _____

Comprehension Score

    Independent reading level _____6_____

    Instructional reading level ____4–5____

    Frustration reading level _3 or fewer_

SELF-MONITORING OF COMPREHENSION

    How well do you think you answered these questions?

    very well _____

    all right _____

    not so well _____

THE DOG WHO RIDES IN A CART*† ☐

I walk with my big tan dog every day. One morning we met a man riding a bicycle. I saw that he was pulling a cart with wheels behind him. I thought that the man was pulling his little boy or girl in the cart.

Just as I was by him I saw what was riding in the cart. I was very surprised to see that it was not a child. It was a big yellow dog who was looking at my dog and me.

I walked on for a while. Later I met the man and the dog again. This time the man stopped, and I asked him why his dog was riding in a cart instead of running or walking. The man said that his dog ran about two miles every day while the man rode his bicycle. Then his dog got too tired to run anymore. The dog then jumped into the cart and rode the rest of the way each day.

I was surprised to see that the dog stayed in the cart all the time that the man and I talked. The dog just looked at my dog and me.

He never barked or tried to get out of the cart. He was a very good dog.

I liked seeing the dog who rode in a cart. I never thought that I would see a dog riding in a cart behind a bicycle.

*The readability level of this passage was computed by the Spache Readability Formula.
†This is a true story that happened in northern Wisconsin in July, 1999.

THE DOG WHO RIDES IN A CART

BEFORE READING

Assessing Prior Knowledge and Interest

1. What do you think a dog could go riding in?

2. Do you like to read stories about dogs? Why? Why not?

AFTER READING

Number of words in this selection _____238_____

Number of word identification miscues _____

Word Identification Miscues

Independent reading level _____0–3_____

Low independent reading level approx. _____4–7_____

High instructional reading level approx. _____8–11_____

Instructional reading level approx. _____12–20_____

Low instructional reading level approx. _____21–24_____

Frustration reading level _____25+_____

Assessing Comprehension

Score 1 for a correct response and 0 for an incorrect response in the appropriate column. Score ✔ for any answers that are clearly illogical or + for any answers that are very good, detailed, or insightful.

	Score	Appropriateness

Reading the Lines (Literal Comprehension)

1. What was riding in the cart?
   (a dog; big yellow dog; yellow dog)   _____ _____

2. How many miles a day did the dog run?
   (two miles)   _____ _____

Reading Between the Lines (Interpretive Comprehension)

3. How do you think the dog showed its owner that it
   was tired after running two miles? **(it lied down; it ran
   [walked] very slowly; it wouldn't run [walk] anymore)**   _____ _____

4. Why do you think the dog stayed so quietly in the
   cart when it was stopped? **(it was well trained; it
   enjoyed riding in the a cart; it minded its owner)**   _____ _____

THE DOG WHO RIDES IN A CART *(Cont'd)*

	Score	Appropriateness

Reading Beyond the Lines (Applied Comprehension)

5. If you had a dog, would you take it riding in a cart? **(any logical answer—some examples: yes, it would be fun; yes, people would enjoy seeing a dog riding in a cart; no, a dog should run or walk, not ride in a cart; no, I don't ride a bicycle well enough to pull a cart and a dog)**   _____ _____

6. Would you like to take a picture of a dog riding in a cart? **(any logical answer—some examples: yes, it would be fun to have a picture like that; yes, maybe the picture would be put in a newspaper or magazine; no, I don't think that the dog would like to have its picture taken)**   _____ _____

Number of comprehension questions correct _____

Comprehension Score

Independent reading level _____6_____

Instructional reading level _____4–5_____

Frustration reading level __3 or fewer__

SELF-MONITORING OF COMPREHENSION

How well do you think you answered these questions?

very well _____

all right _____

not so well _____

JIM HENSON, "FATHER" OF THE MUPPETS*

Most of you have seen the Muppets. This is a story about Jim Henson, the talented creator of those lovable creatures.

Jim was born in 1936 in a small town in Mississippi. He loved to draw even when he was a small boy. Many of the scenes about small towns that later appeared in the Muppets' television shows and movies came from Jim's childhood.

When Jim was in fifth grade, his family moved to Maryland near where his grandparents lived. Jim liked to watch television in high school. He especially liked watching puppets. When he was seventeen, Jim got a job as a puppeteer at a local TV station. While he was in college, he did both puppetry and cartoon drawing. He had his own puppet show by the end of his first year in college.

Jim made his puppets out of soft materials. He changed the way a puppet's face looked as he moved his hand

© 2001 by John Wiley & Sons, Inc.

---

*The readability level of this passage was computed by the Spache Readability Formula.

JIM HENSON, "FATHER" OF THE MUPPETS *(Cont'd)*

around inside the puppet's head. Jim named his creatures "Muppets" because he liked the name. It seemed to fit his creatures.

In 1959 Jim met Jane Nebel, a college friend who was another puppeteer. They got married and later had children. Jim and Jane kept creating new Muppets all the time. They tried to make them more interesting. Some of their most famous Muppets are Elmo, Kermit the Frog, Miss Piggy, Big Bird, Cookie Monster, and Bert and Ernie. Jim and his puppeteers were on the television program *Sesame Street* for many years. Later they also made many Muppet movies.

Jim became ill and died in 1990. The Muppets came to Jim's funeral since he wanted it to be a happy time. Jim and the Muppets brought joy to many children, probably even you!

JIM HENSON, "FATHER" OF THE MUPPETS

BEFORE READING

Assessing Prior Knowledge and Interest

1. Which of the Muppets are your favorites? Why do you like those Muppets so much?

2. What kind of materials do you think the Muppets are made out of?

AFTER READING

Number of words in this selection _____292_____

Number of word identification miscues _____

Word Identification Miscues

Independent reading level _____0–3_____

Low independent reading level approx. _____4–6_____

High instructional reading level approx . _____7–12_____

Instructional reading level approx. _____13–22_____

Low instructional reading level approx. _____23–28_____

Frustration reading level _____29+_____

Assessing Comprehension

Score 1 for a correct response and 0 for an incorrect response in the appropriate column. Score ✔ for any answers that are clearly illogical or + for any answers that are very good, detailed, or insightful.

	Score	Appropriateness

Reading the Lines (Literal Comprehension)

1. In what state was Jim born?
(Mississippi) _____ _____

2. How old was Jim when he got his job as a puppeteer at a local television station? **(seventeen; 17)** _____ _____

Reading Between the Lines (Interpretive Comprehension)

3. Why do you think a person would have to be talented to create a Muppet? **(it would be hard to make a Muppet out of so many different materials; it would be hard to think of characters that could be a Muppet; a Muppet would be hard to move so that it looks alive)** _____

4. Why do you think children like the Muppets so much? **(they are fun to watch and listen to; they do things that children would like to do; they wear interesting costumes)** _____ _____

JIM HENSON, "FATHER" OF THE MUPPETS *(Cont'd)*

	Score	*Appropriateness*

Reading Beyond the Lines (Applied Comprehension)

5. Would you ever like to be a puppeteer like Jim Henson? Why? Why not? **(any logical answer—some examples: yes, it would make me feel good to make little kids [children] happy; yes, I like puppets; no, it would be too hard work; no, I'm not creative; no, I don't like puppets)**   _____   _____

6. Which of the Muppets mentioned in this passage is your favorite? Why? **(any logical answer—some examples: Elmo—he's cute; Kermit—I like frogs, and he's funny; Miss Piggy—she's got nice costumes; Big Bird—it's so big and funny; Cookie Monster—I like to eat cookies too; Bert— he's funny to look at; Ernie—he does funny things)**   _____   _____

Number of comprehension questions correct _____

Comprehension Score

    Independent reading level _____6_____

    Instructional reading level _____4–5_____

    Frustration reading level _3 or fewer_

SELF-MONITORING OF COMPREHENSION

    How well do you think you answered these questions?

    very well _____

    all right _____

    not so well _____

LEARNING ABOUT THE OBJIBWA INDIANS*

The *Objibwa* are a group of North American Indians who lived in the northern part of the United States and Canada many years ago. Today they live near the same areas on reservations in the United States or on reserves in Canada. A reservation or reserve is land that is set aside by the government for Native Americans, who are sometimes called *Indians*. The *Objibwa* also are called *Ojibwe* or Chippewa.

Although today the Objibwa have their own businesses, own gambling casinos, or make clothing, they still practice many of their old traditions. Their schools also teach the Objibwa traditions and often language.

Many years ago, the Objibwa lived in a building called a *wigwam*, which was a round house. To make a wigwam the men bent trees and poles to make a frame, while the women covered it with grasses and bark. In the past the Objibwa ate

© 2001 by John Wiley & Sons, Inc.

---

*The readability level of this passage was computed by the Dale-Chall Readability Formula.

different types of food, including vegetables like corn, squash, and wild rice, and fish and meat.

The Objibwa made their own clothing from animal skins. The men wore shorts, leggings, and moccasins and often a breechcloth, which was a piece of deerskin worn between the legs and tied around the waist with a belt. The Objibwa women wore deerskin dresses and moccasins. The women usually sewed beads or porcupine quills on their clothing.

Family groups were very important to the Objibwa Indians. Large family groups were called *clans*, and clans were spread through many villages. In the past a married couple lived with the wife's family for about a year, and then they moved to their own wigwam.

Today the Objibwa still *spear* fish, which is catching fish with a pole. This pole has sharp pointed ends. Wild rice is still a favorite food of the Objibwa. The rice grows on tall stalks that are found by the shores of lakes. In the fall the Objibwa gather wild rice from their canoes. Perhaps some-day you will be able to eat wild rice. Just cook it and then add maple sugar or syrup to it. It is very, very good.

LEARNING ABOUT THE OBJIBWA INDIANS

BEFORE READING

Assessing Prior Knowledge and Interests

1. What do you know about the Objibwa Indians (Native Americans)?

2. What do you want to learn about the traditions of the Objibwa?

AFTER READING

Number of words in this selection _____350_____

Number of word identification miscues _____

Word Identification Miscues

Independent reading level _____0–4_____

Low independent reading level approx. _____5–9_____

High instructional reading level approx. _____10–16_____

Instructional reading level approx. _____17–28_____

Low instructional reading level approx. _____29–35_____

Frustration reading level _____36+_____

Assessing Comprehension

Score 1 for a correct response and 0 for an incorrect response in the appropriate column. Score ✔ for any answers that are clearly illogical or + for any answers that are very good, detailed, or insightful.

© 2001 by John Wiley & Sons, Inc.

	Score	Appropriateness

Reading the Lines (Literal Comprehension)

1. What is a reservation or reserve? **(land that the government sets aside for the Native Americans to live on and use)**   _____ _____

2. What does wild rice grow on? **(tall stalks by lakes)**   _____ _____

Reading Between the Lines (Interpretive Comprehension)

3. Why do you think the Objibwa made their clothing from animal skins? **(they were easily available; they were comfortable to wear; they were attractive)**   _____ _____

4. Why do you think wild rice is still a favorite food of the Objibwa? **(it tastes good; it is easy to gather; it is good for them)**   _____ _____

LEARNING ABOUT THE OBJIBWA INDIANS *(Cont'd)*

	Score	*Appropriateness*

Reading Beyond the Lines (Applied Comprehension)

5. Would you like to live on a Native American reservation? Why? Why not? **(any logical answer—some examples: yes, I would like to be able to live the customs and traditions; yes, the government helps the people to live; no, I like to live in the city, where there is more to do)** _____ _____

6. Would you like to try spearing for fish?
(any logical answer—some examples: yes, it would be fun to try to do it; yes, I like to eat fish; no, it would be very hard; no, I don't like to handle raw fish) _____ _____

Number of comprehension questions correct _____

Comprehension Scores

   Independent reading level _____6_____

   Instructional reading level _____4–5_____

   Frustration reading level __3 or fewer__

SELF-MONITORING OF COMPREHENSION

   How well do you think you answered these questions?

   very well _____

   all right _____

   not so well _____

CAROLINE QUARLES AND THE UNDERGROUND RAILROAD* ——

Strange as it may sound, the *Underground Railroad* wasn't a railroad at all. This railroad had no steam engines or tracks. Instead what history calls the Underground Railroad was people, freedom workers scattered all over the northern states. These people helped former slaves escape from the brutal life of slavery.

In 1842 one of these runaway slaves was 16-year-old Caroline Quarles. She took $100 and a box of clothes and ran from the St. Louis, Missouri, home of her owner to the Mississippi River and freedom. However, freedom was very difficult for Caroline to find. Because she had light skin and brown hair even though she was Black, she was able to take a riverboat to Illinois. Then she took a stagecoach to Milwaukee in the Wisconsin territory.

In Milwaukee Caroline found a job and a new life with the help of a former slave. However, when a reward of $300 was offered for her return to her owner, this former slave who had seemed to be her friend turned her in.

A young man named Frank Asahel, who believed in freedom for everyone, heard about Caroline, who was then staying in a shack by the river. By

© 2001 by John Wiley & Sons, Inc.

_____

*The readability level of this passage was computed by the Dale-Chall Readability Formula.

CAROLINE QUARLES AND THE UNDERGROUND RAILROAD *(Cont'd)*

that time slave catchers from St. Louis were searching for her. Frank helped her to escape to the river just before the slave catchers arrived.

When the slave catchers arrived where Caroline had been staying, they discovered that she had escaped again. They became extremely angry and looked everywhere for her. To avoid being captured, Caroline hid in a wooden sugar barrel after Frank put the lid on it and quickly left. Caroline sat huddled in that barrel on a sweltering hot August day hour after hour waiting for Frank to come back for her. Finally he returned and pried open the lid of the barrel and freed Caroline.

Later a freedom worker named Lyman Goodnow stowed Caroline under the straw in his wagon and, with the help of other freedom workers, headed for Canada, which was over 500 miles away. There Caroline could be free since Canada did not have slavery.

Caroline remained in Canada as a free woman, married a widower, and had six children. Later in her life in 1880 she wrote to Mr. Goodnow: "I am living and have to work hard; but I have never forgotten you or your kindness."

Always remember how fortunate you are to have been born free. It is a great privilege.

CAROLINE QUARLES AND THE UNDERGROUND RAILROAD

BEFORE READING

Assessing Prior Knowledge and Interests

1. What do you think the Underground Railroad was?

2. How do you think a slave was able to go to Canada to become free?

AFTER READING

Number of words in this selection _____415_____

Number of word identification miscues _____

Word Identification Miscues

Independent reading level ____0–6____

Low independent reading level approx. ____7–13____

High instructional reading level approx. ____14–21____

Instructional reading level approx. ____22–33____

Low instructional reading level approx. ____34–41____

Frustration reading level ____42+____

Assessing Comprehension

Score 1 for a correct response and 0 for an incorrect response in the appropriate column. Score ✔ for any answers that are clearly illogical or + for any answers that are very good, detailed, or insightful.

	Score	*Appropriateness*

Reading the Lines (Literal Comprehension)

1. How old was Caroline Quarles when she began her trip to freedom? **(16; sixteen)** _____ _____

2. What kind of container did Caroline hide in from the slave catchers? **(sugar barrel; barrel)** _____ _____

Reading Between the Lines (Interpretive Comprehension)

3. What about her physical appearance may have helped Caroline to escape? **(she had light skin and brown hair; she probably could pass for a white person)** _____ _____

4. Why do you think Asahel and Goodnow helped Caroline to escape? **(they thought slavery was wrong; they thought slave owners and slave catchers were cruel men; they felt sorry for Caroline)** _____ _____

CAROLINE QUARLES
AND THE UNDERGROUND RAILROAD *(Cont'd)*

© 2001 by John Wiley & Sons, Inc.

Score   Appropriateness

Reading Beyond the Lines (Applied Comprehension)

5. Would you have helped a slave to escape on the
Underground Railroad? Why? Why not? **(any logical
answer—some examples: yes, I think slavery was
wrong; yes, I would want to help slaves since they
deserved freedom; no, I would be afraid to; no,
I wouldn't know what to do)**

_____   _____

6. Would you have tried to escape if you were a slave in 1842?
**(yes, I would want to be free; yes, I could not stand to
live as a slave and do what somebody told me to do; no,
I wouldn't know exactly where to go or what to do
to escape)**

_____   _____

Number of comprehension questions correct _____

Comprehension Score

    Independent reading level _____5_____

    Instructional reading level _____4–5_____

    Frustration reading level _3 or fewer_

SELF-MONITORING OF COMPREHENSION

    How well do you think you answered these questions?

    very well _____

    all right _____

    not so well _____

CASTLES BUILT BY THE NORMANS*

Undoubtedly you have seen many photographs of castles. Many people have toured the Norman castles in France and England and have found them fascinating.

The word *Norman* means *"man from the North,"* and the first Norman people were Vikings from Scandinavia, who invaded an area of northern France that is now called Normandy. The Normans had a *feudal* system of government, which meant that the peasants (working class people) served their local lord or *baron* in exchange for strips of land on which to grow crops. In a similar way all the lords served their king in return for having control over their own area. The Normans were excellent soldiers, and Norman *knights* wore metal armor and rode *war-horses* while fighting their enemies.

The barons built strong castles to defend themselves, and these castles soon became important centers of feudal society. The first Norman castles that were built on lands that the Normans had conquered were only circular banks of earth surrounded by a ditch. Others, which were called *motte-and-bailey castles*, had a square wooden fort or *keep* built on top of a mound of earth called the *motte*. The *keep* was surrounded by a series of sharp wooden stakes and was the safest part of the castle.

---

*The readability level of this passage was computed by the Dale-Chall Readability Formula.

CASTLES BUILT BY THE NORMANS *(Cont'd)*

At the foot of the *motte* was a circular courtyard beside another wooden fence, and this courtyard was called the *bailey*. The *bailey* contained the kitchen, stables, bakery, and chapel.

Later the Normans replaced the wooden castles with stone castles, which were much more secure. Although the Tower of London is the most famous of these stone castles, many others still survive today. These castles have outerwalls as thick as twelve feet and towers and gaps at the top called *battlements* from which *archers* fired arrows at their enemies. A strong stone keep was built inside the walls.

In the ground floor of the *keep* was a storeroom for weapons and armor, and above was the main hall where the lord and lady entertained guests and ate their meals. They slept in the top room of the *keep* called the *solar*. Most castles had a chapel for worshipping. Some castles had a toilet called a *garderobe* (*gard-robe*), which was only a hole in the wall.

Since there was very little machinery, building a stone castle was an enormous task that took thousands of men several years to complete. Castles also were very expensive to build, and they had to be built in locations where there was plenty of food, water, stone, and lumber. However, they were very well built, and some remain intact today.

CASTLES BUILT BY THE NORMANS

BEFORE READING

Assessing Prior Knowledge and Interests

1. How would you describe what a castle looks like?

2. Would you enjoy visiting a Norman castle sometime in the future?

AFTER READING

Number of words in this selection ___435___

Number of word identification miscues _____

Word Identification Miscues

Independent reading level ___0–6___

Low independent reading level approx. ___7–12___

High instructional reading level approx. ___13–20___

Instructional reading level approx. ___21–35___

Low instructional reading level approx. ___36–43___

Frustration reading level ___44+___

Assessing Comprehension

Score 1 for a correct response and 0 for an incorrect response in the appropriate column. Score ✔ for any answers that are clearly illogical or + for any answers that are very good, detailed, or insightful.

Score   Appropriateness

Reading the Lines (Literal Comprehension)

1. What does the word *Norman* mean?
   (man from the North)   _____   _____

2. What was the *garderobe* in a castle?
   (toilet)   _____   _____

Reading Between the Lines (Interpretive Comprehension)

3. Why do you think the Norman knights wore metal
   armor? **(it would be harder to wound or kill them**   _____   _____
   **when they were wearing metal armor; it gave them
   protection against their enemies)**

4. Why did the Norman castles have to be built in locations
   in which food and water were plentiful? **(the people had**   _____   _____
   **to have food and water that were easily available
   since they did not have good transportation there;
   people need food and water to survive)**

CASTLES BUILT BY THE NORMANS *(Cont'd)*

	Score	Appropriateness

Reading Beyond the Lines (Applied Comprehension)

5. Would you have wanted to live in a Norman castle? Why? Why not? **(any logical answer—some examples: yes, it would have been interesting; yes, it seems as if it would have been safe; no, it would have been hard work, unless you were the lord or lady; no, it would have been too primitive)**   _____ _____

6. Would you ever like to visit a castle? Why? Why not? **(yes, it would be fascinating to see one; yes, I would learn a lot about history; no, I really don't like that time in history; no, a castle would be too far to travel)**   _____ _____

Number of comprehension questions correct _____

Comprehension Score

Independent reading level _____6_____

Instructional reading level _____4–5_____

Frustration reading level _3 or fewer_

SELF-MONITORING OF COMPREHENSION

How well do you think you answered these questions?

very well _____

all right _____

not so well _____

Name _____ Grade _____ Teacher _____ Date _____

THE VIKINGS, A FASCINATING PEOPLE*

Most people have heard a great deal about the Vikings although some of what they have heard undoubtedly is inaccurate. For example, the Vikings have a reputation for being violent, ruthless people. While that may be true, many of them were farmers who greatly valued their land.

The Vikings lived about 800 A.D., until 1150 A.D., and at the beginning of that time were content to live as farmers in their native lands of Norway, Denmark, and Sweden. They later launched the first of a series of raids on western Europe, which gave them the reputation for extreme violence that remains today.

Although it is accurate that the Vikings plundered monasteries and towns, they mainly traveled abroad as settlers searching for new lands since their own lands became overcrowded. They desired to continue farming.

Much of what we now know about Viking life is the result of archaeological excavations that have been done. For example, a Viking farmhouse had a main building called a *hall*, which was a rectangle about 40 feet to 100 feet long and was built out of the materials that were available in that area. Wood, stone, and blocks of turf (sod) all were used for walls, while the roof usually was thatched with reeds or straw, but sometimes it was constructed out of turf. The floor of the hall usually was hard packed earth although boards also were

© 2001 by John Wiley & Sons, Inc.

---

*The readability level of this passage was computed by the Dale-Chall Readability Formula.

THE VIKINGS, A FASCINATING PEOPLE *(Cont'd)*

used. While early farmhouses contained only one room, later a farmhouse was divided up into rooms such as a kitchen, bedroom, and weaving room.

Although the inside of a Viking house was simply furnished, it was cluttered. There were shelves to store supplies, and the beams that supported the house also were used for hanging supplies. Foods such as cheeses, butter, and milk were kept in vats and ladled out as needed. Although the Vikings ate beef, veal, lamb, and mutton, they also ate pigs, goats, and horses as well as fish they caught. Their vegetables were cabbages, peas, and onions, and they ate fruit such as raspberries, elderberries, and plums. They drank beer brewed from malt barley and mead brewed from honey. Both were drunk from the horns of cattle.

The early Vikings were *pagans* who believed in a number of different gods and goddesses. Their gods demanded sacrifices, which were made at three major festivals each year. At these festivals the Vikings feasted on horsemeat and drank beer and expected in return for their sacrifices that their gods would provide plentiful harvests and victories in battle. The Vikings later converted to Christianity partially so that they could trade with Christians.

I have visited the excavated Viking city *Jorvik* in what is now York, England, and *Jorvik* was fascinating.

THE VIKINGS, A FASCINATING PEOPLE

BEFORE READING

Assessing Prior Knowledge and Interests

1. What do you know about the Vikings?

2. Are you interested in learning about ancient peoples like the Vikings? Why? Why not?

AFTER READING

Number of words in this selection ____456____

Number of word identification miscues _____

Word Identification Miscues

Independent reading level ____0–6____

Low independent reading level approx. ____7–12____

High instructional reading level approx. ____13–20____

Instructional reading level approx. ____21–36____

Low instructional reading level ____37–44____

Frustration reading level ____45+____

Assessing Comprehension

Score 1 for a correct response and 0 for an incorrect response in the appropriate column. Score ✔ for any answers that are clearly illogical or + for any answers that are very good, insightful, or detailed.

Score *Appropriateness*

Reading the Lines (Literal Comprehension)

1. What is the reputation the Vikings usually have? **(violence; for being violent people)** _____ _____

2. How many rooms did the *early* Viking farmhouses have? **(one room)** _____ _____

3. What is the name of the excavated Viking city mentioned in this passage? **(Jorvik)** _____ _____

Reading Between the Lines (Interpretive Comprehension)

4. Why do you think the Viking farmhouses often had a turf (sod) roof? **(sod was plentiful for them; it was easy to find sod; it would continue to grow, and they could use it)** _____ _____

5. Why do you think the Vikings ate quite a bit of fish? **(they could catch them easily in rivers, streams, or lakes; it was easier to catch fish than to raise animals such as cows or sheep)** _____ _____

THE VIKINGS, A FASCINATING PEOPLE *(Cont'd)*

	Score	*Appropriateness*

6. Why do you think Christians would rather trade with other Christians than with pagans? **(they had more in common with Christians than with pagans; they could discuss their mutual Christian faith)**　　_____　_____

Reading Beyond the Lines (Applied Comprehension)

7. Would you like to have lived in Viking times? Why? Why not? **(any logical answer—some examples: yes, it would have been interesting; no, it was too primitive and not healthy; no, there weren't many medical advances)**　　_____　_____

8. Would you like to visit the excavated Viking city of *Jorvik?* **(any logical answer—some examples: yes, it would be fascinating to see; no, I don't like to travel; no, I'm not interested in history)**　　_____　_____

Number of comprehension questions correct _____

Comprehension Score

    Independent reading level _____8_____

    Instructional reading level _____5–7_____

    Frustration reading level __4 or fewer__

SELF-MONITORING OF COMPREHENSION

    How well do you think you answered these questions?

    very well _____

    all right _____

    not so well _____

THE GREAT CHICAGO FIRE*

If you have ever visited the thriving city of Chicago, you may have a difficult time imagining it as a wasteland of devastation. However, this happened in October 1871, when much of the city was virtually destroyed by the great Chicago fire.

According to legend, the famous fire began during the evening of October 8, 1871, at 137 DeKoven Street when Mrs. Catherine O'Leary's cow kicked over a lantern in the barn. Although it is well documented that the fire began in the wooden barn at that location, there is no evidence that a cow was responsible.

What is certain, however, is that there was a very strong wind coming from the Illinois prairie that day, and it often gusted fiercely. In addition, in 1871 Chicago was a city susceptible to fire since it had about 59,500 buildings, many of them large and ornately decorated, with two-thirds of the buildings constructed entirely of wood. Even though the remainder of the buildings appeared to be fireproof, they were jerrybuilt affairs with stone or brick exteriors but wooden floors and frames, all topped with flammable tar or shingle roofs. Even the sidewalks were wooden as well as cottages, barns, sheds, and outhouses.

It was the gusting swirling winds that drove the flames from the O'Learys' barn into neighboring yards. Since the fire alarms were not sounded correctly, the fire spread quickly.

© 2001 by John Wiley & Sons, Inc.

*The readability level of this passage was computed by the Dale-Chall Readability Formula.

THE GREAT CHICAGO FIRE *(Cont'd)*

As soon as the first shouts of "Fire" were heard, people streamed toward DeKoven Street in the heart of a rather impoverished neighborhood. Most of the neighbors stood watching the yellow-orange flames leaping from roof to roof. Due to the gusting winds, the fire quickly fanned out, destroying such buildings as the courthouse, the *Chicago Tribune* building, the Chamber of Commerce Building, St. Paul's Church, the armory, the waterworks, the post office, and the custom house.

However, the human toll was much more devastating than the destruction of the buildings. It is difficult to imagine the throngs of panicked adults and children fleeing the fire attempting to carry their treasured possessions with them. People trampled those who could not keep up with the panicked crowd. Others were severely burned, and still others died as the fire heated up the area to as much as 1500 degrees as hot air rose and formed a column hundreds of feet high.

The great Chicago fire undoubtedly would have burned until it ran out of city had not a life-saving rain called a miracle begun to fall. As a result of the fire, nearly 100,000 people were homeless, and 17,500 buildings and 73 miles of street were destroyed. However, gradually Chicago was rebuilt into the prosperous city that it is today.

THE GREAT CHICAGO FIRE

BEFORE READING

Assessing Prior Knowledge and Interests

1. What do you currently know about the great Chicago fire of 1871?

2. Are you interested in learning about famous fires? Why? Why not?

AFTER READING

Number of words in this selection ____449____

Number of word identification miscues _____

Word Identification Miscues

Independent reading level ____0–6____

Low independent reading level approx. ____7–12____

High instructional reading level approx. ____13–20____

Instructional reading level approx. ____21–36____

Low instructional reading level approx. ____37–44____

Frustration reading level ____45+____

Assessing Comprehension

Score 1 for a correct response and 0 for an incorrect response in the appropriate column. Score ✔ for any answers that are clearly illogical and + for any answers that are very good, detailed, or insightful.

	Score	Appropriateness

Reading the Lines (Literal Comprehension)

1. In what month of 1871 did the great Chicago fire occur? **(October)**

2. What was the main reason that the fire spread so quickly? **(there was a strong wind blowing the fire)**

3. Why did the fire finally stop burning? **(it started to rain)**

Reading Between the Lines (Interpretive Comprehension)

4. In what ways do you think buildings are less likely to burn today than they were in 1871? **(there is more steel in them; there is less wood in them; they have fireproof roofs)**

5. Why do you think the people were so panic stricken during the fire? **(they thought that might die; they were terrified of fire; they wanted to escape from the fire; they may have lost family members in the confusion)**

	Score	Appropriateness

6. Why do you think some people tried to take their treasured possessions with them? **(they could not bear to have their possessions burned up; they thought their possessions were not replaceable; they loved their possessions)** _____ _____

Reading Beyond the Lines (Applied Comprehension)

7. Would you ever want to become a firefighter? Why? Why not? **(any logical answer— some examples: yes, I could save lives and property; yes, it would be exciting; no, it is too dangerous; no, I am not strong enough to carry someone from a burning building)** _____ _____

8. Would you like to watch a large fire? Why? Why not? **(any logical answer—some examples: yes, it would be exciting; yes, it would be interesting; no, I don't like fires; no, I am afraid of fires)** _____ _____

Number of comprehension questions correct _____

Comprehension Score

Independent reading level _____8_____

Instructional reading level _____5–7_____

Frustration reading level __4 or fewer__

SELF-MONITORING OF COMPREHENSION

How well do you think you answered these questions?

very well _____

all right _____

not so well _____

THE LASER*

A *laser* produces a narrow beam of very bright light, either firing brief pulses of light or forming a continuous beam of light. Laser stands for *Light Amplification by Stimulated Emission of Radiation.* Unlike ordinary light, laser light is *coherent,* which means that all the rays have exactly the same wave length and are all in phase, vibrating together to produce a beam of great intensity or strength.

A *laser* beam may either be of visible light or of invisible infra-red rays. Visible light lasers are used in digital recording and fiber optic communications as well as in surveying and distance measurement and provide results of very high quality and accuracy. The intense heat of a powerful infra-red laser beam is sufficient to cut metal.

In a laser, energy is first stored in a *lasing medium,* which may be a solid, liquid, or gas. The energy excites atoms in the medium, raising them to a high-energy state. One excited atom then spontaneously releases a light ray. The ray of light from the excited atom strikes another excited atom, causing it also to emit a light ray. These rays then strike more excited atoms, and the process of light production grows. The mirrors at the end of the tube reflect the light rays so that more excited atoms release light. All the light rays are in step, and the light beam eventually becomes bright enough to pass through the semi-silvered mirror and leave the laser. The energy then is released as laser light.

© 2001 by John Wiley & Sons, Inc.

*The readability level of this passage was computed by the Dale-Chall Readability Formula.

THE LASER *(Cont'd)*

Lasers have many important applications in a technological society. One application is that of *holography*, which is the production of images that are three dimensional and appear to have depth just like an actual object. In holography the light beam from a laser is split into two beams. One beam, the object beam, lights up the object, while a second beam, the reference beam, goes to a photographic plate or film placed near the object. When it is developed, the plate or film becomes a hologram or three-dimensional image of the object.

A supermarket checkout is a sophisticated input to the store's computer. Each product contains a bar code that has an identification number. As the checker moves the product over a window, an invisible infra-red laser beam scans the bar code. This laser fires a beam of light and only the white spaces in the code reflect the rays. The beam returns to the detector, which connects the on-off pulses of rays onto an electric binary code signal that goes to the computer.

Another application of laser technology is the computer laser printer. Lasers also have unique applications to medicine, greatly helping physicians in a variety of complicated medical procedures. Lasers have countless valuable applications that have enriched our lives in contemporary technological society.

THE LASER

BEFORE READING

Assessing Prior Knowledge and Interests

1. What do you know about lasers?

2. How do you think the scanner in a grocery store works?

AFTER READING

Number of words in this selection _____470_____

Number of word identification miscues _____

Word Identification Miscues

Independent reading level _____0–6_____

Low independent reading level approx. _____7–13_____

High instructional reading level approx. _____14–21_____

Instructional reading level approx. _____22–37_____

Low instructional reading level approx. _____38–46_____

Frustration reading level _____47+_____

Assessing Comprehension

Score 1 for a correct response and 0 for an incorrect response in the appropriate columns. Score ✔ for any answers that are clearly illogical or + for any answers that are very good, detailed, or insightful.

	Score	Appropriateness

Reading the Lines (Literal Comprehension)

1. What is a laser? **(a beam of light)** _____ _____

2. How many dimensions does a *hologram* have? **(three)** _____ _____

3. What kind of computer printer is mentioned in this passage? **(laser printer)** _____ _____

Reading Between the Lines (Interpretive Comprehension)

4. Why do you think a laser can cut metal? **(the beam of light is so very hot; the light is hot enough to cut metal; the beam of light is so strong)** _____ _____

5. In what ways do you think a grocery store scanner is more efficient than having a checker use a cash register or calculator? **(it is quicker; it is less likely to make mistakes; it is easier for the checker to use)** _____ _____

	Score	Appropriateness

6. Why do you think a laser printer is a better printer than other kinds of printers? **(it is faster; it is less likely to make mistakes; the copies turn out better)**   _____ _____

Reading Beyond the Lines (Applied Comprehension)

7. What laser applications have you seen in operation? **(any logical answer—some examples: grocery store scanner, laser printer, a laser at a doctor's office or hospital)**   _____ _____

8. If you were a grocery store employee, would you enjoy using a laser scanner? Why? Why not? **(any logical answer—some examples: yes, it would be easier; yes, it would be more accurate; no, I wouldn't know if it made a mistake)**   _____ _____

Number of comprehension questions correct _____

Comprehension Score

Independent reading level ____8____

Instructional reading level ____5–7____

Frustration reading level __4 or fewer__

SELF-MONITORING OF COMPREHENSION

How well do you think you answered these questions?

very well _____

all right _____

not so well _____

LEARNING ABOUT ROCKS* ≡

Although there are a myriad of different types of rocks, only a minute number of different minerals comprise most of the earth's rocks. Less than ten of the chemical elements known on Earth are found in these rock-forming minerals. The three main types of rocks are *igneous rocks, sedimentary rocks,* and *metamorphic rocks.*

When the Earth became cool enough to have a solid outer skin, *igneous rocks* were the first to appear on the surface. Igneous rocks are still being formed today as volcanoes erupt molten *magma,* which subsequently cools and becomes solid. However, some magma does not reach the Earth's surface but cools as igneous rocks underground. Millions of years later the igneous rocks that cooled several miles (kilometers) down in the Earth's crust may become exposed at the Earth's surface by uplift and erosion. There are many types of rocks that crystallize from different magma under different conditions.

Granite is one of the most common igneous rocks formed at the core of many mountain ranges. Granite contains the minerals *quartz* and *feldspar* along with a small amount of dark minerals such as *mica.* These crystals each

© 2001 by John Wiley & Sons, Inc.

_____

*The readability level of this passage was computed by the Dale-Chall Readability Formula.

contribute a unique color to granite; for example, quartz is gray, feldspar is pink or white, while mica is black.

Basalt is another common type of igneous rock, and most of the solid surface of the Earth is made of basalt. All of the solid ocean crust is basalt, and there are many huge basalt lava flows on the continents. Basalt is formed by molten rock in the Earth's mantle and is fine ground and dark in color because of the dark minerals it contains, primarily *pyroxene* and *olivine*. If basalt magma cools slowly, it forms large crystals called *dolerite*, or if the crystals are very large, they are called *gabbro*.

Sedimentary rocks are formed layer by layer from material that previously made other rocks. This material is created by weathering, which breaks down older rocks into fragments and chemicals into solutions. Then the grains and dissolved rock are transported by wind, rivers, and glaciers and eventually are deposited as layers of *sediment* along with any plant and animal remains that are trapped within them. Over a period of time, the layers are buried and squashed to become *lithified* or hardened into new rocks.

Sandstone is a type of sedimentary rock that is made up of grains of sand that indicate the rock's history. *Limestone's* chemicals are transported invisibly since they are dissolved, which alters the chemical balance of the water. As a result, the chemicals that comprise limestone—*calcium* and *magnesium carbonate*—separate from the water and are deposited in thick layers of limy mud on the seabed to form limestone.

Metamorphic rocks are made from preexisting rocks whether they are sedimentary, igneous, or metamorphic. When a rock metamorphoses, the minerals recrystallize and its original texture changes. Usually these changes happen inside the Earth's crust when it is hot enough and there is enough pressure from the overlying rocks to make rocks recrystallize without melting.

Intense heat changes limestone into *marble*, while heat and pressure change granite into *gneiss*, a rock which shows dark, wispy bands of mica curling around feldspar. Dull gray mudstone can be transformed into sparkling colored crystalline rocks such as *kyinite schist*.

LEARNING ABOUT ROCKS

BEFORE READING

Assessing Prior Knowledge and Interests

1. What do you think are the three main types of rocks?

2. Do you enjoy reading a scientific passage like this? Why? Why not?

AFTER READING

Number of words in this selection _____545_____

Number of word identification miscues _____

Word Identification Miscues

Independent reading level _____0–7_____

Low independent reading level approx. _____8–16_____

High instructional reading level approx. _____17–27_____

Instructional reading level approx. _____28–43_____

Low instructional reading level approx. _____44–54_____

Frustration reading level _____55+_____

Assessing Comprehension

Score 1 for a correct response and 0 for an incorrect response in the appropriate column. Score ✔ for any answers that are clearly illogical or + for any answers that are very good, detailed, or insightful.

	Score	Appropriateness

Reading the Lines (Literal Comprehension)

1. What are the three main types of rocks? **(igneous, sedimentary, metamorphic)** _____ _____

2. What type of rock is granite? **(igneous)** _____ _____

3. What type of rock is sandstone? **(sedimentary)** _____ _____

Reading Between the Lines (Interpretive Comprehension)

4. How do you know the core of a mountain range is very hard? **(it is made of granite, which is a very hard rock; a mountain looks as if it were made of a hard material)** _____ _____

5. Do you think sandstone is a soft or hard rock? Why do you believe as you do? **(a soft rock since it is made up of grains of sand that were deposited as layers of sediment)** _____ _____

LEARNING ABOUT ROCKS *(Cont'd)*

	Score	Appropriateness

6. Do you think marble is a soft or hard rock? Why do you believe as you do? **(hard rock because it was changed from limestone by intense heat)**   _____ _____

Reading Beyond the Lines (Applied Comprehension)

7. Would you ever make a serious study of rocks? Why? Why not? **(any logical answer—some examples: yes, I think it would be interesting; yes, I enjoy all parts of nature; no, I don't like science; no, I'm not interested in science)**   _____ _____

8. Would you like to hunt for gemstones that are embedded in various kinds of rocks? **(any logical answer—some examples: yes, I would like to make gemstone jewelry; yes, I would like to sell the gems that I found; no, I'm not interested in gemstones at all)**   _____ _____

Number of comprehension questions correct _____

Comprehension Score

Independent reading level ____8____

Instructional reading level ____5–7____

Frustration reading level __4 or fewer__

SELF-MONITORING OF COMPREHENSION

How well do you think you answered these questions?

very well _____

all right _____

not so well _____

INFORMAL ASSESSMENT OF WORD IDENTIFICATION SKILLS

As a good informal assessment of a student's word identification skill, you can have him or her read a sample of approximately 100 words from any narrative or content material. If the student mispronounces more than five words (maximum amount) out of the 100-word sample, the material is too difficult for him or her, and easier material should be selected. If you want, you can have the child put down one finger for each word that he or she does not know, and if the child has put down all five fingers on one hand, the material is at the maximum level of difficulty for him or her.

Although this is *not* a foolproof way of determining a student's instructional (with teacher support) level, it may be precise enough in some instances.

SAN DIEGO QUICK ASSESSMENT LIST

The *San Diego Quick Assessment List* is a useful, easy way to assess a child's approximate instructional (with teacher support) level. It is *not* a substitute for a running record, miscue analysis, or an Individual Reading Inventory. However, if a reading teacher or reading tutor wants an easy, quick estimation of a child's approximate instructional reading level, it can be used quite effectively for that purpose.

Administration

1. Type each list of words on index cards.

2. Begin with a card that is at least two years below the child's grade-level assignment.

3. Ask the child to read the words aloud to you. If he or she mispronounces any words on a list, drop down to easier lists until he or she makes no mistakes. This should be the *base level.*

4. Write down all incorrect answers, or use diacritical (phonetic) marks on your copy of the list. For example, the word *grim* might be read and recorded as *grime.* The word *wrest* might be recorded as *west.*

5. Encourage the child to read words that he or she does not know so that you can determine the techniques that he or she uses for word identification.

6. Have the child read from increasingly difficult lists until he or she misses at least three words.

Analysis

1. The list on which the child misses no more than *one of ten words* is the level at which he or she can read independently. Two errors indicate the instructional reading level. Three or more errors indicate material that may be too difficult (frustration reading level).

2. An analysis of the child's errors is useful. Among those that occur most often may be the following:

Error	Example
reversal	*ton* for *not*
consonant	*bump* for *jump*
consonant blend	*bright* for *blight*
short vowel	*grime* for *grim*
long vowel	*rod* for *road*
prefix	*illusion* for *delusion*
suffix	*behaving* for *behave*
miscellaneous	omission of accent, etc.

3. As with all informal assessment devices, teacher observation of student behavior during the assessment is important. Items such as posture, facial expression, and voice quality may signal nervousness, lack of confidence, or frustration while reading.

SAN DIEGO QUICK ASSESSMENT LIST*

Preprimer	Primer	One	Two
see	you	road	our
play	come	live	please
me	not	thank	myself
at	with	when	town
run	jump	bigger	early
go	help	how	send
and	is	always	wide
look	work	night	believe
can	are	spring	quietly
here	this	today	carefully

Three	Four	Five	Six
city	decided	scanty	bridge
middle	served	business	commercial
moment	develop	amazed	abolish
frightened	silent	considered	trucker
exclaimed	wrecked	discussed	apparatus
several	improve	behaved	elementary
lonely	certainly	splendid	comment
drew	entered	acquainted	necessity
since	realized	escaped	gallery
straight	interrupted	grim	relativity

*Word list from "The Graded Word List: Quick Gauge of Reading Ability," Margaret LaPray and Ramon Ross, *Journal of Reading*, January 1969, 305–307. Reprinted with permission of Margaret LaPray and the International Reading Association.

SAN DIEGO QUICK ASSESSMENT LIST *(Cont'd)*

Seven	**Eight**	**Nine**
amber	capacious	conscientious
dominion	limitation	isolation
sundry	pretext	molecule
capillary	intrigue	ritual
impetuous	delusion	momentous
blight	immaculate	vulnerable
wrest	ascent	kinship
enumerate	acrid	conservatism
daunted	binocular	jaunty
condescend	embankment	inventive

Ten	**Eleven**
zany	galore
jerkin	rotunda
nausea	capitalism
gratuitous	prevaricate
linear	risible
inept	exonerate
legality	superannuate
aspen	luxuriate
amnesty	piebald
barometer	crunch

QUICK SURVEY WORD LIST

The *Quick Survey Word List* is a quick test of a student's ability in phonics. To construct it, reproduce it and glue it to a 5" × 8" card. After attaching it to the card, you may want to laminate it so that it will be more durable. The Quick Survey Word List is designed to enable a reading teacher or tutor to assess quickly if a student has the necessary word attack skills to read successfully materials written at the adult level. Therefore, it can be given to students at about the fourth-grade reading level to determine if it is necessary to give the more comprehensive but time-consuming El Paso Phonics Survey.

To give this test, give the student the word list and ask him or her to pronounce each word. Tell the student that the words he or she is going to pronounce are nonsense (make-believe) words or words that are not actual words. Tell the student that these words are difficult, but that you need to know if he or she is able to pronounce them accurately. If the student can pronounce each of the words correctly, it is not necessary to give the El Paso Phonics Survey because the purpose of learning phonic analysis is to help a student successfully attack (decode) unknown words. However, if it becomes clear after one or two words that the student cannot complete this test successfully, you should discontinue it and instead give the El Paso Phonics Survey.

The correct pronunciation of the words on the Quick Survey Word List is given in the following list. The key shows the correct pronunciation as well as the part of each word that should be stressed. However, you must remember that accent rules in the English language are not consistent. Therefore, if a student pronounces the words correctly except for the accent or stress shown on certain syllables, they should be considered correct.

The Quick Survey Word List also is designed to assess a student's knowledge of such phonic and structural skills as syllabication; vowel rules; rules for *c, e,* and *y;* and accent rules. Remember, if a student does not perform well on the first two or three words, discontinue the test. Only if a student is able to pronounce all of the words correctly should you continue through the entire test.

PRONUNCIATION OF THE QUICK SURVEY WORDS

rat'-bel-ing	twā'-fräl
däs'-nit	sprēn'-plit
pram'-min-cil-ling	gōn'-bāt
hwet'-split-tər	strē'-gran
jin'-kyool	glam'-mər-tick-ly
crin'-gāl	gran'-tel-lēn
slat'-run-gəl	āp'-sid

PRONUNCIATION KEY

l—litt<u>le</u>

ə—<u>a</u>bout

ä—f<u>a</u>ther

ə—tamp<u>er</u>

hw—<u>wh</u>at

kyoo—c<u>u</u>te

QUICK SURVEY WORD LIST*

wratbeling	twayfrall
dawsnite	spreanplit
pramminciling	goanbate
whetsplitter	streegran
gincule	glammertickly
cringale	grantellean
slatrungle	aipcid

*Reprinted by permission of Merrill/Prentice Hall, from Eldon E. Ekwall and James L. Shanker, *Locating and Correcting Reading Difficulties*, seventh edition. Columbus, OH: Merrill/Prentice Hall, 1998.

EL PASO PHONICS SURVEY

The *El Paso Phonics Survey* is a very comprehensive informal assessment device for determining a student's specific competencies and weaknesses in phonics. Although it is time-consuming, it is not very difficult to give and evaluate. It just takes a fairly long time to give. It should be given to those students who are weak in phonics; it provides a precise evaluation of their phonic skills.

To construct the El Paso Phonics Survey, reproduce the sample given later in this section and glue it to 5" × 8" cards and then laminate them for durability. Make multiple copies of the Answer Keys so that you can mark each child's response on a separate copy. There are both general directions and specific directions for administering this survey; follow them carefully.

General Directions

1. Before beginning the test, make sure the child has instant recognition of the test words (*in, up, am*) that appear in the box at the top of the first page of the survey. These words should be known instantly by the child. If they are not immediately recognized, the test should be given later when the child has been taught and has mastered them.

2. Give the child a copy of the El Paso Phonics Survey.

3. Point to the letter in the first column and have the child say the name of that letter (not the sound that it represents). Then point to the word in the middle column and have the child pronounce it. Then point to the nonsense word in the third column and have the child pronounce it.

4. If the child can give the name of the letter, the word in the middle column, and the nonsense word in the third column, mark the answer sheet with a plus (+).

5. If the child cannot pronounce the nonsense word after giving the name of the letter and the word in the middle column, mark the answer sheet with a minus (-); or you may wish to write the word phonetically as the child pronounces it. If the child can tell you the name of the letter and the small word in the middle column but cannot pronounce the nonsense word, you may wish to have him or her give the letter sound in isolation. If the child can give the sound in isolation, either the child is unable to blend or does not know the letter well enough to give its sound and blend it at the same time.

6. Whenever an asterisk appears on the answer sheet, refer to the Special Directions.

7. To the right of each blank on the answer sheet is a grade-level designation. This number represents the point by which most basal reader series have taught that sound. By that point, you should expect it to be known. For example, the designation 2.2 means the second month of second grade.

8. When the child comes to two- or three-letter consonant digraphs or blends, as with the *qu* in item 22, she is to say "*q-u*" as with single letters. The child is never to give the letter sounds in isolation while doing actual reading.

9. When the child comes to the vowels (item 59), he or she is to say *"short a"* and so forth and then explain what this means. The same is to be done with the long vowels.

10. All vowels and vowel combinations are put with only one or two of the first eight consonants. If any of the first eight consonants are not known, they should be taught before you attempt to test for vowel knowledge. You will probably find that a child who does not know the first eight consonant sounds rarely knows the vowel sounds.

11. You will notice that words appear to the right of some of the blends on the answer sheet. These words illustrate the correct consonant or vowel sounds that should be heard when the child answers.

12. Included are phonic elements that Ekwall thought were worthwhile to teach to most young children. For example, the vowel pair *ui* is very rare, and when it does appear, it may stand for the short *i* sound in *build* or the long *oo* sound in *fruit*. Therefore, there is no reason to teach it as a sound. However, some letters, such as *oe*, may represent several different sounds, but most often represent one particular sound. In the case of *oe*, the long *o* sound should be used. In such cases, the most common sound is illustrated by a word to the right of the blank on the answer sheet. If the child gives another correct sound for the letter(s), you can say, "Yes, that's right, but what is another way you could pronounce this nonsense word?" The child must then say it as illustrated in the small word to the right of the blank on the answer sheet. Otherwise, the answer must be counted as wrong.

13. Discontinue the test after five consecutive misses or if the child appears frustrated from missing a number of items even though he or she has not missed five consecutive items.

Specific Directions

3. If the child uses another *s* sound as in *sugar* (*sh*) in saying the nonsense word *sup*, ask, "What is another sound?" The child must use the *s* as in the word *soap*.

15. If the child uses the *soft c* sound as in *city* in saying the nonsense word *cam*, ask, "What is another *c* sound?" The child must use the *hard c* as in the word *cup*.

16. If the child uses the *soft g* sound as in *gem* in saying the nonsense word *gup*, ask, "What is another *g* sound?" The child must use the hard *g* as in the word *gate*.

17. Ask, "What is the *y* sound when it comes at the beginning of a word?"

23. The child must use the *ks* sound of *x*, and the nonsense word *mox* must rhyme with *fox*.

35. If the child uses the *th* sound heard in *that*, ask, "What is another *th* sound?" The child must use the *th* sound as in the word *thin*.

44. If the child uses the *hoo* sound of *wh* in saying the nonsense word *whup*, ask, "What is another *wh* sound?" The child must use the *wh* sound as in the word *white*.

72. The child may either give the *ea* sound heard in *head* or the *ea* sound heard in *meat*. Be sure to indicate on the answer sheet which one the child said.

73. If the same *ea* sound is given this time as was given in item 72, say, "Yes, that's right, but what is another way you could pronounce this nonsense word?" Whichever sound was not used in item 72 must be used here. Otherwise, this item should be recorded as incorrect.

81. The child may give either the *ow* sound heard in the word *now* or the *ow* sound heard in the word *blow*. Be sure to indicate on the answer sheet which sound was used.

82. If the same *ow* sound is given this time as was given for item 81, say, "Yes, that's right, but what is another way you could pronounce this nonsense word?" Whichever sound was not used in item 81 must be used here. Otherwise, this item should be recorded as incorrect.

88. The child may give either the *oo* sound heard in *book* or the *oo* sound heard in *goose*. Be sure to indicate on the answer sheet which sound was used.

89. If the same *oo* sound is given this time as was given for item 88, say, "Yes, that's right, but what is another way you could pronounce this nonsense word?" Whichever sound was not used in item 88 must be used here. Otherwise, this item should be recorded as incorrect.

EL PASO PHONICS SURVEY[†]

	in	up	am	

1. p	am	pam		24. pr	am	pram
2. n	up	nup		25. sl	in	slin
3. s	up	sup		26. pl	up	plup
4. r	in	rin		27. fl	in	flin
5. t	up	tup		28. st	am	stam
6. m	up	mup		29. fr	in	frin
7. b	up	bup		30. bl	am	blam
8. d	up	dup		31. gr	up	grup
9. w	am	wam		32. br	in	brin
10. h	up	hup		33. tr	am	tram
11. f	am	fam		34. sh	up	shup
12. j	up	jup		35. th	up	thup
13. k	am	kam		36. ch	am	cham
14. l	in	lin		37. dr	up	drup
15. c	am	cam		38. cl	in	clin
16. g	up	gup		39. gl	am	glam
17. y	in	yin		40. sk	up	skup
18. v	am	vam		41. cr	in	crin
19. z	up	zup		42. sw	up	swup
20. c	in	cin		43. sm	in	smin
21. g	in	gin		44. wh	up	whup
22. qu	am	quam		45. sp	up	spup
23. m	ox	mox		46. sc	up	scup

[†]Reprinted by permission of Merrill/Prentice Hall, from Eldon E. Ekwall and James L. Shanker, *Locating and Correcting Reading Difficulties*, seventh edition. Columbus, OH: Merrill/Prentice Hall, 1998.

47. str	am	stram	69. ee	eem	
48. thr	up	thrup	70. oa	oan	
49. scr	in	scrin	71. ai	ait	
50. spr	am	spram	72. ea	eam	
51. spl	in	splin	73. ea	eap	
52. squ	am	squam	74. ay	tay	
53. sn	up	snup	75. oi	doi	
54. tw	am	twam	76. ou	tou	
55. wr	in	wrin	77. ar	arb	
56. shr	up	shrup	78. er	ert	
57. dw	in	dwin	79. ir	irt	
58. sch	am	scham	80. oe	poe	
59. a	tam		81. ow	owd	
60. i	rin		82. ow	fow	
61. e	nep		83. or	orm	
62. o	sot		84. ur	urd	
63. u	tun		85. oy	moy	
64. a	sape		86. ew	bew	
65. o	pote		87. aw	awp	
66. i	tipe		88. oo	oot	
67. e	rete		89. oo	oop	
68. u	pune		90. au	dau	

Name _____ Grade _____ Teacher _____ Date _____

School _____ Examiner _____

EL PASO PHONICS SURVEY†
Answer Sheet

Mark answers as follows:
Pass +
Fail − (or write word as pronounced)

PEK = point at which element
is expected to be
known

			PEK
Initial Consonants _____			
1. p	pam	_____ 1.3	
2. n	nup	_____ 1.3	
*3. s	sup	_____ 1.3	
4. r	rin	_____ 1.3	
5. t	tup	_____ 1.3	
6. m	mup	_____ 1.3	
7. b	bup	_____ 1.3	
8. d	dup	_____ 1.3	
9. w	wam	_____ 1.3	
10. h	hup	_____ 1.3	
11. f	fam	_____ 1.3	
12. j	jup	_____ 1.3	
13. k	kam	_____ 1.3	
14. l	lin	_____ 1.3	
*15. c	cam	_____ 1.3	
*16. g	gup	_____ 1.3	
*17. y	yin	_____ 1.3	
18. v	vam	_____ 1.3	
19. z	zup	_____ 1.3	
20. c	cin	_____ 1.3	

			PEK
21. g	gin	_____ 1.3	
22. qu	quam	_____ 1.3	
Ending Consonant _____			
*23. m	mox	_____ 1.3	
Initial Consonant Clusters (Blends)			
24. pr	pram	_____ 1.3	
25. sl	slin	_____ 1.6	
26. pl	plup	_____ 1.6	
27. fl	flin	_____ 1.6	
28. st	stam	_____ 1.6	
29. fr	frin	_____ 1.6	
30. bl	blam	_____ 1.6	
31. gr	grup	_____ 1.6	
32. be	brin	_____ 1.9	
33. tr	tram	_____ 1.9	
34. sh	shup	_____ 1.9	
*35. th	thup	_____ 1.9	
	thin		
36. ch	cham	_____ 1.9	
	chin		
37. dr	drup	_____ 1.9	

†Reprinted by permission of Merrill/Prentice Hall, from Eldon E. Ekwall and James L. Shanker, *Locating and Correcting Reading Difficulties*, seventh edition. Columbus, OH: Merrill/Prentice Hall, 1998.

EL PASO PHONICS SURVEY (Cont'd)
Answer Sheet

		PEK				PEK
38. cl	clin	_____ 1.9		63. u	tun	_____ 1.6
39. gl	glam	_____ 1.9		64. a	sape	_____ 1.6
40. sk	skup	_____ 1.9		65. o	pote	_____ 1.6
41. cr	crin	_____ 1.9		66. i	tipe	_____ 1.9
42. sw	swup	_____ 1.9		67. e	rete	_____ 1.9
43. sm	smin	_____ 2.5		68. u	pune	_____ 1.9
*44. wh	whup	_____ 2.5		69. ee	eem	_____ 1.9 (heed)
45. sp	spup	_____ 2.5		70. oa	oan	_____ 1.9 (soap)
46. sc	scup	_____ 2.5		71. ai	ait	_____ 1.9 (ape)
47. str	stram	_____ 2.5		*72. ea	eam	_____ 1.9 (meat)
48. thr	thrup	_____ 2.5		*73. ea	eap	_____ 2.5 (head)
49. scr	scrin	_____ 2.5		74. ay	tay	_____ 2.5 (hay)
50. spr	spram	_____ 2.5		75. oi	doi	_____ 2.5 (boy)
51. spl	splin	_____ 2.5		76. ou	tou	_____ 2.5 (cow)
52. squ	squam	_____ 2.9		77. ar	arb	_____ 2.5 (harp)
53. sn	snup	_____ 2.9		78. er	ert	_____ 2.5 (her)
54. tw	twam	_____ 2.9		79. ir	irt	_____ 2.5 (hurt)
55. wr	wrin	_____ 2.9		80. oe	poe	_____ 2.9 (hoe)
56. shr	shrup	_____ 3.5		*81. ow	owd	_____ 2.9 (blow or now)
57. dw	dwin	_____ 3.5		*82. ow	fow	_____ 2.9 (blow or now)
58. sch	scham	_____ 3.9		83. or	orm	_____ 2.9 (corn)
				84. ur	urd	_____ 2.9 (hurt)

Vowels, Vowel Teams, and Special Letter Combinations

		PEK				PEK
				85. oy	moy	_____ 2.9 (boy)
				86. ew	bew	_____ 2.9 (few)
59. a	tam	_____ 1.6		87. aw	awp	_____ 2.9 (paw)
60. i	rin	_____ 1.6		*88. oo	oot	_____ 2.9 (book or goose)
61. e	nep	_____ 1.6		*89. oo	oop	_____ 3.5 (book or goose)
62. o	sot	_____ 1.6		90. au	dau	_____ 3.5 (paw)

USING PORTFOLIO ASSESSMENT IN ANY READING PROGRAM

A *literacy portfolio* is a collection of a student's work in areas such as reading, writing, and spelling. Using a portfolio is a valuable authentic assessment technique. However, the use of portfolios cannot replace traditional assessment, such as standardized tests of different types, but always should be an important part of evaluation in a reading improvement program. Portfolio assessment is an important aspect of a comprehensive assessment program.

A literacy portfolio, which is a record of a student's progress and self-assessment over time, is usually kept in some type of holder. Often the most common type of holder for a portfolio is an accordion-type device with sections and compartments. The holder also can be a large brown folder, a box, or even a brown paper bag. The holder should be large enough to keep many papers, videotapes, cassette tapes, and drawings. The student can design and illustrate the cover if he or she wants. The folders, boxes, or containers should be easily available to the child in any classroom or tutoring situation in which informal evaluation is stressed. Students must be able to take out their portfolios whenever they wish, look through them, organize them, and add or delete material when they need or want to do so.

Although the use of portfolios in assessment is not new, portfolios are being used more often because they fit in well with our increased understanding of how language develops and, specifically, with a whole language program. Whole language stresses instruction that emphasizes the use of "real" reading materials such as trade books, the integration of reading skills, and the constructing of meaning—all of which are promoted through the use of portfolios.

The concept of using portfolios in instruction and assessment in education probably began with their use by other professionals, such as photographers, artists, and models. For professionals such as these, portfolios are usually *show portfolios*, which display a range of the best work done by that professional over a period of time. However, many of these professionals also have a *working portfolio*, from which the materials in the show portfolio are selected.

Both working and show portfolios can be used in literacy (reading) instruction and assessment. However, working portfolios may be more useful for most students in the elementary school and beyond. A working portfolio contains all of the materials that the student is currently working on. A show portfolio is made by selecting the best materials from the working portfolio (preferably by the student himself or herself, although the teacher also can provide some input if desired). The show portfolio is then shown to parents at parent–teacher conferences, to school administrators, to school board members, or to other groups. A teacher can learn a great deal about a child's abilities and interests by examining his or her portfolio regularly and by having regularly scheduled short conferences with the child about the portfolio. These conferences should be held about four times a year.

Working portfolios normally are much more useful than show portfolios with students in elementary school. The following elements can make up a working portfolio:

➡ A statement of the student's goals for the portfolio

➡ A table of contents to show how the portfolio is organized

➟ A reading/writing log

➟ The drafts of all types of writing that the student has done

➟ Reading response journals

➟ Dialogue journals

➟ Writing done outside of class

➟ Checklists and surveys of different types

➟ Tape-recorded oral reading samples

➟ Videotapes

➟ Audiotapes

➟ Teacher–pupil conference notes

➟ Different types of self-assessment devices

➟ Teacher anecdotes and observations

➟ Graphs of the student's reading, writing, or spelling progress

A reading teacher or tutor always should be aware that the major purpose of using a portfolio is the opportunity for a student to self-assess his or her work as much as possible. If the student does not have the opportunity or direction to make self-assessments, a portfolio may not be very meaningful but may only be a random collection of the student's work. It is important that both the student and his or her teacher or tutor have input into the process of constructing and maintaining the portfolio. Each student should understand that his or her portfolio is going to be available for the teacher, his or her classmates, his or her family members, and others to look at. Sometimes materials from a student's working portfolio can be collected and sent home after the student has decided—with or without teacher or tutor input—that it should no longer be included in the portfolio.

Family members must be informed before a teacher or tutor uses portfolio assessment in any reading improvement program. Such information can be shared via a letter to family members, newsletters, a back-to-school meeting, or in some other way. It is important that family members understand the purpose and content of portfolios before a teacher or tutor attempts to implement them in a reading improvement program.

In summary, portfolios are an important part of a total assessment program. Their use has unique advantages, which are summarized later in this section. You are strongly encouraged to consider using portfolios as one important component of your assessment of literacy skills, including reading skills.

SHOULD STANDARDIZED AND INFORMAL TEST SCORES BE INCLUDED IN A STUDENT'S PORTFOLIO?

Literacy specialists and teachers disagree on whether or not standardized and informal test scores of different types should be included in a student's working portfolio. Some people believe that all of a student's test scores—including standardized test scores of all kinds and all informal test scores (such as the results of running records, miscue analysis, and results from all other informal assessment devices)—should be included.

There are several correct assumptions that may support his view. For example, it can be said that a student has the right to know how well or poorly he or she performed on any type of standardized test. All of these scores are easily available in the student's portfolio to be shown to parents during parent–teacher conferences. Moreover, all such test scores are part of an entire assessment program and should be included in a portfolio because the portfolio is devoted to being a record of a student's progress.

However, there also are equally important reasons why test scores should *not* be included in a student's portfolio. For example, a student's test scores may detract from his or her reactions to reading, writing, and spelling. The inclusion of test scores in a portfolio is a contradiction to the major purpose of using portfolios—that of self-assessment. In addition, a child's test scores should *not* be made available to everyone who may have access to the portfolio.

In summary, each reading teacher and tutor should personally make the decision about whether or not to include standardized and informal test scores in the portfolios of his or her students. Especially with young children, it may not be a good idea to do so.

ADVANTAGES AND LIMITATIONS OF USING PORTFOLIOS

A literacy portfolio has many advantages, including the following:

- It helps the student to develop a positive attitude toward reading, writing, and spelling.

- It supports student ownership in his or her reading, writing, and spelling improvement.

- It improves a student's ability to self-assess, an important skill for reading improvement.

- It provides much useful information about a student for his or her teacher.

- It is useful in parent–teacher conferences and in enlisting parent support for the student's instruction.

- It is useful in conferences about children with principals, supervisors, and consultants.

- It shows the student his or her progress in a concrete, observable way.

- It is an example of authentic assessment since it keeps the focus on student-oriented purposes for reading and writing.

- It promotes teacher–pupil interaction and collaboration among students.

- It emphasizes reading and writing activities that reflect each student's unique background and interests.

Portfolio assessment has limitations, including the following:

➡ It takes much time and effort to implement portfolio assessment in any type of literacy program. Therefore, it is wise to begin portfolio assessment gradually.

➡ It takes quite a bit of time for a student to compile, self-assess, and prepare his or her portfolio.

➡ It is very time-consuming for the reading teacher to conduct twenty to thirty 10- to 15-minute teacher–pupil conferences about the portfolio at least four times a year. This generally is not a limitation for a tutor because the number of students he or she is working with usually is limited.

➡ The portfolio must be carefully explained to both family members and school administrators before it is selected for use in any reading improvement program.

➡ It is difficult to grade a literacy portfolio if this is required by the school system. Ideally, this is not necessary in the primary grades.

In summary, the advantages of portfolio assessment greatly outweigh its limitations. Therefore, I recommend that you consider using it as one means of assessment in a reading improvement program. However, you also should use other informal assessment devices of different types. In addition, you will probably be required to give standardized tests to meet the requirements of your school district or state.

ADVANTAGES AND LIMITATIONS OF USING AUTHENTIC ASSESSMENT DEVICES

Authentic (informal) assessment devices are much more relevant than standardized assessment devices with most students in any reading improvement program. Their advantages for a reading teacher or tutor are as follows:

➡ They usually are authentic in evaluating reading skills.

➡ They usually are well related to the information that is being taught in the classroom reading or special reading program.

➡ They are able to evaluate the student's attitudes toward reading quite well.

➡ They may reflect more accurately the accomplishments and attitudes of children with special needs than do standardized tests. Standardized tests may discriminate against children with many types of special needs.

➡ They emphasize the *process aspects* of reading rather than the *product aspect* in contrast to standardized tests.

➡ They may reflect different styles of teaching and learning more effectively than do standardized tests.

➡ They do not have the prescribed directions and time limits that are found on standardized tests. These tests may penalize the slow, but accurate, reader.

The following are the most important limitations of authentic assessment devices:

➡ Their results often do not meet the requirements of administrators, school districts, school boards, state boards of education, or family members because their results are not "scientific."

➡ They may be time-consuming to construct, give, and evaluate.

➡ They usually are not statistically reliable or valid. That does not mean they are not useful; they simply do not meet the statistical requirements for reliability and validity.

➡ They are not always easy to locate commercially.

➡ They may make it difficult to evaluate students by predetermined criteria, such as traditional report cards and grades. This is why holistic report cards and teacher–parent conferences must be used along with authentic assessment if it is to be successful.

Perhaps this chapter can be best summarized by the following statements:

➡ A reading teacher or tutor should primarily use authentic (informal) assessment devices because they direct instruction.

➡ Standardized devices usually are required for accountability but should not be misused.

FOR ADDITIONAL READING

Burns, P., Roe, B., & Ross, E. (1996). *Teaching reading in today's elementary schools* (pp. 539–575). Boston: Houghton Mifflin.

Cheek, E., Flippo, R., & Lindsey, J. (1997). *Reading for success in elementary school* (pp. 407–438). Madison, WI: Brown & Benchmark.

Clay, M. (1993). *An observational survey of early literacy achievement.* Portsmouth, NH: Heinemann.

Graves, M., Juel, C., & Graves, B. (1998). *Teaching reading in the 21st century* (pp. 476–531). Boston: Allyn & Bacon.

Gunning, T. (1996). *Creating reading instruction for all children* (pp. 486–523). Boston: Allyn & Bacon.

Heilman, A., Blair, T., & Rupley, W. (1998). *Principles and practices of teaching reading* (pp. 452–496). Upper Saddle River, NJ: Prentice Hall.

Johnston, P. (1992). *Constructive evaluation of literate activity.* NY: Longman.

Miller, W. (1995). *Alternative assessment techniques for reading & writing.* West Nyack, NY: The Center for Applied Research in Education.

———. (1986). *Reading diagnosis kit.* West Nyack, NY: The Center for Applied Research in Education.

Rubin, D. (1991). *Diagnosis and correction of reading disabilities* (pp. 31–50). Boston: Allyn & Bacon.

Savage, J. (1998). *Teaching reading & writing: Combining skills, strategies, and literature* (pp. 448–486). Boston: McGraw-Hill.

Shanker, J., & Ekwall, E. (1998). *Locating and correcting reading difficulties* (pp. 339–358). Columbus, OH: Merrill/Prentice Hall.

Walker, B. (1996). *Diagnostic teaching of reading* (pp. 69–88 and 121–134). Columbus, OH: Merrill/Prentice Hall.

WORKS CITED IN CHAPTER 2

Airaisan, P. (1994). *Classroom assessment.* NY: McGraw-Hill.

Argyle, S. (1989). Miscue analysis for classroom use. *Reading Horizons, 29,* 93–102.

Bauman, J. (1988). *Reading assessment: An instructional decision-making perspective.* Columbus, OH: Merrill.

Bauman, J., & Stevenson, J. (1982). Understanding standardized reading achievement test scores. *The Reading Teacher, 30,* 648–654.

Bertrand, J. (1991). Student assessment and evaluation. In B. Harp (Ed.), *Assessment and evaluation in whole language programs* (pp. 17–33). Norwood, MA: Christopher Gordon.

Betts, E. (1946). *Foundations of reading instruction* (pp. 438–485). NY: American Book Company.

Clay, M. (1993). *An observational survey of early literacy achievement.* Portsmouth, NH: Heinemann.

Cohen, M. (1980). *First grade takes a test.* New York: Greenwillow Books.

Donahue, P., Voelke, K., Campbell, J., & Mazzeo, J. (1991). NAEP Report Card for the National and the States. Web site: http://nces.ed.gov/nationsreportcard/pubs/main1998/1999500.shtml.

Duffelmeyer F., & Duffelmeyer, B. (1989). Are IRI passages suitable for assessing main idea comprehension? *The Reading Teacher, 42,* 358–363.

Early, M. (1992–1993). What ever happened to . . . ? *The Reading Teacher, 46,* 302–309.

Goodman, Y. (1987). Kid watching: An alternative to testing. *National Elementary Principal,* 57, 41–45.

Haney, W., & Madaus, C. (1989). Searching for alternatives to standardized tests: Why, whats, and whithers. *Phi Delta Kappan, 70,* 683–687.

Kilgallon, P. (1942). A study of relationships among certain pupil adjustments in language situations. Unpublished doctoral dissertation, Pennsylvania State College.

La Pray, M., & Ross, R. (1969). The graded word list: Quick gauge of reading ability. *Journal of Reading, 12,* 305–307.

Learning Media. (1991). *Dancing with the pen: The learner as a writer.* Wellington, New Zealand: Ministry of Education.

Miller, W. (1995). *Alternative assessment techniques for reading & writing.* West Nyack, NY: The Center for Applied Research in Education.

Neill, D., & Medina, N. (1989). Standardized testing: Harmful to educational health. *Phi Delta Kappan, 70,* 688–697.

Nitko, A. (1996). *Educational assessment of students.* Columbus, OH: Merrill/Prentice Hall.

Short, K. (March 1990). Using evaluation to support learning in process. Paper presented at the spring conference of the National Council of Teachers of English, Colorado Springs, CO.

Stiggins, R. (1994). *Student-centered classroom assessment.* New York: Merrill.

Valencia, S., & Pearson, D. (1987). Reading assessment: Time for a change. *The Reading Teacher, 41,* 726–732.

Weaver, B. (1992). *Defining literacy levels.* Charlottesville, VA: Story House.

Wildsmith, B. (1982). *Cat on the mat.* New York: Oxford University Press.

Chapter 3

IMPROVING ABILITY IN LETTER NAME KNOWLEDGE AND SIGHT WORD RECOGNITION

My teacher-trainees have tutored many kindergarten children who did not know any of the capital or lower-case letter names. Each tutor worked individually with a kindergarten child to learn the letter names. How many letters do you think the children with the greatest amount of difficulty learned during twenty to twenty-five tutoring sessions, each of which lasted from a half hour to forty minutes?

You may be surprised to learn that it was often difficult to get the children to learn as few as *four or five letter names* during that time. This example indicates just how difficult it can be to teach letter names to children, especially those with special needs such as a learning disability. Although it may have been easy for you to learn both letter names and sight words, this is not the case for some children.

This chapter is designed to help you understand the basic characteristics of both letter name knowledge and sight word recognition. It also provides numerous classroom-tested strategies, materials, and reproducibles for improving letter name knowledge and sight word recognition. Although this chapter may be more helpful to teachers and tutors of young children, it may also be relevant for teachers and tutors of older children and adults who have special needs or have not mastered the basic reading skills. It is difficult for a student to be a good reader unless he or she has a large stock of words that are recognized immediately instead of being analyzed by phonics or word structure.

LETTER NAME RECOGNITION AND IDENTIFICATION

Letter name recognition and *letter name identification* are both important beginning reading skills. However, these two emergent literacy skills are *not* a prerequisite to effective beginning reading. For example, most young children learn a number of *environmental print* and *sight words*, such as *STOP, McDonald's Wal-Mart, Crest,*™ *dog, cat, mom,* and *dad* from having these words pointed out to them by adults and other children and having their questions about these words answered. In addition, the use of the language-experience approach (LEA) (discussed later in this chapter) and various types of writing activities should take place before direct reading instruction in the letter names. Because alphabet knowledge always has been important in reading instruction, it probably always will be emphasized in beginning reading programs. However, it should *not be overemphasized.*

As preschoolers, some children learn the names of some letters and also are able to write some of them. By the time they are three years old, a few children can name as many as ten alphabet letters, while by the age of four, some children can write a few recognizable letters, usually those letters found in their first name. Even linguistically adept children who may be able to read and write prior to kindergarten entrance have taken as long as six months to learn all of the letter names, and children may take two or three years to be able to write their names. There is a great deal of difference in children's ability to learn the letter names, and some children entering kindergarten and even first grade are not able to identify any capital or lower-case letters.

It is important for children in kindergarten and beginning first grade to master all of the capital and lower-case letter names for several reasons. For example, family members put great stress on this knowledge, and research has found that the knowledge of letter names in later kindergarten and beginning first grade is the *single most important predictor of subsequent first-grade reading achievement* (Durrell, 1980). In addition, a child cannot always call the letter *b*, for example, "a circle and a long stick," which is a description of its appearance. The child needs an actual name to give the letter.

Even so, it is important to remember that the child who can identify the letter names accurately probably has come from a home environment in which all literacy activities, such as reading on a regular basis to the child, scribbling and writing activities, and development of prior knowledge, have been encouraged. Therefore, the child learns letter names and sight words fairly easily, particularly if he or she has good linguistic aptitude.

Although *letter recognition* is easier for most young children than is *letter identification*, it also is less important in reading achievement. For example, the following is an example of letter recognition:

Put an X on the capital A.
   T A C W

Here is an example of letter identification:

What is the name of this letter?
    A

It is obvious that *letter identification*, not letter recognition, is required in actual reading. Therefore, although letter recognition activities such as the one just illustrated may have some value as a beginning point, letter identification should receive more emphasis in beginning reading instruction.

Obviously, a child needs to have 100% competency in the identification of both the capital and lower-case letter names. Letter naming is an easy task for the child who has good linguistic aptitude, and this type of child seems to learn the letter names almost effortlessly, primarily by being read to and participating in other informal emergent (beginning) literacy activities. However, it can be a difficult and time-consuming task for some children with special needs, especially those with learning disabilities and those who learn slowly. For example, as mentioned previously, it is not unusual for a special needs child to learn to identify only four or five letter names in an entire semester of working with an adult individually for about twenty to twenty-five sessions of a half hour to forty minutes each.

If a child seems to have great difficulty in learning the letter names, it is important to teach *only one letter at a time. Tactile strategies*, such as those described later in this chapter, may be the most helpful, although this is not always the case. If a child does not have a great deal of difficulty, it may be possible to teach two letter names at a time. If you think it is possible, choose two letters that *do not* look like each other. For example, you teach these two letters at the same time:

k c

However, you should not, for example, teach these two letters in the same lesson:

h b

Research has not found any one best order in which to teach the letter names. Usually the child is taught first to recognize, identify, and write the letters in his or her own first name, such as

Kay

After that, a few kindergarten or first-grade teachers or tutors prefer to teach the child to identify all of the lower-case letter names first, followed by the capital letter names. Most teachers or tutors, however, present matching capital and lower-case letters in pairs, such as the following:

W w

Although this may be the most common way of teaching letter names, few teachers or tutors prefer to present letter names in terms of their *usefulness*. For example, such a teacher or tutor probably would present the letters *a* and *s* before presenting the letters *v* and *z* because the latter two letters are much less common. One possible exception to this is the letters *X* and *x*, which are uncommon but often are needed to complete beginning reading workbooks and tests.

It is important that children learn letter names that are meaningful to them. That is why the letters in the child's own first name are usually presented and practiced first. Letters that relate to a thematic unit being presented in kindergarten or first grade also are meaningful to young children. For example, in a unit about zoo animals, the letters *h* for *hippopotamus* and *l* for *lion* could be among those that are taught.

The child also needs to learn the difference between a letter and a word. Many times I have asked kindergarten children to point to a word on an experience chart, and some of the children have pointed to a letter on the chart. Some children do not understand this concept unless it is presented and illustrated for them.

It also is important for a young child to learn the proper terms for the letters. For example, most kindergarten and first-grade teachers and tutors use the terms *capital* and *lower case*, although the term *upper case* also may be used instead of *capital*. Young children should be not be allowed to use the terms *big* and *little (small)* instead of the proper terms as this may be confusing for them. For example, the letters *d* and *h* can be called "big" letters because they are *ascenders* (i.e., they have a part that goes above the main part of the letter). However, they are obviously lower-case letters.

A number of teachers and tutors present the letter names in *D'Nealian script* because of the potential help this may give the children in later making the transition to cursive handwriting. However, a number of early childhood educators and tutors prefer *Zaner-Bloser handwriting* (block handwriting) because family members can teach it properly in the home; it better matches the print found in the books that children read; and it usually is easier to young children to learn.

STRATEGIES, MATERIALS, AND REPRODUCIBLES FOR IMPROVING LETTER NAME KNOWLEDGE

This part of the chapter contains numerous classroom-tested strategies, materials, and reproducibles for improving letter name recognition and letter name identification. Any reading teacher or tutor will find the time-saving materials included in this chapter to be of great benefit.

It is important, however, to remember that all of the materials included in this section can be used in their present form but also can be modified in the light of the needs, abilities, and interests of your own pupils. To do so is consistent with diagnostic-prescription reading instruction whether in the classroom or tutoring sessions.

All kinds of *reading activities* are the most effective way of presenting letter names to many children with the possible exception of those with special needs. As much as possible, however, children should learn and practice both capital and lower-case letter names *in the context* of meaningful words, stories, books, rhymes, and fingerplays.

Print-Rich Environment

It is important that any preschool, kindergarten, or primary-grade classroom have an abundance of print available around the classroom for the children to use. It is equally important that tutors provide the young children with whom they are working with print for them to see also. This print should be placed in a meaningful manner so that each child is able to associate print with meaning. As an example, the print can be labeled with the actual object, thus providing meaning for it. Although a print-rich environment is desirable in any early literacy program, it probably is most closely identified with whole language classrooms. However, it is equally relevant in any early childhood classroom or tutoring situation.

The Alphabet Song

This rhyming song is an easy and fun way for children to learn to recognize letter names. To make it a visual learning experience, you need a long printscript alphabet line such as the following:

Aa Bb Cc Dd Ee Ff Gg Hh Ii Jj Kk Ll Mm Nn Oo Pp Qq Rr Ss Tt Uu Vv Ww Xx Yy Zz

Here is the song:

> *ABCDEFG*
> *HIJKLMNOP*
> *QRSTU and V*
> *WX and Y and Z.*
> *Now I've said my ABC's,*
> *Tell me what you think of me.*

Activity: Have the child or group of children sing the song while one child or the teacher (tutor) touches the corresponding letter on the alphabet line. The teacher or tutor can ask the group to sing slowly or quickly, in a whisper or a loud voice, or in a high or low voice.

TRADE BOOKS FOR EMPHASIZING ALPHABET LETTER NAMES

Many trade books have been published that are designed to emphasize a certain letter of the alphabet or the entire alphabet. They are very helpful if the preschool, kindergarten, or primary-grade teacher or tutor wants to stress a certain letter of the alphabet with the entire class, a small group of children, or an individual child. Many of these books are beautifully illustrated and therefore motivating for young children. Here is a partial list of trade books that you can use for this purpose with your pupils. Many of them also can be used to practice and/or review the sounds *of the letters in context.*

The Letter A

Barry, K. (1961). *A is for everything.* NY: Harcourt Brace Jovanovich.

Boynton, S. (1983). *A is for angry: An animal and adjective alphabet.* NY: Workman.

Ferguson, D. (1977). *Ants.* NY: Wonder Books.

Fowler, A. (1994). *Apple of your eye: Rookie read-about science.* Chicago: Children's Press.

Greenaway, K. (1886). *A—apple pie.* London: Warne.

Hutchins, A. & R. (1994). *Picking apples and pumpkins.* NY: Scholastic.

Learner, H., & Goldhor, S. (1996). *What's so terrible about swallowing an apple seed?* NY: HarperCollins Publishers.

McMillan, B. (1979). *Apples: How they grow.* Boston: Houghton Mifflin.

Russell, C. (1994). *First apple.* NY: Penguin Books USA.

Scarry, R. (1976). *About animals.* NY: Golden Press.

The Letter B

Baker, A. (1982). *Benjamin's book.* NY: Lothrop, Lee and Shephard.

Bottner, B. (1992). *Bootsie Barker bites.* NY: Putnam.

Cox, D. (1985). *Bossyboots.* NY: Crown.

Donovan, M. (1993). *Papa's bedtime story.* NY: The Trumpet Club.

Fox, M. (1993). *Time for bed.* San Diego: Harcourt Brace and Company.

Gretz, S. (1981). *Teddy Bears' moving day.* Chicago: Follett.

Kessler, E. & L. (1957). *Big red bus.* NY: Doubleday.

Lindenbaum, P. (1992). *Boodil my dog.* Elgin, IL: Child's World Publishing.

MacDonald, M. (1996). *Tuck-me-in tales: Bedtime stories from around the world.* Little Rock, AR: August House Littlefolk.

Martin, B. (1983). *Brown bear, brown bear, what do you see?* NY: Holt, Rinehart & Winston.

McCloskey, R. (1948). *Blueberries for Sal.* NY: The Viking Press.

McLeod, E. (1975). *The bear's bicycle.* Boston: Little, Brown & Company.

McPhail, D. (1972). *The bear's toothache.* Boston: Little, Brown & Company.

Moncure, J. (1984). *My "B" sound.* Elgin, IL: Child's World Publishing.

Peet, B. (1977). *Big bad Bruce.* Boston: Houghton Mifflin.

The Letter C

Bridwell, N. (1972). *Clifford, the small red puppy.* NY: Scholastic. (All of the other Clifford books also are appropriate.)

Calhoun, M. (1979). *Cross country cat.* NY: Morrow.

Carle, E. (1969). *The very hungry caterpillar.* NY: Scholastic.

Casey, P. (1994). *My cat Jack.* Cambridge, MA: Candlewick Press.

Crews, D. (1982). *Carousel.* NY: Greenwillow Books.

Freeman, D. (1977). *Corduroy.* NY: Penguin Books.

Gag, W. (1928). *Millions of cats.* NY: Putnam.

Harper, I., & Mosher, B. (1995). *My cats Nick and Nora.* NY: The Blue Sky Press.

Rounds, G. (1991). *Cowboys.* NY: Holiday House.

Schecter, B. (1967). *Conrad's castle.* NY: Harper & Row.

Sun, C. (1996). *Cat and cat-face.* Boston: Houghton Mifflin.

The Letter D

Berenstain, S. & J. (1980). *Dinosaur bone.* NY: Beginner Books.

Capucilli, A. (1996). *Biscuit.* NY: HarperCollins Publishers.

Colbert, E. (1977). *The dinosaur world*. NY: Stravon Educational Press.

Cole, B. (1994). *Dr. Dog*. NY: Alfred A. Knopf.

Cole, J. (1974). *Dinosaur story*. NY: Morrow.

Cole, S., & Calmenson, S. (1996). *Give a dog a bone: Stories, poems, jokes, and riddles about dogs*. NY: Scholastic.

Dupasquez, P. (1988). *Dear daddy*. NY: Puffin.

Geis, D. (1959). *Dinosaurs and other prehistoric animals*. NY: Grosset & Dunlap.

Hoff, S. (1994). *Duncan the dancing duck*. NY: Clarion Books.

McGeorge, C. (1994). *Boomer's big day*. San Francisco: Chronicle Books.

Moncure, J. (1984). *My "D" sound*. Elgin, IL: Child's World Publishing.

Reit, S. (1996). *A dog's tale*. NY: Bantam Doubleday Dell Publishing Group.

Steig, W. (1982). *Doctor Desoto*. NY: Farrar, Straus & Giroux.

White, N. (1995). *Why do dogs do that?* NY: Scholastic.

The Letter E

Barner, B. (1995). *How to weigh an elephant*. NY: Bantam Doubleday Dell Publishing Group.

Eve, E. (1971). *Eggs*. NY: Wonder Books.

Grifalconi, A. (1996). *Don't leave an elephant to go and chase a bird*. NY: Simon & Schuster Children's Publishing Division.

Lobel, A. (1981). *Uncle elephant*. NY: Scholastic.

Paxton, T. (1990). *Engelbert the elephant*. NY: Morrow.

Piper, W. (1961). *The little engine that could*. NY: Scholastic.

Tresselt, A. (1967). *The world in the candy egg*. NY: Lothrop, Lee & Shephard.

Yates, G. (1995). *The elephant alphabet book*. Chicago: Kidsbooks.

The Letter F

Brenner, B., & Chardiet, B. (1994). *Where's that fish?* NY: Scholastic.

Dennis, W. (1973). *Flip*. NY: Scholastic.

Galdone, P. (1975). *The frog prince*. NY: McGraw-Hill.

Hoban, R. (1968). *A birthday for Frances*. NY: Scholastic.

Keller, H. (1992). *Furry*. NY: Greenwillow.

———. (1996). *What's it like to be a fish? Let's-read-and-find-out science*. NY: HarperCollins.

Leaf, M. (1936). *The story of Ferdinand*. NY: The Viking Press.

Lionni, L. (1967). *Frederick.* NY: Pantheon.

Ryder, J. (1979). *Fog in the meadow.* NY: Harper & Row.

Zolotow, C. (1965). *Flocks of birds.* NY: Thomas Y. Crowell.

The Letter G

Arno, E. (1967). *The gingerbread man.* NY: Scholastic.

Bang, M. (1996). *Goose.* NY: Blue Sky/Scholastic.

Blair, S. (1967). *The three billy goats gruff.* NY: Scholastic.

Carle, E. (1996). *The grouchy ladybug.* NY: HarperCollins Publishers.

Fowler, A. (1993). *Wooly sheeps and hungry goats.* Rookie read-about-science. Danbury, CT: Children's Press.

Harrison, S., & Wilks, M. (1980). *In Granny's garden.* NY: Holt, Rinehart & Winston.

Keats, E. (1969). *Goggles.* NY: Holt, Rinehart & Winston.

Kinsey-Warnock, N. (1997). *The summer of Stanley.* NY: Cobblehill Books/Dutton.

Weatherill, S. (1982). *Goosey, goosey, gander.* NY: Greenwillow Books.

Zolotow, C. (1974). *My grandson Lew.* NY: Harper & Row.

The Letter H

Bourgeois, P. (1994). *The many hats of Mr. Minches.* Toronto, Canada: Stoddart Publishing Company, Ltd.

Brenner, M. (1994). *Abe Lincoln's hat.* NY: Random House.

Brett, J. (1997). *The hat.* NY: G. P. Putnam's Sons.

Brown, M. (1969). *How, hippo!* NY: Charles Scribner's Sons.

Burton, V. (1969). *The little house.* Boston: Houghton Mifflin.

Carle, E. (1987). *A house for hermit crab.* Nalick, MA: Picture Book Studio.

Fox, M. (1987). *Hattie and the fox.* NY: Bradbury.

Galdone, P. (1973). *The little red hen.* NY: Scholastic.

Gardella, T. (1997). *Casey's new hat.* Boston: Houghton Mifflin.

Greenstein, E. (1997). *Mattie's hats won't wear that!* NY: Alfred A. Knopf.

Hadithi, M., & Kennaway, A. (1994). *Hungry hyena.* Boston: Little, Brown & Company.

Jeffers, S. (1974). *All the pretty houses.* NY: Macmillan.

Johnson, C. (1958). *Harold and the purple crayon.* NY: Harper & Row.

Pearson, T. (1997). *The purple hat.* NY: Farrar, Straus & Giroux.

Rose, D. (1983). *It hardly seems like Halloween.* NY: Lothrop, Lee & Shephard.

Seuss, Dr. (1940). *Horton hatches the egg.* NY: Random House.

Weatherill, S. (1982). *Humpty Dumpty.* NY: Greenwillow Books.

Zion, G. (1956). *Harry the dirty dog.* NY: Harper & Row.

The Letter I

Bartok, M., & Ronan, C. (1996). *Alaskan Eskimos and Aleuts.* NY: HarperCollins Publishers.

Bornstein, R. (1973). *Indian bunny.* NY: Scholastic.

Dabcovich, L. (1997). *The polar bear son: An Inuit tale.* Boston: Houghton Mifflin.

George, J. (1997). *Arctic son.* NY: Hyperion Books for Children.

Manley, D. (1977). *Let's look at insects.* NY: Derrydale.

Waber, B. (1972). *Ira sleeps over.* Boston: Houghton Mifflin.

The Letter J

Bartocci, B. (1991). *Jungle jumble.* Kansas City, MO: Hallmark.

Degan, B. (1983). *Jamberry.* NY: Harper & Row.

Gray, L. (1994). *Fenton's leap.* NY: Simon & Schuster Books for Young Readers.

Hennessey, B. (1990). *Jake baked the cake.* NY: The Viking Press.

Hru, D. (1996). *The magic moonberry jump ropes.* NY: Penguin Books USA.

Kalan, R. (1981). *Jump frog jump.* NY: Greenwillow Books.

Keats, E. (1966). *Jennie's hat.* NY: Harper & Row.

Steadman, R. (1970). *Jelly book.* NY: Scroll Press.

Stobbs, W. (1965). *Jack and the beanstalk.* NY: Delacorte Press.

Walsh, E. (1993). *Hop jump.* San Diego, CA: Harcourt Brace & Company.

The Letter K

Hogan, P. (1991). *The life cycle of the kangaroo.* Austin, TX: Steck-Vaughn.

Holmelund, M. (1968). *A kiss for little bear.* NY: Harper & Row.

Lepthien, E. (1995). *Kangaroos: A new true book.* Chicago: Children's Press.

Mayer, M. (1973). *What do you do with a kangaroo?* NY: Scholastic.

Payne, E. (1972). *Katy-no-pocket.* NY: Scholastic.

Rockwell, H. (1980). *My kitchen.* NY: Greenwillow Books.

Shapiro, A. (1978). *Kenny's crazy kite.* Los Angeles: Price/Stern/Sloan.

Wood, A. (1985). *King Bidgood's in the bathtub.* NY: Harcourt Brace Jovanovich.

The Letter L

Aardema, V. (1996). *The lonely lioness and the ostrich chicks.* NY: Alfred A. Knopf.

Carle, E. (1996). *The grouchy ladybug.* NY: HarperCollins Publishers.

Cosgrove, S. (1977). *Leo the lop*. Bothell, WA: Serendipity Press.

deRegniers, B. (1989). *Laura's story*. NY: Atheneum.

Kraus, R. (1971). *Leo the late bloomer*. NY: Windmill Books.

London, J., & Long, S. (1994). *Liplap's wish*. San Francisco: Chronicle Books.

Moncure, J. (1984). *My "L" sound*. Elgin, IL: Child's World Publishing.

Nolan, D. (1997). *Androcles and the lion*. San Diego: Harcourt Brace and Company.

Stimson, J. (1997). *Brave lion, scared lion*. NY: Scholastic.

Waber, B. (1969). *Lovable Lyle*. Boston: Houghton Mifflin.

Wolf, G. (1996). *The very hungry lion*. NY: Annick Press Ltd.

The Letter M

Allen, J. (1990). *Mucky moose*. NY: Macmillan.

Bemelmans, L. (1977). *Madeline*. NY: Puffin Books.

Bial, R. (1997). *Mist over the mountains*. Boston: Houghton Mifflin.

Brett, J. (1989). *The mitten*. NY: Putnam.

Bunting, E. (1997). *On call back mountain*. NY: Blue Sky Press.

Burton, V. (1939). *Mike Mulligan and his steam shovel*. NY: Houghton Mifflin.

Eastman, P. (1960). *Are you my mother?* NY: Random House.

Felix, M. (1980). *The story of a little mouse trapped in a book*. La Jolla, CA: Green Tiger Press.

Kiss, A. (1996). *A mountain alphabet*. Toronto, Canada: Tundra Books.

Kraus, R. (1980). *Mouse work*. NY: Windmill.

Lobel, A. (1977). *Mouse soup*. NY: Harper & Row.

Meddaugh, S. (1992). *Martha speaks*. Boston: Houghton Mifflin.

Micklethwait, L. (1994). *I spy a lion: Animals in art*. NY: Greenwillow Books.

Moncure, J. (1984). *My "M" sound*. Elgin, IL: Child's World Publishing.

Morimoto, J. (1986). *Mouse's marriage*. NY: Viking Kestrel.

Morris, N. (1996). *Mountains*. NY: Crabtree Publishing.

Numeroff, L. (1991). *If you give a moose a muffin*. NY: HarperCollins Publishers.

Rockwell, A. (1973). *The awful mess*. NY: Parents Magazine Press.

Seuss, Dr. (1948). *The big hearted moose*. NY: Random House.

Smith-Ayala, E. (1996). *Clouds on the mountain*. NY: Annick Press Ltd.

Walter, M. (1971). *The magic mirror book and magic mirror tricks*. NY: Scholastic.

The Letter N

Allard, H., & Marshall, J. (1977). *Miss Nelson is missing*. Boston: Houghton Mifflin.

Brown, M. (1939). *The noisy book*. NY: Harper & Row.

Erdich, L. (1996). *Grandmother's pigeon*. NY: Hyperion Books for Children.

Gag, W. (1941). *Nothing at all*. NY: Coward, McCann, & Geoghegan.

Jenkins, P. (1995). *A nest full of eggs: Let's-read-and-find-out science*. NY: HarperCollins Publishers.

London, J. (1994). *Condor's egg*. San Francisco, CA: Chronicle Books.

Masner, J. (1989). *Nicholas Cricket*. NY: Harper & Row.

Mayer, M. (1968). *There's a nightmare in my closet*. NY: Dial Press.

Selsam, M. (1979). *Night animals*. NY: Scholastic.

Skofield, J. (1981). *Nightdances*. NY: Harper & Row.

Sugata, Y. (1971). *Good night 1, 2, 3*. NY: Scroll Press.

Swinburne, S. (1996). *Swallows in the bird house*. Brookfield, CT: The Millbrook Press.

Wells, R. (1973). *Noisy Nora*. NY: Scholastic.

Wezel, P. (1967). *The naughty bird*. Chicago: Follett.

The Letter O

Hall, D. (1979). *Ox-cart man*. NY: The Viking Press.

Henkes, K. (1993). *Owen*. NY: Greenwillow Books.

Hoff, S. (1960). *Oliver*. NY: Harper & Row.

Keats, E. (1971). *Over in the meadow*. NY: Scholastic.

Lauber, P. (1990). *An octopus is amazing: Let's-read-and-find-out science*. NY: HarperCollins Publishers.

Most, B. (1980, 1991). *My very own octopus*. NY: Harcourt.

Pringle, L. (1993). *Octopus hug*. Honesdale, PA: Boyds Mills Press.

Turkle, B. (1981). *Thy friend, Obadiah*. NY: The Viking Press.

Yolen, J. (1987). *Owl moon*. NY: Scholastic.

The Letter P

Ahlberg, J. & A. (1978). *Each peach pear plum*. NY: Scholastic.

Atwater, F. & R. (1938). *Mr. Popper's penguins*. Boston: Little, Brown & Company.

Brown, R. (1973). *Pig in the pond*. NY: David McKay.

Bunting, E. (1997). *The pumpkin fair*. NY: Clarion Books.

dePaola, T. (1978). *The popcorn book.* NY: Holiday House.

Duvoisin, R. (1950). *Petunia.* NY: Alfred A. Knopf.

Flack, M., & Wiese, K. (1933, 1961). *The story about ping.* NY: The Viking Press.

Galdone, P. (1970). *Three little pigs.* NY: Scholastic.

Hall, Z. (1994). *It's pumpkin time!* NY: Scholastic.

Henkes, K. (1996). *Lilly's purple plastic purse.* NY: Greenwillow Books.

King, E. (1990). *The pumpkin patch.* NY: Penguin Books USA.

Marzollo, J. (1996). *I'm a seed.* NY: Scholastic.

Rockwell, A. (1993). *Mr. Panda's painting.* NY: Macmillan.

Roth, S. (1966). *Pick a peck of puzzles.* NY: Arnold Norton.

Sendak, M. (1962). *Pierre: A cautionary tale in five chapters and a prologue.* NY: HarperCollins Children's Books.

Wolcott, P. (1975). *Pickle, pickle, pickle juice.* NY: Scholastic.

The Letter Q

Avery, K. (1994). *The crazy quilt.* Glenview, IL: Goodyear Books/Scott, Foresman and Company.

Brown, M. (1950). *The quiet noisy book.* NY: Harper & Row.

Carle, E. (1990). *The very quiet cricket.* NY: Philomel.

dePaola, T. (1977). *The quicksand book.* NY: Holiday House.

Eltings, M., & Folsom, M. (1980). *Q is for duck: An alphabet guessing game.* NY: Clarion Books.

Fleisher, R. (1978). *Quilts in the attic.* NY: Macmillan.

Guback, G. (1994). *Luka's quilt.* NY: Greenwillow Books.

Johnson, A. (1993). *Julius.* NY: Orchard Books.

Johnston, T., & dePaola, T. (1985). *The quilt story.* NY: Putnam's.

Mayer, M. (1971). *The queen wanted to dance.* NY: Simon & Schuster.

Radley, G. (1994). *The spinner's gift.* NY: Alfred A. Knopf.

Turner, A. (1994). *Sewing quilts.* NY: Macmillan.

Zolotow, C. (1963). *The quarreling book.* NY: Harper & Row.

The Letter R

Bate, L. (1975). *Little rabbit's loose tooth.* NY: Scholastic.

Birchfield, D. (1996). *Animal lore and legend—rabbit—American Indian legends.* NY: Scholastic.

Bornstein, R. (1995). *Rabbit's good news.* NY: Clarion Books.

Buringham, J. (1974). *The rabbit.* NY: Thomas Y. Crowell.

dePaola, T. (1992). *Rosie and the yellow ribbon.* Boston: Joy Street Books.

Fisher, A. (1983). *Rabbits, rabbits.* NY: Harper & Row.

Hamilton, K. (1995). *Rockabye rabbit.* Boca Raton, FL: Cool Kids Press.

Heilbroner, J. (1962). *Robert and the rose horse.* NY: Random House.

Ho, M., & Kos, S. (1997). *Brother rabbit: A Cambodian tale.* NY: Lothrop, Lee & Shephard.

Kellogg, S. (1981). *A rose for Pinkerton.* NY: Dial Press.

Kent, J. (1982). *Round robin.* Englewood Cliffs, NJ: Prentice Hall.

Oppenheim, S. (1995). *I love you bunny rabbit.* NY: Bantam Doubleday Dell Books for Young Readers.

Sendak, M. (1975). *Really, Rosie.* NY: Harper & Row.

Shulevitz, U. (1969). *Rain rain rivers.* NY: Farrar, Straus & Giroux.

Thayer, J. (1980). *Applebaums have a robot!* NY: William Morrow.

Watts, M. (1979). *Little red riding hood.* Racine, WI: Golden Press.

Weninger, B. (1996). *What have you done, Davy?* NY: North-South Books.

The Letter S

Ayliffe, A. (1992). *Slither, swoop, swing.* NY: The Viking Press.

Brown, M. (1947). *Stone soup.* NY: Scribner's.

Coxe, M. (1994). *The great snake escape.* NY: HarperCollins Publishers.

Davol, M. (1996). *How the snake got his hiss.* NY: Orchard Books.

Ehlert, L. (1995). *Snowballs.* NY: Harcourt.

Gray, L. (1994). *Small green snakes.* NY: Orchard Books.

Hill, E. (1980). *Where's Spot?* NY: G. P. Putnam's Sons.

Jordan, H. (1960). *How a seed grows.* NY: Thomas Y. Crowell.

Keats, E. (1976). *The snowy day.* NY: Puffin Books.

Kessler, E. & L. (1973). *Slush, slush!* NY: Parents Magazine Press.

Lionni, L. (1973). *Swimmy.* NY: Random House.

Maestro, B. (1992). *Take a look at snakes.* NY: Scholastic.

Shapiro, A. (1978). *Squiggly Wiggly's surprise.* Los Angeles: Intervisual.

Stadler, J. (1985). *Snail saves the day.* NY: Thomas Y. Crowell.

Watkins, S. (1995). *Great snake ceremony.* Tulsa, OK: Council Oak Publishing Company

Zolotow, C. (1967). *Summer is . . .* NY: Thomas Y. Crowell.

The Letter T

Burney, B. (1994). *Tyrassosaurus*. Boston: Houghton Mifflin.

Cosgrove, S. (1984). *Tee-tee*. Vero Beach, FL: Rourke Enterprises.

Guiberson, B. (1996). *Into the sea*. NY: Henry Holt and Company.

Hutchins, P. (1991). *Tidy Titch*. NY: Greenwillow Books.

Lexau, J. (1971). *T for Tommy*. NY: Garrard.

Lloyd, M. (1992). *Look out for turtles: Let's-read-and-find-out science*. NY: HarperCollins Publishers.

Lobel, A. (1979). *A treeful of pigs*. NY: Scholastic.

McPhail, D. (1972). *The bear's toothache*. NY: Penguin Books.

Mosel, A. (1968). *Tikki tikki tembo*. NY: Scholastic.

Pirotta, S. (1997). *Turtle boy*. NY: Farrar, Straus & Giroux.

Seuling, B. (1976). *Teeny-tiny woman*. NY: The Viking Press.

Turner, C. (1991). *The turtle and the moon*. NY: Penguin Books USA.

Udry, J. (1956). *A tree is nice*. NY: Harper & Row.

Wolfe, R. (1981). *The truck book*. Minneapolis: Carolrhoda Books.

The Letter U

Andersen, H. (1965). *The ugly ducking*. NY: Scribner.

Anno, M. (1971). *Upside-downers*. NY: Walker/Weatherhill.

Bright, R. (1959). *My red umbrella*. NY: William Morrow.

Chesworth, M. (1992). *Rainy day dream*. NY: Farrar, Straus & Giroux.

Laser, M. (1997). *The rain*. NY: Simon & Schuster Books for Young Children.

Medearis, A. (1995). *We play on a rainy day*. NY: Scholastic.

Tashima, M. (1971). *Umbrella*. NY: The Viking Press.

The Letter V

Carle, E. (1969). *The very hungry caterpillar*. NY: Philomel.

———. (1995). *The very lonely firefly*. NY: Philomel.

Carrick, C. (1995). *Valentine*. NY: Clarion Books.

Cocca-Leffler, M. (1996). *Lots of hearts*. NY: Grosset & Dunlap.

DeArmond, F. (1963). *The very, very special day*. NY: Parents Magazine Press.

Duvoisin, R. (1961). *Veronica*. NY: Alfred A. Knopf.

Goldreich, G. & E. (1972). *What can she be? A veterinarian*. NY: Lothrop, Lee & Shephard.

Jasapersohn, W. (1978). *A day in the life of a veterinarian.* Boston: Little, Brown & Company.

Marzollo, J. (1996). *Valentine cats.* NY: Scholastic.

Roberts, B. (1997). *Valentine mice!* Boston: Houghton Mifflin.

Shannon, G. (1995). *Heart to heart.* Boston: Houghton Mifflin.

The Letter W

Asch, F. *Water.* San Diego: Harcourt Brace and Company.

Carlstrom, N. (1993). *How does the wind walk?* NY: Macmillan.

George, J. (1995). *To climb a waterfall.* NY: Philomel.

Henkes, K. (1987). *A weekend with Wendall.* NY: Greenwillow Books.

Isadora, R. (1977). *Willaby.* NY: Macmillan.

Jeunesse, G., & Valat, P. (1991). *Water: A first discovery book.* NY: Scholastic.

Keats, E. (1964). *Whistle for Willie.* NY: Viking.

Kennedy, M. (1980). *Wings.* NY: Scholastic.

Marzollo, J. (1996). *I am water.* NY: Scholastic.

Nyblom, H. (1968). *The witch of the woods.* NY: Alfred A. Knopf.

Paz, O. (1997). *My life with the wave.* NY: Lothrop, Lee & Shephard.

Ross, C. (1993). *The Whiryls and the west wind.* Boston: Houghton Mifflin.

Wick, W. (1997). *A drop of water: A book of wonder.* NY: Scholastic.

Yolen, J. (1995). *Water music: Poems for children.* Honesdale, PA: Wordsong/Boyds Mills Press.

Zolotow, C. (1962). *When the wind stops.* NY: Abeland-Schumann.

———. (1972). *William's doll.* NY: Harper & Row.

The Letter X

Bartkowski, R. (1975). *Little Max, the cement mixer.* Chicago: Rand McNally.

Bruchac, J. (1993). *Fox song.* NY: Philomel.

Gregovich, B. (1992). *The fox on the box.* Grand Haven, MI: School Zone Publishing Company.

London, J. (1993). *Gray fox.* NY: Penguin Books USA.

Maloney, C. (1978). *The box book.* Racine, WI: Golden Press.

Moncure, J. (1979). *My "X, Y, Z" sound box.* Elgin, IL: Child's World Publishing.

Robbins, J. (1985). *Addie meets Max.* NY: Harper & Row.

Thomas, P. (1979). *There are rocks in my socks said the ox to the fox.* NY: Lothrop, Lee & Shephard.

The Letter Y

Battles, E. (1978). *What does the rooster say, Yoshio?* Chicago: Albert Whitman.

Marshall, J. (1973). *Yummers.* Boston: Houghton Mifflin.

Seuss, Dr. (1958). *Yertle the turtle and other stories.* NY: Random House.

Weedn, F., & Gilbert, L. (1995). *The magic cape: Inspired by an old Swedish tale.* NY: Hyperion Books for Children.

The Letter Z

Bunting, E. (1974). *We need a bigger zoo.* Lexington, MA: Ginn.

Medearis, A. (1992). *The zebra-riding cowboy: A folk song from the old West.* NY: Henry Holt and Company.

Modesitt, J., & Johnson, L. (1990). *The story of Z.* Boston: Picture Book Studio.

Moss, L. (1995). *Zen, zen, zen: A violin.* NY: Simon & Schuster.

Rojankonsky, F. (1972). *Animals in the zoo.* NY: Alfred A. Knopf.

Seuss, Dr. (1950). *If I ran the zoo.* NY: Random House.

———. (1955). *On beyond zebra.* NY: Random House.

Tallon, R. (1979). *Zoohapets.* NY: Scholastic.

There also are some alphabet trade books that stress all of the alphabet letter names. Here is a partial list of some of these alphabet books:

Agard, J. (1989). *The Calypso alphabet.* NY: Henry Holt & Company.

Alexander, A. (1971). *ABC of cars and trucks.* NY: Doubleday.

Anno, M. (1974). *Anno's alphabet: An adventure in imagination.* NY: Thomas Y. Crowell.

Aylesworth, J. (1992). *The folks in the valley: The Pennsylvania Dutch ABC.* NY: HarperCollins Publishers.

Base, G. (1986). *Animalia.* NY: Henry N. Adams.

Bayer, J. (1984). *My name is Alice.* NY: Dial.

Bowen, B. (1991). *Antler, bear, canoe: A Northwoods alphabet.* Boston: Little, Brown & Company.

Brown, R. (1991). *Alphabet times four.* NY: Dutton Children's Books.

Calemnson, S. (1993). *It begins with an A.* NY: Hyperion.

Ehlert, L. (1989). *Eating the alphabet: Fruits and vegetables from A to Z.* NY: Harcourt.

Feelings, M. (1974). *Jambo means hello: A Swahili alphabet book.* NY: Dial Press.

Gag, W. (1971). *The ABC bunny.* NY: Coward, McCann, & Geoghegan.

Hoban, T. (1982). *A, B, see!* NY: Greenwillow Books.

Isadora, R. (1983). *City seen from A to Z.* NY: Greenwillow Books.

Jonas, A. (1990). *Aardvarks, disembark!* NY: Greenwillow Books.

Lear, E. (1965). *Lear alphabet—Penned and illustrated by Edward Lear himself.* NY: McGraw-Hill.

Lobel, A. (1990). *Allison's zinnia.* NY: Greenwillow Books.

Martin, B., & Archambault, J. (1989). *Chicka chicka boom boom.* NY: Simon & Schuster.

Musgrove, M. (1976). *Ashanti to Zulu: African traditions.* NY: Dial Press.

Provenson, A., & Provenson, M. (1978). *A peaceable kingdom. The Shaker ABECEDARIUS.* NY: The Viking Press.

Rankin, L. (1991). *The handmade alphabet.* NY: Dial Press.

Sendak, M. (1962). *Alligators all around: An alphabet book.* NY: Harper & Row.

Shannon, G. (1996). *Tomorrow's alphabet.* NY: Greenwillow Books.

Tallon, R. (1989). *An ABC in English and Spanish.* NY: Lion Press.

Van Allsburg, C. (1987). *The z was zapped.* Boston: Houghton Mifflin.

Wegman, W. (1994). *ABCs.* NY: Hyperion.

Yolen, J. (1991). *All in the woodland early: An ABC book.* Honesdale, PA: Boyds Mills Press.

STRATEGIES FOR IMPROVING LETTER NAME RECOGNITION

MATCHING CAPITAL AND LOWER-CASE LETTER CARDS

As a beginning point it is often helpful to have young children match letter cards on which are written capital and lower-case letter names. To do so, cut a piece of posterboard into a rectangle 1" × 3". Print a matching capital and lower-case letter pair on each posterboard rectangle with a marking pen. Cut each pair apart using a different pattern so that they can be matched.

Then place all of the cut-apart posterboard pieces into a large brown envelope. Have the child match each of the capital and lower-case pairs by fitting the two pieces together. Because each of the cuts are different, this activity is self-checking (incorrect pairs of letters will not match).

Here is an example of this activity.

COOKING AND BAKING ACTIVITIES TO REINFORCE LETTER NAMES

Cooking and baking activities are a highly motivating way of helping children to review the different letter names. Some of them also can be used to review letter–sound relationships. Here is a sample of the cooking and baking activities that can be used for this purpose. There are many others that can be used equally well.

Two good sources of cooking and baking activities for the letter names are as follows:

Ehlert, L. (1996). *Eating the alphabet*. NY: Red Wagon.

Vietch, B. & Harms, T. (1981). *Cook and learn*. Menlo Park, CA: Addison-Wesley.

Recipes for the starred foods can be found in the book *Cook and Learn*.

The Letter A

apple cobbler   apple pie
apple salad*   apple sauce*
apricot jam

The Letter B

banana bread   bananas and milk
bean salad*   biscuits*
blackberry jam   blueberry jam
butter

The Letter C

cake   candy
cole slaw*   cupcakes*

The Letter D

date cookies

doughnuts (Have one tube-type refrigerator baking biscuit per child. Have the child gently flatten the biscuit and push his or her finger through the center to form a hole. Then heat one inch of cooking oil in an electric fry pan to about 375 degrees. Place the doughnut in the cooking oil and fry it on both sides until it is golden brown. Remove the doughnut from the cooking oil with cooking tongs and have the child shake it in a brown paper bag with powdered sugar.)

dumplings

The Letter E

eggs*   egg salad sandwich
deviled eggs

The Letter F

French fries   fritters*
frosting   fudge

The Letter G

gingerbread person*   grape jelly
grilled cheese sandwich

The Letter H

hamburgers   ham sandwich
hush puppies*

The Letter I

ice cream*   Irish soda bread*

The Letter J

jam sandwich   jelly beans
jelly sandwich   juice*

The Letter K

kabob (Have the child thread cut pieces of fruit on a straw to make the kabob.)

The Letter L

lasagna   latke* (potato pancake)
lemonade*   lollipop

The Letter M

macaroni and cheese   macaroni salad*
meatballs   muffin*

The Letter N

navy bean soup   noodles
nachos (Place tortilla chips in a single layer on a cookie sheet. Sprinkle them with
grated cheese and bake in a 400-degree oven until the cheese melts, which is usually in about five minutes.)

The Letter O

oatmeal ("Three Bears porridge")   oatmeal cookies
omelet   orange juice

The Letter P

pasta   pancakes

peanut butter*

peanut butter and jelly sandwich

popcorn

pizza*

Popsicle

The Letter Q

quesadillas

quince jelly

quick bread

any food that is "fit for a queen"

The Letter R

raisins

raspberries

hot rice salad

raisin cookies

rice

The Letter S

salad*

soup

stone soup (Make stone soup as described in the book *Stone Soup* by Marcia Brown. [NY: Charles Scribner's Sons, 1947].)

strawberry jam

The Letter T

tacos*

tortillas*

tomato catsup*

tuna casserole

The Letter U

upside-down cake (use a packaged mix)

The Letter V

vanilla ice cream*

vegetable soup*

vegetable lasagna

The Letter W

waffles*

The Letter X

Have the child mix fruit or vegetables.

The Letter Y

yogurt*

yogurt shake*

The Letter Z

zucchini bread

zucchini muffins*

zucchini fritters*

TRACING OR TACTILE STRATEGIES

Tracing or tactile (VAK, or visual-auditory-kinesthetic) strategies probably are the single most effective way of presenting letter names to children who have had great difficulty in learning them. Tracing strategies are especially useful with children who have learning disabilities and with other young children who cannot remember the letter names. However, you should remember that all tactile strategies are fairly time-consuming. Here are some tactile strategies that have been found to be the effective with young children with special needs.

➡ **Instant Pudding**—This tactile strategy is highly motivating and effective with young children. Prepare a package of instant pudding and place it in a flat pan (like a cake pan). Have the child draw the target letter name in the pudding, saying its name aloud as he or she does so. Have the child use the terms *capital* or *lower case*. The child may lick his or her fingers after each letter is made. Although chocolate pudding usually is the favorite of young children, strawberry pudding also has been used effectively.

➡ **Colored Chalk and Sand Tray**—Place sand in a flat pan such as a cake pan. Grind a piece of colored chalk and add it to the sand to make it colorful. Have the child draw the target letter in the sand, saying its name aloud as he or she does so. Have the child use the terms *capital* and *lower case*. You can buy commercially colored sand in most places instead of coloring your own if you want.

➡ **Colored Chalk and Salt Tray**—This tactile strategy is identical to the previous one except that salt is used instead of sand. Both work equally well.

➡ **Finger Paints**—Have the child spread finger paint over a sheet of butcher (shiny) paper. Have the child draw each target letter in the finger paint, saying the letter name as he or she does so. The child should indicate whether the letter is a capital or lower-case letter. Because finger paints are fairly messy, some teachers and tutors prefer to use instant pudding, which is less messy. The child also can lick his or her fingers with the pudding. However, you may prefer to use finger paints at least some of the time. Here are two recipes for finger paints.

Finger Paint Recipe 1

$\frac{1}{2}$ cup lump starch

$\frac{1}{2}$ cup cold water

$1\frac{1}{2}$ cups boiling water

$\frac{1}{2}$ cup white soapflakes

1 tablespoon glycerin

food coloring

Dissolve the starch in cold water. Add hot water and cook the mixture until it is clear, stirring constantly. Add soapflakes and stir, and remove from the heat immediately. When cool, stir in glycerin and enough drops of food coloring to give the desired color.

Finger Paint Recipe 2

$\frac{1}{2}$ cup cornstarch

1 cup cold water

1 envelope unflavored gelatin

2 cups hot water

$\frac{1}{2}$ cup mild detergent

Rit® dye (powder form) (If Liquid Rit® dye is used, increase the cornstarch to $\frac{3}{4}$ cup.)

Combine cornstarch and $\frac{3}{4}$ cup of cold water in a medium-sized saucepan. Soak gelatin in the remaining $\frac{1}{4}$ cup cold water. Stir hot water into the starch mixture and cook over medium heat until the mixture comes to a boil and is smooth, stirring constantly. Remove from heat and blend in softened gelatin. Add detergent and stir until thoroughly dissolved. Divide into portions in jars or bowls. Stir in about 1 teaspoon Rit® powder or 1 tablespoon Rit® Liquid Dye for every cup of mixture. If not used immediately, cover mixture tightly for storage. This recipe makes about 3 cups and can be multiplied.

➠ **Finger Painting Letters**—The young child also can use finger paints to paint the target letters on paper at an easel. This is an easy-to-use strategy for tactile reinforcement of the capital and lower-case letter names.

➠ **Oobleck Recipe**—(This is the name for a sticky substance that children enjoy working with.)

6$\frac{3}{4}$ cups water

4 boxes cornstarch

Mix the ingredients together. A half batch is usually plenty. Then have the child draw each target letter in the oobleck, which is spread on a sheet of heavy paper such as butcher (shiny) paper. Read the book *Bartholemew and the Oobleck* by Dr. Seuss (New York: Random House, 1950) either before or after the oobleck is used for letter naming. This is a very popular tactile strategy with older preschool and kindergarten children.

➠ **Shaving Cream**—The child can draw the target capital or lower-case letters in commercially available shaving cream. Shaving cream is less messy than are either finger paints or oobleck.

➠ **Hair Gel**—Place some hair gel in a Zip-Loc™ Freezer Bag. Spread some of the hair gel on a piece of butcher (shiny) paper. Have the child draw each target letter in the hair gel, saying the letter name as he or she does so. Have the child indicate whether it is a capital or lower-case letter.

➠ **Clay**—Have a child form each target letter out of clay, saying the letter name aloud as he or she does so. Have the child indicate whether the letter is a capital or lower-case letter.

→ **Pipe Cleaners**—Have the child bend a pipe cleaner into the shape of each target letter. Then have the child trace over the pipe cleaner, saying the letter name aloud as he or she does so. Have the child state whether it is a capital or lower-case letter.

→ **Playdough or Magic Modeling Clay Recipe**—The child can form the target letters out of the playdough or magic modeling clay.

2 cups salt

$\frac{2}{3}$ cup water

1 cup cornstarch

$\frac{1}{2}$ cup cold water

Mix salt and $\frac{2}{3}$ cup water in a saucepan. Then place pan over low heat, stirring constantly until mixture is thoroughly heated. This will take about 3 or 4 minutes. Remove from heat. Immediately mix cornstarch and $\frac{1}{2}$ cup cold water and add this all at once to the hot salt and water mixture. Stir quickly to combine. Mixture should thicken to about the consistency of stiff dough. If the mixture does not thicken, place the pan over low heat again and stir about 1 minute or until the mixture starts to thicken. Turn out on board or work surface and knead as you would bread dough to form a smooth pliable mass. It can be used immediately, and it will keep pliable indefinitely if it is stored in a tightly closed container or wrapped in plastic or foil. This recipe makes $1\frac{3}{4}$ pounds.

Double Batch:

Double recipe ingredients. Follow the directions given except keep the saucepan over heat when adding cornstarch and water to the hot salt mixture.

How to Color:

Food colors or tempera paint may be added while cooking, or they may be kneaded into the pliable base. Modeled objects may be painted when hard and dry to give surface color.

How to Dry:

Objects will dry and harden at room temperature in about 36 hours, depending on the thickness. To speed drying, preheat oven to 350 degrees. Then turn oven off and place object in oven on wire rack to allow air circulation. Leave in oven until the oven is cold. When dry, surface may be smoothed by rubbing with sandpaper.

→ **Alphabet Pretzels (Edible) Recipe**—Making pretzels in the shape of alphabet letters helps children to remember how to make them.

1 cup lukewarm water

1 cake active yeast or

1 package dry yeast

$4\frac{1}{2}$ cups all-purpose flour

2 teaspoons sugar

$\frac{3}{4}$ teaspoon salt

1 egg yolk beaten with 1 tablespoon water

coarse salt

Preheat oven to 475 degrees. Grease cookie sheet. Slowly stir yeast into 1 cup lukewarm water, following package directions. Set aside. Combine flour, sugar, and salt. Add yeast to mixture to form stiff dough. Turn dough out onto floured counter and knead 8 to 10 times or until it is smooth and elastic. Oil a large bowl. Turn dough in bowl to oil both sides and then cover with clean, damp cloth. Let rise in warm place until double in size. Punch down and shape into letters. Place on cookie sheet. Baste each pretzel with egg yolk mixture. Sprinkle with salt. Let rise again until almost double. Bake for 10 minutes or until golden brown and firm.

➡ **Letters of Dough (Inedible) Recipe**

1 cup salt

2 cups flour

1 cup water

Put all ingredients into a mixing bowl. Mix together and then knead for 10 minutes. Place the letters on an ungreased cookie sheet and bake 40 minutes at 325 degrees. When the letters have cooled, have the child paint them with watercolors. Bake again for 10 to 15 minutes, varnish, and mount them on a board with white glue. Have the child trace each letter mounted on the board for tactile reinforcement. The child's own first name is often used in this tracing strategy.

THE LANGUAGE-EXPERIENCE APPROACH

The language-experience approach is an effective way to help children learn letter names. In this strategy a child or group of children dictate a story or chart about an experience that he or she (they) has had. As the teacher or tutor helps the children read the dictated story or chart aloud, he or she calls the child's attention to various *concepts about print*, including capital and lower-case letter names.

The child (children) is told to circle or underline target capital and lower-case target letters in the story or chart. Usually he or she (they) is able to do this easily because the story or chart has just been dictated. By using this activity, the teacher or tutor also can assess if the child knows the difference between letters and words. Young children sometimes confuse the two unless the concept is presented and practiced meaningfully.

Complete directions about how to use the language-experience approach is found in the section of this chapter devoted to sight word knowledge because it is the most applicable with that reading skill.

LETTER DICTIONARY

Each child can construct his or her personal dictionary. For this activity staple thirteen large sheets of white construction paper, folding them in the middle and stapling them to make a booklet. If you wish, you can have each child decorate the front of his or her letter dictionary. Then print (or have the child print if he or she is able) the capital and lower-case letter pairs on each sheet of paper. Then help the child to draw or cut out a picture to go with each alphabet letter pair. This activity also can improve ability in letter–sound relationships. Here is an example of a page from such a letter dictionary:

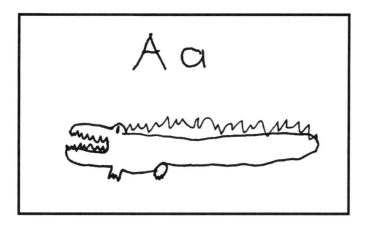

LETTER CUT-OUTS

Letter cut-outs are a useful strategy for stressing target letter names. Cut target capital letters out of construction paper or posterboard. Each letter should be about ten inches high. If the child can do so, he or she can cut out the target letters him- or herself. Then have the child look through old magazines to locate pictures that begin with the target letter (e.g., pictures for the capital letter *D* might be *dog, doll, duck, daisy, dandelion,* and *dish*).

Have the child glue each of the pictures to the large cut-out letter. If you wish, instead you can have the child draw a picture of each object that is to be included in the cut-out letter. Put a string on the large cut-out *D* with the glued-on or drawn-on pictures to make a necklace that the child can wear.

STRINGING LETTERS

Buy a box of macaroni (rigatoni). With a fine-line marking pen, print large capital and lower-case letters on the macaroni. Make five of each capital and lower-case letter. Print the consonants in black and the vowels in red. Dip the ends of pieces of heavy yarn into glue to make the letter stringing easier. When they are still somewhat wet, roll the ends of the yarn to form permanent points.

Have the child string the letters of the alphabet in correct order on the yarn—all capital letters and all lower-case letters. Have the child later pair the letters and make words of the letters on pieces of yarn.

NEWSPAPER AND MAGAZINE LETTERS

Give the child pages from old newspapers or magazines so that he or she can find target letters. Have the child circle each target letter located with a marking pen. As an alternative, the child can cut out the target letters and paste them on a piece of paper to form an interesting collage, which also can be illustrated.

MAGNETIC LETTERS

Magnetic letters are helpful in presenting and reviewing letter names. They are commercially available through many teacher's catalogs as well as in many teacher stores. The child can easily move them around to match capital and lower-case letters. He or she can also construct words by moving the letters around. Magnetic letters are used successfully in the Reading Recovery Early Intervention Program for first-grade children with special needs. They also can be used with older preschool children, kindergarten children, and perhaps even with second-grade children.

You can order magnetic letters from the following source:

Dominie Press
5945 Pacific Center Boulevard
Suite 505
San Diego, CA 92121

This company sells magnetic spelling boards and magnetic letters. However, many stores in your community probably also sell both magnetic spelling boards and magnetic letters.

VISUAL CLOSURE CARDS

To construct visual closure cards, cut strips from white posterboard about 5" × 20" and begin four letters per card. Make only the first stroke. Make dots to show the remaining strokes in the following color coding: 1—red, 2—blue, 3—green, and 4—black. Cover each card with clear self-stick vinyl. Have the child complete each incomplete letter by connecting the dots in the same color code as the writing strokes. Here are several examples of this kind of visual closure activity:

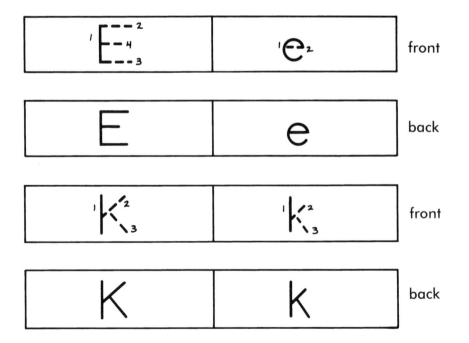

SPECIAL ACTIVITIES FOR EACH LETTER OF THE ALPHABET

There are many motivating activities that can be used for teaching and/or reviewing the different alphabet letters. This section presents one of them for each letter of the alphabet to serve as a model. There are many others that are equally useful and interesting.

The Letter A

Cut an apple horizontally so that the "star" shows. Have children dip the apple half in thick paint and then make a print on a piece of construction paper.

The Letter B

Make a butterfly blotto on a large piece of construction paper. Have children apply paint to the wings on the right-hand side of the butterfly. Have them fold the butterfly in half at the middle and rub gently. Have children open and look at the pattern that is found on the wings.

The Letter C

Have children dip small metal cars in paint and "drive" the cars back and forth over a large sheet of paper to make an interesting design.

The Letter D

Have children make "magic door" pictures. Have each child decorate a "magic door" on construction paper. Have them dictate or write stories about what could be found behind the "magic door."

The Letter E

Have children make "elephant ears" out of construction paper, which can be stapled to headbands for the children to wear. Here is a pattern for the "elephant ears."

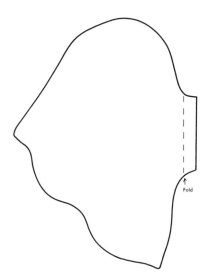

Fold

The Letter F

Have children make a fish pattern similar to the one that follows. Then have them add glue in the pattern of the scales and sprinkle glitter or confetti on the glue to form fish "scales."

The Letter G

Make a goat letter *G* using the pattern that follows with sunflower seeds (or some other type of seeds) to form the letter *G*.

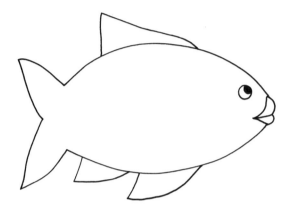

The Letter H

Have the children make headbands out of construction paper, which you then staple to fasten. They can then wear the headbands if they wish at school or at home.

The Letter I

Children can make insects in any creative way in which they wish. All insects have six legs and bodies made up of head, thorax, and abdomen. Have children put these parts together and decorate them as creatively as they wish.

The Letter J

Have children make a jack-in-the-box as in the pattern that follows. Fold construction paper four inches from the top. Place "Jack" under the fold. Open at the fold to see Jack's head.

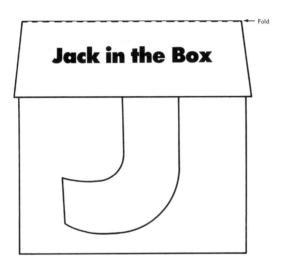

The Letter K

Have the children make a kitchen collage. Have them cut pictures of kitchen items from magazines and paste them on paper to make an interesting kitchen collage.

The Letter L

Have children make a lion puppet. Paste a circle face on a small paper bag. Have children add yarn for the mane and draw in features on the lion puppet to make it as interesting as possible.

The Letter M

Have children make a macaroni collage by gluing different types of macaroni on a sheet of construction paper to make as interesting a collage as possible.

The Letter N

Make a bird's nest by mixing pine needles or shredded wheat and white glue. Have the child mold into a nest shape. Let the "nest" dry and then have children fill the nests with "eggs" made from cornstarch dough.

The Letter O

Have children make oil and water prints. Float oil on water colors in a large flat pan like a cake pan. Have children dip the paper in the mixture to make the print.

The Letter P

Have the children make a pinwheel. Mark an X from corner to corner on a square piece of paper. Cut on the lines almost to the center. Help children attach every other corner piece to the center. Fasten a pin through the center of the pinwheel into the eraser of an unsharpened pencil to make a stick to hold while a child is blowing the pinwheel.

The Letter Q

Have children make a queen's crown from construction paper and glue the crown to the figure of a queen with the letter *Q* placed on it with glue that has glitter sprinkled on it.

The Letter R

Have children make a rainbow. Place the colors red, orange, yellow, green, blue, indigo, and violet paints from left to right in the sections of an empty egg carton.

The Letter S

Have children make a sponge painting by having them dip various sponges into paint containers of different colors. Then have them use the paint-covered sponges to make a pattern on a piece of white construction paper.

The Letter T

Have children make a top by placing a pencil through a cardboard circle.

The Letter U

Have children make an umbrella letter *U*. Have them make an umbrella out of construction paper and then make the letter *U* on it with sunflower seeds or macaroni.

The Letter V

Have the children make a "volcano" from papier mâché around a glass jar. Paint the outside of the volcano. When it is ready, the volcano can be made to erupt by following these two steps:

➡ Mix ¼ cup vinegar, ¼ cup liquid detergent, and red food coloring in the jar.

➡ Add 6 tablespoons baking soda that has been dissolved in warm water.

The Letter W

Have children make a spider web by using white chalk on black paper in interesting designs that could be spider webs.

The Letter X

Make an X-ray by using black paper with white lettering. The white lettering should form the capital letter *X*.

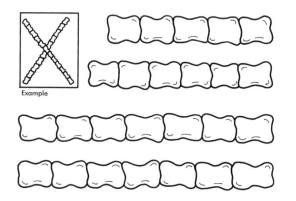

The Letter Y

Have children make a yo-yo letter project. To do so, have them cut a circle out of construction paper, punch two holes near the top of the circle to which a piece of elastic is attached, and make the letter *Y* with construction paper that is glued to the construction paper yo-yo.

The Letter Z

Have children make zinnias by fringing two different-sized circles of paper and pasting them together.

GAMES FOR REVIEWING LETTER NAME KNOWLEDGE

This section presents classroom-tested games that can be used to review the capital and lower-case letter names. Any game that is used to review a reading skill should stress the reading skill that it is devoted to rather than the game. Although games do encourage competition, they were very motivating for many of the students we have tutored. They often are successful with children who have special needs, such as learning disabilties or reading disabilities, when no other type of strategy or material is effective. Therefore, I recommend games as *one* technique that reading teachers and tutors can use to review various reading skills, including that of letter name knowledge.

Research has shown that children have a 53% greater gain in knowledge when participating in active games in comparison with practice using activity sheets. Even passive games result in a 30% better gain than does the use of activity sheets. The games included in this section have been very effective with young children.

Alphabet Apple Tree

TO CONSTRUCT THE GAME

Cut the following tree design from a piece of posterboard 8" × 12".

Print the capital letter names on the tree. Then cut small pieces of posterboard into the shape of apples. Print the lower-case alphabet letter names on the small pieces of posterboard.

TO PLAY THE GAME

To play the game, have the child place the tree on a flat surface. Then have him or her match the letter on each apple with the capital letter on the tree. Either the teacher, the tutor, or another child can check the child's work.

Pick and Match Letter Game

TO CONSTRUCT THE GAME

You need to have pink and red construction paper, marking pens, and clear self-stick vinyl. Make two decks of both the capital and lower-case letters on construction paper cards that are about 3" × 3". On one edge make a black border about ¼" thick. This shows the bottom edge so that the letters will be placed right side up. Cover the cards with clear self-stick vinyl.

Here is an illustration:

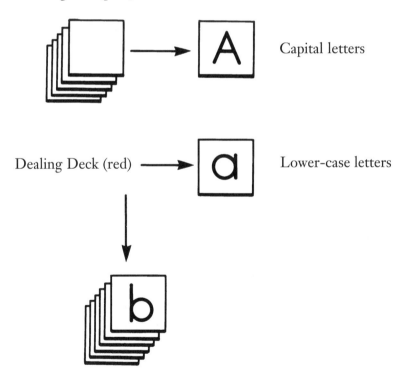

Drawing Pile (pink)

Capital letters

Dealing Deck (red)

Lower-case letters

TO PLAY THE GAME

The letters that are to be reviewed are dealt to two to four children from the red deck of cards. The pink deck will be the drawing pile. Each child draws from this pile and lays the card down so that all the players can see the letter. The player who has the matching letter card lays down the card, names the letter, and keeps both cards. The first child to use all the dealt cards wins if he or she has picked up the most cards.

Bang

TO CONSTRUCT THE GAME

Cover a Pringle™ potato chip can with red self-stick vinyl or red construction paper. Attach a piece of *heavy string* about $1\frac{1}{2}$" to 2" long to the top of the can and use aluminum foil to make a "firecracker" wick. Then print the capital and lower-case letters with a marker on small cards made of tagboard. However, print the word *BANG* on a few of the cards. During the game shake the can often to mix up the cards.

TO PLAY THE GAME

Have children take turns drawing a card and saying each letter name. If the child can correctly say the letter name, he or she keeps the card. If a child draws the word *BANG*, he or she must return all of the cards to the can. The first child to collect ten cards (or any predetermined number of cards) is the winner of the game.

Memory (Concentration)

TO CONSTRUCT THE GAME

Use a marker to make capital and lower-case letter cards out of tagboard. Make two sets of identical cards. Be certain that the children cannot see through the cards when they are turned over.

TO PLAY THE GAME

Place the letter cards face down on a flat surface. Have the child turn up a card in one set and try to find the card that matches it in the other set. When a match is made, have the child say the letter name and keep the card. Points or prizes can be given for the number of cards that the child has.

Alphabet Bingo

TO CONSTRUCT THE GAME

Cut cardboard to make enough $8\frac{1}{2}$" × 11" sheets for each child (any similar size will work just as well). Then each sheet should be divided into 9 to 12 sections. Print an alphabet letter on each section. Make sure each sheet contains a different combination of letters. Then cover the sheets with clear self-stick vinyl. For markers, you can use small pieces of paper, bottle caps, poker chips, or anything similar.

TO PLAY THE GAME

As the caller says a letter name, have the child place markers of some type on his or her card. When a complete row—either horizontal, vertical, or diagonal—is covered, the child calls out "Bingo." If you wish, children can play "Cover the Card" instead. To win the game, the child must be able to identify each letter name as he or she takes off the markers to prove that he or she has won. As an alternative, you can hold up a card with a letter name on it and ask whether any child has that letter on his or her sheet. This version of the game ends when the first child playing the game has "covered" his or her sheet. The first version of Alphabet Bingo reviews letter name identification, while the second version reviews letter name recognition.

Moving with the Alphabet

TO CONSTRUCT THE GAME

You need large newsprint art paper, a felt marker, and masking tape. Print giant letters on the newsprint, one letter per sheet.

TO PLAY THE GAME

To play the game tell the children that you are going to put giant letters around the room. Have the children choose a child to stand by a letter and wait to be told how they should get to the next letter. Have four children choose four friends to walk to the letter *A*, which you point out to them. Select another child to think of a way other than walking that the four children can move to the second letter. Some suggestions might be hopping, skipping, crawling, tiptoeing, dancing, etc. The children clap for the first four children, and another four children are selected and told to walk to another letter.

Eating the Alphabet

TO CONSTRUCT THE GAME

Print the capital and lower-case letter names on small cards about 1" × 1". Then select sturdy boxes on which an animal head and different alphabet strips are glued. Cut holes in the opposite sides of the boxes so children can reach in for the cards.

TO PLAY THE GAME

Have the child select a card and "feed" it to the animal that has a similar alphabet letter on the strip under its mouth. The following illustration should clarify this game.

Walking the Alphabet

TO CONSTRUCT THE GAME

Trace 26 footprints on a large piece of cardboard or cloth. Make cardboard footprint cut-outs each with a printscript alphabet letter written on it with a marking pen.

Make one set of cut-outs for the capital letters and another set of the cut-outs for the lower-case letters. Cover the alphabet letters with clear self-stick vinyl.

TO PLAY THE GAME

Have children place the cutout footprints over the footprint of the correct letter. The following illustration should clarify this game.

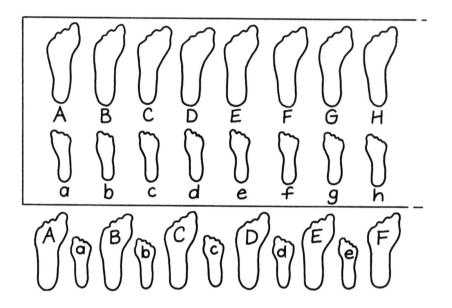

The Letter Chair Game

TO CONSTRUCT THE GAME

Line up some chairs behind each other. Make letter cards with either a capital or a lower-case letter printed on each one.

TO PLAY THE GAME

Have children sit on the chairs that have been lined up behind each other. Begin at the front of the line and show a card with a capital or lower-case letter name printed on it. If the child can give the letter name correctly, he or she can stay in the chair. If a wrong answer is given, the child must go to the end of the line, and all of the rest of the children move up. Children should try to stay at the front of the line so that they can be the "captain."

Tennis Balls and Alphabet Letters

TO CONSTRUCT THE GAME

You need to collect 26 tennis ball cans and lids. You may be able to get them from a tennis club in your area. Then cover all of the cans with self-stick vinyl or prepasted paper. Use a marker to print a capital letter on the side of each can. Gather 26 old tennis balls (you might ask a tennis club for the balls also), and print a lower-case letter name on each one.

TO PLAY THE GAME

Have a child match each lower-case tennis ball with the corresponding letter can and put the correct ball inside it. If you line them up in a row under the chalkboard, the tennis ball cans do not take up much room. As the children sit in a circle, roll a ball to each child. The child should identify the letter and put it in the right can when the letter name is called.

Space Alien

TO CONSTRUCT THE GAME

Write each of the capital letters on a 3" × 5" index card made of tagboard. On one card draw or paste a picture of a "space alien."

TO PLAY THE GAME

Deal each child an even number of the letter cards. Have the children take turns drawing a letter card from the child to his or her right. When a player gets a match, he or she must lay it down. The first player to lay all of his or her cards down except the space alien card, which he or she must have to win, is the winner of the game.

What Is This Letter?

TO CONSTRUCT THE GAME

Trace and cut out the capital letters in sandpaper. Glue the letters to separate sheets of tagboard. Glue one letter to each piece of tagboard.

TO PLAY THE GAME

Give each child those capital letters that he or she does not know. Do not give a child more than five letters at a time. Allow the child to study the pile of letters, and then blindfold him or her. While the child is blindfolded, have him or her feel the letters and tell what they are. When more than one child is playing, the first player to correctly identify the letter is given the point. The child with the most points is the winner.

REPRODUCIBLES FOR IMPROVING LETTER NAME KNOWLEDGE

This section contains several ready-to-use activity sheets you can use to improve various elements of letter name knowledge. You can duplicate and use any of these activity sheets in their present form or modify them in any way you like. Remember that activity sheets can be helpful if they are not overused. Young children often enjoy completing activity sheets (Miller, 1998).

TRACING HARD LETTERS
(Beginning reading level)

These letters may be hard for you to remember. If you *trace* them on the sheet, you may remember them.

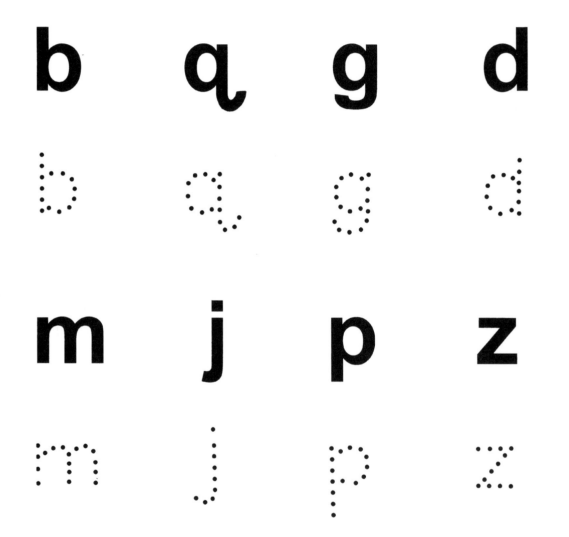

HELP THIS CAT GET HOME
(Beginning reading level)

Fill in the missing letters to help this lost *cat* find its way home.

ALPHABET UMBRELLAS
(Beginning reading level)

Fill in the missing letter on each umbrella.

MATCH THE HUMMINGBIRDS AND FLOWERS
(Beginning reading level)

Draw a line between each hummingbird and the flower that matches it.

MATCH THE HUMMINGBIRDS AND FLOWERS

Draw a line between each hummingbird and the flower that matches it.

MATCH THE HUMMINGBIRDS AND FLOWERS

Draw a line between each hummingbird and the flower that matches it.

179

DOGS AND BONES
(Beginning reading level)

Draw a line between each dog and its matching bone.

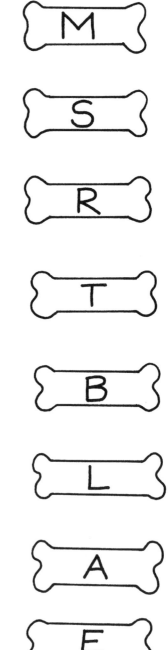

DOGS AND BONES

Draw a line between each dog and its matching bone.

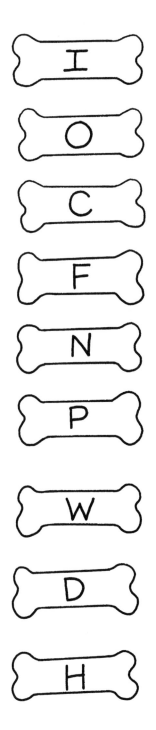

DOGS AND BONES

Draw a line between each dog and its matching bone.

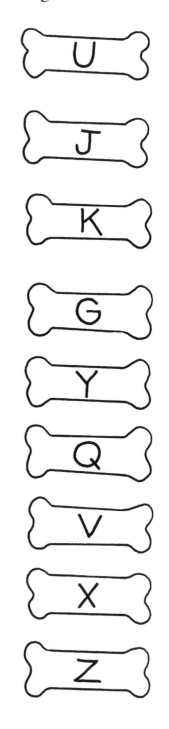

MONKEY LETTERS
(Beginning reading level)

Write the matching capital letter on each card.

SIGHT WORD RECOGNITION AND IDENTIFICATION

Sight word recognition and *sight word identification* are both subskills of *sight word knowledge*. Sight word recognition is recognizing or being able to select a word immediately when it is located with other similar appearing words. However, sight word identification is the ability to say or pronounce a word immediately when it is encountered while reading. Although sight word identification is the more difficult reading skill, it also is the one that is used in reading.

Many sight words do not have a regular *phoneme–grapheme (sound–symbol) relationship* and thus cannot be analyzed by phonics. Such words are more effectively learned as a total unit. Several examples of such sight words are *dog, love, once, said, through,* and *were*.

Sight vocabulary also can be said to be all the words that a reader can identify immediately upon seeing them. Although a reader first may have had to analyze many of these words by phonics, word structure, or context, he or she now has them in his or her sight word bank. A child must have a large sight word bank so that he or she does not have to stop and analyze most of the words while reading, which can interfere with comprehension. It is important that children have mastered all of the basic sight words by the end of third grade so that they can read all grade-appropriate materials with ease and fluency. They also need a mastery of the basic sight words so that they can successfully read the content materials that they will meet in the fourth grade and beyond. An insufficient sight word bank is one important reason why a child who has been an average or good reader in the primary grades may begin to have reading difficulties in fourth grade.

It also is important for a child to master the basic sight words because a small number of them make up a large proportion of the words found in everyday reading for both children and adults. For example, the following ten words make up at least 25% of all the words found in print material:

the	of
and	a
to	in
is	you
that	it

In addition, the most common 25 words found in the English language make up about one-third of all words found in print materials (Fry, Kress, & Fountoukidis, 2000).

For most children the easiest way to learn unknown words is to memorize them (Richek, 1997–1998). However, memorization also is the most limiting way because children have a limit as to how many words they can remember using phonic or structural clues. This limit may be as low as 40 words for some children, a very small number of the words that they must learn to identify.

Sight word identification consists of such subskills as recognizing a word by its total shape, its first few letters, its length, or its special characteristics, such as *ascenders* (letters that reach above the line, such as *h, k, b,* and *d*) or *descenders* (letters that reach below the line, such as *g, p, q,* or *y*). *Configuration* or *drawing a frame* around the entire word is another subskill of sight word identification. Here is an example of configuration:

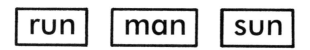

However, configuration is *not* an effective word identification technique in words such as the following because they have no unique configuration or shape. This is the case with a number of common words.

Some subskills of sight word identification may provide unimportant or irrelevant cues to word identification. For example, the double *o* in the word *look* is sometimes said to "be two eyes." However, a number of other words, such as *book, took, hook, stood, goose, noon, moose,* and *moon,* also have a double *o* in the same position. One other incorrect cue is the fairly common practice of having a child look for the small words in a larger word. While this technique may be helpful in the word *another,* it is incorrect in locating the words *fat* and *her* in the word *father.*

Some of the most common words found in reading also are among the most irregular and therefore may be difficult for young children to learn. Many reading teachers and tutors believe that a child may need 120 to 140 meaningful exposures before a word becomes part of his or her sight word bank. Some children with special needs, such as learning or reading disabilities, may need more exposures than that before a word can be recognized immediately.

When selecting words from a sight word list to present to children, probably the two most important factors in deciding which words to present are usefulness and word difficulty. For example, although the sight word *said* is difficult for children, it also is a common and useful word. Therefore, the word *said* probably should be presented and practiced fairly early in a developmental or corrective reading program. Sight words often are *structure* or *function words,* which means that they *have no referent or do not represent any object.* Such words usually are difficult for children to remember because the child is not able to associate such a word with anything concrete. However, a few sight words are *content words* and therefore often are easier for children to remember. The words *father* and *mother* are examples of content words that are common in beginning reading materials.

Sight words should be presented both *in context and in isolation* so that most children can learn them successfully. The presentation of sight words in context is most valuable for most children. However, some children, including those with special needs such as learning or reading disabilities, also should encounter sight words in isolation both for presentation and practice. When words are taught in isolation, children often are able to notice the way they are formed (Samuels, 1967; Singer, Samuels, & Spiroff, 1973–1974). When words are presented in context, children often pay more attention to word meanings and the way in which the word is used. Teaching articles, prepositions, and conjunctions in context is especially important because the most effective way to understand function or structure words is to notice how they are actually used. Presenting sight words in context and isolation helps children learn both their meanings and pronunciation. However, if children already know the meaning of a sight word, a reading teacher or tutor should spend most of his or her time teaching the unique features of the word, including how it is spelled and noticing its pronounceable word parts. Knowing how to spell and/or sound out a word partially or entirely helps students learn and remember new words (Ehri, 1991), but time spent discussing definitions that the child already knows is a waste of time.

Automaticity (immediate recognition of the word) and accuracy are both very important in identifying sight words (Samuels, 1994). In order to reach an acceptable level of accuracy, children must actively process words. They should pay attention as they look at words. Children need different amounts of time to reach a high level of accuracy in word identification. Once they have reached an acceptable level of accuracy in identifying words, they seem to gain automaticity at the same rate (Samuels, 1994). If you are able to swim, for example, you may remember how you tried to remember all the necessary tasks that were involved in learning to swim well. Now that you have practiced swimming for a number of years, you probably perform all of these tasks without even thinking about them. This automaticity is what children should also achieve when they are identifying sight words.

It may surprise you to learn that good readers may be able to learn *four times* as many sight words in a specified period of time as do children with special needs, such as learning or reading disabilities. Children with special needs often need continuous practice to learn sight words. Later sections of this chapter present many strategies, games, and reproducibles for helping children with special needs achieve the necessary automaticity and accuracy in sight word identification that will help them to become effective readers.

SIGHT WORD LISTS

The most common sight words are found in several different *sight word lists*. Although the lists differ somewhat depending on the sources from which the words were taken (children's reading, writing, or both), there is a great deal of overlap among all the lists.

The most common and one of the most useful sight word lists is the *Dolch Basic Sight Word List*, which was compiled by the late Edward Dolch of the University of Illinois in 1941. Although it might appear that this list is outdated, that is not the case because the words included in it are comparable to the words in the newer sight word lists. This list of 220 *service words* is said to make up about 70% of the words found in most first readers and about 65% of the words contained in most second and third readers. As is true with all sight word lists, many of the words contained in the Dolch Basic Sight Word List are structure or function words that have no referent. As stated earlier, structure or function words usually are more difficult for children to remember than are content words, which represent a concrete entity. Children with special needs, such as learning or reading disabilities, often have difficulty remembering these words.

A reproducible copy of the Dolch Basic Sight Word List is included in this section.

Counting the number of words that a child recognizes on a sight word list is one way of assessing his or her *approximate instructional reading level* (the level at which the child can read with some teacher assistance). Here is a table that you can use to estimate a child's *approximate instructional reading level* as indicated by his or her performance on the Dolch Basic Sight Word List (McBroom, Sparrow, & Eckstein, 1944). Although this application has not been researched, these numbers probably also are useful with the *Instant Word List*, which is included later in this chapter as one way of estimating a child's approximate instructional reading level. I have found them to be applicable to other sight word lists because their content overlaps so much.

Words Recognized	Reading Level
0–75	Preprimer
76–120	Primer
121–170	First Reader
171–210	Second Reader
Above 210	Third Reader or above

The following is a reproducible copy of the Dolch Basic Sight Word List. You may copy this sight word list and use it in any way you wish.

Name _____ Grade _____ Teacher _____ Date _____

DOLCH BASIC SIGHT WORD LIST*

List 1	List 2	List 3	List 4
1. _____the	1. _____at	1. _____do	1. _____big
2. _____to	2. _____him	2. _____can	2. _____went
3. _____and	3. _____with	3. _____could	3. _____are
4. _____he	4. _____up	4. _____when	4. _____come
5. _____a	5. _____all	5. _____did	5. _____if
6. _____I	6. _____look	6. _____what	6. _____now
7. _____you	7. _____is	7. _____so	7. _____long
8. _____it	8. _____her	8. _____see	8. _____no
9. _____of	9. _____there	9. _____not	9. _____came
10. _____in	10. _____some	10. _____were	10. _____ask
11. _____was	11. _____out	11. _____get	11. _____very
12. _____said	12. _____as	12. _____them	12. _____an
13. _____his	13. _____be	13. _____like	13. _____over
14. _____that	14. _____have	14. _____one	14. _____your
15. _____she	15. _____go	15. _____this	15. _____its
16. _____for	16. _____we	16. _____my	16. _____ride
17. _____on	17. _____am	17. _____would	17. _____into
18. _____they	18. _____then	18. _____me	18. _____just
19. _____but	19. _____little	19. _____will	19. _____blue
20. _____had	20. _____down	20. _____yes	20. _____red

| /20 | /20 | /20 | /20 |

© 2001 by John Wiley & Sons, Inc.

_____

*Shanker, J., & Ekwall, E. (late). (1998). *Locating and correcting reading difficulties.* Columbus, OH: Merrill, pp. 261 & 263. Reprinted with permission of Merrill.

DOLCH BASIC SIGHT WORD LIST *(Cont'd)*

List 5	List 6	List 7	List 8
1. _____ from	1. _____ away	1. _____ walk	1. _____ tell
2. _____ good	2. _____ old	2. _____ to	2. _____ much
3. _____ any	3. _____ by	3. _____ or	3. _____ keep
4. _____ about	4. _____ their	4. _____ before	4. _____ give
5. _____ around	5. _____ here	5. _____ eat	5. _____ work
6. _____ want	6. _____ saw	6. _____ again	6. _____ first
7. _____ don't	7. _____ call	7. _____ play	7. _____ try
8. _____ how	8. _____ after	8. _____ who	8. _____ new
9. _____ know	9. _____ well	9. _____ been	9. _____ must
10. _____ right	10. _____ think	10. _____ may	10. _____ start
11. _____ put	11. _____ ran	11. _____ stop	11. _____ black
12. _____ too	12. _____ let	12. _____ off	12. _____ white
13. _____ got	13. _____ help	13. _____ never	13. _____ ten
14. _____ take	14. _____ make	14. _____ seven	14. _____ does
15. _____ where	15. _____ going	15. _____ eight	15. _____ bring
16. _____ every	16. _____ sleep	16. _____ cold	16. _____ goes
17. _____ pretty	17. _____ brown	17. _____ today	17. _____ write
18. _____ jump	18. _____ yellow	18. _____ fly	18. _____ always
19. _____ green	19. _____ five	19. _____ myself	19. _____ drink
20. _____ four	20. _____ six	20. _____ round	20. _____ once
/20	/20	/20	/20

DOLCH BASIC SIGHT WORD LIST *(Cont'd)*

List 9	List 10	List 11
1. _____ soon	1. _____ use	1. _____ wash
2. _____ made	2. _____ fast	2. _____ show
3. _____ run	3. _____ say	3. _____ hot
4. _____ gave	4. _____ light	4. _____ because
5. _____ open	5. _____ pick	5. _____ far
6. _____ has	6. _____ hurt	6. _____ live
7. _____ find	7. _____ pull	7. _____ draw
8. _____ only	8. _____ cut	8. _____ clean
9. _____ us	9. _____ kind	9. _____ grow
10. _____ three	10. _____ both	10. _____ best
11. _____ out	11. _____ sit	11. _____ upon
12. _____ better	12. _____ which	12. _____ these
13. _____ hold	13. _____ fall	13. _____ sing
14. _____ buy	14. _____ carry	14. _____ together
15. _____ funny	15. _____ small	15. _____ please
16. _____ warm	16. _____ under	16. _____ thank
17. _____ ate	17. _____ read	17. _____ wish
18. _____ fall	18. _____ why	18. _____ many
19. _____ those	19. _____ own	19. _____ shall
20. _____ done	20. _____ found	20. _____ laugh
/20	/20	/20

THE INSTANT WORD LIST

Edward B. Fry, Professor Emeritus of Education at Rutgers University, has compiled an updated version of the *Instant Word List*, which he first compiled in 1957. This word list was revised in 1980 based on a modification of the Carroll (American Heritage) data. The first 100 words make up half of all print material, and the 300 words together make up 65% of all print materials.

The first one hundred sight words should be mastered by the end of first grade, while both the first and second hundred sight words should be mastered by the end of second grade. It is important for a child to be able to immediately identify all of the words on the Instant Word List by the end of third grade. If he or she cannot do so, the child often has considerable difficulty with reading activities in the fourth grade and beyond.

The following is a copy of Fry's Instant Word List that you can reproduce and use in any way you wish.

THE INSTANT WORDS*†

FIRST HUNDRED

Words 1–25	Words 26–50	Words 51–75	Words 76–100
the	or	will	number
of	one	up	no
and	had	other	way
a	by	about	could
to	word	out	people
in	but	many	my
is	not	then	than
you	what	them	first
that	all	these	water
it	were	so	been
he	we	some	call
was	when	her	who
for	your	would	oil
on	can	make	its
are	said	like	now
as	there	him	find
with	use	into	long
his	an	time	down
they	each	has	day
I	which	look	did
be	do	more	get
this	how	write	made
have	their	go	may
from	if	see	part

Common suffixes: -s, -ing, -ed, -ly, -est

---

*If you want *1000 Instant Words*, the following book contains them: Fry, E., Kress, J., & Fountoudikis, D. (2000). *The reading teacher's book of lists*, fourth edition. Paramus, NJ: Prentice Hall, pp. 47–53.

†If you want more than the 300 sight words, the following is a list of 3000 sight words: Sakiey, E., & Fry, E. (1984). *3000 instant words*. Providence, RI: Jamestown Publishers.

SECOND HUNDRED

Words 101–125	Words 126–150	Words 151–175	Words 176–200
over	say	set	try
new	great	put	kind
sound	where	end	hand
take	help	does	picture
only	through	another	again
little	much	well	change
work	before	large	off
know	line	must	play
place	right	big	spell
year	too	even	air
live	mean	such	away
me	old	because	animal
back	any	turn	house
give	same	here	point
most	tell	why	page
very	boy	ask	letter
after	follow	went	mother
thing	came	men	answer
our	want	read	found
just	show	need	study
name	also	land	still
good	around	different	learn
sentence	farm	home	should
man	three	us	America
think	small	move	world

Common suffixes: -s, -ing, -er, -ly, -est

THE INSTANT WORDS *(Cont'd)*

THIRD HUNDRED

Words 201–225	Words 226–250	Words 251–275	Words 276–300
high	saw	important	miss
every	left	until	idea
near	don't	children	enough
add	few	side	eat
food	while	feet	face
between	along	car	watch
own	might	mile	far
below	chose	night	Indian
country	something	walk	really
plant	seem	white	almost
last	next	sea	let
school	hard	began	above
father	open	grow	girl
keep	example	took	sometimes
tree	begin	river	mountain
never	life	four	cut
start	always	carry	young
city	those	state	talk
earth	both	once	soon
eye	paper	book	list
light	together	hear	song
thought	got	stop	being
head	group	without	leave
under	often	second	family
story	run	late	it's

Common suffixes: -s, -ing, -er, -ly, -est

SURVIVAL WORDS

Survival words are those sight words that older students and adults should recognize immediately for their health and safety. These words are especially important to students with learning and reading disabilities at the middle school level and beyond. They are words that are related to survival in everyday life. This section contains a brief list of the most important survival words that you can reproduce and use in any way you want.

Fry, Kress, & Fountoukidis (2000, pp. 376–384) have compiled a much more comprehensive list of words that older students and adults should be able to identify immediately. Their overall list has been divided into the following sections, and you are encouraged to consult this book if you want a comprehensive list of any of the type of words that are included: Daily Living Words, Travel Words, Application Words, and Work Words (danger words, road signs, signs, want ads, grocery and drug words, menus, income tax, credit terms, hospital, airport, trucking, construction, lumber, and telephone words.)

SURVIVAL WORDS

acid
ambulance
area code
bus
bus stop
cab
cafeteria
cash
caution
combustible
concourse
danger
dentist
dial tone
directory
doctor
do not drink
don't walk
down
drinking water
drug store
elevator
emergency
emergency exit
emergency—911
exit
fire alarm
fire escape
fire exit

first aid
flammable
flight number
fragile
fuel
gas
gentlemen
handle with care
harmful if swallowed
help
high voltage
hospital
keep away
keep off
keep out
ladies
local call
long distance
MD
men
men working
men working above
no admittance
no tresspassing
nurse
open
open door out
operator
out of order

parking
phone
physician
please do not touch
poison
police
post office
private
pull
push
railroad
restaurant
school
school zone
stairs
stairway
STOP
store
taxi
telephone
this way
use other door
walk
warning
watch your step
women
X-ray

STRATEGIES FOR IMPROVING SIGHT WORD KNOWLEDGE

This section contains numerous classroom-tested strategies, materials, games, and reproducibles that reading teachers and tutors can use to improve children's competencies in sight word recognition and identification. The material is designed to be valuable and motivating for beginning readers. However, it may be especially useful with children who have special needs of various kinds, such as learning or reading disabilities.

Although much of the material contained in this section obviously will be the most applicable with young children, a number of the strategies can easily be adapted to older students who have limited sight word knowledge.

ENVIRONMENTAL PRINT

Environmental print should be the first sight words that a young child learns. These are words that are found in the child's everyday environment, such as his or her home, preschool, grocery stores, or shopping malls, among many other places. Environmental print are those words that the child learns by sight because they are part of his or her everyday life.

Children often learn environmental print by looking at words and asking a family member, an older sibling or friend, or another adult, "What does that word say?" The child who has his or her questions about words answered will likely learn a number of environmental words by sight even before starting school.

Some examples of environmental print that a young child might acquire are the following: STOP, Wal-Mart, Target, McDonald's, Hardee's, Crest®, Alpha-Bits®, Cheerios®, and can labels of various kinds such as corn, tomatoes, and soup.

To encourage the learning of environmental print as well as other simple sight words, it is essential for any preschool, kindergarten, or primary-grade classroom to have an abundance of print available around the classroom for the children to see. The print should be placed in a meaningful manner so that each child is able to associate print with meaning. For example, the equipment in the classroom can be labeled so that children associate the abstract symbols with the concrete objects. Some elements of a print-rich environment also can be incorporated into a tutoring or home situation.

READING ACTIVITIES

All types of reading activities are the most effective way of presenting and reviewing sight words for most children. Although sight words may have to be presented and/or practiced in isolation on occasion, as much as possible children should learn and practice sight words in the context of meaningful trade books of all types, poetry, and nursery rhymes.

Wide reading of all kinds of materials undoubtedly is the single best way for children to practice sight word identification. However, some children with special needs, such as learning or reading disabilities, do not enjoy reading any type of material even if the material is easy and interesting. Therefore, it is important for any reading teacher or tutor to provide such students with a wide variety of easy, highly motivating books to read. Children always should be given choices about the books they are going to read. These books usually should be on a child's independent (easy) reading level.

Predictable books usually are effective in helping a child learn sight words. They are useful in small group, partner, or individual reading. Predictable books are valuable for several reasons. They allow children to predict (guess) what will happen next in a book, thus encouraging active participation. They also are easy to read because they have predictable language patterns, thus providing concrete motivation, especially to children who need it the most (e.g., children with special needs).

Predictability can take a number of different forms. A common form is through the use of repeated catch phrases, such as "Brown bear, brown bear, what do you see? I see a yellow duck looking at me" (from *Brown Bear, Brown Bear, What Do You See?* by Bill Martin, Jr. [New York: Holt, Rinehart & Winston, 1967]). Predictable rhyme encourages children to fill in words, as in the book *Cat in the Hat* by Dr. Seuss (New York: Random House, 1957). Cumulative patterns also contribute to predictability, with new events being added with each episode, as in the book *The Jacket I Wear in the Snow* by S. Neitzel (New York: Greenwillow Books, 1989). Conversation also can contribute to predictability, as in the book *Caps for Sale* by E. Slobodkina (New York: Scholastic, 1940).

Because all books become somewhat more predictable as children become familiar with them, *repeated readings* should be done often. Fairy tales may be familiar to many children, so they often are predictable to an extent. Books that have familiar sequences, such as the days of the week, months of the year, letters of the alphabet, and numbers, are predictable to many children. Trade books also become predictable if they have good plots and familiar topics. Books in which pictures exactly match the text usually are predictable to children, especially if the children in a group can easily see the pictures in the book. Today some publishers are publishing simple trade books for young children that are very predictable and therefore are easy to read. Two publishers of such books are Rigby and Modern Curriculum Press.

The following is a simple strategy you can use for helping your pupils acquire various sight words while reading predictable books.

➡ Choose a book that children will enjoy and that contains the sight words you want to review. If possible, use a big (oversized) book version of the trade book so that children will be able to follow along easily while you read.

➡ Preview the book with the children, read it to them, and then discuss it.

➡ Point to each word as you read it aloud.

➡ Reread the book. Invite children to read the repeated parts or other easy parts.

➡ After several rereadings of the book, copy the text onto chart paper or cover the illustrations in the big book. With the pictures covered up, your pupils can concentrate on identifying the words. Have children read the version without the illustrations with your help if necessary.

➡ Duplicate the story and cut the duplicated version into sentence strips. Have children match the individual sentence strips to those contained in that version. Then have the children reassemble the story, sentence by sentence. Sentences can be cut up into individual words, which provides children with the opportunity to match the individual words with the words in the chart story. Have children reconstruct each individual sentence by placing the cut-out words in the proper order.

EASY-TO-READ TRADE BOOKS

This section contains a list of easy-to-read trade books that should be useful in motivating children to identify sight words in a meaningful way. Because this is not a comprehensive list, you should consult many other sources, including other professional books and "Children's Choices," a feature of the journal *The Reading Teacher* that appears in each October issue. This feature of the journal includes an annotated bibliography of children's trade books for students of different ages that have been chosen by professionals with the input of children. The trade books included in the following list are presented in a generally easy-to-hard order, with the books found near the beginning of the list for beginning readers and those found near the end of the list for children reading at about the second-grade level.

Aruego, J. (1971). *Look what I can do!* NY: Scribner.

Carle, E. (1995). *The very lonely firefly.* NY: Philomel.

———. (1987). *Have you seen my cat?* NY: Scholastic.

———. (1992). *Today is Monday.* NY: Putnam.

Cole, J., & Calemnson, S. (1990). *Ready . . . set . . . go!* Garden City, NY: Doubleday.

Hoban, T. (1972). *Push, pull, empty, full.* NY: Macmillan.

Maestro, B., & Maestro, G. (1978). *Busy day: A book of action words.* NY: Crown.

McLenighan, V. (1982). *Stop-go, fast-slow.* Chicago: Children's Press.

Scarry, R. (1963). *Richard Scarry's best word book ever.* Racine, WI: Golden.

Bang, M. (1996). *Goose.* NY: Blue Sky/Scholastic.

Maris, R. (1983). *My book.* Chicago: Children's Press.

Wildsmith, B. (1983). *All fall down.* NY: Oxford.

Keller, H. (1993). *Harry and Tuck.* NY: Greenwillow Books.

Cole, J. (1976). *Fun on wheels.* NY: Scholastic.

Eastman, P. (1960). *Are you my mother?* NY: Random House.

Gordon, S. (1980). *What a dog!* Mahwah, NJ: Troll.

Hutchins, P. (1972). *Good-night, owl.* NY: Macmillan.

Ehlert, L. (1994). *Mole's hill.* NY: Harcourt.

Kraus, R. (1970). *Whose mouse are you?* NY: Macmillan.

Lesieg, T. (1963). *Ten apples up on top.* NY: Random House.

Raffi. (1988). *One light, one sun.* NY: Crown.

Ziefert, H. (1985). *A dozen dogs.* NY: Random House.

Waddell, M. (1992). *Farmer duck.* Cambridge, MA: Candlewick Press.

Blocksma, M. (1992). *Yoo hoo, moon.* NY: Bantam.

Hoff, S. (1959). *Sammy the seal.* NY: Harper & Row.

Brown, M. (1952). *Where have you been?* NY: Scholastic.

Seuss, Dr. (1963). *Hop on pop.* NY: Random House.

Cebulash, M. (1972). *Willie's wonderful pet.* NY: Scholastic.

Hoff, S. (1988). *Mrs. Brice's mice.* NY: Harper & Row.

Lobel, A. (1972). *Frog and toad together.* NY: Harper & Row.

Martin, B. (1967). *Brown bear, brown bear, what do you see?* NY: Holt, Rinehart & Winston.

———. (1972). *Polar bear, polar bear, what do you see?* NY: Holt, Rinehart & Winston.

Cole, J. (1992). *The magic school bus on the ocean floor.* NY: Scholastic.

Hopkins, L. (1984). *Surprises* (a book of poetry). NY: Harper & Row.

Phillips, J. (1986). *My new boy.* NY: Random House.

Robart, R. (1986). *The cake that Mack ate.* Toronto, Canada: Kids Can Press.

Fox, M. (1990). *Possum magic.* NY: Harcourt.

Seuss, Dr. (1957). *The cat in the hat.* NY: Random House.

———. (1958). *The cat in the hat comes back.* NY: Random House.

———. (1960). *Green eggs and ham.* NY: Random House.

Ehlert, L. (1993). *Nuts to you.* NY: Harcourt.

Kasza, K. (1993). *The rat and the tiger.* NY: Putnam.

Van Leeuwen, J. (1979). *Tales of Oliver Pig.* NY: Dial.

——— . (1981). *More tales of Oliver Pig.* NY: Dial.

——— . (1990). *Oliver Pig at school.* NY: Dial.

——— . (1992). *Oliver and Amanda's Halloween.* NY: Dial.

Ericson, J. (1993). *No milk!* NY: Tambourine.

Wiseman, B. (1970). *Morris goes to school.* NY: Harper & Row.

———. (1978). *Morris has a cold.* NY: Dodd, Mead.

Fleming, D. (1996). *Where once there was a wood.* NY: Holt.

Williams, V. (1990). *More, more, more said the baby.* NY: Scholastic.

Giovanni, N. (1996). *The genie in the jar.* NY: Holt.

Henkes, K. (1996). *Lilly's plastic purple purse.* NY: Greenwillow Books.

There are several series of children's books that are specifically designed to give children practice in sight word identification. Here are some of them:

Reading corners. San Diego: Dominie Press. This series features several different basic patterns, such as I do _____; I have _____; I like

_____. These books each have only eight to twelve pages of material, so they are easy for young children to read.

Read more books. San Diego: Dominie Press. This series of books emphasizes a number of basic sentence patterns. The books have limited text and explicitly illustrated color photographs and therefore are easy to read.

Ready readers. (1996). Columbus, OH: Modern Curriculum Press. This is a set of graded readers that includes hundreds of little books. This series has several copies of each title as well as big books.

Seedlings. Columbus, OH: Seedling Publications. This series of books includes sixteen-page booklets in which each page contains one line of material accompanied by an illustration. The vocabulary is somewhat varied.

PREDICTABLE BOOKS

Here is a list of well-known predictable books you can use to review sight words. There are many others that could have been included in the list.

Aardema, V. (1981). *Bringing the rain to Kapiti Plain.* NY: Dial Books.

Ahberg, J. A. (1978). *Each peach pear plum.* NY: The Viking Press.

Arno, E. (1970). *The gingerbread man.* NY: Scholastic.

Aruego, J., & Dewey, A. (1989). *Five little ducks.* NY: Crown Publishers.

Asch, F. (1982). *Happy birthday, moon.* NY: Scholastic.

Bonn, R. (1961). *I know an old lady.* NY: Scholastic.

Brisson, P. (1995). *Benny's pennies.* NY: Yearling Books.

Capucilli, A. (1995). *Inside a barn in the country.* NY: Scholastic.

Carle, E. (1984). *The very busy spider.* NY: Philomel.

———. (1981). *The very hungry caterpillar.* NY: Philomel.

———. (1995). *The very lonely firefly.* NY: Philomel.

Casey, P. (1994). *My cat Jack.* Cambridge, MA: Candlewick Press.

Cowley, J. (1986). *Greedy cat.* Wellington, New Zealand/NY: Richard C. Owen (distributor).

dePaola, T. (1978). *Pancakes for breakfast.* NY: Harcourt Brace Jovanovich.

deRegniers, B. S. (1968). *Willy O'Dwyer jumped in the fire.* NY: Atheneum.

Eastman, P. D. (1960). *Are you my mother?* NY: Random House.

Elting, M., & Folsom, M. (1980). *Q is the duck.* NY: Clarion.

Fitch, S. (1999). *There's a mouse in my house.* NY: Firefly Books.

Fleming, D. (1994). *Barnyard banter.* NY: Henry Holt & Company.

———. (1993). *In the small, small pond.* NY: Henry Holt & Company.

Fox, M. (1987). *Hattie and the fox.* NY: Bradbury.

Galdone, P. (1975). *Henny penny.* Boston: Houghton Mifflin.

———. (1973). *Little red hen.* NY: Scholastic.

———. (1975). *The gingerbread boy.* NY: Seabury.

———. (1972). *The three bears.* NY: Scholastic.

———. (1973). *The three billy goats gruff.* NY: Seabury.

———. (1970). *The three little pigs.* NY: Seabury.

Gordon, J. (2000). *Two badd badies.* Honesdale, PA: Boyds Mills Press.

Gregovich, B. (1992). *The fox on the box.* Grand Haven, MI: School Zone Publishing Company.

Guarino, D. (1989). *Is your mama a llama?* NY: Scholastic.

Hennessy, B. (1992). *Jake baked the cake.* NY: Econ-Clad Books.

Hoberman, M. A. (1978). *A house is a house for me.* NY: Scholastic.

Keats, E. J. (1971). *Over in the meadow.* NY: Scholastic.

King, B. (1995). *Sitting on the farm.* NY: HBJ School Publishers.

Krause, R. (1970). *Whose mouse are you?* NY: Macmillan.

Langstaff, J. (1974). *Oh, a-hunting we will go.* NY: Macmillan.

Leuck, L. (1994). *Sun is falling. Night is calling.* NY: Simon & Schuster.

Lobel, A. (1984). *The rose in my garden.* NY: Greenwillow Books.

MacDonald, E. (1993). *Mike's kite.* NY: HBJ School Press.

Mack, S. (1974). *10 bears in my bed.* NY: Pantheon.

Marzollo, J. (1995). *Sun song.* NY: HarperCollins Juvenile Books.

Mayer, M. (1975). *What do you do with a kangaroo?* NY: Scholastic.

Neitzel, S. (1989). *The jacket I wear in the snow.* NY: Greenwillow Books. (This book has the same pattern as *This is the house that Jack built.*)

Numeroff, L. (1985). *If you give a moose a cookie.* NY: Harper.

———. (1991). *If you give a moose a muffin.* NY: Harper.

Oxenbury, H. (1999). *It's my birthday.* NY: Greenwillow Books.

Poluskin, M. (1978). *Mother, mother, I want another.* NY: Crown.

Piper, W. (1954). *The little engine that could.* NY: Platt & Munk.

Pizer, A. (1992). *It's a perfect day.* Glenview, IL: Scott, Foresman and Company.

Pryor, A. (1990). *The baby blue cat who said no.* NY: Puffin.

Rathman, P. (1996). *Good night, gorilla.* NY: Putnam Publishing Group Juvenile.

Rosen, M. (1989). *We're going on a bear hunt.* NY: McElderry.

Roy, R. (1980). *The three ducks went wandering.* NY: Scholastic.

Ruurs, M. (1996). *A mountain alphabet.* Toronto, Ontario: Tundra Books.

Seuss, Dr. (1957). *Cat in the hat.* NY: Random House.

———. (1958). *Cat in the hat comes back.* NY: Random House.

———. (1965). *Fox in sox.* NY: Random House.

———. (1960). *Green eggs and ham.* NY: Random House.

Slobodkina, E. (1940). *Caps for sale.* NY: Scholastic.

Stevens, J. (1985). *The house that Jack built.* NY: Holiday House.

Strickland, P. (1997). *One bear, one dog.* NY: Dutton Books.

Temple, C. (1992). *On the riverbank.* Boston: Houghton Mifflin.

Tolhurst, M. (1990). *Somebody and the three bears.* NY: Orchard Books.

Tolstoy, A. (1968). *The great big enormous turnip.* NY: Franklin Watts.

Weber, B. (1966). *"You look ridiculous," said the rhinoceros to the hippopotamus.* Boston: Houghton Mifflin.

West, C. (1999). *Have you seen the crocodile?* Cambridge, MA: Candlewick Press.

Wood, A. (1999). *Silly Sally.* NY: Red Wagon Press.

Wood, J. (1992). *Moo, moo brown cow.* NY: Harcourt.

THE LANGUAGE-EXPERIENCE APPROACH

The *language-experience approach (LEA)* is an excellent way for children and older students, including adults who have reading difficulties, to learn and review sight words. LEA dictation can begin as early as the age of three with a child who has good linguistic aptitude. LEA, as it is known today, was mainly researched and publicized by the late Roach Van Allen, Professor Emeritus of the University of Arizona, under whom I studied in the 1960s. At that time Allen was speaking and writing about the language-experience approach in about the same way as it is conceptualized today. According to Allen (1976), LEA is primarily based on the following premise, all from the child's point of view:

> **What I think about is important.**
> **What I can think about, I can say.**
> **What I can say, I can write or someone else can write it for me.**
> **I can read what I have written or what someone else has written for me.**

The language-experience approach is an effective way of teaching and practicing sight words. Children who have dictated language-experience stories and charts usually find them very motivating, interesting, and easy to read. They often can read their own LEA dictated charts and stories much more effectively than they can read any other print materials.

Here is the basic procedure you can follow in using LEA dictation to improve sight word knowledge as well as other reading skills:

1. Give the child or children some type of highly motivating experience so that they will have an interesting experience about which to dictate. Although all children benefit from this, it is especially important for children with special needs, such as learning or reading disabilities. In fact, older disabled readers and even adults have learned many sight words from LEA dictated stories and charts. These dictated materials reflect their own unique experiences.

   Here are some of the initiating experiences that can be used successfully with young children. Older students and adults obviously will need to have different experiences about which to dictate.

   ➠ A trip to an interesting place, such as the police station, fire station, post office, zoo, wildlife preserve, pumpkin patch, grain farm, dairy farm, pig (hog) farm, candy factory, children's section of the local public library, toy store, local shopping mall, among many others. Each community and area has its own unique attractions that can be the basis for a dictated LEA story.

   ➠ An art or construction activity, such as autumn leaf tracings, constructing a simple puppet (see the puppet patterns in Chapter 6), carving a Halloween jack-o'-lantern, making a Thanksgiving turkey out of a potato, building a snowman, making a snowflake, constructing a Valentine or Valentine box, cutting out shamrocks, making paper umbrellas, cutting out spring flowers, making a May basket, or finger painting. Each reading teacher or tutor has his or her own repertoire of art or construction activities that can be used.

   ➠ A cooking or baking activity of some type, such as the ones suggested earlier in this chapter, including fudge, lasagna, zucchini bread, French fries, navy bean soup, oatmeal cookies, cupcakes, cookies, deviled eggs, bread, butter, vegetable soup, applesauce, jam or jelly, muffins, and many others. Each reading teacher and tutor can add many other cooking and baking activities that can be used as motivation for language-experience dictation.

   ➠ A visual or aural activity, such as looking at pictures, watching a videotape, looking at demonstrations, watching experiments, listening to a book being read aloud, or listening to an audiocassette tape.

2. Have an interesting preliminary discussion with the child or children in which the motivation for the LEA dictation is discussed. For example, if a child has visited a local fire station, the teacher and child can discuss the trip in detail using correct vocabulary and emphasizing the order in which the different concepts were seen at the fire station.

3. Have a child or group of children dictate the language-experience chart (on large chart paper) or LEA book (on regular or oversized paper), trying to help the child dictate in complete sentences. An LEA story also can be transcribed in a blank book. Blank regular-sized and big books are available for a low cost from the following source and from teacher's supply stores:

Bare Books
Treetop Publishing Company
220 Virginia Street
Racine, WI 53405

Be careful not to structure the dictation very much or the LEA chart or book will belong to the teacher instead of to the child or children.

The language patterns of the child or children should be used, including their dialect, although any offensive language should be changed. Most specialists in LEA think that if the teacher changes a child's language patterns, the child may feel rejected because that is the only language he or she has.

4. Follow this procedure:

➡ Read aloud the LEA chart or story several times, putting your hand under each word as you read it, being sure to emphasize one-to-one oral language and written word correspondence. The one-to-one correspondence should be stressed, although you can also stress left-to-right progression by moving a hand in a sweeping movement under each sentence as you read it aloud.

➡ Present and/or review a number of beginning reading skills from each LEA chart or story. In addition to sight word knowledge, other reading skills that can be stressed are the concept of words and word boundaries, letter names, beginning phonics, beginning word structure, and knowledge of simple suffixes.

➡ If you want, you can use the LEA story or chart in a number of different ways. It can be duplicated for other children in the class to "read." All of a child's stories then can be bound into a "book," reread several times, and then sent home with the child to read to family members or friends. The LEA charts can be kept on a chart holder and reread a number of times as a class or a group.

➡ Each child can illustrate his or her dictated stories in a creative way using art media such as markers, crayons, colored pencils, finger paints, watercolors, chalk, or tempera paint. Then all of the dictated LEA stories can be bound into a pre-made book and laminated to make them more durable. Here are the names of two books that contain reproducible patterns for ordinary and oversized book covers:

Evans, J., & Moore, J. (1984). *How to make books with children.* Monterey, CA: Evan-Moore.

Evans, J., Morgan, K., & Moore, J. (1989). *Making big books with children.* Monterey, CA: Evan-Moore.

The books can be fastened with a spiral binding (available at printing stores and office supply stores), three large rings, yarn, staples, or a number of other creative, durable ways. The books should be as attractive as possible so that other children and the child's family will find them interesting to look at. This also shows that the teacher or tutor values the child's thoughts.

➡ Each of the "published" LEA books can be put in the literacy center or library corner of the classroom so that other children can look at and read them. Many times children find dictated or child-written books to be among the most interesting of the materials they can read.

➡ Each child can make his or her own *word bank*. A word bank is a collection of all the words that the child has found interesting and useful from his or her LEA charts and stories. The child or the teacher prints each of these words on a piece of tagboard about 1" × 3" with a dark-colored marking pen or crayon. The child then files the words in his or her word bank container, which can be a large brown envelope, a shoe box, or some other suitable container. The child can review these words occasionally, use them in an oral or written sentence, and then return them to the word bank container to be studied again later. The word bank also can serve as an easy-to-locate source for the spelling of some commonly used and meaningful sight words. Here are some words from an LEA story about animals that live in the woods and eat candy: *house, raccoons, woods, candy, ate, bite, animals, wild.*

These are the main steps in LEA dictation of both experience charts and experience stories. They should be modified depending on each child's and each reading teacher or tutor's unique needs. Here are examples of actual LEA stories that were dictated by kindergarten children:

CANDY AND RACCOONS

We stayed in a house in the woods in the summer.

We saw a bunch of raccoons who lived in the woods.

They came by us when they saw us eating candy.

We gave them candy.

They even ate candy out of our pockets.

They didn't bite us.

You shouldn't feed raccoons.

We shouldn't have either.

Raccoons aren't tame animals.

They are wild animals.

You should be careful of them.

CROW

Crow is my neighbor's big black dog.

He's named Crow cause he's black I guess.

Crow is very friendly and tries to lick me all the time.

He likes to chase balls.

He likes "cookies."

His "cookies" really are dog treats.

When I say "Crow, do you want a 'cookie'?" he comes to me.

Then he grabs the dog treat out of my hand.

I really like Crow.

I wish he was my dog.

If you want to learn more about how to use LEA in a classroom or tutoring situation, you can read the following sources, among others:

Combs, M. (1996). *Developing competent readers and writers in the primary grades.* Upper Saddle River, NJ: Prentice Hall.

Cunningham, P., & Allington, R. (1994). *Classrooms that work: They all can read and write.* New York: HarperCollins.

Dixon, C. (1990). *Language experience approach to reading (and writing): LEA for ESL.* Upper Saddle River, NJ: Prentice Hall.

Neuman, S., Copple, C., & Bredekamp, S. (2000). *Developmentally appropriate practices for young children.* Newark, DE: International Reading Association.

Rigg, P. (1989). Language experience approach: Reading naturally. In P. Rigg and R. V. Allen (Eds.). *When they all don't speak English: Integrating the ESL student into the regular classroom* (pp. 65–76). Urbana, IL: National Council of Teachers of English.

Sampson, M., Sampson, M. B., & Allen, R. (1995). *Pathways to literacy.* Orlando, FL: Harcourt Brace College Publishers.

TRACING ACTIVITIES

The tracing strategies described earlier in this chapter for helping children to remember difficult letter names are equally valuable in helping children remember difficult sight words. These tracing strategies usually are the most helpful with children who have learning disabilities or severe reading disabilities and with children who have special reading needs. These children often cannot remember sight words taught by a conventional method. Because tracing is quite time-consuming, it should only be used with the sight words that seem especially difficult and should only be used as long as necessary.

Here are several tracing strategies that were described earlier in this chapter that can be used to help children remember difficult sight words:

➡ Instant pudding (the favorite with most children because they can lick their fingers and eat the pudding)
➡ Colored chalk sand tray
➡ Colored chalk salt tray
➡ Shaving cream
➡ Hair gel
➡ Oobleck
➡ Clay
➡ Pipe cleaners
➡ Playdough
➡ Letters of dough

When using instant pudding, shaving cream, hair gel, oobleck, or a sand or salt tray, have the child print the target sight word in the material, saying it aloud as he or she forms it. Have the child trace the word in the material as many times as necessary to remember the word. In each case have the child also use the word in a sentence. In using playdough, modeling clay, rice, or beans, the child can form the target sight word out of the material. Have the child trace the word enough times to ensure mastery and then use each word in a sentence. Refer to the section titled "Tracing or Tactile Strategies" for additional materials that can be used in tracing.

Puffed Word Cards

As a unique tracing strategy for children who have difficulty remembering sight words, you may want to make puffed word cards. These are three dimensional, textured, and tactile and help children to remember difficult sight words.

Here are the materials you will need to make puffed word cards.

➡ Paint Puffer™
➡ acrylic paint (red, green, or blue)

➡ $\frac{1}{4}$ inch art paint brush

➡ white tagboard or posterboard

Note: Paint Puffer™ is a nontoxic chemical formula that, when added to acrylic paint and heated, causes the paint to expand to 50 times its original volume. Paint Puffer™ can be ordered from most school supply companies. It also can be ordered from the following address (a 4-ounce bottle costs about $6.45):

Watson Place
Building 3-D
Framingham, MA 01701
1-800-365-1333

Here is the procedure to follow in constructing the puffed word cards: Cut white tagboard or posterboard into flash cards about 3" × 5" (3" × 8" if the sight word is long). Mix Paint Puffer™ with acrylic paint in a color of your choice. Mix about two parts of paint to one part of Paint Puffer™. Then, using an art paint brush, print sight words onto the flash cards with the paint/Paint Puffer™ mixture. The thickness of the paint film will determine the height of the "puffed word." The thicker the film, the higher the puffed word. If you want to have a very "tall" word, you can build up layers. Apply several heavy coats of the paint mixture, letting each coat dry several minutes before adding the next coat.

Next, you "puff" the words. The puffing occurs when heat is applied. The paint may be puffed either wet or dry. Heat a convection oven to about 230 degrees. Lay the flash cards on a cookie sheet in a single layer and put the cookie sheet into the oven. Dry paint will puff within seconds, while wet paint takes two or three minutes to puff. However, the puff will flatten out if the flash cards are left in the oven too long or if the oven temperature is above 250 degrees.

Note: The mixture of paint and Paint Puffer™ will keep indefinitely in a closed container. There also is no time limit between paint and puffing. Do not apply the Paint Puffer™ to thin paper as the edges will curl. This does not happen with tagboard or posterboard.

Here is the procedure for using the flash cards with a student who has great difficulty remembering sight words:

1. Show a word card to a student.

2. Tell the student to say the word.

3. Have the student say the word.

4. Have the student trace over the raised letters of the word with his or her index (pointer) finger of the hand with which he or she writes.

5. Have the student say the word again.

6. Have the student use the word in a sentence.

7. Have the student write the word on a sheet of paper, looking at the puffed word only as needed. This procedure should be repeated until the student can pronounce the word immediately.

Screen Board

A screen board is a tracing device that helps children learn difficult sight words. A screen board is made by attaching wire screening to a frame made out of four boards and fastening the screen with masking tape to cover the rough edges. The child then puts lightweight blank paper on top of the screen board. The child makes the target sight word by writing it on the paper with a dark crayon. Writing with crayon on top of the screen provides a raised texture that the child can trace with his or her finger while saying the sight word. Here is an illustration of a screen board.

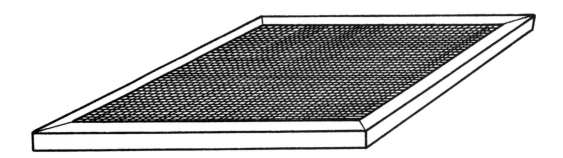

Magnetic Letters

Magnetic letters also can be used as a variation of a tracing strategy. The child should form each target sight word out of magnetic letters, saying the sight word aloud as he or she does so. If the child wants, he or she can form an entire sentence using magnetic letters. This type of activity is used in the contemporary Reading Recovery Program, an early intervention program for first-grade children with special needs. Sources of commercially available magnetic letters were given earlier in this chapter.

FOUR STRATEGIES FOR TEACHING SIGHT WORDS

Here are four teaching strategies that can be used with children who have a difficult time remembering sight words. Most often these are children who have special needs, such as learning or reading disabilities. Although none of these strategies are so time-consuming as tracing, they may be most useful with children who have moderate difficulty remembering sight words.

Cunningham (1980) has explained the following six steps in the "drastic" technique:

1. Write the target sight word on cards and give one card to each child.

2. Tell a story in which the target word is used several times. Have the children hold up their cards every time they hear the word.

3. Have children make up their own stories using the target sight word. As one child reads his or her story, the others hold up their cards when they hear the target word.

4. The word is cut into separate letters. Then children reassemble the letters to form the target word.

5. Write the target sight word on the chalkboard. Have children memorize the word and spell it from memory three times.

6. The word is put into story context.

Here is a useful three-step strategy for teaching difficult sight words to beginning readers:

1. *Seeing*—Write the target word on the chalkboard and pronounce it. Call attention to such features of the word as the initial consonant and word endings that are similar to words that were presented earlier. Use each word in a sentence so that its meaning can be determined from the sentence. When children are better readers, they will not need such a detailed introduction to new words.

2. *Discussing and defining*—When the meaning of the new word is not familiar to the children, you should discuss the word in detail. Students should use their prior knowledge to determine the meaning of the word, and they should consult the dictionary if they are not sure of its meaning.

3. *Using and writing*—Have the children use the new word in their speaking and writing. Ask one or more children to make up a sentence containing the word and write each of the sentences on the chalkboard, chart paper, or an overhead transparency. Beginning readers can include the words in their word banks. New words become completely learned in two ways: through repeated exposure when they occur often in sentences and stories that the children read, and when they are often used in children's writing.

Lapp and Flood (1986) have suggested the following procedure for teaching difficult sight words:

1. If possible, use pictures to illustrate the target sight word. Ask the children to look at the picture carefully and predict what is included in the passage.

2. Ask the children to read along with you as you read the various words. This will help them in deciding whether their predictions are correct or incorrect.

3. Have the children follow along as you reread the passage and point to the picture.

4. Encourage the children to read the passage aloud with you.

5. While the children are following the story visually, ask individual children to read a sentence.

6. When you have finished reading a sentence, stress the individual words by pointing out each of them to the children.

7. Discuss the meaning of each word and explain that some words, such as *a*, *an*, and *the*, serve as helping words to make sentences complete.

8. Emphasize those words with irregular spelling patterns, such as *one*, *once*, *who*, *of*, *off*, *where*, and *were*.

9. Frame each word with your hands so that your pupils become familiar with its length, configuration, beginning letters, ascenders, and descenders.

10. Have children reread the sentence aloud with you.

May (1994, pp. 161–162) has presented a meaning-based interactive procedure to help your pupils learn difficult sight words.

1. The teacher or tutor selects enjoyable predictable books, such as *Polar Bear, Polar Bear, What Do You See?* by B. Martin, Jr. (New York: Holt, Rinehart & Winston, 1972) or *The Cake that Mack Ate* by R. Robart (Toronto, Canada: Kids Can Press, 1986).

2. The teacher or tutor then reads the book aloud.

3. The teacher or tutor reads the book aloud again with the children joining in whenever they can predict what comes next.

4. The children take turns *echoing* (the teacher or tutor reads first and then the children repeat what he or she has read) and *choral reading*.

5. The teacher or tutor reads the text from teacher-made charts with no pictures.

6. The children put matching sentence strips on the charts. (The teacher should make the charts so that a sentence strip can be taped *directly under* each sentence in the chart.)

7. The children later place matching word strips on the charts, saying the words in order the first time this is done and in random order later.

8. The children and teacher or tutor read the entire story aloud together.

9. The teacher or tutor places word strips in random order at the bottom of the chart. The children then come up and match the strips to words in the story, saying each word as they match it to the one in the story.

10. The children write the target words as well as read them. This will help them remember the words.

ANIMAL TACHISTOSCOPE

Using a hand tachistoscope is an effective way to encourage children to practice sight words. Although a tachistoscope can be constructed without an animal theme, most children find it more interesting if it is made in the shape of an animal, such as a lion, dog, cat, pig, or horse. It also can be made to reflect a holiday theme, such as a pumpkin, turkey, Santa Claus, snowman, heart, or shamrock.

How to Construct a Tachistoscope in the Shape of a Lion

Trace a lion pattern on a sheet of tracing paper. Place the tracing paper on top of a sheet of carbon paper. Place these on top of a piece of white posterboard. Trace over the tracing to transfer the lion drawing onto the posterboard. Remove the tracing paper and carbon paper. Color the lion with marking pens or colored pencils and then cut out the lion and laminate it. Trim the laminating film from the cut-out lion. Using an art knife, cut two horizontal slots about $2\frac{1}{2}$" long and 1" apart on the lion's body. Cut a piece of white tagboard into strips about 2" × 12" and laminate them. (See the illustrations.)

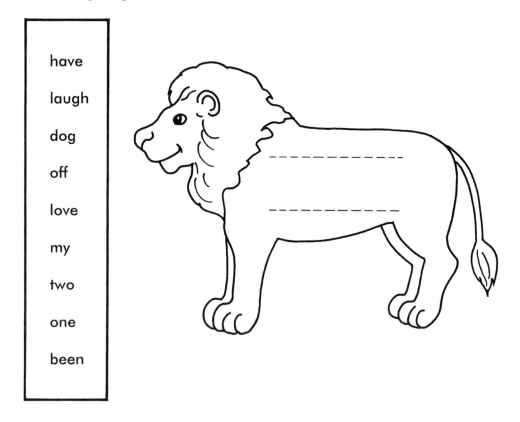

have

laugh

dog

off

love

my

two

one

been

How to Use the Lion Tachistoscope

Choose some sight words with which the child needs review. Using a marking pen, print the sight words on the laminated paper strip, one under the other and about 1" apart. Place the word strip behind the lion tachistoscope and thread it through the bottom slot and then back through the top slot. To use it, slide the word strip up to expose a word. Have the child identify the word. Then pull the word strip up to expose the next word and ask another child to identify that word. Continue in this way.

When you are finished with the sight word practice using the lion tachistoscope, remove the word strip and wipe off the words with a damp paper towel. New words can then be written on the word strip. After some practice, a child can use the tachistoscope for independent practice or for practice with a reading partner(s).

COMPUTER SOFTWARE

Many different types of computer software can be used for meaningful, interesting practice in sight word recognition and identification. Because sight word knowledge is a low-level reading skill, children can easily practice it using computer software.

When evaluating computer software for this purpose, be sure the practice is meaningful and useful. There is no point spending money for software that does not offer worthwhile, appropriate practice. Some of the software packages in this area are not relevant and should not be used.

Computer software packages are being developed and are becoming obsolete almost daily, so this book does not list any of them. Such a list would be outdated almost as soon as it was written. Instead, you should look at the appropriate software catalogs or attend reading conferences when you are ready to select such software packages for your pupils.

OTHER STRATEGIES

The rest of this section briefly describes several other classroom-tested strategies that can be used for improving ability in sight word identification. Use them in their present form or modify any of them to meet the needs and interests of your pupils.

⟼ *Word masking*—This is a variation of the cloze procedure (see Chapter 5) that can be used at the beginning stages of reading. Children can follow along as a big book is being read aloud. During the second reading of the big book, some of the words are covered over by masking tape or sticky notes. When the teacher or tutor reaches one of them, he or she pauses, and the children try to predict what the word might be. After they answer, the word is uncovered, and the children are asked if they were correct or not. In the word-masking cloze procedure, sight word identification, contextual analysis, and comprehension are stressed.

⟼ *Word window*—Cut a window in either a 3" × 5" index card or a small card of posterboard so that the child can hold it directly over words in dictated language-experience charts to frame or isolate the target sight word. A similar window can be made to frame target sight words in children's picture storybooks, although a word window in a book is probably less effective than in an experience chart because the print in the book is so much smaller. Here is an example of a word window.

⟼ *Macaroni sight words*—With a marking pen, write the alphabet letters on macaroni and make ten of each letter. Write the sight words you wish to emphasize on word cards about 3" × 5". Then give each child some heavy, stiff twine and have him or her string the sight words that are found on the word cards. Children should string the letters in the proper order to spell the words on the cards. Here is an illustration of this activity.

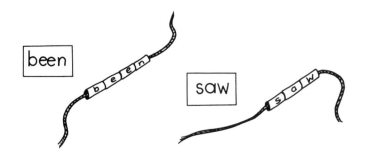

➡ *Writing a sight word story*—Have children create stories about target sight words or draw pictures illustrating them.

➡ *Cut-out sight words*—Have children look in old newspapers and magazines for target sight words and cut them out after finding them. Then have them make a collage using the cut-out sight words.

➡ *Recognizing function (structure) words*—In the humorous trade book *Who Sank the Boat?* by P. Allen (New York: Coward-McCann, 1982), the opening sentence contains a total of 22 words, 10 or 45% of which are function words. Here is the opening sentence: "Beside the sea on Mr. Peffer's place, there lived a cow, a donkey, a sheep, a pig, and a tiny little mouse." The pupil who can recognize function words immediately is well on the way to fluent reading.

➡ *Categorization*—Have a child categorize the sight words found in his or her word bank. They can be categorized as action words, animals, colors, words related to the family, words related to school, words related to home, and feeling words, among others.

➡ *Sentence strip*—Have a pupil write a sentence strip from a language-experience chart or from one of the trade books he or she has recently read. Then have the child cut apart the sentence strip into words and try to reassemble the sentence in correct order. If you want, the cut-apart sentence can be written on very large index cards and placed on the floor to reassemble them. Cut-apart sentence strips are used in the Reading Recovery Early Intervention Program for at-risk first-grade children.

➡ *Word wheel*—Construct a word wheel to provide review in identifying difficult sight words. To make a word wheel, cut out one circular disk about 6" × 8" in diameter and a somewhat larger circular disk. Print target sight words with a marking pen on the larger of the two disks. Cut a sight word window on the smaller disk so that each sight word on the larger disk is visible as the smaller disk is turned. Fasten the two disks with a brad so that the smaller disk can be turned easily, exposing each of the sight words. The child is to immediately pronounce each sight word as it appears in the word window. Here is an illustration of a word wheel.

➡ *Making and breaking sight words*—On 3" × 5" index cards write five sample cards of each target sight word. Use large letters and add cutting lines on each card. Make one model card for each word card. Place each set of cards in a large brown envelope. Have the pupils cut the word cards on each cutting line and then rebuild the words below the model cards. Have children continue practicing each sight word until it is learned. Here is an illustration of this activity.

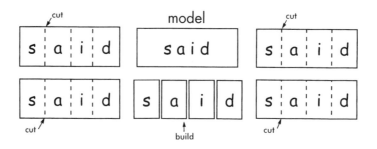

GAMES FOR IMPROVING SIGHT WORD KNOWLEDGE

This section contains several games that reading teachers and tutors have used to improve sight word knowledge. As stated earlier, research has shown that children make good gains in reading skills when they are playing active games in comparison with practice using activity sheets (Dickerson, 1983). However, such games should stress reading skills, not merely playing the games. The games included in this section have proven especially motivating with beginning readers.

Sight Word Checkers

TO CONSTRUCT THE GAME

Obtain six pieces of posterboard about 8" × 8", poker chips (eight of one color and eight of another color), and a marking pen. Using the six pieces of posterboard, lay out six game boards similar to the one illustrated. You should use a different list of target sight words for each of the game boards.

from	which	stop	were	buy	of
woɹɟ	ɥɔıɥʍ	doʇs	ǝɹǝʍ	ʎnq	ɟo
many	they	does	what	how	love
ʎuɐɯ	ʎǝɥʇ	sǝop	ʇɐɥʍ	ʍoɥ	ǝʌol
are	his	any	boy	is	one
ǝɹɐ	sıɥ	ʎuɐ	ʎoq	sı	ǝuo
than	would	there	dog	why	mother
uɐɥʇ	plnoʍ	ǝɹǝɥʇ	бop	ʎɥʍ	ɹǝɥʇoɯ
orange	blue	by	girl	once	said
ǝбuɐɹo	ǝnlq	ʎq	lɹıб	ǝɔuo	pıɐs
spot	star	where	have	off	who
ʇods	ɹɐʇs	ǝɹǝɥʍ	ǝʌɐɥ	ɟɟo	oɥʍ

TO PLAY THE GAME

Have the child choose one of the sight word checkerboards and pick a friend (or the reading tutor) to play the game with him or her. Each player takes a set of colored chips. In order for the child to be able to move, he or she must identify the word he or she has landed on. The other player should be sure the word is pronounced correctly. A player may jump the partner's chips just as in a game of regular checkers. The player with more chips of the opposite color at the end of the game is the winner.

Sight Word Tic-Tac-Toe

TO PREPARE THE GAME

Arrange nine chairs in the center of the room in a tic-tac-toe formation. Then divide the children in a group or the class into two teams—the *X*'s and the *O*'s. Write target sight words on word cards that are large enough for the children to see easily.

TO PLAY THE GAME

Flash a target sight word. The child whose turn it is must pronounce the word correctly. If the sight word is pronounced correctly, the child takes the card with an *X* or *O* depending on his or her team and chooses a chair to sit on. The first team to get three *X*'s or *O*'s in a row is the winner.

Memory (Concentration)

TO CONSTRUCT THE GAME

Make target sight words out of posterboard. Make two sets of identical word cards. Then place the cards face down on a flat surface, such as a table or desk.

TO PLAY THE GAME

Shuffle the two sets of cards and place them separately on the table or desk. Then have a player turn up a card on one set and try to find the card that matches in the other set. When he or she has made a match, have the child pronounce the word and, if correct, keep the card. Then the other player has a turn. The winner is the player who has made the most matches and pronounced the words correctly.

Sight Word Airplane

TO CONSTRUCT THE GAME

Cut an oatmeal carton in half and decorate it to represent an airplane hangar. Draw a spiral path on a sheet of construction paper with the airplane hangar at the end of the path. Divide the path into sections on each of which is printed a target sight word. Make a set of 1" × 2" word cards with target sight words printed on them with a dark marking pen.

TO PLAY THE GAME

Two players should have an object that represents an airplane and duplicate sets of cards with the same target sight words printed on them as are on the path. The game begins with the airplanes at the end of the path and each player's cards placed face up. The first player reads the words on his or her top card. If the word is the same as the one in the first space on the path, his or her airplane is moved to that space. If it is not, the player may not move. His or her card is placed on the bottom of the deck, and the other player takes a turn. The winner is the player whose airplane reaches the hangar first.

Fishing for Sight Words

TO CONSTRUCT THE GAME

Print the target sight words with a dark marker on individual fish about 1" × 2". (See the following fish pattern.) Attach a paper clip to the head of each fish. Construct a "fishing pole" by using a ruler or stick with a string attached to it. Tie a small magnet to the end of the string.

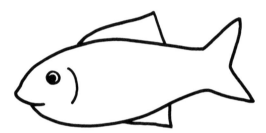

TO PLAY THE GAME

Place all of the "fish" containing the sight words into a container, such as a decorated shoe box or a fish bowl without water. Then have the child fish for each sight word using the fishing pole. As the child is able to "land" a fish, he or she must identify the sight word. If the child can do so, he or she keeps the fish. If the child cannot identify the sight word written on the fish, he or she must "throw" it back into the container.

If you wish, two or more children can take turns fishing for sight words, and the child who has caught the most fish after a specified time period is the winner.

Feed the Chimpanzee

TO CONSTRUCT THIS GAME

Cut out a large stand-up figure of some favorite animal, such as a chimpanzee. Give the chimpanzee a large, wide-open mouth behind which a paper bag is stapled. Print sight words on small cards that are shaped like bananas.

TO PLAY THE GAME

Have the child choose a word card from the stack of word cards. When the child has identified the selected word card correctly (and used it in a sentence if you want), he or she can put the banana into the chimpanzee's mouth (and into the paper bag). When a child cannot identify the word correctly, you can show that word to the child, identify it, and put it back with the other uneaten "bananas." When all of the sight words have been identified, the words can be pronounced again and counted to see how well the chimpanzee has "eaten."

As a variation, only the words correctly identified the first time will be fed to the chimpanzee. These words can then be counted, and you can mention that the chimpanzee probably is still hungry. To help the chimpanzee be "well fed," all of the bananas can again be identified and fed to the chimpanzee.

Bang

TO CONSTRUCT THE GAME

Cover a Pringle™ potato chip can with red self-stick vinyl or red construction paper. Attach a piece of heavy string through the plastic lid and use aluminum foil to make a firecracker wick. Print the letters *BANG* on the can. Cut posterboard into cards about 1" × 2" and print the target sight words on these cards. Print the word *BANG* on several of these cards. Then shake the can often to mix up the words.

TO PLAY THE GAME

Have the children take turns drawing a card and identifying each sight word. If the child can correctly identify the sight word, he or she is able to keep the card. If the child cannot identify the sight word or draws the word *BANG*, he or she must return all of the cards to the can. The first child to collect ten cards (or any other number of cards) is the winner of the game.

Getting Chips

TO CONSTRUCT THE GAME

Divide the words on a basic sight word list into four sections of fifty-five words each. Type or write the sight words on folder labels or masking tape and put them on poker chips of four colors. Put the chips in four small boxes of matching colors.

TO PLAY THE GAME

Have a child begin the game by choosing a color and giving the spinner a whirl. The child then picks as many chips from his or her color section as the spinner indicates. If the child cannot say any one of the words, he or she is told what it is. However, the child must return this chip to the box and pass the spinner to the next player. The winner of this game is the child who has gotten the most chips. The game can be played with several children.

REPRODUCIBLES FOR IMPROVING SIGHT WORD KNOWLEDGE

This section contains several ready-to-duplicate activity sheets that you may want to use to improve your pupils' ability in sight word knowledge. You can duplicate and use any of these activity sheets in their present form or modify them in any way you want. Activity sheets may be of value if they are not overused. Children often enjoy completing activity sheets (Miller, 1998).

FINDING AND WRITING SIGHT WORDS
First-Grade Level

Look at the word on each line. Then put a circle around each letter after it to make the word. Then write the word on the line. The first one is done for you.

1. once   t (o) r v (n) x (c) (e) g l   _____*once*_____

2. laugh   l p c a m u t r g h   _____

3. have   a c h o b a w v s e   _____

4. of   o q g w f y s n t z   _____

5. one   o q s r t n e a b d   _____

6. father   c f a b x t h e y r   _____

7. two   t m w m n o r s w a   _____

8. said   t s a c r y i e d t   _____

9. does   d r p o e r s t w a   _____

10. come   a c e o m e p e t y   _____

SEARCHING FOR LOST ANIMALS
Upper Primary-Grade Level

Circle all the animal names that you can find in this word search. Their names go across, backward, and up and down. The names of the animals that are lost are at the bottom of this sheet.

```
r o f o x q r t s b m o n k e y f a s h
x y r n g o d b y t m r a c c o o n t s
c t t l i o n b l y v m n b h q f t x s
a u n l o p t n b v c g i p w w r f d r
t x e n b h b e a r w w o o e s u o m c
h i p p o p o t a m u s x o f u t m n b
s b y n b c p o e h n m w e s k u n k o
b i e f f a r i g p i j y n b v l o u t
p o r c u p i n e r a c z e b r a c o o
e r s t n a h p e l e r e e q b z x o u
```

zebra	dog	lion	giraffe	monkey
cat	raccoon	porcupine	bear	hippopotamus
mouse	pig	skunk	elephant	fox

221

CAN YOU SOLVE THIS SUMMER PUZZLE?
Upper Primary-Grade Level

Use the words in the box to solve this puzzle.

CANOE	HAPPY
VISITING	FISHING
AUTOMOBILE	BOATING
SWIMMING	LAKE

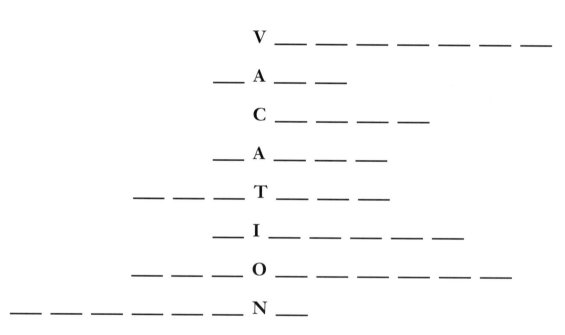

V __ __ __ __ __ __ __

__ A __ __

C __ __ __ __

__ A __ __ __

__ __ __ T __ __ __

__ I __ __ __ __ __

__ __ __ O __ __ __ __ __

__ __ __ __ __ __ N __

Name _____ Grade _____

PICK THE RIGHT WORD
Second-Grade Level

Read each sentence and write the correct word in the blank.

1. Jamie didn't say _____ he was going after school.
                  where   were

2. When I was eating lunch, I spilled my soup and got a _____
                                                      stop   spot

   on my shirt.

3. We hope _____ puppy didn't get out of the yard.
                our   are

4. How has Mr. Black _____ since he went on a trip?
                      been   be

5. Do you think you _____ be able to come to the
                        well   will

   picnic tomorrow?

6. _____ is that woman I saw driving a blue car?
    Who   How

7. Rich _____ going to go to the circus yesterday.
        saw   was

8. Mrs. Jackson's dog only had _____ puppies last month.
                     two   twig

9. _____ one of the children do you like the best?
    When   Which

10. Joey and his family _____ to the lake last summer.
                want   went

RAPID VISUAL TRACKING
Fourth-Grade Level

The word *feather* appears 15 times in this activity sheet. Move your eyes from *left to right* as quickly as possible and circle the word *feather* each time you see it.

fancy feather enormous family fanciful breakfast everyone

lasso feather century mathematics prairie feather octopus

license feather attention prospect fishing supper marry feather

international computer feather difficult word crayon illustration

feather television vacation winter rhythm teacher sponge wolf

mare mountains horizon volcano feather ledge steak autumn

gnaw hippopotamus advantage feather tornado vinegar vanish

puzzle science pride feather fancy factory travel cattle

monkey airport feather paper correct principal reader program

feather fasten difference write chalkboard pencil sentence

birthday comma blank feather frame jacket kitchen something

mammal vowel feather intelligent scientist example float language

study father taught predict locate woman earth disguise feather

learn vegetable knife strong lucky summer suppose

FOR ADDITIONAL READING

Burns, P., Roe, B., & Ross, E. (1996). *Teaching reading in today's elementary schools* (pp. 94–103). Boston: Houghton Mifflin.

Chall, J. (1996). *Learning to read: The great debate.* Fort Worth: Harcourt Brace College Publishers.

Gunning, T. (1996). *Creating reading instruction for all children* (pp. 55–58 & 122–132). Boston: Allyn & Bacon.

Heilman, A., Blair, T., & Rupley, W. (1998). *Principles and practices of teaching reading* (pp. 151–161). Upper Saddle River, NJ: Prentice Hall.

Machado, J. (1995). *Early childhood experiences in language arts* (pp. 373–383). NY: Delmar Publishers.

May, F. (1998). *Reading as communication* (pp. 142–172). Upper Saddle River, NJ: Prentice Hall.

McAllister, E. (1987). *Primary reading skills activity kit* (pp. 124–134). West Nyack, NY: The Center for Applied Research in Education.

Miller, W. (2000). *Strategies for developing emergent literacy* (pp. 79–127). Boston: McGraw-Hill Higher Education.

Muncy, P. (1995). *Complete book of illustrated reading and writing activities for the primary grades* (pp. 3–14 & 119–172). West Nyack, NY: The Center for Applied Research in Education.

Shanker, J., & Ekwall, E. (late). (1998). *Locating and correcting reading difficulties* (pp. 29–30, 245–249, 91–100, & 251–269. Columbus, OH: Merrill/Prentice Hall.

Vacca, J., Vacca, R., & Gove, M. (1995). *Reading and learning to read* (pp. 134–135 & 270–277). NY: HarperCollins College Publishers.

WORKS CITED IN CHAPTER 3

Allen, R. (1976). *Language experiences in communication.* Boston: Houghton Mifflin.

Cunningham, P. (1980). Teaching were, with, what, and other "four-letter" words. *The Reading Teacher, 34,* 160–163.

Dickerson, D. (1983). A study of the use of games to reinforce sight vocabulary. *The Reading Teacher, 36,* 46–49.

Durrell, D. (1980). Letter-name value in reading and spelling. *Reading Research Quarterly, 16,* 159–163.

Ehri, L. (1991). Development of the ability to read words. In R. Barr, M. Kamil, P. Rosenthal, & P. D. Pearson (Eds.), *Handbook of reading research: volume II* (pp. 383–417). NY: Longman.

Fry, E., Kress, J., & Fountoukidis, D. (2000). *The reading teacher's book of lists*, fourth edition. Paramus, NJ: Prentice Hall.

Lapp, E., & Flood, J. (1986). *Teaching students to read.* NY: Macmillan.

May, F. (1998). *Reading as communication.* Upper Saddle River, NJ: Prentice Hall.

McBroom, M., Sparrow, J., & Eckstein, C. (1944). *Scale for determining a child's reading level.* Iowa City, IA: Bureau of Publications, Extension Service, University of Iowa, p. 11.

Miller, W. (1998). First-grade children's perceptions of reading. *Arizona Reading Quarterly, 25*, 7–12.

Richek, M. (1997–1998). Readiness skills that predict initial word learning using two different methods of instruction. *Reading Research Quarterly, 13*, 200–222.

Samuels, J. (1967). Attentional process in reading: The effect of pictures in the acquisition of reading responses. *Journal of Educational Research, 58*, 337–342.

————. (1994). Toward a theory of automatic information processing in reading revisited. In R. Ruddell, M. Ruddell, & H. Singer (Eds.), *Theoretical models and processes in reading* (pp. 816–837). Newark, DE: International Reading Association.

Shanker, J., & Ekwall, E. (late). (1998). *Locating and correcting reading difficulties* (pp. 261 & 263). Columbus, OH: Merrill/Prentice Hall.

Singer, H., Samuels, J., & Spiroff, J. (1973–1974). The effect of pictures and contextual conditions on learning responses to printed words. *Reading Research Quarterly, 9*, 555–567.

Chapter 4

IMPROVING ABILITY IN PHONICS

"Schools are not teaching phonics today, and that is why so many kids are just not learning to read." Have you heard anyone make a statement like this? It is likely that you have. This probably is the most common criticism leveled at elementary schools today. Is this a valid criticism or a convenient excuse for the falling reading test scores that are common today in a number of schools?

Certainly, too many children are not learning to read well, and part of the reason *may be* the lack of systematic phonic instruction in the primary grades. However, because reading is a complex process, there are many other reasons for poor reading achievement in addition to the lack of phonics instruction.

However, phonics is an important word identification skill that should be mastered by most children at least to an extent. The lack of structured phonic instruction that may occur in a total whole language program may have contributed to lowered reading scores. Most children should be competent in the most important phonic elements by the time they are in the intermediate grades.

This chapter provides information about the importance of phonics, phonic elements, and many classroom-tested, easy-to-use strategies and materials for teaching phonics. The chapter also includes a number of motivating phonic games and reproducibles that can be used for reviewing various phonic elements. After reading this chapter, you should feel competent to teach phonic skills to any students whom you are teaching or tutoring, including children with special needs such as learning or reading disabilities.

PHONEMIC AWARENESS

Phonemic awareness is an important skill in which children should be competent before being exposed to phonics instruction. In the past, phonemic awareness was called auditory discrimination. It is an emergent literacy skill that is helpful in preparing children for success in phonics whether phonics is taught using integrated themes or in isolation.

Phonemic awareness consists of skills such as the following:

➡ Listening for and repeating the rhyming patterns found in the material.

➡ Listening to predictable books and then "reading" them along with the teacher or tutor.

➡ Being able to discriminate between pairs of words that are pronounced orally or on cassette tape. Some word pairs should be alike while some should be different. The child should indicate whether the pairs of words are alike or different. Here are several word pairs that can be used for this purpose:

run—ran	bit—bet
man—man	pat—pet
tub—tug	got—pot
cube—tube	fast—fast
ten—ten	top—tap

➡ Being able to discriminate among objects, some of which begin with the target sound and some which do not. Some objects—for example, for the phoneme /d/— are *doll*, *duck*, ball, *dish*, fork.

➡ Being able to discriminate between pictures that represent minimal pairs of words. Each pair of pictures should be placed on a table or desk and the child should point to the picture whose word you say. For example, for the word pairs *bat* and *hat* ask the child to point to the picture of the *hat*.

➡ Being able to rhyme words. The child should understand the concept of rhyming words and be able to provide several rhyming words for the target word. Some of these can be nonsense words. Here are some rhyming words for the target word *bump: dump, fump, gump, hump, lump, mump, nump, pump, sump,* and *wump.*

THE RELATIONSHIP BETWEEN PHONICS AND READING

The lack of systematic phonic instruction has been blamed for causing many reading problems. Reading is complex, so it is important to remember that lack of phonic instruction is only one cause. Certainly, a person can read adequately or even well with limited or no phonics skills. However, some knowledge of phonics is extremely helpful for readers as they attempt to identify unknown words. Although phonics is an important word identification technique, used alone it is not the most important one. It becomes the most important technique when it is combined with context, as in the following examples:

Josef would like to receive a _____ for a pet.

Josef would like to receive a k_____ for a pet.

It is obvious that the addition of the consonant *k* helps the reader determine that *kitten* is the most likely answer. Therefore, phonics is the most effective when it is combined with context while reading.

It is true that young children in the primary grades who have systematic phonic training perform more effectively on reading achievement tests than those who do not. Systematic phonic training is usually provided most effectively by some type of formal phonic program, such as those mentioned later in this chapter. Although such children outperform children without formal phonic training in the primary grades, this initial advantage often does not continue through the intermediate grades, middle school, or high school. The students without formal phonic training often catch up in reading performance.

Phonics instruction can be taught in isolation, as is done in most formal phonic programs, or in context, as is done in whole language programs and in many basal reader programs. Although integrated phonics instruction may be successful for children with good or even average linguistic aptitude, often it is not successful with children who have special needs, such as learning or reading disabilities. Such children usually need a structured phonic program with much concrete repetition and overlearning of the phonic skills.

Whole language programs without the inclusion of much phonics often are not successful in teaching reading to children with special needs. Although they may be effective with linguistically adept children, they are not effective with most special needs children. A number of states, notably California, currently are mandating the teaching of many more phonic skills than has been done in the recent past due to falling reading test scores. These lowered test scores were thought to be the result of the use of total whole language programs. This may or may not be the case.

In any case, this author (along with many other reading specialists) believes that the important phonic elements and rules should be taught to all children who can learn them. A possible exception may be children with very poor phonemic awareness skills. It also is most helpful to teach phonics in both integrated and isolated settings to benefit the most students. It is important for all children with special needs, such as learning disabilities and reading disabilities, to have a structured phonic program with plenty of meaningful repetition.

A BRIEF DESCRIPTION OF PHONICS

Phonics (also known as *graphophonics* or *graphonics)* is the study of speech sounds and their relation to decoding in reading. Decoding literally means "breaking the code," which in the case of reading refers to the alphabetic code. Many reading specialists, including this author, believe that competency in phonics is necessary to ensure a child's success in reading. For example, Adams (1990) has stated the following after completing a comprehensive study on beginning reading that was commissioned by Congress:

> In summary, deep and thorough knowledge of letters, spelling patterns, and words, and of the phonological translations of all three, are of inescapable importance to both skillful reading and its acquisition. By extension, instruction designed to help children's sensitivity to spellings and their relations to pronunciation should be of paramount importance in the development of reading skills (p. 416).

In summarizing Adams's research, Stahl, Osborne, and Lehr (1990) stated the following:

> Insufficient familiarity with the spellings and spelling-to-sound correspondence of frequent words and syllables may be the *single most common source of reading difficulties* [emphasis mine] (p. 115).

Reading teachers and tutors should understand that phonics is *a means to effective reading, not an end in itself.* Phonic analysis is only *one technique* that children should use in identifying words, although it is an important one. Adams (1990) summarizes the usefulness of phonics:

> The goal of teaching phonics is to develop students' abilities to read connected text independently. For students, however, the strongest functional connection between these two skills may run in the reverse direction. It is only the nature of reading that can make the content of a phonic lesson seem sensible; it is only the prospect of reading that can make them seem worthwhile (p. 272).

GUIDELINES TO PHONICS INSTRUCTION AND THE TWO MAIN APPROACHES TO TEACHING PHONICS

There is no real purpose for a child to know that the */i/* in the word *did* is short unless the child is able to decode the word successfully. In addition, a phonic skill that children already know should *not* be taught to them as this is a waste of time. Any student who is reading on the fourth-grade level or above probably already possesses most, if not all, of the phonic skills that he or she ever will need to know. As much as possible, the phonic skills that are taught should be related to the reading tasks in which students currently are participating or soon will be participating. For example, a good time to teach the sound of the consonant */d/* is when the children are going to read the interesting trade book *Duncan the Dancing Duck* by S. Hoff (New York: Clarion Books, 1994). Sometimes children are taught phonic skills before they are given the opportunity to use them. Research has shown that children do not use phonic information unless the skills that they have been taught are applicable to the present reading instruction (Adams, 1990).

To summarize, phonics instruction should be *systematic, but also should be meaningful, functional, and contextual.* However, it is especially important that it be *systematic* for children with special reading needs, such as learning or reading disabilities.

The two main approaches to teaching phonics are *analytic* and *synthetic.* In *analytic phonic analysis,* which also is called *implicit phonics,* consonants usually are not taught in isolation because researchers think the consonant sounds are distorted in isolation. Consonants are taught instead within the context of an entire word. For example, the sound */b/* is referred to as the sound that is heard at the beginning of the words *baby, ball,* and *boy.* In analytic phonics the sound */b/* is not pronounced in isolation as *buh* because that is distorted, because there is no *"buh"* syllable in *baby, ball,* or *boy.*

In *synthetic phonic analysis*, which also is called *explicit phonics*, each word is decoded sound by sound, and both consonant and vowel sounds are pronounced in isolation. For example, in saying the word *cat*, the child would say *"cuh-a-tuh."* In this approach the consonant sounds often are distorted because they cannot be pronounced without a vowel sound being added. A number of children have great difficulty determining how a word is pronounced using synthetic phonic analysis because they are not proficient in *auditory blending* and because the consonant sounds are distorted.

Although most contemporary basal reader series recommend using only analytic phonic analysis, *this author recommends using a combination of analytic and synthetic phonic analysis.* Some children, especially those with learning or reading disabilities, are unable to discriminate between the individual sounds unless they are presented and practiced in isolation. This is especially true in the case of the short vowel sounds, and it also is the case to some extent with consonant sounds. A number of reading specialists, including this author, believe that the single best way of teaching young children to decode words is by *analogy (word families)*. Analogy involves using *onsets (beginning consonants, consonant blends, or consonant digraphs)* and *rimes (word families)*.

Analogy is a technique in which words are taught in *rimes*, such as the following:

m-an

p-an

c-an

f-an

r-an

v-an

pl-an

Usually the first word in a group of words is taught as the *header*, and the children are then helped to generalize (determine) the identification of the words in that group. Usually an *onset* composed of an initial consonant is attached to the rest of the word (the rime). Consonant blends or consonant digraphs can be added later. Here are a few examples of rimes to which initial consonants, consonant blends, or consonant digraphs can be added:

-ab, -ack, -ad, -ade, -ag, -ake, -alk, -ame, -all, -am, -an, -ark, -ate, -eat, -eld, -end, -id, -ift, -ink, -oke, -old, -ook, -oon, -ub, -uck, -ump, -unk, -it, oad, -oat, -op, -ot -ote, oud,

THE MOST COMMON PHONIC ELEMENTS AND RULES

Because the area of phonics and phonic analysis is complex, this book provides only a brief introduction to the subject. An interested reading teacher or tutor should refer to one or more of the useful resource books on this subject that are included later in this chapter. Many books have been devoted solely to the subject of phonics.

Phonemes are defined as the *sounds* that occur in a language. There are forty-four or forty-five phonemes in English depending on what source is consulted. A phoneme is either written as a letter or, more often, as a phonetic symbol between slash marks: /*m*/. A *grapheme* is the written symbol for a phoneme or sound. A grapheme can be composed of one or more letters. For example, it takes the two letters *s* and *h* to represent the single phoneme /*sh*/. There are about 251 graphemes in written English. Thus, English does *not* have a regular phoneme–grapheme relationship.

CONSONANTS

A *consonant* is caused when the outgoing breath stream is blocked by an organ of speech. The organs of speech are the hard palate, the soft palate, the larynx, the tongue, the teeth, the lips, and the vocal cords. When the blockage is complete, the resulting sounds are known as *plosives* or *stops*. Those in which the blockage is partial are called *continuants*. Continuants also are classified as voiced or voiceless depending on whether or not the vocal cords vibrate while producing the sound.

Here are some examples of plosives:

k	kite	g	go
p	pay	b	baby
t	toy	d	did

These nasal sounds are one type of continuants:

m	mitten	n	nose

Fricatives are continuants that are made when the outgoing breath escapes with audible friction:

f	for	v	violet
s	sell	z	zebra
h	him		
th	think (voiceless)		them (voiced)
ch	chain	j	joy
sh	shoe		

The *liquids* are the following:

r	rabbit	l	like

The *glides* are as follows:

y	yellow	w	wish

CONSONANT BLENDS

A *consonant blend* (*consonant cluster*) consists of two or three consonant letters that appear together. Each consonant retains some element of its own sound while blending with that of the others. Although most consonant blends occur at the beginning of words, they also can be found at the end.

Here are examples of common consonant blends:

bl	black	br	break	cl	clap
cr	crow	dr	drum	fl	fly
fr	fry	gl	glass	gr	grow
pl	play	pr	price	sc	score
sk	skip	sm	smile	sn	snake
sp	spot	spl	split	spr	spring
st	stay	str	string	sw	swing
tr	tray	tw	twin		

CONSONANT DIGRAPHS

A *consonant digraph* is composed of two consonants that record a single sound that is different from the sound that either one would record separately. Here are examples of consonant digraphs:

ch	chin	sh	ship
th (voiceless)	thin	th (voiced)	these
wh	what	ph	photograph
ng	ring	gh	tough

VOWELS

Vowels result when the organs of speech modify the resonance chamber without stopping the flow of the outgoing breath. All vowels are voiced, and there are no nasal vowels in English. One vowel is distinguished from another by the quality of its sound. Here are examples of the vowels:

a	apron	a	ant	a	air
a	walk	a	far		
a	father				
e	me	e	egg	e	learn
e	her	e	bear	e	sergeant
i	ice	i	igloo	i	skirt

o	rope	o	ostrich	o	often
o	or	o	word		
u	use	u	cube	u	umbrella
u	burn				
y	try	y	baby	y	hymn

w   cow (diphthong—see the explanation in the following discussion)

y   toy (diphthong—see the explanation in the following discussion)

THE SCHWA SOUND

The *schwa sound* ə is the unstressed vowel sound in a word of more than one syllable. Any one of the five vowel letters can be the schwa sound when it is found in an unaccented syllable. The schwa sound has a sound that is similar to that of the short *u*. Here are some words that contain the schwa sound:

a	bedlam	e	label	i	pencil
o	beckon	u	minus		

DIPHTHONGS

A *diphthong* is composed of two vowel sounds that together record one sound that is different from the sound that either of them would have recorded separately. Here are several examples of words that contain a diphthong:

ow cow	ou out	oy soy	oi oil
ew new			

VOWEL DIGRAPHS

A *vowel digraph* occurs when two adjacent vowels record one sound. Here are some words that contain a vowel digraph:

ai train	ay pay	
ee beet	ea beat, head, great	
ie pie		
oa boat	oe hoe	ow crow
oo cook	oo noon	oo blood
ui fruit		

RIMES

A *rime (word family, phonogram,* or *graphemic base)* is a group of vowels and consonants that usually are pronounced and learned as a unit. These are used in teaching phonics with the use of analogies. It is a group of letters to which onsets (initial consonants, initial consonant blends, or consonant digraphs) are attached. Earlier in this chapter we listed a number of rimes. A comprehensive listing of rimes is found in the following resource:

Fry, E., Kress, J., & Fountoukidis, D. (2000). *The reading teacher's book of lists,* Fourth Edition. Paramus, NJ: Prentice Hall, pp. 55–63.

HOMOPHONES

A *homophone* is a word that is pronounced the same as another word but has a different spelling and meaning. Here are some examples:

air—heir	ant—aunt	ate—eight
bail—bale	bare—bear	bazaar—bizarre
boar—bore	burro—burrow	bread—bred
broach—brooch	capital—capitol	cereal—serial
close—clothes	deer—dear	desert (v.)—dessert
ewe—yew—you	flew—flu—flue	grate—great
hail—hale	heal—heel—he'll	hoarse—horse
hole—whole	knead—need	knot—not
lie—lye	made—maid	miner—minor
muscle—mussel	pair—pare—pear	plain—plane
rain—rein—reign	right—rite—write	sale—sail
suite—sweet	throne—thrown	wait—weight
week—weak	would—wood	yoke—yolk

HOMOGRAPHS

Homographs are words that are spelled the same but have different meanings and different origins. Here are a few examples:

Jeremy *read* that book last week. Pauli will *read* the local newspaper this afternoon.

That is a *minute* amount of money. I don't like to be even one *minute* early for a party.

The *wind* is blowing very hard today. We have to *wind* our cuckoo clock every day.

My father will *present* a *present* to me on my birthday tomorrow.

CLYMER'S PHONIC RULES

There are many phonic rules that sometimes are taught to children. However, Clymer (1963) suggested that only eighteen phonic rules are consistent or regular enough to warrant teaching to primary-grade children. He conducted a well-known research study in which he attempted to determine the reliability or consistency of forty-five commonly taught phonic rules. Clymer used sets of basal readers to determine the phonic rules that were commonly presented in the primary grades at that time. Then he arbitrarily decided that a phonic rule should be at least 75% consistent to be presented to children. Out of the forty-five rules that Clymer studied, he found only eighteen that were at least 75% consistent and therefore should be presented to children. Some of the most common phonic rules, such as "When two vowels go walking, the first one does the talking" (when two vowels are located next to each other, the first one is usually long and the second is usually silent), were not found to be consistent. However, it may be helpful to present a few of these anyway if they are commonly contained in the reading materials you are using.

The eighteen rules that Clymer thought should be presented to children in the primary grades are as follows:

The *r* gives the preceding vowel a sound that is neither long nor short.

Words having the double *e* usually have the long *e* sound.

In *ay* the *y* is silent and gives *a* its long sound.

When *y* is the final letter in a word, it usually has a vowel sound.

When *c* and *h* are next to each other, they make only one sound.

Ch is usually pronounced as it is in *kitchen*, *catch*, and *chair*, not like *sh*.

When *c* is followed by *e* or *i*, the sound of *s* is likely to be heard.

When the letter *c* is followed by *o* or *a*, the sound of *k* is likely to be heard.

When *ght* is seen in a word, *gh* is silent.

When two of the same consonants are side by side, only one is heard.

When a word ends in *ck*, it has the same last sound as in *look*.

In most two-syllable words, the first syllable is accented.

If *a*, *in*, *he*, *ex*, *de*, or *be* is the first syllable in a word, it is usually unaccented.

In most two-syllable words that end in a consonant followed by *y*, the first syllable is accented and the last is unaccented.

If the last syllable of a word ends in *le*, the consonant preceding the *le* usually begins the last syllable.

When the first vowel element in a word is followed by *th*, *ch*, or *sh*, these symbols are not broken when the word is divided into syllables and may go with either the first or second syllable.

When there is one *e* in a word that ends with a consonant, the *e* usually has the short sound.

When the last syllable is the sound *r*, it is unaccented.

ADDITIONAL INFORMATION ABOUT PHONICS

If you want more information about phonics, you can read one or more of the following resources, all of which I have found useful.

Cunningham, P. (1995). *Phonics they use: Words for reading and writing.* NY: HarperCollins.

Fry, E., Kress, J., & Fountoukidis, D. (2000). *The reading teacher's book of lists,* Fourth Edition. Paramus, NJ: Prentice Hall.

Gaskins, I., Cress, C., O'Hara, C., & Donnelly, K. (1986). *Benchmark word identification/vocabulary development program.* Media, PA: Benchmark School.

Goodman, K. (1993). *Phonics phacts.* Portsmouth, NH: Heinemann.

Heilman, A. (1998). *Phonics in proper perspective.* Columbus, OH: Merrill/Prentice Hall.

Hull, M., & Fox, B. (1998). *Phonics for the teacher of reading.* Columbus, OH: Merrill/Prentice Hall.

Rinsky, L. (1997). *Teaching word recognition skills.* Upper Saddle River, NJ: Gorsuch Scarisbrick Publishers.

Wilson, R., & Hall, M. (1997). *Programmed word attack for teachers.* Columbus, OH: Merrill/Prentice Hall.

TRADE BOOKS FOR IMPROVING PHONICS ABILITY IN CONTEXT

There are a number of interesting trade books that a reading teacher or tutor can use for teaching or reviewing various phonic elements in the context of actual reading. Even children with special needs, such as learning or reading disabilities, need to have practice in reading trade books that review the various phonic elements. Although the phonic skills often should be presented to such children in isolation, it is important that they be reinforced by reading appropriate books.

Trade Books for Reviewing Initial Consonants*

B

Berenstain, S. & J. (1971). *The Berenstain B book.* NY: Random House.

Bottner, B. (1992). *Bootsie Barker bites.* NY: Putnam's.

Casey, P. (1994). *My cat Jack.* Cambridge, MA: Candlewick Press.

Donovan, M. (1993). *Papa's bedtime story.* NY: The Trumpet Club.

Lindenbaum, B. (1992). *Boodil my dog.* NY: Tern Enterprises.

Miller, J. (1993). *Go to bed.* Cambridge, MA: Candlewick Press.

---

*A number of the trade books listed in Chapter 3 for learning and practicing letter names may also be helpful in reviewing phonics.

Moncure, J. (1984). *My "B" sound*. Elgin, IL: Child's World Publishing.

Peet, B. (1977). *Big bad Bruce*. Boston: Houghton Mifflin.

Rounds, G. (1991). *Cowboys*. NY: Holiday House.

Sun, C. (1996). *Cat and cat-face*. Boston: Houghton Mifflin.

Soft C

McPhail, D. (1974). *Cereal box*. Boston: Little, Brown & Company.

Wildsmith, B. (1970). *Circus*. NY: Franklin Watts.

D

Cole, B. (1994). *Dr. Dog*. NY: Alfred A. Knopf.

Lexau, J. (1987). *The dog food caper*. NY: Dial Books.

McNeal, T. & L. (1996). *The dog who lost his Bob*. Morton Grove, IL: Albert Whitman and Company.

Moncure, J. (1984). *My "D" sound*. Elgin, IL: Child's World Publishing.

Reit, S. (1996). *A dog's tale*. NY: Bantam Doubleday Dell Publishing Group.

Zemack, H. & M. (1973). *Duffy and the devil*. NY: Farrar, Straus & Giroux.

F

Brenner, B., & Chardiet, B. (1994). *Where's that fish?* NY: Scholastic.

Littledale, F. (1987). *The farmer in the soup*. NY: Scholastic.

McKissack, P. (1992). *A million fish . . . more or less*. NY: Alfred A. Knopf.

Hard G

Burningham, J. (1976). *Mr. Grumpy's motor car*. NY: Thomas Y. Crowell.

Chardiet, B. & J. (1993). *The rough gruff goat brothers rap*. NY: Scholastic.

Keats, E. (1969). *Goggles*. NY: Collier Books.

Kinsey-Warnock, N. (1997). *The summer of Stanley*. NY: Cobblehill Books/Dutton.

Seuss, Dr. (1960). *Green eggs and ham*. NY: Beginner Books.

Soft G

Galdone, P. (1975). *The gingerbread boy*. NY: Clarion Books.

Lionni, L. (1979). *Geraldine, the music mouse*. NY: Random House.

Rey, H. (1973). *Curious George*. Boston: Houghton Mifflin. (Other titles in this series are *Curious George goes to the circus, Curious George rides a bike,* and *Curious George learns the alphabet.*)

H

Bancroft, C., & Gruenberg, H. (1993). *Felix's hat.* NY: Macmillan.

Gardella, T. (1997). *Casey's new hat.* Boston: Houghton Mifflin.

Hadithi, M., & Kenneway, A. (1994). *Hungry hyena.* Boston: Little, Brown & Company.

Johnson, C. (1955). *Harold and the purple crayon.* NY: Harper & Row.

Kuskin, K. (1979). *Herbert hated being small.* Boston: Houghton Mifflin.

J

Cole, J. (1987). *Norma Jean jumping bean.* NY: Random House.

Degan, B. (1983). *Jamberry.* NY: Harper & Row.

Hennessy, B. (1992). *Jake baked the cake.* NY: Econ-Clad Books.

Hru, D. (1996). *The magic moonberry jump ropes.* NY: Penguin Books USA.

Moncure, J. (1984). *My "J" sound.* Elgin, IL: Child's World Publshing.

Walsh, E. (1993). *Hop jump.* San Diego: Harcourt Brace & Company.

K

Hogan, P. (1991). *The life cycle of the kangaroo: A new true book.* Chicago: Children's Press.

Maestro, B. & G. (1982). *The key to the kingdom.* NY: Harcourt Brace Jovanovich.

Moncure, J. (1984). *My "K" sound.* Elgin, IL: Child's World Publishing.

Wood, A. (1985). *King Bidgood's in the bathtub.* NY: Harcourt Brace Jovanovich.

L

deRegniers, B. (1989). *Laura's story.* NY: Atheneum.

Gliori, D. (1993). *Alion at bedtime.* Hauppauge, NY: Barron's Educational Series.

Krauss, R. (1971). *Leo the late bloomer.* NY: Windmill Books, Simon & Schuster.

London, J., & Long, S. (1994). *Liplap's wish.* San Francisco: Chronicle Books.

Moncure, J. (1984). *My "L" sound.* Elgin, IL: Child's World Publishing.

Wolf, G. (1996). *The very hungry lion.* NY: Annick Press Ltd.

M

Bemelmans, L. (1977). *Madeline.* NY: Puffin Books.

Johnston, T. (1994). *Amber on the mountain.* NY: Dial Books for Young Readers.

Kellogg, S. (1976). *Much bigger than Martin.* NY: Dial Press.

Numeroff, L. (1991). *If you give a moose a muffin.* NY: HarperCollins.

Ruurs, M. (1996). *A mountain alphabet.* Toronto, Ontario: Tundra Books.

Wolcott, P. (1974). *Marvelous mud washing machine.* Reading, MA: Addison-Wesley.

N

Jenkins, P. (1996). *Falcons nest on skyscrapers: Let's-read-and-find-out science.* NY: HarperCollins Publishers.

Kitchen, B. (1993). *And so they build.* Cambridge, MA: Candlwick Press.

Masner, J. (1989). *Nicholas Cricket.* NY: Harper & Row.

McGovern, A. (1967). *Too much noise.* Boston: Houghton Mifflin.

P

Brown, R. (1973). *Pig in the pond.* NY: David McKay.

Duvoisin, R. (1950). *Petunia.* NY: Alfred A. Knopf.

Hall, Z. (1994). *It's pumpkin time!* NY: Scholastic.

Rockwell, A. (1993). *Mr. Panda's painting.* NY: Macmillan.

Roth, S. (1966). *Pick a peck of puzzles.* NY: Arnold Norton.

Zawwyn, D. (1995). *A pumpkin blanket.* Berkeley, CA: Tricycle Press.

Q

Carle, E. (1990). *The very quiet cricket.* NY: Philomel.

Hurd. T. (1978). *The quiet evening.* NY: Greenwillow Books.

Johnston, T., & dePaola, T. (1985). *The quilt story.* NY: Putnam's.

Turner, A. (1994). *Sewing quilts.* NY: Macmillan.

Zolotow, C. (1963). *The quarreling book.* NY: Harper & Row.

R

Fisher, A. (1983). *Rabbits, rabbits.* NY: Harper & Row.

Han, S. (1995). *The rabbit's escape.* NY: Henry Holt & Company.

Heilbroner, J. (1962). *Robert and the rose horse.* NY: Random House.

Kent, J. (1982). *Round robin.* Englewood Cliffs, NJ: Prentice Hall.

Shulevitz, U. (1969). *Rain, rain, rivers.* NY: Farrar, Straus & Giroux.

Stevens, J. (1995). *Tops and bottoms.* San Diego: Harcourt Brace & Company.

S

Ayliffe, A. (1992). *Slither, swoop, swing.* NY: The Viking Press.

Gray, L. (1994). *Small green snake.* NY: Orchard Books.

Lionni, L. (1973). *Swimmy.* NY: Random House.

Robinson, F. (1996). *Great snakes!* NY: Scholastic.

Stadler, J. (1985). *Snail saves the day.* NY: Thomas Y. Crowell.

T

Berger, M. (1992). *Look out for turtles! Let's-read-and-find-out science.* NY: HarperCollins Publishers.

Birney, B. (1974). *Tyrassosaurus Tex.* Boston: Houghton Mifflin.

Lexau, J. (1971). *T for Tommy.* NY: Garrard.

MacGill, S. (1991). *And still the turtle watched.* NY: Dial Books for Young Readers.

Ness, E. (1965). *Tom tit tot.* NY: Scribner's.

Preston, E. (1969). *The temper tantrum book.* NY: The Viking Press.

V

Carle, E. (1969). *The very hungry caterpillar.* NY: Philomel.

Carrick, C. (1995). *Valentine.* NY: Clarion Books.

Cocca-Leffler, M. (1996). *Lots of hearts.* NY: Grosset & Dunlap.

DeArmond, F. (1963). *The very, very special day.* NY: Parents' Magazine Press.

Shannon, G. (1995). *Heart to heart.* Boston: Houghton Mifflin.

W

Arnold, T. (1996). *No more water in the tub.* NY: Dial Books for Young Readers.

Carlstrom, N. (1993). *How does the wind walk?* NY: Macmillan.

Keats, E. (1964). *Whistle for Willie.* NY: The Viking Press.

Locker, T. (1997). *Water dance.* San Diego: Harcourt Brace and Company.

Nyblom, H. (1968). *The witch of the woods.* NY: Alfred A. Knopf.

Sendak, M. (1963). *Where the wild things are.* NY: Harper & Row.

Simon, N. (1995). *Wet world.* Grand Haven, MI: School Zone.

X

Gregovich, B. (1992). *The fox on the box*. Cambridge, MA: Candlewick Press.

Mason, C. (1993). *Wild fox: A true story*. Camden, ME: Down East Books.

Robbins, J. (1985). *Addie meets Max*. NY: Harper & Row.

Y

Castenada, O. (1993). *Abuela's weave*. NY: Lee & Low Books.

Lecher, D. (1992). *Angelita's magic yarn*. NY: Farrar, Straus & Giroux.

Marshall, J. (1973). *Yummers*. Boston: Houghton Mifflin.

Seuss, Dr. (1958). *Yertle the turtle and other stories*. NY: Random House.

Z

Seuss, Dr. (1950). *If I ran the zoo*. NY: Random House.

———. (1955). *On beyond zebra*. NY: Random House.

Tabor, N. (1994). *Cincuenta en la cebra: Contando con los animales/Fifty of the zebra: Counting with the animals*. Watertown, MA: Charlesbridge Publishing.

Trade Books for Reviewing Target Phonic Elements

Long and Short A

Bayer, J. (1984). *A, my name is Alice*. NY: Dial Press.

Hiawyn, O. (1982). *Angry Arthur*. NY: Harcourt Brace Jovanovich.

Maestro, B. (1992). *How do apples grow? Let's-read-and-find-out science*. NY: HarperCollins Publishers.

Moncure, J. (1984). *Short a and long a: Play a game*. Elgin, IL: Child's World Publishing.

Russell, C. (1994). *First apple*. NY: Penguin Books USA.

Turner, A. (1993). *Apple valley year*. NY: Macmillan.

Ziefert, H. (1988). *Cat games*. NY: Puffin.

Long and Short E

Backstein, K. (1992). *The blind man and the elephant*. NY: Scholastic.

Barner, B. (1995). *How to weigh an elephant*. NY: Bantam Doubleday Dell.

Freschet, B. (1977). *Elephant and friends*. NY: Scribner's.

Gregorich, B. (1984). *Nine men chase a hen*. Grand Haven, MI: School Zone.

Johnson, D. (1995). *Never ride your elephant to school*. NY: Henry Holt & Company.

Moncure, J. (1984). *Short e and long e: Play a game*. Elgin, IL: Child's World Publishing.

Shaw, N. (1986). *Sheep in a jeep.* Boston: Houghton Mifflin.

Thaler, M. (1994). *Never mail an elephant.* Mahwah, NJ: Troll.

Yates, G. (1995). *The elephant alphabet book.* Chicago: Kids Books.

Ziefert, H. (1988). *Dark night, sleepy night.* NY: Puffin.

Long and Short I

Gelman, R. (1977). *More spaghetti I say.* NY: Scholastic.

Greydanus, R. (1988). *Let's get a pet.* Mahwah, NJ: Troll.

Hoff, S. (1988). *Mrs. Brice's mice.* NY: HarperCollins.

Kendall, R. (1992). *Eskimo boy: Life in Inupiaq Eskimo.* NY: Scholastic.

Moncure, J. (1981). *Word bird makes words with pig.* Elgin, IL: Child's World Publishing.

Reynolds, J. (1993). *Frozen land: Vanishing cultures.* San Diego: Harcourt Brace & Company.

Long and Short O

Keller, H. (1990). *An octopus is amazing: Let's-read-and-find-out science.* NY: HarperCollins.

Moncure, J. (1981). *No! no! word bird.* Elgin, IL: Child's World Publishing.

Oppenheim, J. (1992). *The show and tell frog.* NY: Bantam.

Pringle, L. (1993). *Octopus hug.* Honesdale, PA: Boyds Mills Press.

Long and Short U

Chesworth, M. (1992). *Rainy day dream.* NY: Farrar, Straus & Giroux.

Gregorich, B. (1984). *The gum on the drum.* Grand Haven, MI: School Zone.

Laser, M. (1997). *The rain.* NY: Simon & Schuster Books for Young Readers.

Lewison, W. (1992). *Buzz said the bee.* NY: Scholastic.

McKissack, P., & McKissack, F. (1988). *Bugs!* Chicago: Children's Press.

Medearis, A. (1995). *We play on a rainy day.* NY: Scholastic.

Moncure, J. (1984). *Short u and long u: Play a game.* Elgin, IL: Child's World Publishing.

R-Controlled Vowels

Coxon, M. (1991). *The cat who lost his purr.* NY: Penguin Books USA.

Penner, R. (1991). *Dinosaur babies.* NY: Random House.

Wynne, P. (1986). *Hungry, hungry sharks.* NY: Random House.

Consonant Digraphs

CH

Dupre, R. (1993). *The wishing chair.* NY: Carolrhoda Books.

Hesse, K. (1993). *Poppy's chair.* NY: Macmillan.

Hoff, S. (1961). *Little chief.* NY: Harper & Row.

Kwitz, M. (1983). *Little chick's breakfast.* NY: Harper & Row.

Martin, B. Jr & Archambault, J. (1989). *Chicka chicka boom boom.* NY: Scholastic.

PH

Govan, G. (1988). *Phinney's fine summer.* NY: World Publishing.

SH

Adams, A. (1981). *Shoemaker and the elves.* NY: Macmillan.

Amato, C. (1995). *The truth about sharks: Young readers' series.* Hauppauge, NY: Barron's Educational Series.

Cowley, J. (1988). *Shoo.* Bothell, WA: Wright Group.

Fowler, A. (1995). *The best way to see a shark: Rookie read-about science.* Chicago: Children's Press.

Kline, S. (1984). *SHHH!* NY: Whitman Publishers.

Shaw, N. (1989). *Sheep on a ship.* Boston: Houghton Mifflin.

Walker, N., & Kalman, B. (1997). *Sharks.* NY: Crabtree Publishing.

TH

Cowley, J. (1987). *One thousand currant buns.* Bothell, WA: Wright Group.

Ketchersid, S. (1996). *Thumbelina: Ladybird favorite tales.* NY: Penguin Books USA.

Loedhas, S. (1962). *Thistle and thyme.* Toronto, Canada: Alger.

/Aw/ Vowels

Oppenheim, J. (1991). *The donkey's tale.* NY: Bantam.

———. (1993). *"Uh-oh!" said the crow.* NY: Bantam.

/Oo/ Vowels

Blocksma, M. (1992). *Yoo hoo, moon.* NY: Bantam.

Cohlene, T. (1990). *Ka-ha-si and the loon: An Eskimo legend.* Mahwah, NJ: Watermill Press.

Cowley, J. (1991). *The kangaroo from North Woolloomooloo.* Sydney, Australia: Murdock Magazines Pty. Ltd.

Wiseman, B. (1959). *Morris the moose.* NY: HarperCollins.

Diphthongs

Goode, D. (1988). *I hear a noise.* NY: Dutton.

Jaffe, N. (1996). *The golden flower: A Taino myth from Puerto Rico.* NY: Simon & Schuster for Young Readers.

Lobel, A. (1975). *Owl at home.* NY: Harper & Row.

Oppenheim, J. (1989). *Not now! said the cow.* NY: Bantam.

Word Families

Casey, D. (1994). *The cat Jack.* Cambridge, MA: Candlewick Press.

Cowley, J. (1990). *Dan the flying man.* Bothell, WA: Wright Group.

Patrick, G. (1974). *A bug in a jug.* NY: Scholastic.

Seuss, Dr. (1957). *The cat in the hat.* NY: Random House.

Young, E. (1995). *Cat and rat: The legend of the Chinese zodiac.* NY: Henry Holt and Company.

WELL-KNOWN PHONICS MATERIALS

There are numerous phonics programs and materials on the market today. You can find over 300 listed on the World Wide Web. However, three widely publicized ones are briefly described here.

THE BENCHMARK WORD IDENTIFICATION PROGRAMS

The Benchmark School is a private school in Media, Pennsylvania, that is designed to help children with special needs of various types. The faculty at this school researched and developed a program that was designed to help poor readers learn the important word identification skills.

This program emphasizes phonics instruction *using analogies.* In the analogy approach students are taught to decode words by comparing an unknown word to known words. (See the material on analogies contained earlier in this chapter.) Students are taught interesting one-syllable key words that represent each rime (phonogram) and in this way become aware of the common rimes.

When students meet an unfamiliar word while reading in this program, they are taught to look for spelling patterns (rimes) within the word. Next they think of known key words that have the same spelling patterns as those in the unknown word. Instruction in how to apply the analogy strategy is teacher directed and grounded in the explicit (direct)-instruction model. Each day teachers tell students *what* they are going to teach, *why* it is important, *when* it can be used, and *how* to use it. Teachers then *model* the process, and this is followed by *guided practice with teacher feedback*. Every-pupil response techniques and teacher feedback are important characteristics of the program, characteristics that help keep the teacher and students involved for every minute of the lesson. Other important characteristics of the program are gradual release of responsibility from teacher to students and a high level of success through learning from teacher feedback about errors in decoding.

Briefly, here are the major materials contained in this program:

Benchmark Word Identification/Vocabulary Development Program, Beginning Level, 1986—This program contains 30-minutes-a-day lessons for students ages 5–11 who are beginning readers through mid-second-grade level and who are able to learn at least five words by sight. The program uses key words to decode unknown words by analogies and develops phonemic awareness. Cost: $150.

Benchmark Word Identification/Vocabulary Development Program, Revised Beginning Level, 1997—This program includes a teacher's guide, worksheets, and 53 story sheets. It contains 30-minutes-a-day lessons for students ages 5–11 who are beginning readers through mid-second-grade level. It stresses letter–sound matches for initial consonants and initial consonant combinations, developing a concept of rhyme, fully learning key words, decoding unknown words by using key words, and reading predictable stories with words containing the target rimes. Cost: $200.

Word Detectives; Benchmark Extended Word Identification Program for Beginning Readers, 1996—This program includes six videotapes, teacher's guide, worksheets, and 50 story sheets. It contains 45- to 60-minutes-a-day lessons for students ages 5–11 who have experienced difficulty learning to read. This program provides more detail and more reinforcement than do the two previous programs. Cost: $500.

Benchmark Word Identification/Vocabulary Development Program, Intermediate Level, 1986—This program contains 20-minutes-a-day lessons for students of all ages who are reading on mid-second-grade reading level to those reading at the intermediate level. Emphasis is on decoding multisyllabic words by analogy as well as learning about meaning units in our language. Cost: $150.

Intermediate Word Detectives Program, 2000—This program includes a teacher's guide, worksheets, and nonfiction selections. It contains 30-minutes-a-day lessons for students who have completed the *Word Detectives Beginning and Transitions Program* or who are reading on a third-grade reading level or above. In the intermediate program more emphasis is placed on spelling than on decoding. Cost: $200.

The Benchmark Program also contains a set of 50 Little Books to accompany the Word Detectives Program and a set of 53 Little Books to accompany the Revised Beginning Program. The costs of each of these sets are $180 and $190, respectively. In addition, the Program has a series of six videotapes, one presenting an overview of

Benchmark School's beginning literacy program, and five presenting each element of the Revised Beginning Program and the Beginning Word Detectives Program. The cost of each videotape is $200. These videotapes would be helpful for a reading teacher or tutor who is using this program.

Evaluation of the Benchmark Program

The Benchmark Program is firmly grounded in theory about how students most effectively learn phonics skills. It is based on the analogy approach to the teaching of phonics, which is effective with most students in comparison to either analytic or synthetic phonic analysis. The reading teacher or tutor also is given detailed instructions about how to implement this program. Therefore, in spite of its relatively high cost, I recommend it for students who have specials needs, such as learning or reading disabilities, *if they are able to develop phonemic awareness skills. The Benchmark Word Identification/Vocabulary Development Program, Revised Beginning Level, 1997,* contains a number of features not included in the earlier edition that probably make it the more useful of the two.

If you want more information about the Benchmark Program, you can visit Benchmark's Web site at www.benchmarkschool.org or call Benchmark at 610-565-3854. Benchmark's mailing address is 2107 N. Providence Road, Media, PA 19063.

HOOKED ON PHONICS—LEARN TO READ

Although *Hooked on Phonics—Learn to Read* is a phonics program designed for parents of children who have reading difficulties, according to the Hooked on Phonics Web site about 3,400 schools are currently using it along with about 2,000,000 families. The original program recently has been revised by adding a reading component to the phonics component. In general, the program costs between $200 and $250.

Hooked on Phonics—Learn to Read contains color-coded boxes that correspond to the different reading levels of children. Each of the five reading levels is contained in its own color-coded box. Each also contains a Parent's Toolbox, filled with materials to help family members guide the child's reading program. In addition, the program includes 10 audiotapes and five sets of flash cards. Each audiotape and deck of flash cards introduces the child to the sounds that letters make and how to combine the sounds to form words. The program also includes five workbooks to help a child sound out words with different letter–sound patterns. The workbooks contain stories that give the child practice reading words with those patterns and also include games and comprehension questions. There also are four sets of helper word play cards that are designed to give the child practice spelling words in "interactive" ways. In addition, the program contains posters and stickers to help parents track a child's progress and motivate him or her to read. The child places another sticker on the poster each time a story or book is read.

The Web site states that this program is based on research findings that a child's word identification ability predicts up to 90% of what his or her comprehension will be in third grade. Although research has shown that children who have a strong decoding program in the primary grades outperform children who do not, this initial advantage usually disappears in the intermediate grades and beyond. In addition, the Web site merely lists the names of researchers and the dates of studies, but no actual citation is given for verification of the claims.

The Web site states that a phonics program that does not emphasize actual interesting reading is "a prescription for failure." Therefore, in contrast to the previous program, this new version incorporates real books created by award-winning authors and illustrators. They are said to be "books that call out to your children with enchanting pictures, friendly characters, and clever stories—books that not only engage their reading skills, but their imaginations."

In addition, a parent report card on the program is reported on the Web site that states that 80% of parents saw an improvement in their child's reading in 4 weeks as well as other positive statements. However, the only citation that is provided for these statements is this: "Independent research, Shapiro & Associates, June, 1998." It does not state if all parents who purchased the program participated in the research study. The money comes with a 90-day money-back guarantee.

Evaluation of Hooked on Phonics—Learning to Read

The Web site provides no concrete evidence of the usefulness of the program in the form of complete research citations. It probably is a better program than was the original program, which did not emphasize actual reading. It may be useful in a few instances in which children have the phonemic awareness to succeed in the program but have just not been successful in school reading. However, a better alternative for a reading teacher or tutor may be the Benchmark Program, while a better alternative for family members may be reading to the child; reading with the child; providing many easy, motivating materials; constructing or duplicating interesting activity sheets; and playing simple homemade or commercial phonics games with the child.

If you want more information about *Hooked on Phonics—Learning to Read*, you can visit the Web site at www.hookedonphonics.com or call 1-888-222-3334. The mailing address is Gateway Learning Corporation, 665 Third Street, Suite 225, San Francisco, CA 94107.

THE PHONICS GAME

The Phonics Game consists of six phonics games that children play with family members. Although this program is primarily designed for home use, it can be used by reading teachers and tutors. The games are said to be an important way to learn phonics, thus resulting in improved reading skills.

The content of the six phonics games included in this teaching aid are as follows:

Game 1: In the Beginning—Mainly devoted to vowels and consonants.

Game 2: Silent Partners—Stresses long vowel words, the silent /e/, beginning spelling by using the sounds, and learning the "two vowels located together" rule.

Game 3: Copy Cats—Learning the sounds of letters that copy each other, learning the /c/ and /g/ rule, learning /s/ when it sounds like /z/, learning the sounds of /y/, and learning how words rhyme.

Game 4: Double Trouble—Learning about special vowel sounds such as diph-thongs, vowel digraphs, and *r*-controlled vowels.

Game 5: Odd Balls—Learning how to use phonics to decode words "even on the few words that break a rule of phonics."

Game 6: Divide and Conquer—Learning the sounds made by /tion/, /sion/, /tial/, and /cial/, sounding out three- and four-syllable words, and learning about contractions.

Each game is accompanied by a videotape, an audiotape, or a Play Book that intro-duces the rules of phonics practiced by that game. After each game the spelling exercises on the "Sounds and Spelling" audiotape and the reading samples in the "Reading Selections" envelope provide a "workout" on what has been learned.

The Web site includes a number of testimonials by satisfied parents who apparently have used the games successfully. The game can be purchased in two ways. *The Phonics Game* sells for $199.95 and includes the following: three videotapes, seven audiotapes, six progressive double-deck card games, Sound Code Chart, Audio Spelling Lesson, Reading Selections, Play Book, and Phonetic Rules Cards. For a cost of $284.85, in ad-dition to *The Phonics Game*, the following is included: *The Phonics Fun Zone* CD-ROM for Mac or PC and a set of 10 phonetic readers.

The Phonics Game Junior, for ages 3–6, sells for $159.95. The company also offers *The Phonics Game Start K* for $79.95. This package includes a videotape, three "fun and progressive" card games, a Play Book, Phonetic Rules Cards, three Phonetic Readers, and Quick Start Instructions.

Evaluation of The Phonics Game

The Phonics Game may be a useful review tool for family members and reading teachers or tutors of children who need help in phonics *if* they have the necessary phone-mic awareness skills to benefit from it. However, it is not inexpensive. In many cases the money could be better spent on constructing homemade games or buying less expensive games for reviewing phonics. Because the games are motivating, many children proba-bly will enjoy playing them simply for the undivided attention of a family member if for no other reason. This one-on-one attention may be one important reason for reading improvement. Of course, phonics is only one component of reading and is the only com-ponent stressed in this game.

I do not recommend *The Phonics Game Junior* as most children are not ready for any phonic skills except beginning phonemic awareness skills at the age of three or four. To teach very young children phonic skills may be detrimental for a number of them.

The company provides a *"Promise"* in addition to the 60-day guarantee. It promises that "your child will receive a minimum one-letter grade improvement on his or her next report card." The *"Promise"* has some conditions, which are given on the Web site. For more information you can visit the Web site at thephonicsgame.com or call 1-888-713-4263. The e-mail address is customerservice@Games2Learn. The company is located at Games 2 Learn, 150 Paularino Avenue, Suite 120, Costa Mesta, CA 92626.

STRATEGIES FOR IMPROVING ABILITY IN PHONICS

This section now contains classroom-tested strategies and materials for teaching and/or reviewing phonics. You should adapt all of the suggestions if necessary in light of your students' needs and interests.

PRESENTING THE VOWEL PATTERNS

Vowel letters are difficult to decode because vowel sounds can be spelled in many different ways. For example, the long /e/ sound can be spelled in seventeen ways. Most children who are taught to recognize vowel *patterns* do better in identifying words than those who do not.

Here are the main vowel patterns and their prediction power (May, 1998):

VC (short vowel) pattern (*bit*) 86% regular

VCC (short vowel) pattern (*neck*) 89% regular

VCE (long vowel—silent /e/) pattern (*cake*) 81% regular

VVC (long vowel) pattern (only *ai, ea, ee, oa*) 77% regular

CV (long vowel) pattern (*so, he, fly*) 77% regular

According to May, teaching these patterns to children can make a significant difference in their reading fluency and comprehension.

Here is a brief list with examples of each pattern. You can add many more to each list.

Short *VC*	Short *VCC*	Long *VCE*	Long *VVC*	Long *CV*
bad	sand	lake	paid	me
get	nest	game	beak	hi
hid	pick	nine	mail	my
top	block	hope	goat	so
nut	bump	cube	seen	he
hat	rang	bake	train	go
pet	band	kite	toad	be
run	bell	bone	beet	fly
sun	will	cake	road	we

Briefly, here are the steps you can use to teach these vowel patterns:

➡ Use the term *VC pattern*, for example, instead of the term *Vowel-Consonant pattern*, which is harder for children to say and remember.

➡ Print words from each of the five vowel pattern groups on separate cards so that children can use them to practice the type of vowel pattern that they are.

➡ Select eight VC words and read them to your pupils, pointing out that each word ends with a vowel followed by a consonant. Tell them that these are all VC words.

➡ Hand each of the children five cards that have a word from each of the five vowel pattern groups on them. For example, you may hand Mario these words: *nut, hint, bake, pail,* and *my.* Ask the children to hold up the word card that illustrates one of the vowel patterns that you put on the chalkboard. You can help those children who have held up the wrong card to find the right one.

➡ When the children all have the correct pattern, have them each read their word (with your help if necessary) and put it on the chalkboard railing. As each child comes to the board, ask him or her what kind of word he or she has (such as the VC pattern) and have the child point to the vowel letter and the consonant letter.

➡ If you want, let the children play a game with the VC words. Divide the class into pairs to play a game of "Concentration." Have the partners first make two cards for each of the ten words in the VC column. Use more of the words for a more difficult game.

WORD WALL

A *word wall* is a very useful strategy for reviewing word patterns and high-frequency words. Put words on a wall in alphabetical order, and add about five new words a week to the wall. Perhaps a reading tutor can make a variation of a word wall on chart paper. These words can be chosen from experience charts and stories, basal readers, trade books, and other materials. They should be high-frequency words that the children will use many times in their reading and writing. Because these words are located on the wall, they can be used as a type of dictionary. For example, if the child wants to find out how to spell the words *friend, one,* or *school,* he or she needs only to look at the right place on the wall. Difficult-to-remember words also can be reviewed by using the word wall on a regular basis.

For example, after a rime such as *-ake* has been introduced, put the *-ake* pattern words on the wall. However, you should put them on a different place on the wall and arrange them alphabetically by *rime.* For example, the *-ab* pattern should be first, followed by the *-ack* and *-ad* patterns, etc. The first word in each column should be the model (header) word accompanied by an illustration so that the children can refer to the illustration if they forget how to identify the model word. When children have difficulty with a pattern word and cannot use a pronounceable word part to unlock the word's pronunciation, they should consult the word wall. Encourage them to identify the model word and then use the analogy strategy to help them identify the unknown word.

Have the children review the pattern words on the wall regularly by using strategies such as these:

➡ Pantomime an action (*rake, talk, throw, bend*) or use gestures to indicate an object or other item (*pig, cake, cat)* and then have the children write the appropriate rime on an every-pupil response card and hold it up for you to see. Have a child point to that word on the word wall and identify it. Before pantomiming the word, tell children the model word of the rime.

➡ Use the "secret word" strategy. (Cunningham & Allington, 1994). Select a pattern word from the word wall and write it on the sheet of paper but do not tell children what it is. Have children number the sheet of paper from 1 to 5 and then give a series of five clues about the identity of the word. After each clue, have the children write down their guess. The object of this activity is for a child to guess the secret word from the least clues. The clues might be as follows:

1. The secret word is in the -*ake* rime.
2. It has four letters.
3. It is something for children to eat.
4. It often is eaten with ice cream.
5. Freddy is looking forward to seeing his birthday _____ this Friday.
(cake)

CROSS-CHECKING WORD IDENTIFICATION STRATEGIES

It is important for children to learn the value of *cross-checking word identification* by using more than one cueing system. Children can identify many words by thinking about what word would make sense in that sentence and noticing whether the initial consonant, consonant blends, or consonant digraphs in that word match what they are thinking of. The ability to use the initial consonants in a word along with the context is the most important decoding strategy. The child should learn to do two things together—think about what word would make sense in context and think about the letters and sounds. Many children like to use one or the other but not both. Thus some children may guess an unknown word by supplying a word that makes some sense in context, while others guess with a word that begins with the correct consonants but makes no sense in the sentence. In order to help children cross-check meaning with sound, first have them guess the word using no letters. Then show some of the letters and finally show the entire word and help them to confirm which guess makes sense and contains the correct letters.

For each cross-checking lesson using different cueing systems, you should write sentences on the chalkboard or an overhead transparency. Then cover the word to be guessed with two pieces of paper, one of which only covers the first letter. You can use magnets to hold the pieces of paper on the board. Here are some simple sentences. You can use the children's own names to make this activity more motivating for them.

Sarah likes to go to the circus.

Tanyanika likes to see the clowns.

Joanie likes to eat popcorn.

Kim Li likes to look at the trained dogs.

Eve likes to watch the elephants do tricks.

Show the children the sentences and tell them that they should read each sentence and try to guess what word is covered up. Have the children read the first sentence and guess the hidden word. They may guess *zoo, mall, park, store, fair,* etc. Next to each sentence write each guess that makes sense. When they have made several guesses, uncover the letter *c*. Erase any guesses that do not begin with this letter and ask if there are any more guesses that begin with *c* and make sense. If there are any more such guesses, write them down. However, be sure that the guesses begin with *c* **and** make sense. Some children may begin guessing anything that begins with a *c* whether or not it makes sense. Say, "Celery does begin with a *c*, but I can't write that word because people don't go to the celery."

When you have written all the guesses that make sense and begin with the correct letter, uncover the word. See if the word that you have uncovered is one that the children guessed. If it is, praise them; if it is not, tell them that it was hard and you are sure they will be able to do it correctly the next time. Continue with each sentence by going through these same steps.

➡ Read the sentence and write any guesses that make sense.

➡ Uncover the first letter and erase any guesses that do not begin with that letter.

➡ Have the children make more guesses and write only those that make sense *and* also begin with the correct letter.

➡ Uncover the entire word and determine whether any of their guesses were correct.

THE ELKONIN STRATEGY AND ELKONIN BOXES

The *Elkonin strategy* and *Elkonin boxes* are useful if children have difficulty learning to segment words phonetically. Elkonin (1973) developed this strategy, which is used regularly in the Reading Recovery Early Intervention Program for first-grade children with special needs. Elkonin tried to make the difficult skill of *segmenting* (analyzing phonetically) words more concrete by using drawings and markers. In this strategy the child is given a drawing of a short word below which are blocks that correspond to the number of sounds in the word. Below the drawing of the word *sun*, for example, there would be three blocks. A token is placed in each block to represent the three sounds in *sun*.

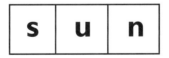

Here is a brief summary of the steps in the strategy:

➡ Explain the task, model it, and guide the child through it.

➡ Give the child a drawing of the *sun*. Remind the child to say the word that names the picture and stretch the word out so that he or she can hear the separate sounds. If the child has difficulty hearing the sounds, pronounce the word very deliberately. Although you emphasize each sound, try not to distort them.

➡ Have the child place a token in each square while saying each sound. The child should say /s/ and put a marker in the first block, then say /u/ and put a marker in the second block, and finally put a marker in the third block while saying /n/.

➡ Using the blocks shows the child how many separate sounds there are in a word. As the child becomes more adept at this strategy, he or she can tell you how many different sounds there are in a word.

➡ Finally, the child can learn to segment words by drawing boxes such as these, which clearly illustrate how many sounds are found in any particular word. These are called *Elkonin boxes*. Each square of the box should contain the grapheme(s) that represent the phoneme for which it (they) stands. Here is an example of two boxes that illustrate this concept. This part of the strategy is often used in Reading Recovery lessons.

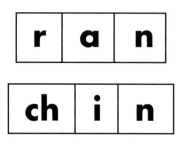

➡ Notice that the word *ran* is composed of three sounds and three letters; the word *chin* is composed of three sounds but four letters because the consonant digraph /ch/ is only one phoneme (sound) but is represented by two letters.

TONGUE TWISTERS

Tongue twisters are helpful for reviewing consonants because they give many word examples for the sound and are enjoyable to say. Just say them at first and have children repeat them after you without letting them see the words. Then have the children say them as quickly as they can and as slowly as they can. When the children have said them enough times to memorize them, have the children watch you write the tongue twisters on a piece of chart paper. Underline the first letter of each tongue twister with a different color marker. Then have the children reread them. If you are making posters of the tongue twisters, you can have one or several children illustrate each of them.

Add one or two new tongue twisters every day. You always should say them first and write them only *after* the children have memorized them. After you write the new ones, review all of the old ones. Leave the charts or posters displayed and refer the children back to them if they forget or become confused about a sound.

Here are some tongue twisters to use as examples. You can easily make your own additional ones. You can use your pupils' names in the tongue twisters if their names contain the correct letters and sounds.

Becca's big boy brought bright boxes.

Carol came clapping clearly.

Dirty Dale didn't dig.

Father's friend fried French fries.

Greg's grandma's goat got gout.

Happy Henry had hamburgers.

Jessie's jewelry jammed.

Katie's kitten kicked.

Let Louie light little lamps.

Millie's mother made mousse.

Nine neighbors need nice noses.

Perry picked pretty pink peaches.

Quack quickly.

Rosa's red rocket roared.

MAGNETIC LETTERS

We discussed *magnetic letters* and where to purchase them in Chapter 3. However, magnetic letters also are useful in teaching phonic skills. Magnetic letters are commonly used in the Reading Recovery Early Intervention Program.

Magnetic letters can easily be used as an effective manipulative activity in which children put letters together to form words. Therefore, they provide meaningful practice for word building using onsets and rimes. Children are able to assemble ten or more words beginning with two-letter words and extending to five-letter or even longer words (Cunningham & Cunningham, 1992). The last word that the children assemble should contain all of the letters they were given. For example, give the children the letters *a*, *d*, *n*, *s*, and *t* and ask them to

➡ Use two letters to make *at*.

➡ Add a letter to make *sat*.

➡ Take away a letter to make *at*.

➡ Change a letter to make *an*.

➡ Add a letter to make *Dan*.

➡ Change a letter to make *tan*.

➡ Take away a letter to make *an*.

➡ Add a letter to make *and*.

➡ Add a letter to make *sand*.

➡ Now break the word apart and see what word you can make with all the letters (*stand*).

HINKS PINKS

Hinks Pinks is a highly motivating strategy to use in teaching and/or reviewing rhyming. These are rhyming pairs that children love to make up, illustrate, and then use to solve riddles. Teachers also like them because they emphasize the spelling pattern–rhyme relationships and provide children with a real purpose for looking for and manipulating rhyming words.

Here are several illustrations for Hinks Pinks. They are followed by a number of Hinks Pinks you can use in your classroom. Of course, children will be eager to construct many of their own Hinks Pinks once they understand their purpose and have started doing so. A reproducible example of Hinks Pinks is provided later in this chapter.

bank sank	flat cat	like bike
spill pill	tall hall	fish dish
bake cake	nice mice	press dress
nice ice	pink drink	wide ride
man ran	quick pick	dark park
rude dude	hot tot	pig jig
stuck truck	hunk junk	hay play
loose goose	sick Dick	king ring
bell fell	cap flap	sup cup
fat rat	light night	fix mix
wet set	rub tub	goat coat

IMPROVING AUDITORY BLENDING

There are several strategies that will help a child blend various sounds, which is often a difficult skill especially for a child with learning disabilities. Tell children that they will be doing a kind of "ice skating" to help them sound out words. The use of analogies, as explained earlier, minimizes the need for blending.

Put large letters on the floor and have the child "skate" slide from one to another while saying the letter sounds out loud or have the child stretch a rubber band between words. You also can use letter tiles or other moveable letters that may be gradually moved apart while a word is sounded slowly and then brought back together as the entire word is pronounced. Teach the child to use his or her voice to "slide" through the sounds of unfamiliar words.

WORD SORT

Obtain a number of shoe boxes. Put an initial *s*, a consonant blend with an initial *s*, such as *st*, or a consonant digraph with an initial *s*, such as *sh*, on each shoe box. Then obtain some small objects that begin with these various sounds. Some objects may be a *sock, spoon, scarf, shell, soap,* and *sailboat.*

VARIABILITY STRATEGY

It is important that children learn to be flexible in their approach to decoding. They can be taught the following *variability strategy:*

1. First try the main pronunciation of the letter—the one that the letter usually stands for.

2. If the common pronunciation gives a word that is not a real word or one that does not make sense in the sentence, try the other pronunciation.

3. If you still get a word that is not a real word or does not make sense in the sentence, ask for help.

A STRATEGY FOR CHILDREN WITH LEARNING DISABILITIES

Harwell (1989) uses a strategy for teaching beginning phonic elements to children with learning disabilities that you may want to consider using. She wrote that if a child has acquired few or no phonic sounds from prior phonic instruction, the process usually takes about 20 consecutive days, with forty days being the longest time that it has ever taken. She also wrote that the teacher may work with one child at a time for 30 minutes daily, but that it was possible to work with up to four beginning readers at a time. Harwell also said that it was necessary to give adequate blending and feedback time to each child. Briefly, here is how the system is used. If you want more information about Harwell's system, you should consult her book, *Complete Learning Disabilities Handbook* (West Nyack, NY: The Center for Applied Research in Education, 1989), pp. 119–123.

➡ Print each alphabet letter on the chalkboard or a sheet of paper. Say, "The letter's name is *a*. Repeat, please." Be sure that the children repeat "The letter's name is *a*," rather than just saying "*a*."

➡ Say, "The letter's sound is _____." (Give the short /a/ sound. At the same time, draw an *apple* on the chalkboard. If you are working with a group, the children can each draw his or her own apple. Do not allow them to say, "The letter's name is *apple*."

➡ Say, "*Apple* is a word that starts with _____" (again pronounce the short /*a*/ sound—really overemphasize it) "but it takes the five letters to spell *apple*." Write *apple*, point, count to the five letters, and then repeat, "The letter's sound is _____."

➡ Harwell then continues this same procedure for each of the other symbol–sound relationships.

SOUND–SENSE STRATEGY

The *sound–sense strategy* (Houghton Mifflin, 1981) is a helpful strategy that should be taught to all children as soon as they have mastered beginning reading. Teach the child to pause briefly at an unknown word and then follow these steps:

➡ Skip the unknown word and read to the end of the sentence.

➡ Return to the unknown word and associate appropriate sounds for initial and final letters of the word.

➡ Return to the beginning of the sentence and reread, attempting to identify the unknown word.

ADDITIONAL STRATEGIES

There are many additional strategies for reviewing phonics. Some are briefly described here.

➡ Type a short story omitting all the vowels. Have the child try to read the story silently or orally, mentally adding the omitted vowels. You also can have the child write in each of the omitted vowels if you want. Here is a brief example of this activity:

> Today it _s a v_ry bea_tiful sunny d_y. I _m going t_ t_ke my d_g for a w_lk l_ter this afterno_n. I r_ally enjoy w_lking my dog on a n_ce day. However, I also t_ke her for a walk on a ra_ny day. Th_n it is n_t so m_ch f_n but I do _t anyw_y!

➡ Print two columns of words on the chalkboard. One word in each column should contain the same vowel sound as a word in the opposite column, although the spellings can be different. Have the child draw a line between the two words that contain the same vowel sound.

➡ Write a number of words on the chalkboard that have been spelled phonetically. Have children pronounce each of these words by interpreting the phonetic spellings.

➡ Write a number of words on the chalkboard that contain either the hard *c* or soft *c*. Have the child place a check mark besides the words that contain the target sound. A similar activity can be constructed for the hard *c* or soft *g*. Here is an example of this activity.

Put a check mark in front of each word that begins with a soft *c*.

_____ cedar		_____ cell	
_____ card		_____ cane	
_____ ceiling		_____ cut	
_____ cent		_____ candy	
_____ cord		_____ cone	

➡ Make five decorated boxes and label each box with a short vowel. Have the children locate pictures or objects whose names contain the short vowel sounds and file them in the appropriate boxes. Each day take out the pictures and objects and review the vowel sounds.

➡ Use riddles to practice rhyming words. Here is an example:

This is a word that rhymes with *ball*.

A child and dog can play with it.

It is called a _____.

(ball)

➡ Have students create *secret messages* by substituting onsets in familiar words and then putting the newly constructed words together to make a a secret message (QuanSing, 1995). In addition to being motivating, secret messages help students focus on the onsets and rimes in words and improve comprehension. Once students become familiar with this procedure, they can construct their own secret messages either individually or as a cooperative learning activity. Here is a sample secret message:

Take *B* from *By* and put in *M*. _____

Take *s* from *sat* and put in *c*. _____

Take *p* from *pan* and put in *c*. _____

Take *d* from *day* and put in *pl*. _____

Take *w* from *wall* and put in *b*. _____

Secret Message: *My cat can play ball.*

➡ *Word wheels* can be used to practice attaching an initial consonant or later a consonant blend or digraph (onset) to various rimes (phonograms). A word wheel is made

by cutting two inches of tagboard, one of which is slightly larger than the other. Fasten the two disks with a brass fastener. Print rimes on the large disk, and the initial consonant, blend, or digraph on the smaller disk. (See illustration.) The child spins the disk and pronounces each of the newly formed words. For example, a word wheel using the consonant *s* can be used to form the words: *sat, sit, sup, sell, sold, sail,* and *sake.*

⟶ Use a jump-rope rhyme to review analytic phonic analysis using authentic material. Duplicate this rhyme and let the children read and sequence it using sentence strips. Then cover up target words and have the children figure out what these words are. Ask them to predict which letters would represent the beginning and ending sounds of the target words. You can continue to use the poem for reading and writing activities to keep the review of sounds in context. You can use the procedure with jump-rope rhymes or ball-bouncing rhymes (Olenski, 1992).

⟶ Print a common rime on a cardboard disk like the one in the illustration. Pull a strip of cardboard with initial consonants on it through an opening cut in the disk. Show the children how to pull the strip through the disk, pronouncing each word as it is formed.

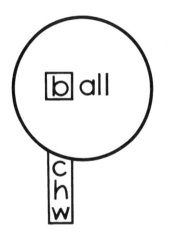

⟶ Divide the children into groups. Give half of them initial consonant, consonant blend, or consonant digraph cards. Give the other half word-ending cards. Tell the children to pair up with other children, holding word parts that combine with their parts to form real words. Have each pair hold up their cards and pronounce the word they have made when they have located a combination. Then let them search for other possible combinations for their word part.

⟶ Phonics is a lower-level reading skill, so use computer software to practice various phonics skills. You can locate many useful software programs by visiting the World Wide Web, consulting appropriate educational software catalogs, or visiting the computer software booths at local, state, regional, or national reading conventions or software conventions. Because any list of computer software becomes outdated almost as soon as it is published, this book does not contain a such a listing.

GAMES FOR REVIEWING PHONICS SKILLS

Phonics usually is not inherently interesting to most children, so games can be a good way of reviewing phonic elements or rules in a motivating way. Of course, the games always should emphasize the phonic skill to be reviewed instead of the game. As much as possible, competition should be minimized in the games so that children, especially those with special needs, do not become discouraged.

The games included in this section have been used successfully countless times by both reading teachers and tutors. You should adapt any of the games in the light of your pupils' needs and interests.

Here are the names of two commercial phonics games you may want to consider purchasing. I recommend that a reading teacher or tutor use both homemade and commercial phonics games, as each offers unique advantages and limitations.

Road Race, 1987
Curriculum Associates
Telephone 1-800-225-0248
E-mail—cainfo.curriculumassociates.com

Word Trek, 1977
DLM Teaching Resources
One DLM Park, P.O. Box 4000
Allen, TX 75002

Phonic Bingo

TO CONSTRUCT THE GAME

Make cards that look like Bingo cards out of cardboard. (See the illustration.) Print initial consonants, consonant blends, and consonant digraphs on the cards in random order. Have children make tokens out of small squares of colored construction paper or any other appropriate materials.

s	f	ch	br
g	sl	th	v
d	dr	w	tr
r	h	j	sh

bl	gr	fr	ch
t	z	y	b
r	pl	str	n
n	m	j	l

TO PLAY THE GAME

Pronounce a word beginning with one of the consonants, consonant blends, or consonant digraphs. Tell the children to look at their cards for the letter or letter combination that represents that word's initial sound. Tell those children who have a word beginning with that letter or letter combination to cover it up with a token of some kind. Continue to pronounce words until one child has covered his or her entire card. The first child who does this is the winner, or the game may continue until all the cards are covered.

Searching for Buried Treasure

TO CONSTRUCT THE GAME

You should construct a game board similar to the illustration on the next page. Each word on the game board should be a word that has a silent final /e/ that makes the vowel long. It also should have a counterpart without the silent final /e/ that has a short medial vowel. The child needs to pronounce both words if he or she lands on a space. Some directions that you might want to include on the game board are as follows:

Can't find treasure map—Go back to start

Found one gold coin lying on the ground—Take 1 more turn

Became ill—Go back to start

Got caught in a rainstorm—Go back 2 spaces

Sunny weather today—Go ahead 1 space

You can use any other directions that you want.

Some word pairs that you might want to use on the game board are as follows:

cape—cap	*hate—hat*	*rate—rat*
cane—can	*mane—man*	*mate—mat*
tape—tap	*hope—hop*	*pale—pal*
fade—fad	*shame—sham*	*pane—pan*
vane—van	*bite—bit*	*made—mad*
pale—pal	*fate—fat*	*rode—rod*
tape—tap	*slide—slid*	*ride—rid*

The players can make a "gold coin" out of yellow construction paper or use any other kind of token.

TO PLAY THE GAME

The players roll the die to see who goes first, and the highest number goes first. Each player rolls the die and moves his or her token the number of spaces indicated. When a player lands on a word, he or she must read the word aloud as it is printed and then cover up the silent final /e/ and read the word aloud again (i.e., *made, mad*). If a player does not read it correctly and in correct order, he or she must move back to the previous position. If you want, the player also must say the patterns, such as *VCE, made; VC, mad*. There can be more than one player in each space. To reach the treasure chest, the player must roll the exact number on the die. The first child to reach the treasure chest is the winner. This game combines chance and skill, and any child can win even if he or she has special reading needs.

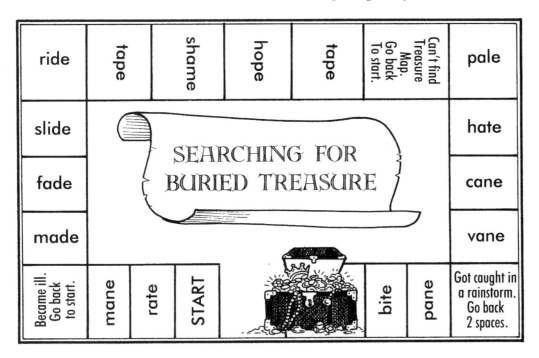

Guess the Mystery Word

TO PLAY THE GAME

This is a game in which children try to guess a mystery word, which has letters in the same location as do three clue words. Divide the children into two groups. Each word is worth 10 points. With each "no" answer to a question, the turn goes to the other team, and a point is subtracted.

Write each sentence and its clue words on the chalkboard. Then read the sentence, saying "blank" for the mystery word. Pronounce the clue words and have the children pronounce them. Children can ask, "Does the mystery word begin like [one of the clue words]? Does it end like . . . ?" Here is an example:

My favorite food to eat is _____. (*pizza*)

Teacher: Listen while I read this sentence and try to decide what word might fill in the blank. The clue words are *parade*, *zoo*, and *zebra*. Say them after me. Rhonda's team won the toss, so they can go first. The mystery word is worth 10 points.

Rhonda's team member: Does the word begin like *zebra?*

Teacher: No, it doesn't.

Willie's team member: Does the word begin like *parade?*

Teacher: Yes, it does. [Write *p* on the chalkboard near the beginning of the blank line.] You now get another turn.

Willie's team member: Does the word end like *zoo?*

Teacher: No, it doesn't.

Rhonda's team member: Does the word end like *zebra?*

Teacher: Yes, it does. [Write *a* on the chalkboard near the end of the blank line.] You can meet now with the rest of your team and try to figure out what the word is.

Rhonda's team confers and decides that the word probably is *pizza* because this type of food has a *p* at the beginning and an *a* at the end. Rhonda's team receives 8 points for this win, and the game continues with more mystery words and clue words.

Phonic Rummy

TO CONSTRUCT THE GAME

Make a deck of cards with the phonic elements you want to review. On each card write one phonic element and four words that use the particular phonic element. Underline one of the four words. The deck may consist of 36, 40, 44, 48, or 52 cards. For each phonic element there will be 4 cards, each of which has a different word underlined. A deck of 36 cards would involve 9 phonic elements, and 40 cards would involve 10 phonic elements, etc.

Here are examples of words and phonic elements for the cards:

o	**bl**	**ch**
top	**black**	**chin**
not	**blend**	**chip**
fox	**blow**	**cheek**
hop	**blue**	**chose**

TO PLAY THE GAME

The dealer shuffles the cards and then deals eight cards face down to each player. The rest of the cards are then placed face down in the center of the table. The first player to the left of the dealer asks for a word using a certain phonic element on which he or she wants to build. For example, the child might say, "I want Latasha to give me *not* from the *o* group" and pronounces the short /o/ sound. If Latasha has that card, she would give it to the caller. The player (caller) then continues to call for certain cards from different people. If the person called on does not have the card, the caller takes a card from the center pile, and the next player to his or her left has a turn. When a player completes a "book" (that is, when he or she has all four cards from a certain phonic pattern), the player lays it down. Players only can lay down "books" when it is their turn to draw. The player who gets the most "books" before someone else empties his or her hand is the winner.

Going to the Grocery Store

TO CONSTRUCT THE GAME

You need five large shopping bags labeled *a, e, i, o,* and *u* and many empty containers (boxes, cartons, or cans) of food whose names include the target vowel sounds.

TO PLAY THE GAME

Have the children sort the food items into the correct shopping bag. Tell them whether they are to listen for and then sort by long or short vowel sounds. Here are some suggested foods that can be used for this game.

Long Vowels

tomato	pie	beans	grapes
peaches	raisins	cheese	cake
Coke®	rice	peas	ice cream
sweet potato	oatmeal	grape juice	potato

Short Vowels

cabbage	apple	jam	eggs
fish	pickles	olives	ham
chips	muffin	nuts	Popsicle
stuffing	pumpkin	salad	dressing

Think

TO CONSTRUCT THE GAME

This game provides practice with initial consonants, vowels, and consonant blends. Make enough small cards out of tagboard so that each alphabet letter and initial consonant blend can be printed on them. There may be more than one card for each vowel.

TO PLAY THE GAME

The cards should be placed face down on the table. Have players take turns selecting a card and naming a word that begins with the same letter or blend. If a player cannot name a word in about 5 seconds, he or she puts the card back. The winner is the person who has the most cards after the entire pile has been drawn.

Pizza Board Game

TO CONSTRUCT THE GAME

You need the following to construct this game:

8" pizza boards (you may be able to obtain them from a local pizza restaurant) clothespins

marking pens

old workbooks or catalogs

scissors

glue

clear self-stick vinyl

Around each pizza board, glue pictures that represent the vowel combinations being studied. On the back side, write each word. Write words on the clothespins for these pictures. Write the vowel elements in red letters. Cover the pizza board with clear self-stick vinyl. Here are several illustrations that will help you construct the board:

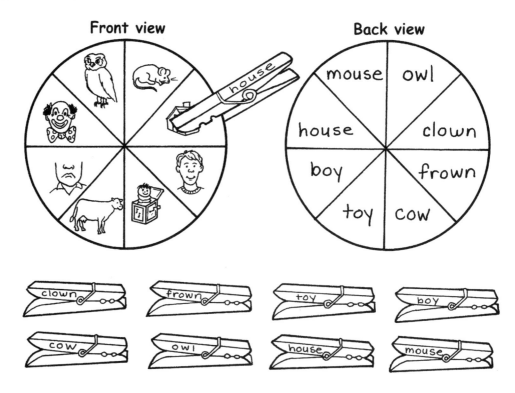

TO PLAY THE GAME

Have the child clip the correct clothespin to each picture around the board and then read the word. The back of the wheel may be referred to for self-checking.

REPRODUCIBLES FOR IMPROVING PHONICS ABILITY

This section contains several reproducibles that you can use to improve your pupils' ability in the various elements of phonics. Such sheets can be helpful and motivating if they are not overused.

HINKS PINKS
Fourth-Grade Level

A Hink Pink is made up of two rhyming spelling patterns that make a funny description. Read each definition and see if you can make up a Hink Pink for it. You can work with a partner(s) if you wish. When you are done with this activity sheet, make up your own Hink Pink for Number 20. The first one is done for you.

1. loud bell   *strong gong*

2. closer/distant automobile   _____

3. impolite man   _____

4. royal jewelry   _____

5. aquatic meal   _____

6. colored beverage   _____

7. ill boy   _____

8. rotund feline   _____

9. uncontrollable youngster   _____

10. touch rodent   _____

HINKS PINKS *(Cont'd)*

11. view insect _____

12. primate's coat _____

13. heavenly body _____

14. unpleasant supervisor _____

15. dark bag _____

16. excellent home _____

17. large hog _____

18. naughty father _____

19. water wave _____

20. _____ _____

Answer Key: far car, rude dude, king ring, fish dish, pink drink, sick Dick, fat cat, wild child, pat rat, see bee, ape cape, far star, cross boss, black sack, best nest, big pig, bad Dad, lake wake

WHAT'S THE RIGHT WORD?
First-Grade, Second-Semester, or Second-Grade Level

Read each question and circle the right answer. The right answer will be one of the underlined words.

1. What can you eat with peanut butter and jelly, dread or bread?

2. What is part of a lion's head, a mane or a cane?

3. What do you use on a letter to mail it, a tramp or a stamp?

4. What is a very large fish, a spark or a shark?

5. What do you use to think with, a brain or a strain?

6. Where does a person keep money, a bank or a tank?

7. What is a person, a van or a man?

8. What is a color, black or track?

9. What is a kind of fruit, a drape or a grape?

10. What do you use to go fishing, bait or wait?

11. Where can you find pigs and cows, on a harm or a farm?

12. What can you do in the winter, state or skate?

13. What can you have for dinner, neat or meat?

14. What is a kind of insect, a bee or a tree?

15. What can you take to get clean, a path or a bath?

TRY TO MAKE NEW WORDS
Second-Grade Level

Read each sentence and follow the direction.

1. **sleep**   Change one letter and get the name of an

animal.   _____

2. **ate**   Add one letter and get a part of a fence.

_____

3. **star**   Take off one letter and get something black and

sticky.   _____

4. **sail**   Change one letter and get something many

animals have.   _____

5. **sink**   Change one letter and get a color.

_____

6. **dish**   Change one letter and get something you can

eat.   _____

7. **loon**   Change one letter and get something you can

see in the sky at night.

_____

8. **block**   Change one letter and get something that tells

you the time.   _____

9. **fog** Change one letter and get an animal.

   _____

10. **five** Change one letter and get a place that bees live in.

   _____

11. **our** Add two letters and get something that bread is made out of. _____

12. **out** Add two letters and get a very loud sound.

   _____

13. **crush** Change one letter and get something you use to clean your teeth. _____

14. **us** Add one letter and get something that children ride in to school. _____

15. **trunk** Change two letters and get the name of a black and white animal. _____

RHYMING ANIMAL NAMES
Second- or Third-Grade Level

Read each of the key words on this sheet. Then write the name of an animal that rhymes with the key word on the line beside it. You can work with a partner(s) if you want to. Check the spelling if you need to.

1. blouse _____

2. cantaloupe _____

3. box _____

4. log _____

5. sat _____

6. fog _____

7. pen _____

8. mitten _____

9. float _____

10. sale _____

11. keep _____

12. loose _____

13. pear _____

14. trunk _____

15. how _____

FILL IN THE MISSING VOWELS
Second- or Third-Grade Level

This is a true story about a raccoon family that lived in the big woods. There are some missing vowels (*a, e, i, o, u*) in the story that you should fill in. After you have finished, reread the story to be sure you have done it correctly. You can work with a partner(s) if you want to.

RACCOONS IN A SWING

I have a friend n____med Shirley who lives in the big woods in the summer. Shirley put p____pcorn and leftovers on her deck e____ch evening for the raccoons. One n____ght a raccoon c____me, and Shirley named it Willie.

Later Willie came b____ck with three b____by raccoons. Because it was a m____ther raccoon, Shirley then named it Wilhelmina (Wĭl/hĕl/mēn/ə). Shirley saw the three b____by raccoons s____tting on an iron sw____ng and swinging b____ck and forth.

One evening Shirley m____xed p____ncake syrup and w____ter and put it in a bowl for the raccoons. Mama raccoon p____cked up the bowl and drank it wh____le standing on her two hind l____gs. Then she g____ve a b____g burp! The baby r____ccoons then j____mped off the sw____ng and dr____nk the rest of the syrup and water. What a f____nny sight all the raccoons were!

WHAT IS THE ANSWER?
Third-Grade Level

Read this story to yourself. It contains five words with diphthongs. When you read a word with a diphthong (*oi, oy, ou, ow, ew*), underline the word and print the first letter of that word on the first blank under the story. Then continue finding four more words with diphthongs and writing the first letter of each word on the blank lines. When you are finished, you will know what happened to Mike. You can work with a partner(s) if you want to.

WHAT HAPPENED TO MIKE?

Mike is a third-grade student who likes to play with his toys, especially his model cars. One Saturday Mike took his model cars out to play with them in his driveway.

His friend Shun came over and asked him to go to the ice cream store with him for a sundae with nuts on it. On the way there the boys saw a big hoot owl in a maple tree.

When Mike and Shun got to town, they went into the ice cream store, where they each had a sundae. Mike asked for extra nuts in his sundae because he loved them.

Shun said, "I don't know how you can eat all those nuts." All of a sudden Mike exclaimed, "Hey, there must have been a hard nutshell in this sundae. I broke a _____!"

— — — — —

Answer Key: toys, out, owl, town, how; t o o t h

274

FOR ADDITIONAL READING

Burns, P. (late), Roe, B., & Ross, E. (1996). *Teaching reading in today's elementary schools* (pp. 110–136). Boston: Houghton Mifflin.

Cunningham, P. (1991). *Phonics they use.* NY: HarperCollins Publishers.

Fry, E., Kress, J., & Fountoukidis, D. (2000). *The reading teacher's book of lists*, fourth edition. Paramus, NJ: Prentice Hall.

Gunning, T. (1996). *Creating reading instruction for all children* (pp. 77–119). Needham Heights, MA: Allyn and Bacon.

———. (2000). *Phonological awareness and primary phonics.* Needham Heights, MA: Allyn and Bacon.

Heilman, A. (1998). *Phonics in proper perspective.* Columbus, OH: Merrill/Prentice Hall.

Heilman, A., Blair, T., & Rupley, W. (1998). *Principles and practices of teaching reading* (pp. 161–183). Upper Saddle River, NJ: Prentice Hall.

May, F. (1998). *Reading as communication* (pp. 173–203). Upper Saddle River, NJ: Prentice Hall.

McAllister, E. (1987). *Primary reading skills activities kit* (pp. 147–165). West Nyack, NY: The Center for Applied Research in Education.

Miller, W. (2000). *Strategies for developing emergent literacy* (pp. 128–157). Boston: McGraw-Hill College Publishers.

Muncy, P. (1995). *Complete book of illustrated reading & writing activities for the primary grades* (pp. 25–101). West Nyack, NY: The Center for Applied Research in Education.

Shanker, J., & Ekwall, E. (late). (1998). *Locating and correcting reading difficulties* (pp. 101–122). Columbus, OH: Merrill/Prentice Hall.

Vacca, J., Vacca, R., & Gove, M. (1995). *Reading and learning to read* (pp. 277–290). NY: HarperCollins College Publishers.

WORKS CITED IN CHAPTER 4

Adams, M. (1990). *Beginning to read: Thinking and learning about print.* Cambridge, MA: MIT Press.

Clymer, T. (1963). The utility of phonic generalizations in the primary grades. *The Reading Teacher, 12,* 252–258.

Cunningham, P., & Allington, R. (1994). *Classrooms that work: They all can read and write.* NY: HarperCollins Publishers.

Cunningham, P., & Cunningham, J. (1992). Making words: Enhancing the invented spelling-decoding connection. *The Reading Teacher, 46,* 106–115.

Elkonin, D. (1973). Reading in the USSR. In J. Downing (Ed.), *Comparative reading* (pp. 551–579). NY: Macmillan.

Harwell, J. (1989). *Complete learning disabilities handbook.* West Nyack, NY: The Center for Applied Research in Education.

Houghton Mifflin. (1981). *Sound–sense strategy.* Boston: Houghton Mifflin.

May, F. (1998). *Reading as communication.* Upper Saddle River, NJ: Prentice Hall.

Olenski, S. (1992). Using jump rope rhymes to teach reading skills. *The Reading Teacher, 46,* 173–175.

QuanSing, J. (1995). *Developmental teaching and learning using developmental continua as maps of language and literacy development which link assessment to teaching.* Paper presented at the annual meeting of the International Reading Association, Anaheim, CA, May, 1995.

Stahl, S., Osborne, J., & Lehr, F. (1990). *Beginning to read: Thinking and learning about print—A summary.* Champaign, IL: Center for the Study of Reading.

Chapter 5

IMPROVING ABILITY IN WORD STRUCTURE AND CONTEXT

Are you able to identify this fairly unusual word—*hypothyroidism*? If you know that the prefix *hypo* means "under" or "little," you may be able to figure out that *hypothyroidism* means a person has thyroid functioning that is below normal. If you are able to do that, you are using word structure to help you identify the word. However, if you see this word in the following sentence, you are able to determine its meaning from its use in sentence context: *I am going to the doctor for tests for possible hypothyroidism because I have gained weight and feel tired so much of the time.* However, a reader may or may not be able to pronounce the word correctly. The pronunciation is not so important as is the meaning of the word.

This chapter explains the basic characteristics of both *word structure*, sometimes called *structural analysis*, and *context*, sometimes called *meaning* or *semantic clues*. It also contains many classroom-tested teaching strategies, materials, games, and reproducibles that will help you teach and reinforce both of these important word identification techniques. It is important that all students in the elementary school, including those with special needs, master both word structure and context to the limits of their ability. To do so will best enhance their reading comprehension.

WORD STRUCTURE

Word structure or *structural analysis* is using *word parts* to determine the meaning and pronunciation of unknown words. This word identification technique can be helpful in improving a child's meaning vocabulary, especially if it is used along with context clues and phonics. Although it may be useful in the primary grades, it is most helpful with older students in the intermediate grades and beyond.

Word structure (structural analysis) is composed of several subskills. One subskill is attaching a *prefix* or *suffix* (*affix*) to a *base* or *root word* to form a *derivative*. Derivational suffixes change the part of speech of a word or its function in some way. Common derivational suffixes can form *nouns*, as in the words *marriage* and *annoyance*, while others can form *adjectives*, as in words such as *pleasant* and *thoughtful*. Still others change the function of a verb so that it indicates a *person*, as in the words *painter* and *farmer*. A few of the most common suffixes presented in the primary grades are *-er*, *-less*, *-y*, and *-ness*. Several common suffixes discussed in the intermediate grades are *-al*, *-tion*, *-ion*, *-ology*, *-ious*, and *-ward*.

Inflectional suffixes indicate grammatical items and include plural *-s*, as in *dogs*; third-person singular, as in *works*; present participle *-ing*, as in *singing*; past tense *-ed*, as in *jumped*; past participle *-en*, as in *tighten*; comparisons *-er* and *-est*, as in *shorter* and *short-est*; and the *-ly*, as in *slowly*. Young children learn some of the inflectional suffixes early in the primary grades. For example, *-s*, *-ed*, and *-ing* are commonly found in beginning reading materials of all types and therefore are taught in first grade. The suffixes *-er*, *-est*, and *-ly* are taught in most basal reader systems in second grade (Harris & Jacobson, 1982). Although Harris and Jacobson's research study is not current, its findings probably still are accurate.

Structural analysis is related to the term *morpheme*, which is the smallest unit of meaning in a language, and a morpheme can be either *free* or *bound*. A *free morpheme* is a group of letters that make up any meaningful word, such as *school*, *computer*, *store*, *man*, or *girl*. A *bound morpheme* is composed of one or more letters that cannot function alone as do real words. Several examples of bound morphemes include the suffix *-ing* in the word *walking*, the prefix *re-* in the word *rework*, and the prefix *sub-* in the word *submarine*.

Understanding the use of *compound words*, *syllabication*, *accent (stress)*, and *word origins* are several other subskills of word structure. *Contractions* usually are considered a part of word structure, although they should be learned as *sight words*, especially in beginning reading instruction. Often it is not very helpful for a child to determine what two or three letters are omitted when the contraction is formed. It is more helpful to learn the contraction as a sight word that is instantly identified.

Discussing prefixes, suffixes, root words, and compounds may remind you of memorizing lists of word elements. However, learning morphemes is a *constructive process* that children begin as early as age two (Brown, 1973). For example, a young child around the age of four may make a statement such as this: *"Mikey goed to the store last night."* This is an example of a young child *overgeneralizing* a grammatical concept of which he or she is becoming aware. The child has constructed a rule for the past tense of the verb *go* that makes sense to him or her. Later the child will understand the process and say *went*.

Clymer's list of phonic generalizations was included in Chapter 4. Because a number of these rules also deal with word structure, you are encouraged to refer to this list when necessary. There is a direct link between generalizations about suffixes and the reader's ability mentally to separate suffixes from word roots in order to identify the total derived or inflected word, so it is helpful to teach older primary-grade children the following rules:

➡ When adding a suffix beginning with a vowel to a word that ends with an *e*, the *e* is usually dropped (i.e., *rose* is *rosy* and *escape* is *escapade*). However, in a word such as *manageable*, the *e* is not dropped because to do so would give the *g* a hard sound.

➡ When adding a suffix beginning with a vowel to a word that ends in one single consonant with a short vowel before it, the last consonant is usually doubled (i.e., *skip* + *ing* = *skipping* and *tap* + *ing* = *tapping*). In the case of *tap* this enables the reader to differentiate between the words *tapping* and *taping*. However, *y* is not changed to an *i* when adding *ing*, as in the words *try/trying*. English does not permit two *i*'s together and without the *y* the word would be spelled *triing*.

➡ When adding a suffix to a word that ends with *y* preceded by a vowel, the *y* is not changed (i.e., *donkey + s = donkeys* and *turkey + s = turkeys*).

This process of becoming aware of oral and written grammar continues through elementary school as children better understand the concepts of past tense and third-person plural. The use of word structure as a word attack skill should build on these *constructive elements*. The instruction given to children should be functional rather than mechanical and isolated. For example, even many primary-grade children can use their knowledge of the meaning of the prefix *un-*, which means "*not*," to construct meaning for such words as *unable*, *unfold*, and *unhappy*.

If a child always reads for meaning and uses grammatical (syntactical) clues as well as meaning clues, translating letters into sounds happens automatically. For example, a child's innate grammatical sense will tell him or her that a /z/ sound is used in the underlined words in the following sentence: *Our class has eleven boys and twelve girls.* It also is not necessary to tell him or her that the suffix *-s* is represented by the /z/ sound in other common words such as *cars*, *toys*, *teachers*, *jars*, and *farmers*. Children usually can pronounce the *-ed* suffix correctly in these words, although three different pronunciations are possible: *talked*, *played*, and *wanted*. Therefore, it is not necessary to teach children to identify the pronunciations of /t/, /d/, or /id/ that *-ed* represents.

Compound words are one element of word structure that receive much emphasis in the primary grades beginning in first grade. One way of forming new words is to put two words together to form a new composite word. The English language has been expanded with thousands of compound words. For example, according to Rinsky (1997, p. 87), about 60% of the new words that come into English are compound words (e.g., *network*, *cyberspace*, *megabyte*, and *spaceship*).

Remember that even though compound words may look easy to adults, they can be difficult for children. For example, a child who can identify both of the words *skate* and *board* may have a harder time in identifying the word *skateboard* because it looks both long and difficult. Children should learn to identify each word of which a compound word is composed separately and then pronounce them together. They also should learn that the meaning of the compound word is a composite meaning of the two words of which it is composed. However, they also should understand that the meanings of the individual words that make up a compound word do not always give a clue to the meaning of the compound word, as in the words *dragonfly* and *cattail*.

Here are the title of several children's trade books that can be used to reinforce compound words:

Berenstain, S., & Berenstain, J. (1969). *Inside, outside, upside down*. NY: Random House.

Carlson, N. (1994). *K is for kiss goodnight: A bedtime alphabet*. NY: Bantam Doubleday Dell Publishing Group.

Carle, E. (1977). *The grouchy ladybug*. NY: Scholastic.

Cox, D. (1985). *Bossyboots*. NY: Crown.

Ehlert, L. (1995). *Snowballs.* NY: Harcourt.

James, S. (1991). *Dear Mr. Blueberry.* NY: Macmillan.

Kessler, L. (1986). *Old Turtle's riddle and joke book.* NY: Greenwillow Books.

Moncure, J. (1988). *The biggest snowfall.* Chicago: Children's Press.

Rice, E. (1980). *Goodnight, goodnight.* NY: Greenwillow Books.

Some reading specialists do not believe that traditional syllabication is useful in either word identification or spelling because computer word processing programs are so common today. One such reading specialist is Groff (1981), who thinks it usually is more helpful to divide a word into *"chunks of meaning"* rather than into traditional syllables that match those of a dictionary. For example, Groff probably would "chunk" the word *ladder* as *ladd/er* instead of the syllabic division *lad/der*, which is the more common one. I agree with Groff on this point.

On the primer reading level only 15% of the words have more than one syllable; in first grade 25% of the words are polysyllabic; and by sixth grade 80% of the words contain more than one syllable. Therefore, you can see that children in the primary grades should begin to understand how to divide words either into "chunks of meaning" or traditional syllables. The next section of this chapter provides suggestions for doing this.

As stated earlier, word structure is often most helpful when it is used *along with* meaning clues and phonics. For example, if a child attacks a word of more than one syllable using word structure, he or she first must be able to decode each of the "chunks of meaning" or syllables phonetically and then blend them into a recognizable word that is in his or her meaning vocabulary. After the word has been analyzed both structurally and phonetically, the child then must use meaning clues to determine whether or not it makes sense in sentence context.

In conclusion, children in the primary grades should begin to learn word structure, which is then continued and refined in the intermediate grades and beyond.

COMMON PREFIXES, SUFFIXES, AND WORD ROOTS

Because there are far too many prefixes, suffixes, and word roots to be included in this book, you are encouraged to consult the following teacher's resource book for a comprehensive listing of each of them.

Fry, E., Kress, J., & Fountoukidis, D. (2000). *The Reading Teacher's Book of Lists,* Fourth Edition. Paramus, NJ: Prentice Hall.

   Lists of Prefixes, pp. 85–92

   Lists of Suffixes, pp. 93–99

   Greek and Latin Roots, pp. 106–111

   List of Plurals, pp. 326–327

Here is a Scope and Sequence Chart for the most common prefixes in grades 3–8 (Harris & Jacobson, 1982).

Grade	Prefix	Meaning	Example
3	*un-*	not	unclear
	un-	opposite	undress
	under-	under	undercover
4	*dis-*	not	dishonor
	dis-	opposite	disembark
	re-	again	reinvent
	re-	back	replay
5	*im-*	not	immovable
	in-	not	invisible
	pre-	before	prewar
	sub-	under	submarine
6	*ex-*	out, out of	export
	ex-	former	explayer
	inter-	between	interurban
	mis-	not	misunderstood
	mis-	bad	misgivings
7	*en-*	forms verb	enlarge
	ir-	not	irrational
	trans-	across	transport
8	*anti-*	against	antisocial
	pro-	in favor of	prowar
	super-	above	superhuman

Here is a Scope and Sequence Chart for the most common derivational suffixes in grades 2–8 (Harris & Jacobson, 1982).

Grade	Suffix	Meaning	Example
2	-en	made of	golden
	-er	one who	teacher
	-or	one who	sailor
3	-able	is, can be	lovable
	-ible	is, can be	gullible
	-ful	full of, having	truthful
	-ness	having	happiness
	-(t)ion	act of	fascination
	-y	being, having	rainy
4	-al	having	maternal
	-ance	state of	annoyance
	-ence	state of, quality	violence
	-ify	make	vilify
	-less	without	worthless
	-ment	state of	management
	-ous	having	joyous
5	-ian	one who is in a certain field	musician
	-ic	of, having	volcanic
	-ish	having the quality of	childish
	-ive	being	negative
6	-ian	one who	barbarian
	-ist	a person who	physicist
	-ity	state of	hilarity
	-ize	make	sanitize
7	-ar	forms adjective	muscular
	-age	forms noun	baggage
	-ess	female	goddess
8	-ary	forms adjective	military
	-ette	small	majorette
	-some	forms adjective	worrisome

Here is a Scope and Sequence Chart for common word roots in grades 3–8 (Harris & Jacobson, 1982).

Grade	Root	Meaning	Example
3	*graph*	writing	telegraph
	tele	distance	telephone
4	*port*	carry	portable
	saur	lizard	dinosaur
	phon	sound	phoneme
	vid, vis	see	video
5	*astro*	star	astronomer
	cred	believe	credible
	duct	lead	conduct
	tri	three	triple
6	*aud*	hear	audiologist
	auto	self	autobiography
	bi	two	bifocal
	ology	study of	zoology
	scrib, script	writing	transcript
	therm	heat	thermal
7	*mid*	middle	midway
	ped	foot	pedometer
	chrono	time	chronological
	dict	say	verdict
	hemi	half	hemisphere
	manu	hand	manual
8	*bio*	life	biography
	geo	earth	geography
	micro	small	microsurgery
	mono	one	monotonous
	semi	half, part	semiliterate
	some	group	twosome

STRATEGIES FOR IMPROVING ABILITY IN WORD STRUCTURE

This section contains many classroom-tested strategies and materials for improving ability in word structure. You are encouraged to use any of them in their present form if they seem applicable and to modify them in light of the needs, abilities, and interests of your students.

THE ANALOGY STRATEGY AND RIMES

Using the analogy strategy and rimes (phonograms) greatly helps students to pronounce words of more than one syllable. Students with learning or reading disabilities often "freeze" when they reach large words. Typically they either do not try to identify the words or else they guess wildly at them.

Using the analogy strategy with rimes helps students combine vowel patterns (phonics) and syllabication (word structure). For example, examine the two following words and the two different ways that each word theoretically could be pronounced.

CV Pattern	**VC Pattern**
∪	‾
stup/id	stu/pid

CV Pattern	**VC Pattern**
∪	‾
riv/er	ri/ver

The student should learn to read aloud or silently a word such as those in the preceding list *in context* and then select the correct pronunciation (i.e., the pronunciation that makes sense in sentence context). The analogy approach with rimes should be a tool that is used in a thoughtful, flexible way—not simply drawing lines between syllables with no regard for whether or not the pronounced word makes sense in context.

A GENERALIZATION STRATEGY FOR TEACHING SYLLABICATION

Gunning (1996) has provided the following syllabication strategy using the generalization approach.

Step One: Auditory Perception of Syllables. Explain to students that many words have parts that are called *syllables.* Pronounce a group of words and have children clap once for each syllable that they are able to hear: *tur-tle, teach-er, lad-der, ta-ble, gir-affe, pic-ture, ti-ger,* etc. Once students understand this concept, have them join in.

Step Two: Perception of Printed Syllables. Present one- and two-syllable words that contrast with each other so that students can understand printed syllables.

a	*tall*	*jump*	*rain*	*through*
about	*taller*	*jumping*	*rainbow*	*throughout*

Step Three: Perception of a Syllable Generalization. Once students understand what syllables are, present words that illustrate a syllable generalization. For example, the following words illustrate the suffix *-ing* generalization:

walk	*do*	*be*	*sleep*	*throw*
walking	*doing*	*being*	*sleeping*	*throwing*

Then have students read the words and contrast them. Help them to see that the words on the top have only one syllable while the words on the bottom contain two syllables. Read each word on the bottom and have the students clap as they hear the separate syllables in each word. Encourage students to discover that the *-ing* at the end of a word makes up a separate syllable. In subsequent lessons help them discover other prefixes and suffixes and broaden the generalization.

Step Four: Guided Practice. Have the students read poems, signs, and short selections and sing songs that contain words illustrating the target generalization. Have them complete review exercises in which they use both syllabication clues and context to select the word that correctly completes a sentence. The following should illustrate this activity:

Honey will go *walk, walking* with her owner tomorrow morning.

I wonder if Tanya will *do, doing* her homework tonight.

My puppy is *be, being* very stubborn today.

A child should *sleep, sleeping* about ten hours a night.

Sami's father hurt his arm *throw, throwing* a ball.

Step Five: Application. Have students read all types of narrative and content selections that contain words with more than one syllable. Encourage them to apply the generalization(s) they have learned.

TEACHING SYLLABICATION USING THE PATTERN APPROACH

In a *pattern approach* students look at a number of words that contain a common syllable. For example, many words that begin with a consonant and are followed by a long */o/* can be presented in a pattern form. Using this approach, students learn to recognize pronounceable units in words and also to apply the open-syllable generalization in a specific situation. The pattern can be introduced with a one-syllable word that is then contrasted with multisyllabic words to make it easier for the children to understand. Here is an example of this concept:

go	*voted*
total	*motel*
hotel	*global*
vocal	*totem*

Gunning (1996) presented the following main steps to use in the pattern approach to syllabication.

Step One: Introduce the Pattern. Write the word *go* on the chalkboard and have the children pronounce it. Next write the word *ago* directly under it and have them pronounce it. Contrast *go* and *ago* by stressing the sound that each syllable makes. If you want, you can write the two words in different colors to help students contrast them. Then have the students pronounce *ago*. Then present the words *alike, about, away, around,* and *alone.* As students read the separate syllables in each word, point to each one. Help children notice the similarities among the words.

Step Two: Formulate a Generalization. Help students to understand that *a* at the beginning of a word may have the schwa (ə) sound of /uh/. Because the schwa sound only is found in a word of more than one syllable, give students a multisyllabic model word for the *a* spelling of the schwa sound. Tell students that *ago* (or any other selected word) can be the model word for this pattern. If they forget the pattern, they can use the model word to help them remember. It is a good idea to start a model words chart.

Step Three: Guided Practice. Have students read a second set of schwa /a/ words such as *along, across, alive, asleep, awake, abound.* Have students do any activity such as this:

Construct words by putting together two of the three syllables found in each row.

sleep	*a*	*play*	_____
a	*live*	*drive*	_____
round	*a*	*work*	_____
long	*bake*	*a*	_____
a	*wake*	*dream*	_____

Circle the word that makes sense in each sentence.

My dog Kersti can fall *sleep, asleep* anytime.

Hope's sister is very lucky to be *alive, live* after that automobile accident.

Please take me *long, along* with you to the mall today.

Elizabeth doesn't want to go *away, way* from home for more than one day.

I couldn't get Becky *awake, wake* when she was sleeping on Wednesday afternoon.

Step Four: Application. Have students read all types of narrative and content selections that contain the schwa /a/ sound.

PLAYDOUGH AND MODELING CLAY

Playdough and modeling clay are effective in giving children practice with inflectional endings at the beginning reading level. Have the child use playdough and modeling clay to make objects that illustrate comparisons. For example, have the children use either material to show the following:

thin, thinner, thinnest

big, bigger, biggest

little, littler, littlest

long, longer, longest

tiny, tinier, tiniest

short, shorter, shortest

Variation

The same concept can be shown by having the child fold a sheet of 12" × 18" newsprint or manila paper. Then have the child print words such as the following on the paper: *thin, thinner, thinnest; big, bigger, biggest; little, littler, littlest; long, longer, longest; tiny, tinier, tiniest; short, shorter, shortest*. Have the child draw pictures to illustrate each of these comparisons. Here is an illustration of the first comparison mentioned:

ARE THESE REAL OR MADE-UP COMPOUND WORDS?

Write a number of compound words on the chalkboard or a transparency. Some of them should be real compound words, while others should be made-up compound words. Have the child then write all the words in two columns on a sheet of paper—those that are the actual compound words and those that are not. If you want, this activity also can be placed on an activity sheet for a child to complete independently or with a partner(s).

Here are some words that you might want to use for this activity.

Actual Compound Words	Made-Up Compound Words
wheelchair	*catpaw*
blueberry	*dognose*
spacecraft	*boatoar*
earring	*birdsong*
baseball	*greengrass*
doorbell	*grayhair*
sunshine	*bookcover*
blackbird	*televisionset*
tablecloth	*flowerpetal*
playhouse	*treebark*

STRUCTURAL GRAFFITI

Cover an area of the classroom or tutoring area, such as part of a bulletin board, with butcher paper. Label the paper with some part of word structure, such as compound words, contractions, prefixes, or suffixes. Throughout the week in their free time, have children write appropriate words containing that structural element on the paper. Have the entire class discuss and evaluate their structural "graffiti" at the end of the week. This activity is most appropriate for children in the upper primary grades or possibly fourth grade.

TYING WORDS TOGETHER

You need a sheet of 8" × 10" posterboard, a marker, scissors, and eight pairs of 16" shoelace. Print the first half of appropriate compound words on the left of the poster-board and the second half of the words on the right side of the posterboard in scrambled order. Punch holes by each of the word halves. Have the child thread a shoelace through the hole beside half of each compound word to the other part to make a complete compound word. Have the child continue until he or she has matched all of the words and made correct compound words.

WHAT KIND OF COMPOUND WORDS ARE THESE?

To increase children's knowledge of compound words, construct a large wall chart with five headings, such as *Kinds of Living Creatures, People, Things, Places*, and *Time*, written on the top. Then ask the children to find compound words that fit under these and/or other appropriate headings. Here is a sample of compound words that children could include on such a list.

Kinds of Living Creatures	People	Things	Places	Time
blackbird	*frogman*	*motorcycle*	*sidewalk*	*Thanksgiving*
starfish	*grandfather*	*basketball*	*airport*	*sunrise*
goldfish	*lifeguard*	*buttermilk*	*backyard*	*sunset*
bluebird	*gentleman*	*cupcake*	*ballpark*	*afternoon*
bulldog	*landlady*	*drugstore*	*uptown*	*birthday*
copperhead	*grandmother*	*flashlight*	*downtown*	*breakfast*
grasshopper	*housewife*	*newspaper*	*downstairs*	*nighttime*
dragonfly	*firefighter*	*pancake*	*vineyard*	*daytime*
woodpecker	*salesperson*	*waterfall*	*cockpit*	*midnight*
rattlesnake	*shortstop*	*streetcar*	*railroad*	*weekend*

WEB FOR A WORD ROOT

You can construct a web for a word root that you place on the chalkboard or a transparency. Later you can give students, especially those who are average or above in reading, word roots and have them try to construct their own webs independently or with a partner(s) for the various word roots. This activity is most appropriate for students in the intermediate grades and beyond. It is probably too difficult for students who have learning or reading disabilities. Here is an example of this type of web that was constructed from the root word *port*, which means "carry."

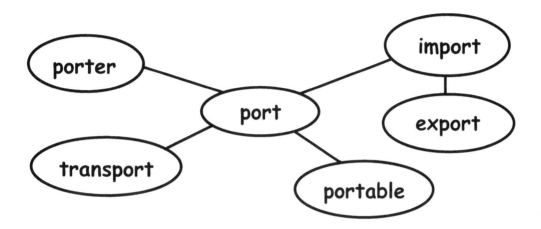

Here are some other root words and words that are derived from them that can be included in such a web.

aqua (meaning water)—*aquatic, aquarium, aquamarine, aqueous, aquifer*

biblio (meaning book)—*bibliography, bibliophile, Bible*

bio (meaning life)—*biography, biology, biochemistry, biopsy*

man (meaning hand)—*manufacture, manuscript, manual, manipulate*

miss (meaning send)—*missile, mission, remiss, dismiss, missionary*

mort (meaning death)—*mortuary, mortal, immortal, mortician*

numer (meaning number)—*numeral, numerator, numerous, enumerate, innumerable*

pater (meaning father)—*paternal, patriarch, paternity, patricide*

phob (meaning fear)—*acrophobia, claustrophobia, xenophobia*

phon (meaning sound)—*phonics, phoneme, phonograph, telephone, microphone, symphony*

pug (meaning fight)—*pugilist, pugnacious, impugn, repugnant*

rad (meaning ray, spoke)—*radius, radio, radiate, radium, radiology*

scribe (meaning write)—*script, transcribe, scriptures, scribble*

spec (meaning see)—*spectator, inspect, suspect, respect, spectacle*

terr (meaning land)—*terrarium, territory, terrestrial, terrace*

therm (meaning heat)—*thermometer, thermal, thermostat, thermos*

urb (meaning city)—*urban, suburb, suburban, urbane*

The teacher's resource book by Fry, Kress, and Fountoukidis that was mentioned earlier contains a comprehensive list of word roots that can be used in this activity.

USING WORD ROOTS, PREFIXES, AND SUFFIXES TO CREATE NEW WORDS

Able readers in the intermediate grades and beyond probably would enjoy using word roots, prefixes, and suffixes to create new words that are not currently in the dictionary. First present this concept to them and then they can practice this strategy either independently or preferably with a partner(s).

If you want, this activity can be placed on an activity sheet that will challenge good readers. Obviously, this type of activity is too difficult for most students with learning or reading disabilities.

Here are several examples that could be included in this activity.

a *hyrobile*—a vehicle that runs on water

a *bibliohom*—a man (person) who likes to read

a *quadocular*—a person who wears glasses (four eyes)

thermacqua—hot water

computergram—letter sent by E-mail

STRATEGY FOR LONG WORDS

Students with difficulties in word structure cannot decode or attack long words. They should use the following strategy when trying to identify such words.

1. Look for any prefixes and suffixes in the word and try to use its meaning to help identify the word.

2. Look for the word root and try to use its meaning to help identify the word.

3. Read to the end of the sentence. Think of a word with those parts that makes sense in the sentence.

4. Try other sounds, syllables, and accents until you form a word that makes sense in sentence context.

5. If you still are not able to identify the word, ask someone or use the dictionary to help you identify it.

GAMES FOR IMPROVING ABILITY IN WORD STRUCTURE

This section includes several classroom-tested games for improving ability in word structure. Because such games are motivating, they often are especially useful with students who have learning or reading disabilities, who may be difficult to motivate. You can modify the games in any way you want in light of the interests and needs of your students.

Contraction Pizza Board

TO CONSTRUCT THE GAME

You need pizza boards, which usually can be obtained inexpensively or for free from a local pizza restaurant. You also need wood clothespins, marking pens, and clear self-stick vinyl.

With a marking pen, divide the pizza board into sections. Write two words that can comprise a contraction in each section of the pizza board. Then write the corresponding contractions on the clothespins. Cover the pizza board with clear self-stick vinyl. Here is an illustration of a contraction pizza board.

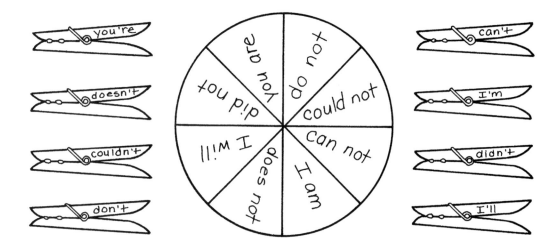

TO PLAY THE GAME

Have the child match the contraction to each set of double words by clipping the corresponding clothespin to the correct section.

The Prefix and Suffix Game

TO CONSTRUCT THE GAME

Make 3" × 5" cards with a prefix such as *un*-_____, *re*-_____, or *dis*-_____ printed on them. In addition, make 3" × 5" cards with a suffix such as _____-*ing*, _____-*ly*, or _____-*ed* printed on them. Be sure to include the line to show children whether it is a prefix or a suffix.

TO PLAY THE GAME

You should not use this game until children are knowledgeable about prefixes and suffixes. Children who are nonnative English speakers probably will have considerable difficulty with this game.

Each of the two teams chooses a pitcher, who will "pitch" a word to the "batter." The batter then thinks of a word to go with the prefix or suffix and pronounces it. If the student does this but cannot use the word in a sentence, he or she has hit a "single." If the student can think of a word, pronounce it, and use it in a sentence, he or she has hit a "double." After the students have become more adept at the game, you may want to limit the hits to singles to slow down the game.

Try to Spin for Suffixes

TO CONSTRUCT THE GAME

Select a heavy piece of cardboard or a piece of plywood. Then cut it in a circle about 2 to 3 feet in diameter. Write a few suffixes around the edge of the board so that they occupy the same positions as the numbers on the face of a clock or watch. However, you only need about six or eight suffixes, not twelve.

You also need extra overlays to attach to the face of the circle. These overlays will enable you to readily change the suffixes that you are stressing at that time. Place a pointer in the center of the circle that can be spun.

Construct a number of 3" × 5" word cards that can be used with each overlay. For example, for the suffixes -s, -ed, -ing on the overlay, you can write the word *walk* on a word card. Here is an illustration of this game board.

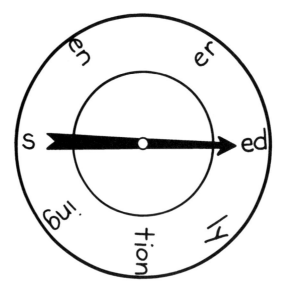

TO PLAY THE GAME

Pass out an equal number of word cards to each player in a group. You or a student then spins the pointer, which stops on a suffix. You call on each member of the group and ask him or her to take his or her top card and try to attach that suffix. The student can be asked to spell and pronounce the formulated word. When a student has done so correctly, he or she puts the card in the box. The student who has his or her cards in the box first is the winner.

Cutting Contractions

TO CONSTRUCT THE GAME

You need unlined newsprint, marking pens, and scissors. On strips of the unlined newsprint, write two words that will form the new contractions being presented. Give these word strips and a pair of scissors to each child. For each set make small cards, each of which contains an apostrophe. The following illustration should clarify the construction of this game.

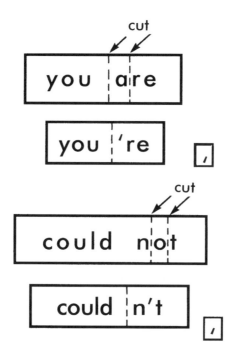

TO PLAY THE GAME

To help children remember which letters are to be taken away in order to form the contractions, have each child cut away these letters and replace them with an apostrophe card. Two children can work informally to make this activity gamelike.

Making Compound Words

TO CONSTRUCT THE GAME

You need cardboard, different colors of marking pens, belt eyelets, an eyelet tool, clear self-stick vinyl, heavy yarn or shoelaces, and cellophane tape. Use 9" × 12" cardboard pieces. On the left edge of the cardboard draw or cut out pictures that form a compound word. On the right side write the compound word in a scrambled order. Cover with clear self-stick vinyl. On each edge beside the picture and words, insert a belt eyelet. Attach a piece of knotted yarn and tape the end of each piece. The following illustration should clarify the construction of this game.

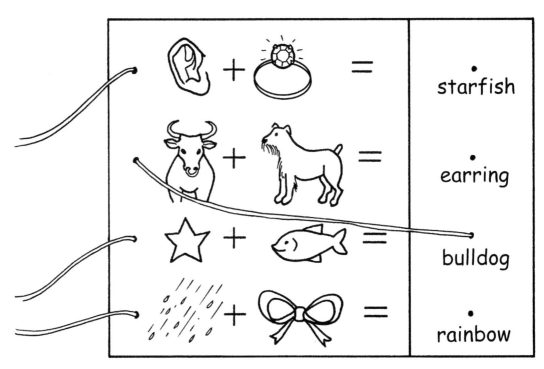

TO PLAY THE GAME

Have the student match the pictures to the correct compound word by inserting the yarn into the correct eyelet on the right side. To make this activity gamelike, you can have one child do the activity and another child check the work.

REPRODUCIBLES FOR IMPROVING ABILITY IN WORD STRUCTURE

This section contains several reproducibles that you can use for improving your students' ability in various elements of word structure. You can use them in their present form or modify them in any way you wish.

CHOOSE THE RIGHT WORD
Second-Grade Level

Read each sentence to yourself. Circle the word that makes sense in each sentence.

1. The fur on Fluffy the cat is the *soft, softer, softest* of all.

2. Bob is *tall, taller, tallest* than Kurt.

3. Salli is the *short, shorter, shortest* child in our family.

4. That new baby really is *tiny, tinier, tiniest* and very cute.

5. It was very hard for my older brother to pass that *wide, wider, widest* truck with his small car.

6. Today is the *lovely, lovelier, loveliest* day I have ever seen.

7. I think my mother is very *pretty, prettier, prettiest*.

8. I have never seen anyone *angry, angrier, angriest* than Ms. Jackson was today.

9. Mr. Swanson is a very *heavy, heavier, heaviest* man.

10. Emily's new puppy that she named Honey is very *fat, fatter, fattest*.

11. Barry is the *old, older, oldest* boy on Parkside School's soccer team.

12. My sister seems very, very *happy, happier, happiest* today.

13. Jake's grandmother's funeral was the *sad, sadder, saddest* day of his life.

14. I thought Wednesday was a very *long, longer, longest* day.

15. Susie is the *young, younger, youngest* child in our class.

MAKING NEW COMPOUND WORDS
Third-Grade Level

There are two compound words under the blank in each sentence. Write part of one word and part of the other word to make a new compound word. The new compound word should make sense in the sentence. The first one is done for you.

1. Molly really likes to eat_____**blueberry**_____ pie for dessert.
   strawberry/bluebird

2. A _____ is supposed to save people
   lifeguard/sailboat
   from drowning if a steamship should accidentally sink.

3. A _____ is a lovely yellow flower
   teacup/buttermilk
   that can be seen in the woods in the summer.

4. My mother needs to buy a new _____
   boardwalk/teacup
   for the kitchen because she doesn't have enough space to
   put all of the groceries.

5. I really like the _____ so that I
   daydream/nighttime
   can stay outside and play.

6. My brother Dave bought a new _____
   outfield/boardwalk
   motor for his motorboat.

7. A shiny _____ is a very pretty kind
   bluebird/blackboard
   of bird.

8. Molly enjoys going _____ on
   downpour/uptown
   Saturday mornings.

9. Our _____ team won almost all of
   footprint/baseball
   the games that it played this year.

10. That store has a _____ machine
    volleyball/pinpoint
    that is fun to play.

11. Patti's mom just had their _____
    mailroom/bathtub
    remodeled, and it is very pretty.

12. A _____ is another name for a
    landfill/woodpecker
    forest.

FILL IN THE BLANK WITH THE WORD CONTAINING THE CORRECT PREFIX
Fourth-Grade Level

Fill in the blanks with the correct word in each set of six sentences. The words that you can choose from are printed above the six sentences.

replay	relive
rewrite	redo
reappear	repack

1. I had to _____ the dusting as I had been very careless.

2. Yetti had to _____ his writing assignment as he made so many grammar mistakes.

3. Elizabeth really likes to _____ her favorite CD.

4. The sun may _____ almost as soon as it stops snowing.

5. I hope Jill doesn't _____ her car accident over and over again.

6. Carolyn had to _____ her suitcase over and over again on her trip to South Africa.

FILL IN THE BLANK WITH THE WORD CONTAINING
THE CORRECT PREFIX *(Cont'd)*

unhappy	unkind
unroll	unhealthy
unlike	unpack

1. When everyone forgot my grandmother's birthday, she was

    very _____.

2. When Shamika returned home from her trip to the lake,

    she had to _____ her suitcase.

3. Because Betti doesn't ever eat properly, she is an

    _____ person.

4. Although Wesley and Wendy are twins, they are

    _____ in many ways.

5. Please _____ that tube of aluminum

    foil for me.

6. Mr. Flanders is always so mean and _____

    to me.

FILL IN THE BLANK WITH THE WORD CONTAINING
THE CORRECT PREFIX *(Cont'd)*

disagree	**disloyal**
disappear	**disrepair**
dislike	**dismount**

1. That old house is in a terrible state of

   _____.

2. Kathy and her brother _____ about

   almost everything.

3. My puppy just seemed to _____ from

   our backyard this morning.

4. It is very hard for some people to _____

   from a horse.

5. Frankie seems to be a very _____

   person.

6. I really _____ doing homework every

   evening.

Name _____ Grade _____

MY REACTION TO WORDS WITH THE *PRO-* OR *ANTI-* PREFIX
Fourth-Grade Level

Circle the prefix **Pro-** or **Anti-** that indicates your reaction to each of the following words.

1. **Pro-** Anti- swimming
2. **Pro-** Anti- homework
3. **Pro-** Anti- pizza
4. **Pro-** Anti- broccoli
5. **Pro-** Anti- shoveling snow
6. **Pro-** Anti- recess
7. **Pro-** Anti- hamburgers
8. **Pro-** Anti- school bus
9. **Pro-** Anti- headache
10. **Pro-** Anti- science
11. **Pro-** Anti- reading
12. **Pro-** Anti- art
13. **Pro-** Anti- television
14. **Pro-** Anti- computer games
15. **Pro-** Anti- dogs
16. **Pro-** Anti- cats
17. **Pro-** Anti- math
18. **Pro-** Anti- ice skating
19. **Pro-** Anti- candy
20. **Pro-** Anti- studying
21. **Pro-** Anti- snakes
22. **Pro-** Anti- camping
23. **Pro-** Anti- fishing
24. **Pro-** Anti- ice cream
25. **Pro-** Anti- winter

CONTEXT CLUES

The use of *context clues* is a word identification technique in which a reader determines the meaning and sometimes the pronunciation of unknown words by examining the context in which they are located. That context can be the sentence, the nearby sentences, the paragraph, or the entire passage. It usually also involves grammar clues.

Sometimes context clues are not very helpful (Schatz & Baldwin, 1986). An informal survey of difficult words in children's magazines, textbooks, and trade books indicates that usable context clues are provided only about one-third of the time (Gunning, 1990). Some reading specialists estimate that the average reader is able to use context successfully only between 5 and 20% of the time (Jenkins, Matlock, & Slocum, 1989; Nagy, Anderson, & Herman, 1987).

Even when context is helpful, some children do not take advantage of it. However, children usually become more adept in its use as they progress through the elementary grades. They also must be given direct instruction and practice in the use of context clues if they are to use them effectively. A teacher cannot just tell children to use context clues without giving them direct instruction and much motivated practice in their use. They also must be given feedback to let them know that they are correct (Carnine, Kameenui, & Coyle, 1984).

Reading specialists have determined that there are a number of different kinds of context clues. Although the categories of context clues differ somewhat, here is one classification that commonly has been used (Herber, 1967, p. 16).

- *Experience clues*—A reader uses his or her prior knowledge to determine the meaning of the unknown word. This is why it is very important for a child to have much appropriate prior knowledge to be an effective reader either of narrative or content material.

- *Association clues*—A reader attempts to associate the unknown word with the known word. Example: Today I have a *voracious* appetite and have been as hungry as a bear.

- *Synonym clues*—There is a synonym to the known word in the sentence to explain it. Example: Because Mrs. Stark needed to have an eye examination to fit her for glasses, she went to an *ophthalmologist*.

- *Summary clues*—Several sentences can be used to summarize the meaning of the unknown word.

- *Comparison or contrast clues*—There is a comparison or contrast to the unknown word in the sentence or paragraph that gives the word its meaning.

- *Previous contact clues*—The child can determine the meaning of the unknown word from previous experiences that he or she has had with a similar word.

Other similar classification schemes for context clues are found in Gunning (1996) and Rinsky (1997). You may want to consult one or both of them for additional information.

With the current emphasis on reading as a global, meaning-based process that emphasizes comprehension from the beginning, it is obvious that context clues are *the single most useful technique of word identification.* However, context clues are the most helpful when used along with word structure and phonics and when there are not many unknown words in the reading material. Usually there should be *no more than one in fifty unknown words in the material* if context clues are to be used effectively.

Context clues can be presented as early as the beginning reading level, when you orally give a sentence with an omitted word. Then ask the children to suggest a word orally that makes sense in that sentence. This activity also ensures readiness for the *cloze procedure.* At the primary-grade level, explain the importance of context clues to the pupils, and encourage them to use context clues to deduce the meaning of unknown words that they meet while reading. In addition, ask primary-grade children to read simple sentences and select the omitted word that makes sense in each sentence from the options that are supplied. For example,

Evie bought her mother a beautiful _____ for her birthday.
scare, scream, scarf

It is important to encourage students both in the primary and intermediate grades to supply words that make sense while reading, both silently and orally, even if the provided words are not the actual words found in the reading material. All students should be taught that using context clues is not merely guessing at the meaning of unknown words, but rather is a *calculated estimate* of the meaning of unknown words that demands inferential thinking on the student's part.

Especially in the primary grades, children often are discouraged from risk taking, which may hinder their reading progress because too much stress then is placed on word-perfect oral reading. However, the practice of word substitution can be carried to an excess when students mispronounce up to half of the words in the reading material. Such students should continue to have practice and/or review in sight word identification, word structure, or phonics depending on their weaknesses.

Here are the advantages of using context clues:

➡ Most students can identify words in context that they cannot identify in isolation.

➡ Readers who can use context clues become independent decoders much more quickly. They learn to be good predictors of what words might be. They then are able to confirm or reject their predictions depending on whether or not they make sense in the context of what they are reading. Then they rapidly read on.

➡ Words that do not have a consistent sound–symbol relationship may be more easily generalized by using context clues.

➡ Children who have difficulty with phonic skills that require closer attention to visual features may identify unknown words more easily in this way.

Here are some of the limitations of using context clues:

➡ Beginning readers have a limited reading vocabulary, so they often have difficulty in using context clues effectively.

➡ Because there are many synonyms in English that could make sense in different contexts, when context clues are used alone, their use may not result in accurate word identification. When the exact word is required for some reason, a child must also use other clues, such as word structure or phonic clues, along with context clues.

➡ In a number of cases, the surrounding context may not be enough to provide accurate word identification or may provide misleading information about the word.

In summary, context is the one technique of word identification that best represents the concept of reading as a language-based process that emphasizes comprehension. Therefore, it usually should receive the most emphasis as a word identification technique with the possible exception of children with learning disabilities, who may need more emphasis placed on the other word identification techniques, such as phonics. However, these children also need to understand the importance of using context clues.

STRATEGIES FOR IMPROVING ABILITY IN CONTEXT CLUES

This section includes several strategies and materials that reading teachers and tutors can use to improve the context skills of their students. All of them have been used successfully by many reading teachers and tutors.

WIDE READING

Wide reading of various kinds of materials undoubtedly is the single best way of improving ability in context clues. This reading can take place in predictable books (see the list of predictable books in Chapter 3); dictated language-experience stories; child-written books; trade books of various types, including picture storybooks, chapter books, adolescent novels, and informational books; and children's magazines and newspapers.

Reading is a skill that makes the most improvement using materials that students can read fairly easily. Therefore, it is obvious that the more a student reads, even if it is from simple materials, the better reader he or she should become. However, children who have difficulty with reading activities, such as children with learning disabilities or other special needs, often do as little reading as possible and therefore do not make good reading progress. Although it may be hard to motivate such children, it should be possible to do so by having them read very interesting, easy materials that are especially chosen for them. You may be successful with such students by encouraging them to read self-selected, fairly easy material that reflects their interests. Predictable books, including Dr. Seuss books, usually have been effective with various kinds of special needs children, including those with learning disabilities. Older students with special reading needs may enjoy books about sports, animals, space, other boys and girls, or mysteries.

SELF-MONITORING

It is important for students to learn to monitor their silent and oral reading. The concept of self-monitoring is explained briefly in the next chapter. It is a mind-set in which a reader consistently thinks about what he or she is reading. If the reader is not successfully understanding the material, he or she should learn how to apply fix-up strategies, which also are briefly explained in the next chapter. Good readers of all ages monitor their comprehension much more effectively than do poor readers.

LISTENING FOR READING MISCUES

Children can be helped to become aware of *miscues* (errors) that interfere with comprehension by having them listen to material (either teacher-read or tape-recorded), indicate when miscues occur, and state why the miscue is inappropriate. When a student meets an unknown word in context or is not aware that a disruptive miscue (one that interferes with comprehension) has occurred, he or she usually should finish reading the entire sentence because it may provide additional useful information. Usually the words *after the unknown word* provide more help than the words before it. A *place-holder* (a word that makes sense and is grammatically appropriate) can be used until new information makes it necessary to try another response. If neither strategy is effective, rereading the sentence containing the unknown word may help. However, before doing so, the student should examine the unknown word by using phonic clues along with context clues (an effective combination method of word identification). If none of these strategies is effective, it may be useful to read the sentence before or after the sentence containing the unknown word.

Dahl and Samuels (1974) have presented the following strategy for using context clues:

1. Use information from the passage, prior knowledge, and language clues.

2. Make a prediction as to which word is the most likely to occur.

3. Compare the printed and predicted words to see if they fit.

4. Accept or reject the prediction.

Taylor and Norbush (1983) also have recommended a four-step procedure for encouraging students to self-correct disruptive miscues:

1. On a one-to-one basis the student reads a 100- to 300-word passage at the appropriate instructional level to the teacher, who gives very little feedback.

2. The teacher praises the student for something well done in this oral reading, especially his or her self-correction.

3. One or two uncorrected miscues are shown to the student by reading his or her rendition to him or her and having the student tell what word did not make sense or sound right.

4. The student is helped to recognize the miscued (miscalled) words by showing how context and graphic (sight or phonic) clues could have been used.

A WORD IDENTIFICATION STRATEGY THAT EMPHASIZES CONTEXT CLUES

Shanker and Ekwall (1998) suggested a strategy that is an effective way to teach students to use context clues when they are reading independently.

When you come to a word that you don't know

1. Say the beginning sound.

2. Read the rest of the sentence. THINK.

3. Say the parts that you know. GUESS.

4. Ask someone to help you and go on.

Step 1 emphasizes phonics and is useful because beginning sounds are often the most useful in identifying an unknown word. Step 2 requires the student to use context clues before using additional phonic or structural clues. It is useful because the words that come *after* the unknown word are helpful more often than words that come *before* an unknown word. Step 3 requires the student to use other word attack clues, such as ending sounds, vowel sounds, and word structure. The last step encourages the student to ask for help or continue reading if there is no other alternative. *If students must use Step 4, the material probably is too difficult for them, and they should be given easier material to read.*

Shanker and Ekwall suggest that you use the following steps in presenting this strategy:

1. Present the steps using a written chart that students can remember and refer to.

2. Model and use the steps yourself with simple sentences.

3. Tell students that this strategy really works.

4. Give students sentences that they can use to apply the steps as you provide help.

5. Ensure that students use the steps as they practice reading.

Here are some sample sentences you can use to present and give students practice in this four-step word identification strategy. They are models of sentences you can formulate for your own students. They illustrate the four steps mentioned earlier.

1. Some *nights* it is hard for me to go to sleep. (1, 2)

2. Milo can *throw* a baseball very straight and fast. (1, 2)

3. My mother baked me a *birthday* cake for my ninth birthday. (1, 2, 3)

4. *Chocolate* fudge certainly is my favorite candy. (1, 2, 3)

5. The *piranha* is a very ferocious fish that eats flesh. (1, 2, 3, 4?)

6. A *volcano* destroyed two ancient cities in Italy hundreds of years ago. (1, 2, 3, 4)

TEACHING THAT CONTEXT CLUES ARE NOT ALWAYS EFFECTIVE

It is important for students to learn that context clues are not always effective in determining the meaning and/or pronunciation of unknown words. The student should look at the following three groups of words with your help. He or she should understand that some sentences provide very good context clues, others provide only a little help, and still others provide no help at all.

Group I (Context is effective for the student)

1. When a p_____ grows up, it will be a dog.

2. When the sun comes out and it gets warm, a snowman will m_____.

3. In the summer I like to go swimming in the l_____.

Group II (Context provides some clues for the student)

1. My mother bakes the best c_____ that I have ever eaten. (*cake, cookies, cupcakes*)

2. My favorite month of summer is J_____. (*June, July*)

3. I would like to receive a d_____ for my birthday. (*dog, doll*)

Group III (Context provides no help)

1. We had many cl_____ days during the month of November. (*clear, cloudy*)

2. Linda is very h_____ today. (*happy, hot, hopeful, healthy*)

3. That woman is very l_____. (*little, likable, lovable*)

REBUSES

A beginning reading activity is to have the child dictate (or the teacher construct) a chart that uses *rebuses* (pictures) in place of some of the difficult but interesting vocabulary words. One of the most effective ways to use rebuses is by putting them in recipes for cooking or baking activities. The recipe is written on chart paper. Baking cookies, gingerbread figures, or bread, or making butter, among other foods, are all appropriate for this kind of activity.

OMITTING WORDS THAT CAN BE DETERMINED FROM CONTEXT

Construct sentences or short paragraphs, omitting selected words that students should be able to determine from their context. In place of each target word, insert an initial consonant and then *x*'s for the rest of the letters in the words. The following are examples of this activity:

Allison sxx many interesting animals on her trip to the Brookfield Zoo.

When students are able to get most of the deleted words by replacing the *x*'s with letters, the next step is to replace target words with *x*'s for *each* letter.

My xxxx sister cries when she is hungry or needs to have xxx diaper changed.

After students are able to get most of the deleted words by replacing the *x*'s with letters, leave blank lines to replace entire omitted words.

Today is a beautiful _____ day, and the _____ is shining brightly.

VARIATIONS OF THE CLOZE PROCEDURE

The *cloze procedure* was developed by Wilson L. Taylor (1953) and is based on the psychological theory of *closure*, which states that a person wants to finish any incomplete pattern. The cloze procedure is based on the *prediction* aspect of reading, which indicates that a reader tries to predict the unknown words he or she may meet in a passage. Therefore, the cloze procedure makes use of both context clues and grammar clues to help a reader identify unknown words.

The cloze procedure has a number of different variations, each of which can be helpful in improving a student's contextual and comprehension skills. One variation can be used as an alternative for determining a student's independent, instructional, and frustration reading levels.

No matter for what purpose a cloze procedure is used, it is constructed in the same basic way. Construct a cloze procedure from a content textbook, a trade book, a basal reader, or any other supplementary reading materials. Select a passage of about 250 words at what is believed to be the child's approximate instructional or high independent reading level. Then type the first and last sentences of the passage with no deletions. Every *n*th word is omitted throughout the rest of the passage unless the selected word is a proper noun or a very difficult word. I recommend that about every tenth word be omitted at the primary-grade reading level, every eighth word at the intermediate-grade reading level, and every fifth word above the intermediate-grade reading level. When the cloze procedure is used to improve ability in context clue usage, you should count as correct *any word that makes sense in the passage* and satisfies any other specific requirements. Incorrect spelling is not penalized in any version of cloze.

A young child should have completed a number of readiness activities before being exposed to actual cloze procedures. As one reading activity, select sentences from experience stories and print each sentence on a strip of tagboard, omitting one word. Then print each omitted word on a word card. Have the child place the proper word card in each sentence strip. You can make slits in each sentence strip if you want. Then have the child read each sentence aloud. As another example, print a short passage on the appropriate reading level and put masking tape over the words to be omitted. Have the children guess each omitted word. After each guess is made, remove the masking tape and have the children compare the actual word with their guesses. As one other example, *zipper cloze* involves printing some sentences on an overhead projector transparency with one word covered by a small piece of cardboard. Place a piece of tape across the cardboard to fasten it to the transparency so that the tape serves as a hinge. Then when you want to show the word to children after having them guess what the word might be, lift the tagboard flap. In the upper primary grades children should be able to discuss why various answers may or may not be acceptable in terms of context or grammar clues.

An easy version of cloze for use in the primary grades has all the omitted words written in random order in columns at the bottom of the sheet containing the passage.

Then the child selects the proper word to complete each blank as he or she reads the passage and prints it in the blank. Another simple option for use in the primary grades has each of the omissions with two or three options being placed under it or after it. Most children at this level like this variation of cloze very much. One other fairly easy variation for use in the upper primary or lower intermediate grades combines phonic clues and context clues. In this variation the beginning letter or the first two letters (consonant blend or consonant digraph) are written at the beginning of the omission. This variation is called a *partial word deletion*. In addition to the version just mentioned, the student can be given ending consonants or ending consonant digraphs in addition to the initial part of the words. As a third modification, only consonants are given and the vowels are deleted. Various modifications of this version emphasize various phonic elements. One other fairly easy version has random deletions, with the omitted word easy to figure out.

In selective word omission, important nouns, verbs, adjectives, or adverbs can be deleted. These words carry the meaning of the author's writing. When selected nouns, verbs, adjectives, or adverbs are deleted, the emphasis is on meaningful information from the passage. In addition, the special vocabulary of a subject is emphasized. The students we have tutored found that this variation requires considerable prior knowledge in the subject from which the cloze procedure was constructed.

A version often used at about the third- or fourth-grade reading level combines word length clues and context clues. Each omitted word is replaced by a typewritten space as long as the omitted word. For example, here is how the word *donkey* would look if it were deleted from this type of cloze procedure: _ _ _ _ _ _.

Note: In all of the other versions of the cloze procedure, the length of each blank space should be about fifteen typewritten spaces long.

Still other contemporary variations of cloze include deleting entire sentences in a random manner, deleting more than one word at a time, deleting an entire phrase (such as a prepositional phrase), or deleting the unimportant words in the passage. You can construct your own variations of the cloze procedure that are as useful as the versions described here.

Several variations of the cloze procedure are found later in this chapter in the reproducibles section.

CRYPTOGRAPHY AND MUTILATED MESSAGES

Many students enjoy figuring out codes and writing messages in codes. When something is written in code, something has been done to change the graphic display, so context is used to break the code.

Here are several ways messages can be changed or mutilated. You and your students can think of many more ways. There also are trade books on cryptology that your students can consult.

➡ Color names are added: *My purple dog is green big and very red friendly.*

➡ The bottom of all the letters is cut off:

My father really enjoys fishing at the lake.

➥ No spaces are left between words and a letter is added between words: *Sallibwouldoreallyplikeqtorgetsazkittenyforpherobirthday.*

HETERONYMS

Create a series of sentences using words that are spelled alike but may have different pronunciations or meanings. Have students read the sentences aloud or silently, pronouncing each word correctly.

REPRODUCIBLES FOR IMPROVING ABILITY IN CONTEXT CLUES

This section contains several reproducibles that you can use to improve your students' abilities in context clues. Any of them can be used in their present form or modified in any way you wish. It is important that you make these reproducibles compatible with your reading program.

CLOZE PROCEDURE WITH THE OMITTED WORDS
AT THE BOTTOM OF THE SHEET
Second-Grade Level

Read this story about skunks to yourself. As you read it, pick a word from the "Answers" that fits in each blank space. Then print the word in the blank space. When you are done, read the story again to be sure it is all correct.

SKUNKS

Have you ever seen a skunk? A skunk is a pretty animal with a black _____ white coat. Skunks often live in the woods.

Most other _____ in the woods have learned to leave skunks alone. _____ can spray other animals with a scent _____ smells just terrible. This smell is so strong that _____ takes a long, long time to go away.

Sometimes _____ try to get close to a skunk. The skunk _____ sprays the dog, and the dog runs home howling. _____ dog's owner usually has to wash the dog with _____ soup! Nothing else will take that awful smell away.

_____ a skunk sprays a person, the person usually has _____ throw away all the clothes that he or she _____ wearing.

That is why the story you are _____ to read now is so interesting. It is a _____ story that happened to one of my friends about _____ years ago.

SKUNKS

Many years ago people did not have _____ inside their houses. They had to go outside to _____ "outhouse" to go to the bathroom. When Shirley and John _____ building their new house in the woods, they used _____ outhouse for a while.

One day Shirley was in the _____. All of a sudden she saw a skunk coming _____ the outhouse. Skunks cannot see very well. The skunk _____ up on the platform of the outhouse and walked _____ and forth across Shirley's feet.

What would you have _____? Well, Shirley just stayed very, very still. Finally the _____ jumped down and walked away. Shirley thinks the _____ never did see her. Anyway it didn't spray her!

Shirley _____ very lucky, don't you think? It's a good thing for her that skunks aren't able to see clearly!

ANSWERS

animals	tomato	Skunks	thirty	done	going
that	and	to	an	then	was
it	If	true	were	jumped	skunk
dogs	skunk	toilets	an	was	back
The	toward	outhouse			

ANSWER KEY

SKUNKS

Have you ever seen a skunk? A skunk is a pretty animal with a black **and** white coat. Skunks often live in the woods.

Most other **animals** in the woods have learned to leave skunks alone. **Skunks** can spray other animals with a scent **that** smells just terrible. This smell is so strong that **it** takes a long, long time to go away.

Sometimes **dogs** try to get close to a skunk. The skunk **then** sprays the dog, and the dog runs home howling. **The** dog's owner usually has to wash the dog with **tomato** soup! Nothing else will take that awful smell away.

If a skunk sprays a person, the person usually has **to** throw away all the clothes that he or she **was** wearing.

That is why the story you are **going** to read now is so interesting. It is a **true** story that happened to one of my friends about **thirty** years ago.

Many years ago people did not have **toilets** inside their houses. They had to go outside to **an** "outhouse" to go to the bathroom. When Shirley and John **were** building their new house in the woods, they used **an** outhouse for awhile.

One day Shirley was in the **outhouse** . All of a sudden she saw a skunk coming **toward** the outhouse. Skunks cannot see very well. The skunk **jumped** up on the platform of the out-house and walked **back** and forth across Shirley's feet.

What would you have **done** ? Well, Shirley just stayed very, very still. Finally the **skunk** jumped down and walked away. Shirley thinks the **skunk** never did see her. Anyway it didn't spray her!

Shirley **was** very lucky, don't you think? It's a good thing for her that skunks aren't able to see clearly!

WHAT IS THE MYSTERY WORD?
Third-Grade Level

Read this entire story to yourself. As you read it, try to figure out what *one word has been omitted* from the whole story. After you have read the whole story, write the one mystery word in each blank in this story so that it will make sense.

Emily likes to eat almost all kinds of food. Even when she was little, she was a good eater.

Now Emily is in third grade, and her favorite food most definitely is _____. She could eat _____ for lunch and dinner nearly every day. However, her mother doesn't let her eat _____ very often, just once in a while for a special treat.

Sometimes Emily's mother makes _____ at home, while other times she orders it over the telephone. Emily likes either kind of _____ equally well.

When Emily's mother makes _____ at home, she uses a prepackaged _____ mix. However, her mother usually adds ground beef or sausage to the ingredients in the mix.

When they order _____ in, Emily asks for _____ with cheese and sausage for the family. Sometimes this is the kind of _____ that the restaurant delivers. Once in a while Emily's mother orders _____ with anchovies, a kind of fish. Emily definitely doesn't like anchovies!

Sometimes the family goes to the _____ restaurant and eats _____ there. That really is a lot of fun. Emily can see the _____ maker throw the _____ dough up in the air and catch it as it comes back down. Emily has never seen him drop it.

Is _____ your favorite food, too? It is a favorite with many children.

Answer: pizza

WHAT IS THE REAL WORD?
Fourth-Grade Level

Read each sentence to yourself. Then try to figure out what the actual underlined word is and write it on the line below the sentence. You can work with a partner(s) if you want to. The first one is done for you.

1. The beautiful white, fluffy sugy fell looking almost like a blanket where it landed. _____**snow**_____

2. Sarah is allowed to watch only one hour of terapine each evening as she also has to do her homework.

   _____

3. Patsy has always wanted to learn to ride a hemet so that she can vacation on a ranch someday. _____

4. Many children like to go for a swim in the pote that is in our city park. _____

5. When I had the flu, I had to take aspirin and drink orange juput. _____

6. Carol really likes peanut butter and jelly sabenwens.

   _____

7. I had a birthday cate and ice cream on my birthday, which is March 8. _____

WHAT IS THE REAL WORD? *(Cont'd)*

8. Joanie likes to see the elephants pick up things with their tenks. _____

9. On Thanksgiving the tumkie always looks golden brown and yummy. _____

10. I think our tembey always gives us too much homework.

_____

11. When Tommy goes firstng, he uses worms for bait.

_____

12. My job in the summer is always to cut the grett.

_____

13. That bors fell out of its nest last week and was injured, but it is all right now. _____

14. Most boys and gifls like to play baseball.

_____

15. Winfield always is happy when scrotl is out for the summer, and he can sleep later in the mornings. _____

Answers: television, horse, pool, juice, sandwiches, cake, trunks, turkey, teacher, fishing, grass, bird, girls, school

© 2001 by John Wiley & Sons, Inc.

THESE WORDS LOOK ALIKE, BUT SOUND DIFFERENT
Fourth-Grade Level

Read each pair of sentences to your partner. The two underlined words in each pair are spelled the same but pronounced differently. Be sure to use the context to help you decide how each one is pronounced.

1. Mr. Michaels read a book to our class yesterday afternoon.
2. Mr. Michaels will read another book to our class tomorrow afternoon.

3. That is a minute piece of cake that you gave me.
4. Please wait a minute for me.

5. This sofa feels as heavy as lead.
6. Guide dogs are used to lead the blind.

7. My father has a bass voice.
8. Donna caught a large-mouthed bass on Birch Lake.

9. Jim shot a deer with his bow and arrow.
10. The bow is the forward part of a ship.

11. Please close the door.
12. Please don't sit too close to me as I have a cold.

13. A desert is a very dry climate.
14. Please don't desert me at the party.

15. Cherie saw two beautiful does in the woods yesterday.
16. Marie does not always use good sense.

THESE WORDS LOOK ALIKE, BUT SOUND DIFFERENT *(Cont'd)*

17. My grandmother is an invalid since she had a stroke.
18. That story is invalid and untrue.

19. A primer is a book that young children read.
20. A primer is the first coat of paint that a person applies.

21. I know how to row a boat very well.
22. Tommy and Mitch had a terrible row.

23. Farmers sow seeds in the spring so that they can harvest a crop in the fall.
24. A sow is a large female hog.

25. We have a large console television set.
26. My mother tried to console the woman who was involved in an automobile accident.

27. Do is the first note on the musical scale.
28. Do you like to have hamburgers and french fries for lunch?

29. Marianne dove off the high diving board at the pool.
30. The dove flew away when it saw a cat.

CLOZE PROCEDURE USING WORD LENGTH AS A CLUE
Fifth-Grade Level

Read this story about cheetahs silently. Complete each of the omitted words in the story with the correct word. In each omission the word has as many letters as there are blank spaces. When you are finished, read the entire story again to be sure it is correct. You can work with a partner(s) if you want.

CHEETAHS

You may be surprised to read that I petted a cheetah when I was in South Africa. Although it was a tame cheetah, it _ _ _ _ _ was a little dangerous to pet it. _ also saw a group of four cheetahs _ _ _ _ _ _ _ _ a gazelle when I was visiting East Africa _ _ _ _ _ four years earlier.

Cheetahs are very beautiful _ _ _ _ _ _ _ that in some ways look like very _ _ _ _ _ cats. They have a tawny coarse coat _ _ _ _ round black spots; "tear stripes" down the _ _ _ _ of their nose; and a slender, long-legged _ _ _ _ with blunt, nonretractable claws. Cheetahs also have _ _ _ _ _ heads, high-set eyes, and small ears. They _ _ _ about 44–53 inches long and weigh about 86–143 _ _ _ _ _ _.

Cheetahs have a flexible spine, an oversized liver, _ _ enlarged heart, and a slender, muscular body. _ _ _ of these physical characteristics enable them to _ _ the fastest animal on land and the _ _ _ _ _ _ _ _ hunter in Africa. Unbelievably, cheetahs can run _ _ fast as 60 miles an hour.

CHEETAHS

Although _ _ _ _ _ _ _ _ were once found throughout Africa and Asia, _ _ _ _ are now scattered only through eastern Africa _ _ _ a small region in southwestern Africa.

Cheetahs _ _ _ _ gazelles, impala, wildebeest calves, and other hoofed _ _ _ _ _ _ _ that weigh up to 88 pounds. They _ _ _ _ _ _ drag their prey to a hiding place _ _ protect their kill from other animals.

Female _ _ _ _ _ _ _ _ live alone except when they are raising _ _ _ _, and male cheetahs live alone or with _ small group of brothers from the same litter. _ _ _ _ _ _ _ _ hunt in late mornings and early evenings _ _ _ suffocate their prey by biting underneath the _ _ _ _ _ _. A cheetah's chase for prey lasts from 20 seconds _ _ one minute, and only half are successful. _ _ _ _ _ _ _ _ make chirruping sounds, hiss or spit, and _ _ _ _ when content.

They are an endangered species. _ _ help cheetahs survive, humans must protect their habitat, stop illegal poaching (hunting), improve livestock management, and increase public education and awareness.

Answers: still, I, stalking, about, animals, large, with, side, body, small, are, pounds, an, All, be, swiftest, as, cheetahs, they, and, hunt, animals, always, to, cheetahs, cubs, a, Cheetahs, and, throat, to, Cheetahs, purr, To

FOR ADDITIONAL READING

Burns, P. (late), Roe, B., & Ross, E. (1996). *Teaching reading in today's elementary schools* (pp. 103–110 & 137–146). Boston: Houghton Mifflin.

Cheek, E., Flippo, R., & Lindsey, J. (1997). *Reading for success in elementary schools* (pp. 122–129). Madison, WI: Brown & Benchmark Publishers.

Fry, E., Kress, J., & Fountoukidis, D. (2000). *The reading teacher's book of lists*, Fourth Edition (55–63, 65–74, 85–99, 106–113). Paramus, NJ: Prentice Hall.

Gunning, T. (1996). *Creating reading instruction for all children* (pp. 132–150). Boston: Allyn & Bacon.

Heilman, A., Blair, T., & Rupley, W. (1993). *Principles and practices of teaching reading* (pp. 183–194). Upper Saddle River, NJ: Prentice Hall.

McAllister, E. (1987). *Primary reading skills activities kit* (pp. 166–183). West Nyack, NY: The Center for Applied Research in Education.

Miller, W. (1993). *Complete reading disabilities handbook* (pp. 161–170, 298–331). West Nyack, NY: The Center for Applied Research in Education.

———. (1999). *Ready-to-use activities and materials for improving content reading skills* (pp. 134–137, 151–154). West Nyack, NY: The Center for Applied Research in Education.

———. (2000). *Strategies for developing emergent literacy* (pp. 156–173). Boston: McGraw-Hill Higher Education.

Muncy, P. (1995). *Complete book of illustrated reading & writing activities for the primary grades* (pp. 102–115, 250–260). West Nyack, NY: The Center for Applied Research in Education.

Rinsky, L. (1997). *Teaching word recognition skills* (pp. 81–108). Upper Saddle River, NJ: Gorsuch Scarisbrick Publishers.

Shanker, J., & Ekwall, E. (late). (1998). *Locating and correcting reading difficulties* (pp. 123–138). Columbus, OH: Merrill/Prentice Hall.

Vacca, J., Vacca, R., & Gove, M. (1995). *Reading and learning to read* (pp. 290–298). New York: HarperCollins College Publishers.

WORKS CITED IN CHAPTER 5

Brown, R. (1973). *The first language: The early stages.* Cambridge, MA: Harvard University Press.

Carnine, D., Kameenui, E., & Coyle, G. (1984). Utilization of contextual information in determining the meaning of unfamiliar words. *Reading Research Quarterly, 19,* 188–204.

Dahl, P., & Samuels, S. (1974). A mastery based experimental program for teaching poor readers high speed word recognition skills. Unpublished paper, University of Minnesota.

Groff, P. (1981). Teaching reading by syllables. *The Reading Teacher, 14,* 659–664.

Gunning, T. (1996). *Creating reading instruction for all children.* (pp. 132–150) Boston: Allyn & Bacon.

———. (1990). How useful is context? Unpublished study. New Haven, CT: Southern Connecticut State University.

Harris, A., & Jacobson, M. (1982). *Basic reading and writing vocabularies.* New York: Macmillan.

Herber, H. (1967). *Teaching reading in content areas.* Englewood Cliffs, NJ: Prentice Hall.

Jenkins, J., Matlock, B., & Slocum, T. (1989). Approaches to vocabulary instruction. *Reading Research Quarterly, 24,* 215–235.

Nagy, W., Anderson, R., & Herman, P. (1987). Breadth and depth of vocabulary knowledge: Implications for acquisition and instruction. In M. McKeown & M. Curtis (Eds.), *The nature of vocabulary acquisition* (pp. 19–35). Hillsdale, NJ: Lawrence Erlbaum.

Rinsky, L. (1997). *Teaching word recognition skills.* Upper Saddle River, NJ: Gorsuch Scarisbrick Publishers.

Schatz, E., & Baldwin, R. (1986). Context clues are unstable predictors of word meanings. *Reading Research Quarterly, 21,* 439–453.

Shanker, J., & Ekwall, E. (late). (1998). *Locating and correcting reading difficulties.* Upper Saddle River, NJ: Prentice Hall.

Taylor, B., & Norbush, L. (1983). Oral reading for meaning: A technique for improving word identification skills. *The Reading Teacher, 39,* 234–237.

Taylor, W. (1953). Cloze procedure: A new tool for measuring readability. *Journalism Quarterly, 39,* 234–237.

Chapter 6

IMPROVING VOCABULARY AND COMPREHENSION SKILLS

A number of people not in the reading field believe that if a student has good phonic skills, he or she will automatically be an excellent reader who understands everything that is read. Do you believe this is the case?

Unfortunately, competency in word identification, including phonics, does not ensure competency in reading comprehension. This is because comprehension is a complex process that also requires abstract intelligence, good prior knowledge, a good meaning vocabulary, and an understanding of the relationships between words. Although it is true that a student usually cannot be a good comprehender without good word identification skills, much more than word identification is required for the student to understand what he or she reads.

This chapter briefly explains the characteristics of both meaning vocabularies and reading comprehension. It also provides many classroom-tested strategies, materials, and reproducibles for improving ability in these two important reading skills. After reading this chapter, you should be able to help all students, including those with learning and reading disabilities as well as other special needs, to improve their vocabulary and comprehension skills.

TYPES OF READING VOCABULARIES AND THEIR RELATION TO READING ACHIEVEMENT

It is useful to explain the different kinds of *conceptual (meaning) vocabularies.* These refer to the words to which an individual child or adult can attach one or more meanings. There are several different types of meaning vocabularies. For example, the *listening vocabulary* is the first type of vocabulary a young child acquires. It is mainly learned in the home by hearing family members and others with whom the young child comes in contact speak. Obviously, if a young child attends any type of early childhood facility, the adults there also are important in learning the listening vocabulary. The young child next learns the *speaking vocabulary* by imitating the speech of family members, other adults, and older children with whom he or she comes in contact. This is why it is important for a young child's speech models to use correct grammar and interesting, precise vocabulary. This is also the reason the child may learn to speak a dialect such as the African American dialect or the Latino dialect.

Next, the child often learns the *reading vocabulary*, although he or she may learn the *writing vocabulary* first. In addition, the reading vocabulary and the writing vocabulary may develop at the same time. The reading vocabulary is primarily learned in school unless the child is an early reader, in which case it can be learned in the home or in a child-care facility. By the time the child is in the intermediate grades, his or her reading vocabulary usually is larger than the speaking vocabulary unless the child is disabled in reading. The writing vocabulary also is mainly learned in school, although a beginning can be made before school entrance, especially if the child is encouraged to use *invented spelling*. Usually the writing vocabulary is the smallest because a person normally does not use many words in writing that are used in speaking or met while reading.

The *potential* or *marginal vocabulary* is composed of all the words the child *may be able* to determine the meaning of by using context clues; by knowing the meaning of prefixes, suffixes, or word roots; or by understanding the derivatives of words. It usually is impossible to determine the size of a student's potential vocabulary because the context in which a word is located may determine whether or not the child will know its meaning. It is important for every student to understand context clues and to know the meaning of affixes and word roots so that he or she will have a large and useful potential vocabulary. This is especially important with students in the intermediate grades and beyond.

Research studies have found that meaning vocabulary knowledge is highly related to reading comprehension. However, this conclusion also can be made by logical analysis. In one well-known study, Davis (1944) researched the reading process and found by factor analysis of reading comprehension that it was composed of two major skills—*word meanings (vocabulary)* and *reasoning ability*, which probably is the same as comprehension.

Chall (1987) estimated that the average child begins first grade with about 5,000 to 6,000 words in his or her meaning vocabulary and that during twelve years of schooling, the typical child learns about 36,000 more words. However, other researchers have found results different from Chall's. For example, according to Chall, in 1897 Canton found that six-year-old children had a vocabulary of 2,000 words, and in 1941 Smith wrote that children in first grade had a vocabulary of about 24,000 words. Shibles (1959) stated that the vocabulary of first-grade children was about 26,363 words. Over the years other researchers have found different results. It is obvious that young children today probably have a more extensive meaning vocabulary than they did in the past because of the influence of television, computer software (including computer games), the World Wide Web, and radio, among many other things. However, it is important to remember that whether children "know" a word or are just able to repeat it superficially in context should be determined by each teacher (Dale, 1965).

The size of a child's meaning vocabulary correlates positively with school success. Meaning vocabulary consists of such elements as knowledge of the multiple meanings of words, knowledge of synonyms and antonyms, knowledge of homonyms and homographs, and understanding of relational terms.

According to Dale and O'Rourke (1971), knowing a word is not an either/or proposition. For example, they wrote about four stages in word knowledge (p. 3):

1. I never saw this word before.
2. I've heard of this word, but I don't know what it means.
3. I recognize this word in context—it has something to do with . . .
4. I know this word. (p.3)

Graves (1987) expanded the stages of learning words to include the following:

Task 1: Learning to read known words

Task 2: Learning new meanings for known words

Task 3: Learning new words that represent known concepts

Task 4: Learning new words that represent new concepts

Task 5: Classifying and enriching the meaning of known words

Task 6: Moving words from receptive (listening and reading) to expressive (speaking and writing) vocabulary

As can be seen from the six tasks that were just listed, even when a child "knows" a vocabulary word, it may be a matter of degree. For example, a person who has performed a double lutz in ice skating obviously has a much better understanding of just what is involved in this skating maneuver than a person who has not.

At any grade level, developing vocabulary is not simply a process of listing vocabulary words and having students look up the definition of each one. Instead, it is a part of living. For example, young children learn the approximately 6,000 words they know when entering first grade by interacting with family members, other adults, and other children, gradually learning the names of people, animals, objects, and concepts that are found in their environment. As children grow and continue to have many varied experiences, their vocabularies continue to develop. For example, they learn such terms as *foul ball, strike, strike zone, out, first base, second base, third base, outfield, home run, pitcher, catcher,* and *shortstop,* among others, by being involved in baseball either as a participant or spectator.

It also is important to understand that a word is seldom "known" in isolation. Instead it usually is "known" in the context of a phrase, a sentence, a paragraph, or an entire passage. That is why it often is more effective to learn the meanings of new words in a whole language setting rather than in isolated lists of words. For example, the word *drive* has a number of different meanings depending on the context in which it is located. The following illustrate a few of the meanings for this fairly abstract word:

I am really glad that I can *drive* a car.

That man in the flea market usually likes to *drive* a hard bargain.

My father can *drive* a golf ball a very long distance.

Amber doesn't like her mother to *drive* her to clean every room every Saturday.

Ranch hands sometimes still go on a cattle *drive.*

The local symphony had a membership *drive* last month.

Shaundra has a great deal of *drive.*

To summarize, development of meaning vocabularies is a complex process that should continue over many years. However, students in elementary school can make a substantive beginning in this important part of reading.

THE CONE OF EXPERIENCES

Dale (1969) has developed a *cone of experiences* that is useful for reading teachers and tutors. This cone of experiences shows the importance of what are called *"activities of action,"* through which students learn vocabulary and concepts by direct experiences whenever possible. However, when hands-on experiences are not possible, children need *"activities of observation,"* such as school trips, scientific experiments, demonstrations, interactive computer software, the World Wide Web, models, graphics, and visuals. Dale stated that learning concepts and vocabulary by beginning with written language—the *product*—is very difficult for students with learning disabilities and for disabled readers.

Dale has constructed a helpful visual representation of his beliefs that he called the *Cone of Experiences Model for Vocabulary Building*. (It is reprinted here with the permission of Holt, Rinehart and Winston.)

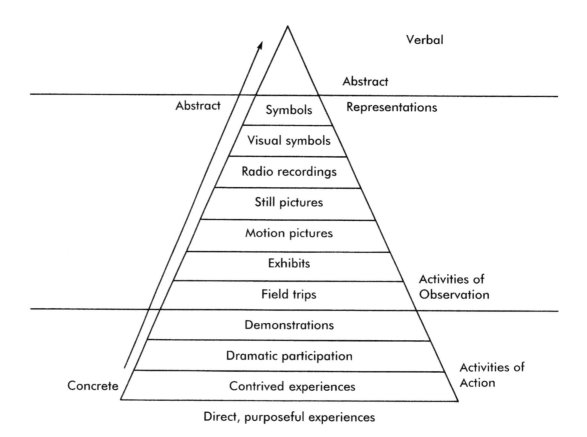

STRATEGIES FOR IMPROVING COMPETENCY IN MEANING VOCABULARY

Strategies, ready-to-use activity sheets, and games for improving competency in many of the items included in Dale's cone of experiences are included in this section. Modify any of these strategies and materials to suit the needs, abilities, and interests of your own students.

DIRECT EXPERIENCES

Direct experiences undoubtedly are the single most effective way of developing students' meaning vocabulary and conceptual knowledge. Obviously, it is not always practical to use direct experiences. When using direct experiences of any kind for vocabulary and concept development, parents, reading teachers, or reading tutors should attempt to build vocabulary and concepts prior to the experience, during the experience, and after the experience. For example, before a third-grade class takes a trip to the planetarium, the teacher should discuss with the students the demonstrations and exhibits they are likely to see there. He or she also should write some of the important vocabulary terms related to the planetarium on the chalkboard, a piece of large chart paper, or a transparency. During the experience, the teacher can point out the concepts and models that were discussed in school. After the class returns to school, the students as a large group, a small group, or individually (if there is a teacher's aide, or volunteer available) can review the vocabulary. Sometimes the students can write an account of the experience, emphasizing the vocabulary and concepts.

Several examples of places that are interesting to students for school or family trips are as follows. However, each community has its own unique sites for direct experience and excursions.

> zoo, wildlife preserve, forest preserve, pet shop, veterinary hospital, courthouse, small claims court, traffic court, hospital, nursing home, museum, planetarium, aquarium, greenhouse, post office, police station, fire station, dairy farm, grain farm, pig farm, ranch, airport, train station, train trip, park, playground, candy-making facility

SECOND-HAND OR VICARIOUS EXPERIENCES

Obviously, not all experiences for students can be direct experiences. Some must be second-hand or vicarious experiences. Although such experiences are not a true substitute for direct experiences in vocabulary and concept building, often they are more practical than are direct experiences. For example, when a third-grade class is studying about the tropical rain forests of the world in a whole language thematic unit, they obviously cannot take a trip to see all of the rain forests of the world. However, researching and constructing a likeness of a rain forest in the classroom should teach them a great deal about it.

Second-hand experiences that can be used for vocabulary and concept development include using the World Wide Web, watching a videotape, watching films, looking at slides, using interactive computer software, using other computer software, watching scientific experiments or demonstrations, examining models and realia, looking at pictures, examining actual objects and artifacts, looking at dioramas, listening to cassette recordings, and listening to CDs. As in the case of direct experiences, a reading teacher or tutor must emphasize conceptual and vocabulary development while using any type of second-hand experience.

WIDE READING

Wide reading, both to students and by students, is one of the most effective ways of developing concepts and vocabulary. Think about all of the concepts and vocabulary that a student can learn about space, for example, by reading a good informational book about the solar system. It is important that young children hear all types of materials read aloud to them on a daily basis and that older students read all types of narrative and informational materials regularly to ensure optimum vocabulary and conceptual development.

According to research, students who are identified as voluntary or wide readers demonstrate high levels of reading achievement in both vocabulary and reading comprehension (Anderson, Wilson, & Fielding, 1985; Greaney, 1980; Taylor, Frye, & Marayama, 1990). In addition, Nagy and Herman (1987) found that the *number of words children learn through context during periods of sustained silent reading far outnumbers the words they learn from direct instruction.* In another study, Anderson, Wilson, and Fielding (1988) found that the amount of "free reading" done by a student was the best predictor of vocabulary growth between grades 2 and 5. Therefore, encouraging students to read for pleasure and information is important in the primary grades and continues into the intermediate grades and beyond for vocabulary and conceptual development.

BOOKS TO PROMOTE THE ENJOYMENT OF WORDS

Words can be used in school to create enjoyment and pleasure. Tell appropriate riddles, jokes, limericks, puns, and fingerplays to your students and encourage them to share their favorites also. Here are some books that can be used to encourage word play and word enjoyment. There also are many others in your school library and local public library.

Berenstain, J., & Cohen. P. (1988). *Grand-slam riddles.* NY: Whitman. This book contains baseball riddles.

Bourke, L. (1994). *Eye spy: A mysterious alphabet.* NY: Chronicle Books. In this beautifully illustrated alphabet book, each letter appears with three vividly colored panels, which depict a word beginning with that letter, and a fourth panel, which depicts a homonym beginning with that letter and cues the word used to represent the next letter.

Burns, D. (1988). *Snakes alive!* Minneapolis: Lerner. This book contains a number of riddles about snakes.

Clark, E. (1991). *I never saw a purple cow and other nonsense rhymes.* Boston: Little, Brown & Company. This collection contains about 120 rhymes about animals.

Defty, J. (1992). *Creative fingerplays and action rhymes.* Phoenix, AZ: Oryx Press. This is an index of fingerplays and action rhymes. It also includes a helpful teacher's guide.

Degan, B. (1983). *Jamberry*. NY: Harper & Row. This is a book with highly motivating vocabulary.

Eichenberg, F. (1992). *Ape in a cape: An alphabet of odd animals*. NY: Harcourt Brace Jovanovich. This is a book with interesting words about animals.

Gwynne, F. (1988). *A little pigeon toed*. NY: Simon & Schuster. This is a very interesting collection of ambiguous phrases and amusing illustrations depicting the incorrect interpretations of those phrases. Other similar books by Fred Gwynne are *Chocolate moose for dinner* (Windmill Books, 1976) and *The king who rained* (Simon & Schuster, 1970).

Heller, R. (1998). *A cache of jewels and other collective nouns*. NY: Putnam. This book has rhyming text and illustrations that introduce a variety of collective nouns. Other books by the same author (both 1998, Putnam) are *Many luscious lollipops* (adjectives) and *Up, up, and away* (adverbs).

Juster, N. (1961). *The phantom tollbooth*. NY: Random House. In this book a young boy makes a fantastic journey through Dictionopolis, a city where interesting words of all kinds live.

Martin, B. J., & Archambault, J. (1989). *Chicka chicka boom boom*. NY: Simon & Schuster. This book contains creative language and is very appealing to young children.

Parish, P. (1964). *Thank you, Amelia Bedelia*. NY: HarperCollins Publishers. Amelia has a problem with homophones and often confuses literal and figurative meanings. When asked to make a jelly roll, for example, Amelia puts a jar full of jelly on the floor and tries to make it roll. It is a highly amusing book. Other books in the Amelia Bedelia series are *Play ball, Amelia Bedelia!* (HarperCollins, 1972) and *Come back, Amelia Bedelia* (HarperCollins, 1971).

Rosenbloom, J. (1988). *The world's best sports riddles and jokes*. NY: Sterling. This book contains riddles and jokes from different sports.

Spier, P. (1967). *To market, to market*. NY: Doubleday. This is a traditional book for young children that uses creative, interesting language.

WORD ORIGINS AND HISTORIES

The study of word origins and histories is called *etymology*. Etymology only appeals to students in the intermediate grades and beyond who are good readers and who have demonstrated an interest in learning about words. Those students will enjoy learning about the kinds of changes that have taken place in the English language by studying words and definitions that appear in very old dictionaries and by studying the differences among American English, British English, and Australian English, among others. Several examples of such words are as follows:

American English	British English	Australian English
vacation	*holiday*	
elevator	*lift*	
truck	*lorry*	

American English	British English	Australian English
candy	*sweets*	
friend		*mate*
sweater		*jumper*
pond		*billabong*

A useful source of word origins that good readers will find interesting is as follows:

Funk, W. (1992). *Word origins and their romantic stories.* Avenal, NJ: Outlet Book Company.

In addition, teachers need to help students understand the different ways that words can be formed. For example, *portmanteau* words are formed by merging the sounds and meanings of two different words (for example, *smog* from *smoke* and *fog*). *Acronyms* are words formed from the initial letters of a name or by combining initial letters or parts from a series of words (for example, *radar* from *r*adio *d*etecting *a*nd *r*anging).

Some words are shortened forms of other words (*phone* from *telephone*) and a number of words are borrowed from other languages (*hors d'oeuvres* from French). Students who are capable and interested should discuss the origins of such words when they meet them while reading. In addition, students can think of other words that have been formed in a similar manner. You can add other examples.

If you wish, place a "word tree" on the bulletin board, with limbs labeled *Latin, Greek, Spanish, Anglo-Saxon, French, Native American, Dutch,* and so forth. The students then put appropriate words that they locate in various sources in the correct place on each limb. A word tree such as this can be allowed to "grow" as a unit of study on words continues.

FIVE-STEP GUIDE TO VOCABULARY INDEPENDENCE IN CONTENT AREAS

There are five basic steps that can be used as a general guide to vocabulary independence.

1. Trigger prior knowledge. Have the student ask himself or herself, "What do I already know about these words?"

2. Preview the reading material for cues as to what the words might mean.

3. Read the material.

4. Refine and reformulate predicted meanings of the vocabulary based on information gained from reading the material.

5. To make the new word permanent, the student must read and use it. Have him or her use new vocabulary in writing and watch for the word in future reading and writing.

SEMANTIC MAPPING (WEBBING)

Semantic maps are a useful strategy for students to use in improving meaning vocabulary knowledge, in improving reading comprehension, and in motivating writing. Semantic maps or webs for vocabulary or conceptual development can be used both *before* and *after* reading. Semantic webs can be called semantic webs, story webs, advance organizers, and think-links, among others. Although there are slight variations among all of these strategies, they are very similar. Students often prefer to use semantic maps rather than semantic webs because with the latter they have to write the vocabulary terms *inside the circles* on the web, which is often difficult to do. They often become frustrated when parts of the words do not fit inside the circles.

In formulating a map or web, you should first display a completed map on the chalkboard, transparency, or a large sheet of chart paper using the vocabulary terms you want to highlight. With young children the map obviously should be a simple one, while with older students it can be considerably more complex and sophisticated. Illustrate to the students how the map shows the relationships among the vocabulary terms. Then place a partially completed semantic map on the chalkboard or transparency and help the students to complete it.

Only after they have had many experiences with completing semantic maps or webs with teacher or tutor support should students be asked to construct or complete a map with a partner(s). If semantic mapping is not presented carefully and with much preparation, a student will likely become frustrated and never want to use this strategy again.

Here is an example of a semantic map for students in the intermediate grades that has been constructed about Yellowstone National Park.

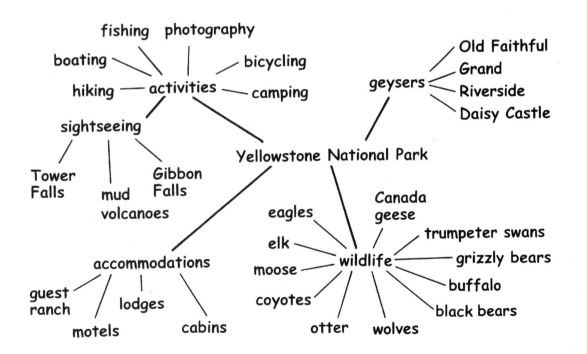

A SYNONYM OR ANTONYM WEB

You can have students in the upper primary and intermediate grades construct their own synonym or antonym web. To do so, give the student the target word for the middle of the web and have him or her, either independently or with a partner(s), add as many synonyms or antonyms for the target word as possible. Each web should be devoted solely to synonyms or antonyms. The student can consult a thesaurus for help if he or she wishes. This strategy encourages students to use alternative vocabulary terms in their writing. Here are two examples of synonym webs and two examples of antonym webs:

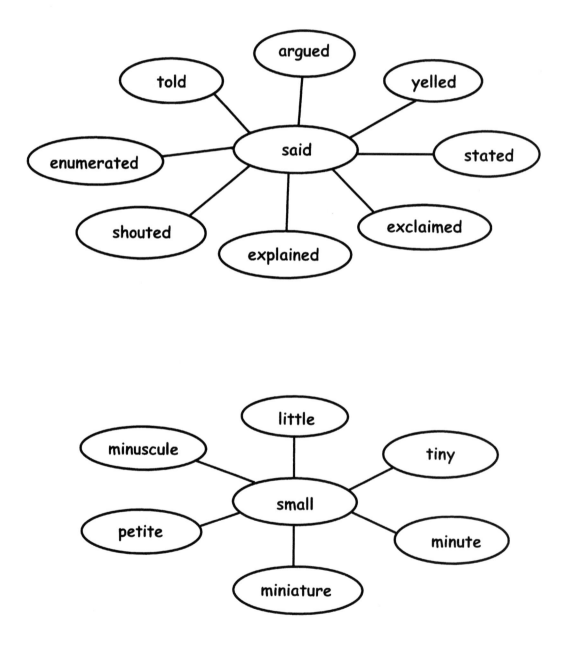

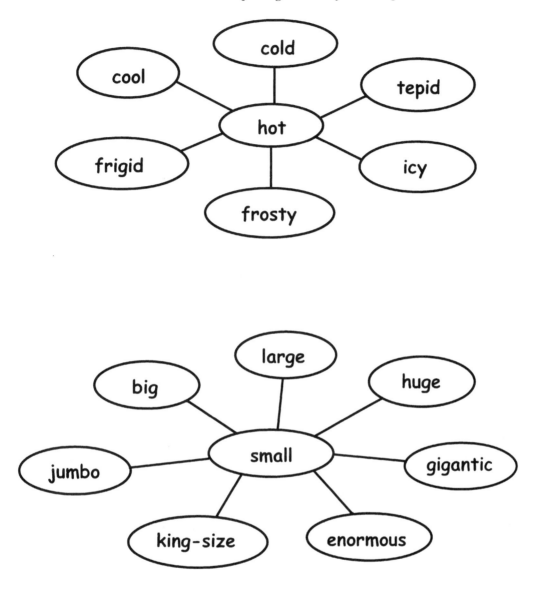

CONCEPT OF DEFINITION MAP

A concept of definition map is a procedure that Schwartz and Raphael (1985) formulated to help students in the intermediate grades and beyond acquire a concept of definition. This is a variation of a semantic map. In this strategy Schwartz and Raphael recommend direct instruction emphasizing three questions about a concept being studied: "What is it? What is it like? What are some examples?"

Here is an example of this type of map.

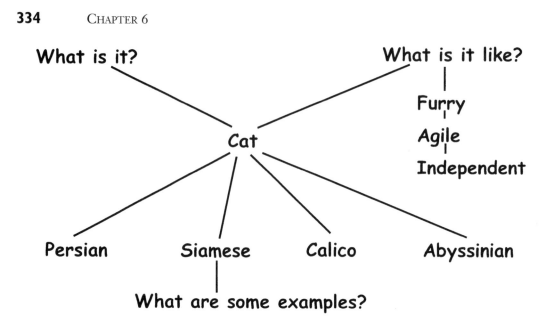

KEY WORD OF THE DAY

You can use the key word of the day as one strategy to improve students' meaning or conceptual knowledge. In this strategy, select a word that could be used in daily conversation. Then attach the key word to a word mobile that is hanging at some location in the classroom or tutoring setting. In addition, write the word on the "Interesting Word Chart" that is found in the classroom or tutoring location. Then use the word many times in different contexts and have the students do the same.

Many of the students will try to guess the meaning of the word before the group time, which takes place at the end of the school day or tutoring session. Always discuss the key word of the day near the end of the day or tutoring session. Predicting the meaning of the key word of the day becomes a game for the students. After the first week of school, they understand that their teacher or tutor will use a new word each day or at least three times during the week.

CONTEXT REDEFINITION STRATEGY

The context definition strategy encourages students to predict word meanings and then use context clues to confirm their predictions. This strategy consists of the five following steps:

1. *Select* about four key words from a story or textbook chapter (try to pick at least one word that students are likely to know).

2. *List* these key words on the chalkboard, transparency, or sheet of chart paper with a blank space for the students' predictions.

3. Have students *predict* what they think each word means, write their predictions, and then vote on the most likely prediction.

4. Have the students read to *verify* their predictions.

5. After reading, have the students *edit* or *redefine* their initial predictions to reflect contextual meanings. (Students can copy these definitions in their own glossaries or vocabulary notebook.)

Here is an example of context redefinition:

Write a definition or synonym for these two italicized words:

1. *randag*

2. *haplive*

Now read the following paragraph to see if you need to change your initial predictions:

She *randag* off the high diving board and made a beautiful swan dive right into the middle of the pool. However, as she was climbing out of the pool on the small stairway, unfortunately she slipped and *haplive* in the pool, making a big splash.

THE FOUR-SQUARE STRATEGY

The four-square strategy will help students use prior knowledge to increase vocabulary. First, select four important words from a content assignment that students are going to read and have the students fold four papers into quarters. Have the students write the first word in square 1 (for example, *laudable*).

Use the word in appropriate context so that students will have some clues to its meaning; for example, "Graduating from college and becoming a teacher is a *laudable* goal." Then ask the students: "Is there anything you believe you do that is *laudable?*" Label these student examples as *laudable*.

Have students write something in the second square that they believe to be *laudable*. In the third square, have students write a *nonexample* for *laudable* (for example, *smoking*). In the fourth square, have students write a definition of the word in *their own words*. The following illustration should clarify the four-square strategy.

laudable 1	studying 2
anything that is worthy of praise 4	smoking 3

SCAFFOLDING

Scaffolding is effective with students in encouraging the development of concepts and vocabulary. Scaffolding in reading is somewhat based on the technique that house painters or carpenters use in their work. For example, typical house painters do not simply stand on a ladder. Instead they construct a scaffold by placing a wooden plank between two sawhorses or something similar. Then the house painters stand on the scaffold. This is both safer and easier for them.

In the same way scaffolding provides help to students instead of requiring them to complete a task on their own. For example, in scaffolding an adult provides a verbal response for a young child who is not yet able to make that response himself or herself. When the baby says *kitty*, the adult can say, "Do you see that kitty sleeping on the sofa? It looks fluffy and cuddly, doesn't it? It looks as if its fur is very soft." In addition to expanding the child's vocabulary knowledge, the adult can ask the child to do something that extends his or her knowledge and demonstrates his or her understanding. Questions that consist of more than one word are preferable, such as "What does the kitty look like?" or "Why do you think the kitty likes sleeping on the sofa?" Questions beginning with *what, who, when,* and *where* usually result in one-word answers, while *why* questions are likely to elicit more complete answers that have required thought. As a student's vocabulary knowledge develops, the adult needs to provide much less scaffolding.

INVENTED SPELLING

Using invented spelling can help improve the vocabulary knowledge of children in the primary grades. Using invented spelling while writing for any purpose frees children from having to ask their teacher or tutor how to spell an unknown word. When invented spelling is used, the child simply is encouraged to spell any unknown words phonetically. In many cases, this invented spelling is understandable both to adults and to other children and allows children to explore new vocabulary.

UNDERSTANDING RELATIONSHIPS BETWEEN WORDS

Give students several words that are related and ask them to identify others appropriate to the given words. The words given by the students can be similar or opposite in meaning and should be based on their reading of stories and books.

Here are several examples of similar meanings:

large, huge	(big, gigantic, king-sized, enormous)
small, little	(tiny, miniature, wee, petite)

Here are several examples of opposite meanings:

fast, rapid	(slow, plodding, lethargic)
whisper, quiet	(yell, shout, exclaim, roar, deafening)

Here are several examples of combinations of meaning:

dark, light	(pitch black, bright)
large, small	(little, gigantic)

WORD PLAY

Word play is an interesting strategy for students to use in motivating vocabulary development. It can provide multiple exposures to words in different contexts that are important to students for word meaning mastery. For example, Gale (1982) wrote that "Children who play with words show a stronger grasp of meaning than those who do not. To create or comprehend a pun, one needs to be aware of a word" (p. 220).

Here are some ways to motivate students to engage in word play:

➠ Use Hinks Pinks (see Chapter 5).

➠ Ask students silly questions about the new words they have been learning. For example, "Would you like to have a *squid* for a pet?"

➠ Have students in the upper primary and intermediate grades write words in ways that demonstrate their meanings. For example, they may write the word *up* slanting upward, *down* slanting downward, or *round* in a circle.

➠ Explain to students what puns are and provide some examples. Then ask students to make up their own puns or find puns to bring to school. Let them explain the play on words that puns make to their classmates who do not understand them. Example: *If a turtle doesn't have a shell, is it homeless or naked?*

➠ *Riddles* are motivating to students. To use riddles, students must interact with others. To construct riddles, students must organize information and decide how this information can be presented in the form of a riddle. Riddles can be helpful in moving students from the literal to the interpretive level of understanding (Gale, 1982). Tyson and Mountain (1982) have written that riddles encourage students to use both context clues and high-interest material, both of which can encourage vocabulary learning.

➠ Have students use what Ruddiman (1993) calls the *"Vocab Game"* to develop their meaning vocabulary knowledge. For this game, have each student bring in a word from their reading each week. Have the students try to stump you with their words. In addition, other students can try to figure out their classmates' words. While they are doing this, they can use a dictionary. Students also can use their knowledge of synonyms and antonyms. The class can earn points by stumping you or by figuring out another student's word. Have a student, who acts as a recorder, keep a record of the information about the words, which you can then duplicate for the class. This activity is the most applicable in the upper primary or intermediate grades.

➠ Students in the upper primary and intermediate grades usually enjoy completing crossword puzzles, hidden-word puzzles, acrostics, and anagrams. These also can be used to improve sight word identification.

SEMANTIC FEATURES ANALYSIS GRID

A strategy that helps students to learn the meanings of the vocabulary terms found in content areas by relating them to known words is called a *semantic features analysis grid*. This technique involves looking at the similarities and differences of related concepts. Semantic features analysis has proven useful for improving students' knowledge of specialized vocabulary terms found in all the content fields.

As a simple example of this strategy for vocabulary development, in semantic features analysis the reading teacher or tutor selects a category such as *dogs* and lists in the left-hand column of the grid some members of this category, such as *golden retriever, Labrador retriever, toy poodle, basset hound, pomeranian, Old English sheepdog, sheltie, collie, cocker spaniel, papillon, greyhound, saluki, bloodhound, springer spaniel*, and *miniature pincher*.

Features that may be common to the category, such as *mammal, fur coat, sporting group, sight hound, scent hound, herding group, working group*, or *companion animal*, can be listed in a row across the top of the grid. The teacher and student can use a system of pluses and minuses to determine which members of the category being studied contain which features.

A plus in a semantic features analysis grid means *yes* (that the category members have this feature), a minus means *no* (that it does not have the feature), and a question mark means perhaps or maybe it has this feature. If one of the category members is a new vocabulary term, the students should be able to see how this new term is similar to, yet different from, the other words that the student already knows.

For example, the teacher writes the new vocabulary terms at the top of the column of category members and asks the students to add other examples of category members to the grid. The students then are asked to add features of the category members to the grid. The students then complete the grid by using pluses and minuses to match members and features, as explained previously.

WORD DERIVATION

Students in the intermediate grades and beyond can study words of recent origin. This can motivate word learning and writing activities. Introduce students to new words and then have them place the new words into categories.

Here are some words of recent origin that can be used in this activity.

desktop	*SCUD missile*	*Netscape*	*Yahoo*
cellular telephone	*fax*	*byte*	*ram*
digital	*ergonomics*	*gigabyte*	*inline skates*

IDIOMATIC EXPRESSIONS

You can have students study figurative language. Students can try to translate each idiomatic expression into its actual meaning. Here are some examples of idiomatic expressions that can be used in the intermediate grades and beyond.

gets up with the chickens	*dead to the world*
a green thumb	*to come clean*
keep this under your hat	*afraid of his own shadow*
lost her marbles	*cost an arm and a leg*
head in the clouds	*cracked a book*
forever and a day	*half-baked ideas*
give my right arm	*got up on the wrong side of the bed*
walking on air	*song and dance*
really opened my eyes	*take the cake*
not playing with a full deck	*get the picture*
nose in a book	*out of the woods*
burns a hole in his pocket	*get hung up*
down in the dumps	*days were numbered*
coughed up	*dead to the world*
forever and a day	*don't see eye to eye*

Several Other Strategies

→ Computer software lends itself well to improving both conceptual and vocabulary knowledge. Simple crossword puzzles are effective with young children for improving vocabulary knowledge. Crossword puzzles may be most valuable if they are based on a theme that is part of a whole language unit. With younger students, begin with crossword puzzles that have only five to ten words and expand them as students develop proficiency in this technique. *Crossword Magic* (The Learning Company School Division, Cambridge, MA) or a similar piece of computer software can easily be used to create crossword puzzle grids. All you have to do is supply the words and the word definitions.

   To obtain a complete listing of computer software for improving vocabulary knowledge, consult *The Educational Software Selector* (TESS) from the EPIE Institute (Hampton Bays, NY). This resource describes more than 16,000 pieces of software and videodisks. TESS is available on CD-ROM. Computer software is reviewed on a regular basis in the journals *Electronic Learning* and *Technology and Learning*.

→ With the student(s), brainstorm other words for common words, like *said*, and write them on charts. Then have students use the alternative word when writing.

→ Have students make vocabulary cards. When a student finds a new word, have him or her write it on a card in sentence context. Then the student should file the cards in a shoebox and review them periodically.

→ Select six to eight difficult words and four to six familiar words. Then have students provide possible sentences that use at least two of the new words. After reading them, have the students change the sentences if they are not accurate.

➡ Have primary-grade students illustrate new vocabulary words to demonstrate their understanding of them.

➡ Construct a time line to show the relationships between words. These time lines are very similar to the number lines used for numbers.

Here is an example:

boiling	hot	warm	tepid	cool	cold	frigid

GAMES FOR IMPROVING ABILITY IN MEANING VOCABULARY

This section includes several games for improving ability in meaning vocabulary. Such a game can be motivating and useful with students if the competition in the game is not overemphasized.

Concentration Using Homonyms

TO CONSTRUCT THE GAME

Make a set of about 8 to 10 word cards with a corresponding set of about 16 to 20 homonym cards. Some of the homonyms that can be used in this game are as follows: *be, bee, to, too, two, hear, here, course, coarse, red, read, ate, eight, air, heir, aloud, allowed, bail, bale, base, bass, bear, bare, pear, pare, herd, heard, horse, hoarse, knew, new, not, knot, mail, male, or, oar, one, won, passed, past, pause, paws, peace, piece, pedal, peddle, rain, rein, wring, ring, so, sew, some, sum, tail, tale, their, there, week, weak, weather, whether, wood, would.*

TO PLAY THE GAME

This game is played the same as conventional "Concentration." Shuffle the cards and place them face down in rows on a table or on a "Concentration" board. Two students play this game. One begins by turning over a card. Then the student tries to find its homonym by turning over another card. If the words are not homonyms, the student must turn both cards face down, and the next student gets a turn. When a student turns over a pair of homonyms, he or she is allowed to keep the two cards. The student with more cards at the end of the game is the winner. This same game can be played with antonyms or synonyms.

Matching Definitions with Words

TO CONSTRUCT THE GAME

Make envelopes that contain slips of paper with numbered words printed on them. The envelopes also should contain a larger set of slips with a definition of each of these words, numbered on the back to match the first set.

TO PLAY THE GAME

Have students each take an envelope and empty it on their desk. Then the students should place the word slips in a column in numerical order—for example,

> *epidemic*
>
> *prairie*
>
> *trail*

The students then try to match the definition slips with the words. When they have finished, they can check the accuracy of their work by seeing if the numbers match. Number each envelope and give students a number sheet corresponding to each envelope. Have them check off each number as they complete the words in each envelope. Then each student will be certain that he or she has done all of the envelopes.

Homonym "Old Maid" Game

TO CONSTRUCT THE GAME

Print homonyms on word cards. You can use the homonyms given earlier along with any others you want.

TO PLAY THE GAME

Have the children take turns drawing word cards from each other as in the game of "Old Maid." A student who has a pair of homonyms can put them down if he or she can give a correct sentence using each of the words. The student who has the most pairs at the end of the game wins.

The Classification Game

TO CONSTRUCT THE GAME

Divide the students into groups of three or four and make category sheets like the one illustrated on the next page for each group.

Several other categories that can be used in this game are *Mammals, Reptiles, Birds, Insects; Cities, States, Countries; TV Cartoons, Other TV Shows; Movies; Sports of Various Types, such as Baseball, Football, Basketball.*

TO PLAY THE GAME

When you give the signal, the students start writing as many words as they can think of that belong in each category. When you signal that the time is up, a student from each group reads the group's words aloud to the class. Have the students compare their lists and discuss why they placed particular words in particular categories.

Meats	Fruits	Vegetables

REPRODUCIBLES FOR IMPROVING MEANING VOCABULARY KNOWLEDGE

This section includes several reproducibles for improving ability in meaning vocabulary knowledge. You can use any of these in their present form if you wish or modify them in any way you like.

Name _____   Grade _____

THINK OF A SYNONYM
Second- or Third-Grade Level

A synonym is a word that means about the same thing as another word. Read each sentence to yourself and write a synonym to the underlined word on the line below the sentence. You can work with a partner(s) or use a thesaurus if you want. The first one has been done for you.

1. A cheetah is a wild animal in Africa that can run very

   <u>fast.</u>   <u>quickly</u>

2. That really is a lovely sheltie puppy.

   _____

3. Jeremy has always been scared of thunderstorms.

   _____

4. I would be glad if my family could go to Walt Disney
   World next summer.   _____

5. Elena is the brightest student in Ms. Washington's
   third-grade class.   _____

6. Ted fell and injured his knee on the playground at school
   yesterday.   _____

7. This January certainly has been a very frigid and snowy
   month.   _____

8. I was very angry when my telephone rang during the middle of the night last week.

   _____

9. Joanie had a fever and felt ill at school yesterday.

   _____

10. Billie always likes to tell really silly jokes.

    _____

11. I never want a tiny piece of cake for dessert.

    _____

12. Elian shouted when he won the spelling bee in our class.

    _____

13. That moving van is a gigantic vehicle to drive.

    _____

14. During the race Callie sprinted to the finish line first.

    _____

15. I wonder how many ladies will come to the luncheon tomorrow.

    _____

16. Everyone is unhappy that our class cannot go to the museum this year because of a lack of money.

    _____

17. It is a very black night tonight because there is no moon.

    _____

18. It is his birthday, so Kent is joyful today.

    _____

19. The pizza we had for lunch was very tasty.

    _____

20. The lemonade my mother made was very frosty.

    _____

Name _____   Grade _____

VOCABULARY WORD PUZZLES
Third-Grade Level

Here are some vocabulary words about animals you should know. Fill in the missing letters of each word. When you are finished, check each word to be sure it is correct. You can work with a partner(s) if you want.

1. k _ n g/ _ r/ _ o

2. g _/ z e l _ e

3. g _/ r _ f _ e

4. r _ i/n _ c/ _ r/ o _ s

5. e l/ _/ p _ a n _

6. s _u i r _/ e _

7. _ o y/o t/ _

8. b l _ o d/_ o u n _

9. t _/g _ r

10. o/ p _ s s/ _ m

11. h _ p/p _/p o _/a/ _ u s

12. l e _ p/_ r d

13. r _ c/ c _ _ n

14. h a _/ s _ e r

15. d _n/k _ y

16. f _ r/ r e _

17. m o n _/ _ y

18. f _ x

19. p _ r/ c _/ p i _ e

20. z _ / b r _

© 2001 by John Wiley & Sons, Inc.

WHAT DO THESE MEAN?
Fourth-Grade Level

Choose the best explanation of the underlined idiomatic expression from the choices below it by circling the correct letter in front of the sentence. The first one has been done for you.

1. My father was as happy as a lark when he finished shoveling the snow in our driveway.
   a. My father was as happy as a meadow lark bird.
   b. My father was happy that the snow shoveling was done.
   c. My father likes to see meadow larks.

2. Patsy seems to eat like a bird during school lunch.
   a. Patsy does not eat well during school lunch.
   b. Patsy likes to eat food that a bird would like.
   c. Patsy seems to eat only as much as a bird.

3. That repairman pulled a fast one when he repaired our television set yesterday.
   a. The repairman fixed our television set very quickly yesterday.
   b. The repairman was efficient as he fixed our television set yesterday.
   c. The repairman wasn't honest when he repaired our television set yesterday.

4. Juana let her hair down at Kersti's birthday party yesterday.
   a. Juana seemed to have a very good time at Kersti's birthday party yesterday.
   b. Juana unbraided her long hair and let it hang down at Kersti's birthday party yesterday.
   c. Juana unpinned her long hair and let it hang down her back at Kersti's birthday party.

WHAT DO THESE MEAN? *(Cont'd)*

5. I suppose I will have to eat crow after my mistake.
    a. I suppose I will have to actually eat a crow after my mistake.
    b. I suppose I will now have to admit my mistake.
    c. I suppose I will now have to find a crow because I made a mistake.

6. My new P.E. teacher needs to get her feet wet.
    a. My new P.E. teacher needs to get used to her new job.
    b. My new P.E. teacher should get her feet wet.
    c. My new P.E. teacher should not wear boots when it is wet outside.

7. Kendra needs to make a move about her problems.
    a. Kendra needs to try to solve her problems.
    b. Kendra needs to move to solve her problems.
    c. Kendra needs to move away from her problems.

8. Carol should let sleeping dogs lie.
    a. Carol should leave things the way they are.
    b. Carol should not bother a dog that is sleeping.
    c. Carol should never wake up a sleeping dog.

9. My father put his foot down about my brother's driving the car.
    a. When my brother wanted to drive the car, my father stamped his foot.
    b. My father put his foot down when my brother wanted to drive the car.
    c. My father would not let my brother drive the car.

10. Our family can hardly keep the wolf from the door.
    a. A wolf tried to get in our house.
    b. Our family doesn't have much money.
    c. A wolf was seen near the door of our house.

11. Craig took the rap for his friend's mistake.

    a. Craig took the blame for his friend's mistake.

    b. Craig listened to rap music with his friend.

    c. Craig told his friend that he made a mistake.

12. I got cold feet about making a speech at the convention.

    a. I was nervous about making a speech at the convention.

    b. My feet got cold when I had to make a speech at the convention.

    c. When I have to make a speech at the convention, I always get cold feet.

13. Our science test yesterday was duck soup.

    a. Our science class yesterday made duck soup.

    b. Our science test yesterday was like soup made with cooked duck.

    c. Our science test yesterday was easy.

14. Dinner at the restaurant was on the house.

    a. Dinner at the restaurant was free.

    b. Dinner at the restaurant was near our house.

    c. Dinner at the restaurant was fine.

15. My brother always gets up with the chickens.

    a. My brother always gets up when the chickens get up.

    b. My brother always gets up very early.

    c. My brother gets up very near to the chickens.

16. My mother certainly had a green thumb.

    a. My mother was a very good gardener.

    b. My mother got a green thumb from dying a garment green.

    c. My mother has a stained green thumb.

WHAT DO THESE MEAN? *(Cont'd)*

17. Becky didn't know the ropes at her new school.
    a. Becky didn't know where ropes at her new school were located.
    b. Becky didn't know the routine at her new school.
    c. Becky didn't know if her new school had ropes for P.E.

18. Do you get the picture?
    a. Do you take pictures with your camera?
    b. Do you understand what's going on?
    c. Did you get the pictures you were supposed to?

19. Win's birthday party was for the birds.
    a. Win's birthday party was not very good.
    b. Win had birds at his birthday party.
    c. Win had a party for some birds.

20. Marilyn has been down in the dumps since her husband died.
    a. Marilyn has been unhappy since her husband died.
    b. Marilyn had to go to the dump herself since her husband died.
    c. Marilyn has gone down to the local dump since her husband died.

USING MAGIC SQUARES
FOR VOCABULARY IMPROVEMENT

Magic squares are a motivating way to improve the knowledge of specialized vocabulary terms in the content fields. Magic squares can be used at any level from the upper primary through secondary. Magic squares are special arrangements of numbers that, when added across, down, and diagonally, always equal the same sum.

Reading teachers or tutors can construct magic squares by having students match a lettered column of words to a numbered column of definitions. Letters on each square of the grid match the lettered words. Students try to find the magic number by matching the correct word and definition and entering the number in the appropriate square on the grid. A magic square is fairly easy to construct, and some students in middle school and beyond may enjoy constructing their own magic squares, either independently or preferably with one or more partners.

REPRODUCIBLE

The following is a reproducible magic square about weather definitions. You may duplicate and use it with your students if it seems applicable. It can serve as a model for the magic squares you and your students construct using the specialized vocabulary from the content materials your students read.

MAGIC SQUARE
Sixth-Grade Level

Select from the numbered statements the best match for each vocabulary term. Put the number in the proper box. The total of the numbers will be the same across each row and each column. Try to find the Magic Number!

Weather Terms

A. air mass

1. a tornado-like formation over water, usually much smaller and less vigorous than a true tornado

B. dew point

2. a line on a weather map that surrounds an area with the same atmospheric pressure

C. isobar

3. a narrow band of winds blowing high in troposphere at speeds in excess of 57 miles per hour or greater

D. jet stream

4. a large body of air with nearly uniform temperature and moisture content

E. occluded front

5. a boundary between cold and warm air masses that acts like a cold front in some areas and a warm front in others

F. saturation

6. a measure of the amount of water vapor actually held by a specific volume of air in comparison to the maximum water vapor it can hold at a constant temperature

G. squall line

7. a condition of the atmosphere in which a certain volume of air holds the maximum water vapor it can hold at a specific temperature

H. waterspout

8. a line of thunderstorms that forms along a front

I. relative humidity

9. the temperature to which a certain volume of air must be cooled to bring the relative humidity to 100 percent

© 2001 by John Wiley & Sons, Inc.

MAGIC SQUARE *(Cont'd)*

A	B	C
D	E	F
G	H	I

C	B	A
2	9	4
F	E	D
7	5	3
I	H	G
6	1	8

Answer Key:
The Magic Number is 15.

READING COMPREHENSION

Reading comprehension is a complex process that is related to the thinking process, so it is difficult to explain simply. Briefly, comprehension is *constructing meaning from the printed material*. It is an *interactive process* that requires using *prior knowledge* along with *printed material*. When this definition is used, a reading teacher or tutor must consider the characteristics of both the reader and the printed material. In the case of the reader, his or her prior knowledge of the material, interest in reading the material, purpose for reading the material, and ability to pronounce the words found in the material should be considered. In the case of the printed material, the number of difficult words, the sentence length, and the format must be taken into account.

Although both prior knowledge and features of the print material are important, the reader's prior knowledge is usually the most important. In addition, the more prior knowledge that a reader has, the less need he or she has of the printed material. This is the reason that a specialist in a particular area (history, biology, anthropology, sociology) usually is able to read material in that area much more rapidly and with better comprehension than does a person with less prior knowledge.

Another definition of comprehension describes it as a process of making connections between what the reader knows and what he or she does not know, between the new and the old (Searfoss & Readence, 1994). However, Shanklin and Rhodes (1989) have written that comprehension is an *evolving process*, often beginning before a book is opened, changing as the material is read, and continuing to change even after the book is completed. The developmental nature of comprehension is increased when the reader interacts with others about aspects of the material after it has been read. Therefore, classroom (or teacher–student) interaction about reading materials is important to comprehension development and should be planned carefully.

Contemporary research in reading comprehension also describes *schema theory*. Schema theory attempts to explain how a person stores information or knowledge in his or her mind, how the knowledge that is possessed is used, and how new knowledge is acquired. For example, Anderson, et al. (1988) wrote that comprehension involves activating or constructing a *schema* that accounts for the elements in the text, similar to constructing the outline of a script. Thus a script outline for reading about South Africa might include the following categories (also called *slots): Soweto, gold, diamonds, zebras, apartheid, giraffes, game preserve, Table Mountain, Indian Ocean, Atlantic Ocean*, among others (Rumelhart, 1980). Comprehending the material then involves filling these slots with particular examples or instances.

Although activating a schema is necessary, reading is more complex than simply filling in slots. As they *transact* (interact) with printed material, competent readers constantly relate what they are reading to other experiences they have had and other information they have read. In addition, their interest in the material is very important in the web of linkages they construct (Hartman, 1994).

Another recent focus of comprehension is *metacognition (self-monitoring)*, which is concerned with a reader's awareness of his or her own thinking as he or she tries to understand the printed material. It is important that a student learns how to monitor his or her own reading comprehension. Research has consistently found that *good readers are much better at monitoring their comprehension than are poor readers.* Later this chapter provides several strategies for helping students learn to monitor their comprehension.

Research also has shown close relationships between comprehension and decoding (word identification) (Adams, 1991). Thus, developing decoding (word identification) strategies to competency is important. However, you should remember that the use of decoding strategies is only a means of accessing the meaning of the printed material. When good decoders have problems with comprehension, they need help in developing language proficiency and listening comprehension.

DIFFERENT LEVELS OF COMPREHENSION

In the past, comprehension skills usually were divided into four major categories: *literal*, *interpretive*, *critical*, and *applied*. Today most researchers consider comprehension to be a language-based process that cannot be divided into arbitrary categories. Instead, they state that there are only two major categories of comprehension: *vocabulary knowledge (word meaning)* and *understanding the reading material*.

Some contemporary reading specialists have stated that because comprehension cannot be accurately divided into subskills in research studies, the various levels of comprehension should not be taught to students. I believe that it is important to try to teach the most important aspects of comprehension separately, at least to most students, especially to students with learning disabilities and reading disabilities.

Here are the various levels of comprehension and the more important subskills that comprise them (Miller, 1999).

Textually Explicit (Literal or Factual— "Right There") Comprehension

➡ answering "right there" questions found in the reading material

➡ locating directed stated main ideas

➡ locating significant and irrelevant details

➡ placing items in correct sequence or order

➡ reading and carrying out directions

Textually Implicit (Interpretive or Inferential— "Think and Search") Comprehension

➡ answering "think and search" questions (the reader has to deduce the answers from reading the materials)

➡ answering questions that call for interpretation (the answer is not found directly in the material)

➡ drawing conclusions and generalizations

➡ predicting the outcomes

➡ summarizing what was read

➡ sensing the author's mood and purpose

➡ locating implied main ideas

Critical (Textually Implicit or Evaluative—"Think and Search") Comprehension

➡ responding to questions in which the reader must *evaluate* the reading material

➡ discriminating between fact and fantasy (real and make-believe)

➡ evaluating the accuracy or truthfulness of the reading material

➡ sensing an author's biases

➡ recognizing propaganda techniques such as the bandwagon effect, testimonials, the halo effect, emotionally toned words, and card stacking

Scriptally Implicit (Script Implicit, Schema Implicit, Applied, or Creative) Comprehension

➡ answering "on my own" questions (the reader has to combine his or her prior knowledge with the printed material to arrive at new knowledge or actions)

➡ applying knowledge gained from reading to one's own life for problem solving

➡ bibliotherapy (solving a problem through reading about a similar problem)

➡ cooking and baking after reading recipes

➡ participating in art activities as a follow-up to reading

➡ creative writing of prose and poetry (including using invented spelling if necessary)

➡ participating in construction activities as a follow-up to reading

➡ participating in rhythm activities as a follow-up to reading

➡ putting on creative dramatics and sociodrama

➡ puppetry

➡ conducting scientific experiments

➡ creative book reports

➡ reading material that appeals to the emotions (the affective aspects of reading)

Some subskills of reading comprehension are not applicable with young children but are relevant only for older students in middle school and beyond. However, *all students* can make a beginning in all four levels of comprehension and should be given many opportunities to do so.

STRATEGIES FOR IMPROVING ABILITY IN READING COMPREHENSION

This section contains numerous classroom-tested strategies, materials, and reproducibles that can be used to improve students' abilities in the various aspects of reading comprehension. Modify any of these strategies or materials in light of your students' needs, interests, and abilities.

WIDE READING

Wide reading of interesting, motivating, relevant, easy material is the single best way to improve reading comprehension. The major purpose of such reading always should be to understand what is read. Comprehension improves the best if the student always has specific purposes for the reading. Such reading can take place in trade books, including predictable books, easy-to-read books, chapter books, informational books, supplementary readers, poetry, children's magazines and newspapers, and relevant computer software. The student always should have purposes for reading, monitor his or her comprehension as the reading is being done, and be prepared in some way to show that he or she has understood the material.

POETRY

Children's poetry is an enjoyable way of improving both comprehension and listening skills. Poetry is condensed, which makes every word important. It also encourages visual imagery because of its sensory descriptions and introduces enchanting stories. In addition, poetry provides opportunities for a student to learn new words, ideas, and attitudes and to experience life through the eyes of a poet. It has form and order and is easy to learn.

To summarize, poetry can be used for the following purposes:

➡ demonstrating the pleasure of hearing sounds

➡ giving pleasure through the use of poetry containing silly words and humor

➡ improving students' imaginations

➡ enhancing students' self-worth and confidence

➡ improving the understanding of rhyming

Here are some types of poetry:

➡ *lyric*—Melodic, descriptive poetry that usually has a song quality.

➡ *narrative*—Poetry that tells a story or describes an event or happening.

➡ *limerick*—Poetry with five lines of verse set in a specific rhyming pattern that is usually humorous.

➡ *free verse*—Poetry that does not rhyme.

➡ *nonsense*—Poetry that is often ridiculous and whimsical.

➡ *haiku*—An ancient but currently popular Japanese verse that contains three lines consisting of seventeen syllables and often dealing with the topic of nature.

Placing poems in prominent places in the classroom or tutoring setting may help to create interest in poems, especially if pictures or illustrations are placed by the poems. For example, a poetry tree made by placing a smooth tree limb in plaster of Paris can have paper leaves with poems on the back that can be chosen at group sharing times. A "poem of the day" has been effective in a number of classrooms. Pictures and flannel boards can be used in presenting poetry in an interesting way. A poem can be enjoyed either indoors or outdoors or as a valuable learning resource at the end of a lesson or when students are waiting in line.

You also can create your own personalized poems for your class or the student whom you are tutoring. The following suggestions for writing poems for students may be helpful:

➡ Use frequent rhyming.

➡ Vary the rhythm.

➡ Use themes and ideas that are familiar to students.

➡ Use definite rhythms that encourage chanting, moving, or singing.

➡ Use words that students are able to easily understand.

➡ Make each line an independent thought.

➡ Use many action verbs.

➡ Try to include visual images in each line.

Here are several books of poetry you may want to use. There are, of course, many others that are equally useful.

Adoff, A. (1982). *All the colors of the race*. NY: Lothrop, Lee & Shepherd. (I*: 5–9).

Baylor, B. (1981). *Desert voices*. NY: Scribner. (I: All ages)

Brooks, G. (1967). *Bronzeville boys and girls*. NY: HarperCollins Publishers. (I: 8–11)

Ciardi, J. (1985). *Doodle soup*. Boston: Houghton Mifflin. (I: 6–8)

Cole, W. (Ed.). (1981). *Poem stew*. NY: Harper Trophy. (I: 6–10)

———. (Ed.). (1992). *A zooful of animals*. Boston: Houghton Mifflin. (I: 5–7).

deRegniers, B., Moore, E., White, M., & Carr, J. (Eds.). (1988). *Sing a song of popcorn: Every child's book of poems*. NY: Scholastic. (I: 7–12)

---

*Indicates the interest level by age.

Esbensen, E. (1995). *Dance with me.* NY: HarperCollins Publishers. (I: 5–12)

Farjeon, E. (1951). *Eleanor Farjeon's poems for children.* Philadelphia: Lippincott. (I: 7–11)

Giovanni, N. (1985). *Spin a soft black song.* NY: Farrar, Straus & Giroux. (I: 8–12)

Harrison, M., & Stuart-Clark, C. (Eds.). NY: Farrar, Straus & Giroux. (I: 8–12)

Hopkins, L. (Ed.). (1986). *Best friends.* NY: Harper. (I: 10–12)

Hughes, L. (1995). *The book of rhythms.* NY: Oxford University Press. (I: 7–11).

Kennedy, X., & Kennedy, D. (Eds.). (1982). *Knock at a star.* Boston: Little, Brown & Company. (I: 9–YA [Young Adult])

Larrick, N. (Ed.). (1968). *Piping down the valleys wild.* NY: Dell. (I: 9–YA)

Lear, E. (1946). *The complete book of nonsense.* NY: Dodd, Mead. (I: 5–9)

Livingston, M. C. (Ed.). (1987). *Cat poems.* NY: Holiday. (I: 5–8)

Merriam, E. (1969). *The inner city Mother Goose.* NY: Simon & Schuster. (I: 9–YA)

McCord, D. (1986). *One at a time.* Boston: Little, Brown & Company. (I: 9–YA)

Nye, N. (Ed.). (1995). *The tree is older than you: Bilingual poems from Mexico.* NY: Simon & Schuster. (I: 8–YA)

O'Neill, M. (1969). *My fingers are always bringing me news.* NY: Doubleday. (I: 6–10)

The Oxford treasury of children's poems. NY: Oxford University Press. (I: 6–11)

Prelutsky, J. (1984). *The new kid on the block.* NY: Greenwillow Books. (I: 5–9)

Rylant, C. (1989). *But I'll be back again.* NY: Orchard. (I: 12–YA)

Sandburg, C. (1928). *Good morning, America.* NY: Harcourt. (I: 10–YA)

Schwartz, A. (1992). *And the green grass grew all around: Folk poetry for children.* NY: HarperCollins Publishers. (I: 6–YA)

Silverstein, S. (1986). *The giving tree.* NY: HarperCollins Publishers. (I: 4–8)

———. (1981). *A light in the attic.* NY: HarperCollins Publishers. (I: 12 and up)

———. (1974). *Where the sidewalk ends.* NY: HarperCollins Publishers. (I: 5–12)

Strickland, D., & Strickland, M. (1994). *Families: Poems celebrating the African American experience.* Honesdale, PA: Wordsong/Boyds Mills. (I: 7–12)

Viorst, J. (1981). *If I were in charge of the world and other worries.* NY: Atheneum. (I: 12–YA)

Watson, C. (1987). *Father Fox's Pennyrhymes.* NY: HarperCollins. (I: 6–9)

Yolen, J. (1996). *Sky scrape/City scrape, poems of city life.* Honesdale, PA: Boyds Mills Press. (I: 6–10)

PREDICTION STRATEGIES

There are several prediction strategies that can greatly improve a student's comprehension skills. For example, encouraging students to use prediction both before and during reading is one of the easiest and effective ways of improving comprehension. This simple strategy requires no special materials but merely a mind-set on the part of readers. If students make predictions about the content of the material before and during reading, their comprehension greatly improves. Prediction can begin as early as the preschool level, when students are asked to make simple predictions about story content from hearing the title of a book read to them and during the reading aloud of the book. Before listening to a trade book being read aloud or reading it for themselves, students can answer questions such as these:

What do you think this book (story) will be about?

What do you think will happen in this book (story)?

What would you like to have happen in this book (story)?

During the reading of the material, questions such as the following can be asked:

What do you think will happen next in this book (story)?

What would you like to have happen next in this book (story)?

What do you think (story character) will do next in the book (story)?

What do you think (story character) should do next in this book (story)?

Two other effective prediction strategies that are applicable for use in both the primary and intermediate grades are the *Directed Listening-Thinking Activity (DL-TA) and Directed Reading-Thinking Activity (DR-TA)*. These two prediction strategies follow mainly the same format except that in the former the students listen to the material, while in the latter they read it for themselves. Both were developed in some form by the late Russell G. Stauffer of the University of Delaware (1975, 1980). Both are useful strategies because they involve prediction and reading (listening) with specific purposes. Briefly, DL-TA and DR-TA encourage *active involvement* with the reading material by having students make predictions about the material and then checking the accuracy of their predictions. That is why either strategy can improve understanding and remembering so effectively.

Here are the basic steps of DL-TA and DR-TA. In the former the student listens to the material, while in the latter he or she reads the material.

1. Have students listen to (read) the title of the narrative or informational book and then, on the basis of this title and their own prior knowledge, make predictions about the content of the book. If you wish, in the DR-TA the student or teacher writes the predictions.

2. Tell the students that they should read (listen to) the trade book to see if the material confirms or does not confirm the predictions that they made. Then have the student read (listen to) the book a section at a time.

3. After the book is completed, have the students discuss each of their predictions, indicating which ones were confirmed and which ones were not. Help the students to determine what criteria should be used in deciding whether or not the predictions were confirmed. This portion of the DR-TA also can be written if you wish.

4. If the book was not read at one time, alternate periods of silent reading and discussion until the entire book has been read. In each case, emphasize the validity of the student's reasoning rather than the correctness of the original predictions.

The *Anticipation Guide*, which was developed by Readence, Bean, and Baldwin (1981, 1992), is another interesting strategy that can be used with students in the upper primary and intermediate grades to improve their prediction abilities and thus the comprehension of what they are going to read. This prereading strategy helps students to activate their prior knowledge before reading and uses statements instead of questions as an initial way to get students more involved in their learning. Briefly, here are the steps in this prediction strategy:

1. *Identify the major concepts*—The teacher or tutor first identifies the major concepts in the reading selection (either a narrative trade book or informational book) by careful reading of the material and the teacher's manual, if one is available.

2. *Determine students' knowledge of these concepts*—The teacher or tutor should try to determine how the main concepts in the reading material support or refute what the students already know about the material.

3. *Create statements*—The teacher or tutor then creates three to five statements about the material. The students should have enough knowledge to understand what the statements say, but not enough to make any of them completely known.

4. *Decide statement order and presentation*—The order of the statements should follow the order of the statements presented in the material. The Anticipation Guide can be presented on the chalkboard, a transparency, or a reproducible activity sheet.

5. *Present guide*—When giving the guide to students, the reading teacher or tutor either should read the directions orally or have the students read them silently. Students also should be told that they will later share their thoughts and opinions about each statement by defending their agreement or disagreement with each statement. Students can work individually or with a partner(s) while making the responses.

6. *Discuss each statement briefly*—The reading teacher or tutor should first ask for a show of hands from students to indicate their agreement or disagreement with each statement.

7. *Have students read the material*—The students then read the material with the purpose of deciding what the author may say about each statement.

8. *Conduct follow-up discussions*—After they have read the material, the students can respond again to the material. The Anticipation Guide serves as the basis for an important postreading discussion in which students can share the new information gained from reading and talk about how their previous thoughts may have been modified by what they believe the author said.

STORY IMPRESSIONS

The use of story impressions is a helpful strategy for improving comprehension of narrative material such as narrative trade books. Story impressions can be used effectively with students in second grade and beyond. This strategy consists of the following easy-to-implement steps (McGinley & Denner, 1987).

➡ Select an interesting narrative trade book at the appropriate grade level with a clearly defined plot and clearly defined characters.

➡ As you read this trade book, select about six to eight key words from the book that will serve as the *story* impression clues. These clues should be about story characters or important story events.

➡ Place these clues on the chalkboard or a transparency in the following way:

story clue

⇓

story clue

⇓

story clue

⇓

story clue

⇓

story clue

⇓

story clue

⇓

story clue

⇓

story clue

➡ Have the students formulate a prediction about the reading material from each of the story clues. You should write each prediction on the chalkboard opposite the numbers of 1, 2, 3, and so on. Encourage the students to make logical predictions.

➡ Have each student who is participating in the story impressions activity read the material, focusing on determining whether or not the predictions were correct. Thus, this strategy encourages purposeful, motivated reading, which should lead to improved comprehension.

➡ After the students have finished reading the entire trade book, they again should look at their predictions. Each prediction that proved to be accurate is allowed to remain, with nothing else written opposite it. However, each prediction that proved to be inaccurate should be corrected by having the students dictate the correct story summary statement opposite the inaccurate prediction.

The strategy of story impressions has these advantages:

➠ It provides students with *specific purposes* for reading, and therefore their comprehension often is improved significantly.

➠ It helps students learn to make valid and logical predictions.

➠ It motivates students to read relevant, appropriate materials.

As an example, I have chosen the children's chapter book entitled *The Canada Geese Quilt* by N. Kinsey-Warnock (New York: Cobblehill Books/Dutton, 1989). This book is about a young girl named Ariel who lives in Vermont and is very close to her grandmother. Ariel made a sketch of Canada geese flying that her grandmother is going to make into a quilt for the family's new baby. When her grandmother has a stroke, Ariel helps her grandmother finish the quilt. Her grandmother also helps Ariel accept the grandmother's illness and eventual death.

Here are the story impression clues for this book:

Story Impression Clues

Ariel, a young girl who lives in Vermont

⇓

artist

⇓

new baby

⇓

sketch of design for baby quilt

⇓

stroke

⇓

completed Canada geese quilt

⇓

Ariel's gift quilt from Grandma

If you want, you can write your own predictions in the Predictive Summary portion of the following reproducible activity sheet. Then locate this trade book from your local public library, school library, or university library and read it. After you have read it, do not add anything to the correct predictions, but write the correct story summary opposite any incorrect predictions. You may find that this activity is fairly challenging for you even as an adult. If you make multiple copies of the following story impressions activity sheet, use only one of them at this time and use the others later for the students whom you are teaching or tutoring.

STORY IMPRESSIONS ACTIVITY SHEET
Primary- or Intermediate-Grade Level

Predictive Story Summary	Actual Story Summary

K-W-L AND K-W-H-L

The study strategies of K-W-L and K-W-H-L are helpful in the upper primary and intermediate grades after you have carefully modeled them and provided sufficient scaffolding. They are study strategies that can be used only with content material such as social studies and science. Good readers in the primary grades should be exposed to them so that their use can be refined in the intermediate grades. They are valuable strategies to use in improving comprehension and retention of content material.

K-W-L is an acronym for *What I Know—What I Want to Learn (Know)—What I Have Learned.* Developed by Ogle (1986, 1989) K-W-L stresses a student's prior knowledge, encourages him or her to construct questions to read to answer, directs the student to look for answers to these specific questions, and enables him or her to effectively summarize what was read. The strategy is mainly helpful because it helps students to use their prior knowledge while reading and gives them specific purposes for reading.

The strategy should be presented in a group or an individual setting to those readers who seem able to benefit from using it. First identify the most important concepts in the material and ask students to state what they already know about these concepts. Write these concepts on the chalkboard or a transparency under a heading titled "What I Know." In the second step provide motivation by focusing on what the students want to learn about these concepts that they do not currently know. Write these questions under a column labeled "What I Want to Learn (Know)." Once the students have determined their purposes for reading, they should read the material to locate the answers to their questions.

In the final part of K-W-L, have the students orally or in writing summarize what they have learned from reading the material. They can dictate this portion of the activity sheet to you, and you write it down under the column headed "What I Have Learned." Have them do this without referring to the material that they read.

K-W-H-L adds a step before the final step called "How I Can Find Out." In this step, with your help the students brainstorm for resources that they can use to locate the needed information. In addition to content textbooks, other resources that may be used are as follows: informational trade books, children's newspapers and magazines, the World Wide Web, computer software, videotapes, films, and classroom visitors.

The following is a sample K-W-L activity sheet that you can use with your students. You can duplicate as many copies of this activity sheet as you wish for use with your students.

K-W-L ACTIVITY SHEET

What I Know	What I Want to Learn	What I Have Learned

VISUAL IMAGERY

Formulating visual images, sometimes called mental images, is a good strategy for improving comprehension. It is especially effective if students are given material that lends itself well to formulating mental images of what they read. Many students do not use this strategy unless they have had specific instruction and practice in exactly how to do it. Creating mental images promotes the use of prior knowledge and improves the ability to make predictions and inferences. In addition to improving comprehension, imaging can help retention of what is read.

One reason that visual imaging is effective is that it is an *active, generative process.* For example, in a research study comparing fourth-grade students who read a story without illustrations and created their own images while reading with fourth-grade students who made use of the illustrations included in the story, the group that created its own images seemed to remember the story better (Gambrell & Javitz, 1993). It appeared that creating one's own images is more effective than using someone else's creations. Imaging is a fairly easy strategy to teach and use.

One way of improving mental imaging ability is to have students read high-interest material and ask them to try to picture the main character, the setting, or the events in the story. Some trade books that can be used for this purpose with elementary students are as follows. There are many others that are equally valuable for this purpose.

Alexander, L. (1995). *The Arkadians.* NY: Dutton. (*I: 11–13)

Barrett, J. (1978). *Cloudy with a chance of meatballs.* NY: Atheneum. (I: P–8)

Chetwin, G. (1994). *Jason's seven magical night rides.* NY: Bradbury. (I: 11–YA)

Conrad, P. (1993). *The tub grandfather.* NY: HarperCollins Publishers. (I: P–8)

Coville, B. (1992). *Jeremy Thatcher, dragon hatcher.* San Diego, CA: Harcourt and
    Company. (I: 9–12)

Dahl, R. (1964). *Charlie and the chocolate factory.* NY: Alfred A. Knopf. (I: 8–10)

———. (1961 & 1996). *James and the giant peach.* NY: Alfred A. Knopf. (I: 7–11)

Eastman, P. (1960). *Are you my mother?* NY: Random House. (I: P–6)

Gilson, J. (1981). *Can't catch me: I'm the gingerbread man!* NY: Lothrop, Lee and Shephard.
    (I: 8–10)

Henkes, K. (1991). *Chrysanthemum.* NY: Greenwillow Books. (I: P–6)

Hoban, F. (1960). *Bedtime for Frances.* NY: Harper & Row. (I: P–7)

Hoffman, E. (1816 & 1984). *The nutcracker.* NY: Crown. (I: 8–11)

Jones, D. (1993). *The crown of Dalemark.* NY: Greenwillow Books (I: 12 + up)

Kellogg, S. (1981). *A rose for Pinkerton.* NY: Dial. (I: 6–9)

Kinsey-Warnock, N. (1992). *Wilderness cat.* NY: Dutton. (I: 5–9)

Klause, A. (1993). *Alien secrets.* NY: Delacorte. (I: 10–YA)

---

*Indicates the interest level by age.

Mayer, M. (1969). *There's a nightmare in my closet.* NY: Dial. (I: P–7)

McCloskey, R. (1948). *Blueberries for Sal.* NY: The Viking Press. (I: P–7)

Meddaugh, S. (1995). *Hog-eye.* Boston: Houghton Mifflin. (I: 6–9)

Polacco, P. (1991). *Applemando's dreams.* NY: Philomel. (I: 6–9)

SanSouci, R. (1992). *Sukey and the mermaid.* NY: Four Winds. (I: 6–9)

Sendak, M. (1963). *Where the wild things are.* NY: Harper & Row. (I: P–8)

Seuss, Dr. (1937). *And to think I saw it on Mulberry Street.* NY: Vanguard. (I: P–8)

Showers, P. (1991). *The listening walk.* NY: HarperCollins Publishers. (I: 5–7)

Silverstein, S. (1992). *The giving tree.* NY: HarperCollins Publishers. (I: P–8)

Stevenson, J. (1980). *The terrible Halloween night.* NY: Greenwillow Books. (I: P–7)

Turner, A. (1985). *Dakota dugout.* NY: Macmillan. (I: 5–8)

Van Allsburg, C. (1981). *Jumanji.* Boston: Houghton Mifflin. (I: 7–10)

———. (1985). *The Polar Express.* Boston: Houghton Mifflin. (I: 5–8)

Viorst, J. (1972). *Alexander and the terrible, horrible, no good, very bad day.* NY: Atheneum. (I: P–8)

Williams, M. (1922 & 1983). *The velveteen rabbit.* NY: Holt. (I: 6–9)

Winthrop, E. (1985). *Castle in the attic.* NY: Holiday House. (I: 6–10)

USING PUPPETS

Puppets are an extremely useful tool to use in both teaching and tutoring reading, especially for younger students. For example, I was working with a first-grade pupil a few years ago and was having a difficult time getting my tutee to talk. No matter what strategies I used, the little girl just would not respond. One day I brought a honeybee puppet to the session, and the little girl pretended that she was a honeybee. She responded well that day to the reading instruction, including answering comprehension questions about the material that she read. After a while she was talking a great deal. I tutored her again the next year in second grade, and at our first meeting she said, "Do you remember me from last year? I didn't talk at all then, and now I talk all the time!" This certainly was true. A puppet had performed a miracle for her.

Koos (1986) said this about puppets:

> Imagine a lifeless puppet lying on a table. Suddenly, a child slips his [her] hand into the puppet and it awakens to a life and personality of its own. Magic happens, and the world of make-believe begins. Children love to pretend, and puppetry allows them to create their own magic (p. 56).

Using puppets is an example of *applied* or *creative reading*—the highest level of the reading process. Here are some ways you can use puppets in your classroom or tutoring sessions:

➡ Have the students present puppet plays and skits. Some of these plays and skits can be follow-ups to trade books or stories that have been read or heard.

➡ Provide props and puppet theaters so that students can use them in puppet plays and skits.

➡ Find community resources that give puppet presentations: puppeteer groups, high school and elementary classes, and skilled individuals.

➡ Have students use puppets when reading the parts orally in a trade book or story.

➡ Have shy children use puppets when talking with each other or with the reading teacher or tutor.

Puppets can be divided into two general categories—those worked with the hands and fingers or those that dangle on a string. Hand puppets are popular with young children because they are practical and easy to use. Moving arms and pliable faces on puppets increase the possibilities for characterization and action. Rubber, plastic, and papier-mâché puppet heads are durable, and cloth faces permit a wide variety of facial expressions.

Here are several ways to construct common puppets.

Sock Puppets

MATERIALS NEEDED:

Old sock, felt, and a sewing machine

CONSTRUCTION PROCEDURE:

1. Use an old wool sock or other thick sock. Turn it inside out and spread it out with the heel on top.

2. Cut around the edge of the toe (about three inches on each side).

3. Fold the mouth material (red felt) inside the open part of the sock and draw the shape. Cut the mouth piece out and sew into the proper place.

Paper Bag Puppets

MATERIALS NEEDED:

Paper bags, scissors, crayons or marking pens, paste, yarn or paper scraps, and paint (optional)

CONSTRUCTION PROCEDURE:

1. Paper bag puppets are easy to make. Give each student a small paper bag.

2. Show the students how the mouth works and let them color or paste features on the bag.

3. You may want to have them paste on a circle for the face. Paste it on the flap part of the bag and then cut the circle on the flap portion so that the mouth can move again.

4. Many students will want to add special features to their paper bag puppets.

Stick Puppets

MATERIALS NEEDED:

Paper, glue, scissors, tongue depressors or Popsicle sticks

CONSTRUCTION PROCEDURE:

1. Students draw characters and scenery. Depending on the age of the students, the characters and scenery can be simply colored or cut out.

2. Older students can create their own figures.

Papier-Mâché Puppet Heads

MATERIALS NEEDED:

Styrofoam egg or ball (a little smaller than the size you want for the finished head) and soft enough to have a holder inserted into it

neck tube (made from cardboard five inches long and rolled into a $1\frac{1}{2}''$ tube and taped closed or a plastic hair roller)

bottle (to put the head in while it is being created and to hold it during drying)

instant papier-mâché (purchased from a craft store)

poster paints

gloss coat spray (optional)

white glue

CONSTRUCTION PROCEDURE:

1. Mix instant papier-mâché with water (a little at a time) until it is like clay—moist, but neither wet nor dry.

2. Place Styrofoam egg (or ball) on neck tube (or roller) securely. Then place egg (or ball) on bottle so that it is steady.

3. Put papier-mâché all over head and halfway down the neck tube. Coating should be about a half inch thick.

4. Begin making the facial features, starting with the cheeks, eyebrows, and chin. Then add eyes, nose, mouth, and ears.

5. When you are finished with the head, allow it to dry at least 24 hours in an airy place.

6. When the head is dry, paint the face with poster paint. When that is dry, coat it with spray gloss finish to seal the paint.

7. Glue is useful for adding yarn hair if you want.

Other types of puppets that students in the elementary school can make are as follows: cloth hand puppets, pop-ups, jumping jack puppets, box puppets, and bird and frog puppets. Many teacher resource books contain directions for constructing these kinds of puppets along with many others.

MODELING STRATEGIES FOR PARAGRAPH MEANING

When modeling strategies for paragraph meaning, model and then direct students in the use of a code for marking reactions to chosen paragraphs. This is one of the most effective methods of teaching students to monitor their thought processes while they are reading. This technique can be used with individuals, small groups, or the entire class. Although it is the most effective with intermediate-grade or older students, it also can be modified and used with primary-grade students. The code system probably should vary somewhat depending on the grade level of the students involved.

Here is how to prepare the materials for this strategy.

1. Select two or more passages of about 200 to 400 words depending on the age and ability of your students. This technique probably is the most successful with material that is on a student's low independent or high instructional reading level. Choose interesting passages from books on science or social studies.

2. The first passage should be triple spaced with wide margins and placed on an overhead transparency for you to use in modeling the strategy. Other passages should be prepared as hard copies for students to read on their own and as overhead transparencies.

3. You also may want to prepare accompanying photographs or illustrations in color on a transparency.

4. Make an overhead transparency or enough hard copies for each student of the symbols that you will be using to describe your own comprehension monitoring. Select seven or fewer symbols, such as the ones illustrated here:

GVI = Got a Visual Image

RA = Read again

☺ = No Sweat!

MBI = Must Be Important

HW = Hard Word

LAP = Look at Picture

? = I Don't Understand

Teaching Steps

The technique can be taught to the entire class or a small group of students in the following way:

1. Present the first selection to the students on an overhead transparency or on copied pages (for them to read silently). Prior to reading you may discuss the title briefly and ask a few questions to activate prior knowledge.

2. Have the students read the passage silently.

3. Present and describe the symbols to the students.

4. Place another transparency of the same passage on the overhead projector. This transparency consists of the passage triple spaced with wide margins and with your strategy symbols inserted in the passage in appropriate places.

5. Model how you would read the selection by telling the students what you did; that is, what you were thinking when you wrote your symbols on the passage. Discuss with the students why you made the choices you did and talk about the passage with the students, demonstrating your interest and enthusiasm in the material being read. **Note:** There is not just one "correct" way to place your symbols. Any logical approach you use will work well.

6. Introduce a second selection. You may show a photograph or illustration on the overhead projector to increase interest and use other techniques to activate students' prior knowledge about the topic.

7. Pass out the second selection and have the students read it, either on their own or in pairs. The students usually should have a choice about this matter. Encourage the students to monitor their own thinking as they read and explain to them that they may use your symbols or their own symbols to mark this selection as they read it.

8. Circulate around the room while the students are working, giving praise and encouragement for their efforts.

9. Go over the second selection and discuss which symbols the students used and why. Explain to them that different people may read and understand the same material

in different ways, and that is good. Answer questions about the material as they are posed.

10. Present a follow-up lesson a day or two later. Have the students read another selection and repeat steps 6 through 9. In addition, locate future opportunities to inquire about students' use of comprehension-monitoring strategies when you are working with them individually or in small groups. Also find additional occasions to model your own strategies with other kinds of material.

Although this procedure may seem complicated, students usually adapt to it quickly and are highly motivated to participate. It will help them to monitor (think about) their reading comprehension and to learn effective comprehension strategies from their teacher. It also will help less able readers to learn strategies from their classmates who are better readers.

Tell students that it is important to be able to recognize words for which they do not know the meaning while they read. Encourage them to try to determine the meaning of unknown words from their context. If a student is not able to determine the meaning of an unknown word from context, encourage him or her to ask for help or to use the dictionary. Many readers often omit or ignore words for which they do not know the meaning. Being aware of this habit may help them to break it. For example, if you look up the meaning of a word in the dictionary, chances are that you will be aware of it in the future even if you had ignored the word many times in the past.

Teach students to learn to distinguish when the material does or does not make sense to them. You may want to provide practice in this skill by rewriting a passage and adding sentences within the text that contribute nothing to the meaning. Then have students read the material and try to locate those sentences that do not contribute to the overall comprehension of the material. This may help them to monitor their comprehension in the future.

DISCRIMINATING BETWEEN REAL AND MAKE-BELIEVE AND BETWEEN FACT AND OPINION

Discriminating between real and make-believe and between fact and opinion are both elements of *critical* or *evaluative reading*, which is a high level of comprehension. Critical or evaluative reading is a very important skill in a democratic society, so it is vital that students be provided with many opportunities to understand and practice this skill.

Although only a few children in first grade may be able to discriminate between real and make-believe, many children in second grade should be able to learn this reading skill. One good way of doing this is to ask children if they think a trade book or story that they have listened to or read for themselves is real or make-believe and to give the reasons why they believe as they do. For example, children are able to understand that books and stories in which animals talk or behave like humans in other ways could not be real because animals cannot behave that way in actual life.

By third grade students can be given a series of statements orally and asked to determine if they are fact or opinion. This is a fairly difficult reading skill for children to master, so it should be presented thoroughly. Later students can be given activity sheets that are devoted to this reading skill so that they can practice. Here are several sample items from such a sheet:

Fact or Opinion?

An ostrich lays very large eggs that are about equal to a dozen or more chicken eggs. (F)

A poodle is the smartest of all dog breeds. (O)

A female (girl) dog always is a better pet for a child than a male (boy) dog. (O)

Every animal in the woods is cautious when meeting a skunk. (F)

A snake makes a good pet for a child. (O)

Camels can go days or even weeks without water. (F)

Kittens usually are cuter than puppies. (O)

A black rhinoceros can be a dangerous animal. (F)

Some key phrases can alert students to the fact that they are reading a make-believe book or story. Students can be taught such key phrases as *once upon a time, many years ago in a land far away, in the beautiful make-believe land of . . . , the animals in this book talk to each other.*

Older students can learn subskills of critical reading such as evaluating the truthfulness and accuracy of the reading material, comparing reading material from several sources, sensing an author's biases, interpreting figurative language, and recognizing such propaganda techniques as the bandwagon effect, testimonials, cardstacking, the halo effect, repetitive words, emotionally toned words, and glittering generalities.

Most students in elementary school can achieve some degree of competency in the various elements of critical reading within the limits of their prior knowledge and abstract intellectual ability. The elements of critical reading should receive increasing emphasis as the student progresses into the intermediate grades and beyond. Critical reading skills perhaps are more commonly taught now than they have been in the past because they have been stressed in college classes for preservice and inservice teachers and in teachers' materials.

In the past, critical reading may not have received so much stress in some elementary classrooms as it should have. This may have resulted in part because some teachers did not want to encourage divergent responses. Then, too, some teachers were somewhat cautious about discussing controversial issues in the classroom. However, it is encouraging to note that many contemporary reading teachers and tutors are encouraging critical, divergent responses.

There are many strategies that can be used to improve ability in the various subskills of critical reading. Some of them are as follows:

➡ Answering questions that call for critical or evaluative responses

➡ Participating in small group discussion about topics that encourage divergent responses

➡ Comparing materials from different sources, such as content textbooks, trade books, the World Wide Web, newspapers, or magazines

➡ Analyzing newspaper and magazine advertisements

RECOGNIZING MAIN IDEAS

You can teach students to locate the main idea and supporting details of a story. You can list the main idea as well as the supporting details, as illustrated by the following paragraph.

It was a beautiful warm summer day with sunny cloudless skies. The temperature was nearly 85 degrees, and I could wear my new shorts. I put on some sunscreen so that I would not get a sunburn.

Main Idea: **It was a beautiful warm summer day with sunny cloudless skies.**

Supporting Details: **The temperature was nearly 85 degrees. I could wear my new shorts. I put on some sunscreen so that I would not get a sunburn.**

A way of illustrating the relationship between the main idea and the supporting details in a paragraph is to draw the paragraph in a diagram, as follows.

Some paragraphs have one main idea.

It was a beautiful warm summer day with sunny cloudless skies.
The temperature was nearly 85 degrees.
I could wear my new shorts.
I put on some sunscreen so that I would not get a sunburn.

Other paragraphs may have two main ideas.

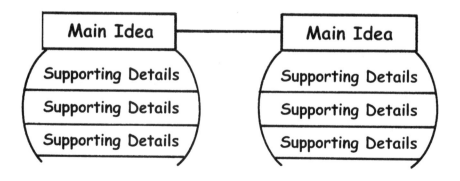

Other kinds of paragraphs may look like the following:

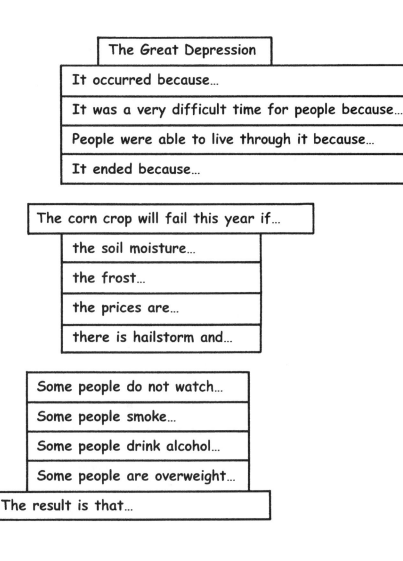

ACTIVITIES TO DEVELOP SEQUENCE ABILITY

There are several strategies that can be used with students to help them develop the ability to place a number of items in correct sequence or order. Sequencing is a complex reading skill that takes students considerable time and practice to master. Therefore, you should begin by having students place only two or three items in correct sequence in the early primary grades and then progress to having them place about five to eight (the maximum) items in correct order by the time they are in third grade. In the intermediate grades students can place perhaps ten items in correct order. Even at that grade level, some students will find this a difficult task. This reading skill can be practiced using both actual objects and activity sheets. It often should be begun with actual objects and then progress to activity sheets.

Here are several activities for providing instruction and/or practice in placing items in the correct sequence:

➡ Find a simple comic strip that has five or fewer frames. Cut the comic strip apart by frames and then laminate the frames to make them more durable and long-lasting. Have students try to reassemble the comic strip by putting it in correct sequence. If you want, each comic strip that is to be used for this purpose can be placed in a large envelope. This is a good activity to use in the reading center as an independent activity. If you want to make this a self-checking activity, you can place the correct sequence number on the back of each comic strip frame before laminating it.

➡ There are many commercially available sets of cards that are designed to help students learn sequential ability. They usually can be checked out of an elementary school's media center or purchased in a school supply store. In each case the student simply places the cards in correct sequential order. If you want, the student also can describe the action that is taking place on each of the cards after he or she has put them in correct order. In this way these cards also can be used to improve oral language ability. Such cards may be appropriate for older students if the cards contain material that is relevant for them.

Here are several other suggestions for using comic strips to improve sequence ability that are designed to integrate reading and writing.

➡ Delete a frame from the comic strip and have students infer what is missing and then write a description for it.

➡ Delete the ending frame and have students infer and write an ending for the strip.

➡ Remove some of the balloons of dialogue and have students infer and write in the appropriate dialogue.

➡ You also can construct your own activity sheets or purchase commercial activity sheets that emphasize placing items in correct order. This kind of activity sheet usually is constructed as follows:

Place the items on this activity sheet in the correct order.
_____ Jan and Emily decided to go outside to play in the snow.
_____ There was a snowstorm last night.
_____ The sun came out in the afternoon, and the weather got much warmer.
_____ By the end of the day, Jan and Emily's snowman had almost melted.
_____ After they had played in the snow a while, Jan and Emily built a big snowman in the front yard.

Place the items on this activity sheet in the correct order.
_____ By the time the tour bus took me home, I was tired.
_____ I took a tour bus to a small town in northern Mexico on Sunday.
_____ Because the girls rode the horses in rough gravel, some of the gravel sprayed up and hit the people in the lower stands who were watching them.
_____ Near the end of the exhibition one of the riders had to quit as her horse acted sick.

_____ Therefore, it was much safer to sit high up in the stands farther away from the horses.

_____ I enjoyed the tour, during which I watched the Mexican girls riding their horses.

_____ I saw two teams of young girls, who were each dressed in identical costumes, riding beautiful white horses.

STRATEGIES FOR IMPROVING ABILITY TO FOLLOW DIRECTIONS

The ability to read and carry out directions is *not* a skill that traditionally has been taught effectively in elementary schools. Many adults, including this author, have considerable difficulty reading and following directions successfully. Therefore, it is imperative that this important reading skill be taught more effectively by reading teachers and tutors.

Here are several strategies that can be used effectively for this purpose.

➡ Help students to become aware of key words that indicate a series of instructions, such as *first, second, then,* and *finally.* Discuss in this case that there actually are four steps, although the writer used only the terms *first* and *second.* As students read the directions, have them reinforce this knowledge by having them make lists of words that were used to indicate the steps.

➡ Write directions for recess activities on the chalkboard. Try to get the students into the habit of following these directions without an oral explanation from you.

➡ Write directions for paper folding or other activities the students can do at their seats. Have the students read and follow these directions step by step.

➡ Ask the students to write the directions for playing a game. Have them read their directions and analyze whether they could learn to play the game from a student's written directions.

➡ Encourage the students to read and follow written directions, such as those in workbooks and certain arithmetic verbal problems, *without your help.*

➡ Write directions for certain designs to be drawn on paper. For example, the following directions may be given:

1. Make an *X* on your paper halfway between the top and bottom and 2" from the left-hand side.

2. Make a *Y* halfway between the top and the middle of the paper and 2" from the left-hand side.

3. Make a *Z* halfway between the middle and the bottom of the paper and 2" from the left-hand side.

4. Draw a line that will connect the *X, Y,* and *Z.*

5. Write your name on the bottom right-hand side of the paper in printed capital letters.

After these steps are completed, have students examine their pictures in relation to a picture that is drawn correctly on the chalkboard and then discuss the reasons for their errors in following these directions.

SEMANTIC MAPS AND WEBS

Semantic maps and webs can be used in both the primary and intermediate grades as an effective way of developing specialized vocabulary and comprehension as well as motivating writing. Semantic maps and webs can be used both before and after reading any type of content or narrative material. Their use enables students to understand the relationships between vocabulary terms, helping them to remember them and comprehend the material more effectively. Semantic maps or webs also can be called *story maps, story webs, advance organizers,* and *think-links.*

Although there may be slight variations among all of these strategies, they are very similar. They are graphic representations of the relationships among the important vocabulary terms in the material and are designed to organize prior knowledge and vocabulary. There are as many variations of semantic maps or webs as there are reading researchers, teachers, and tutors, and you are encouraged to experiment with your own version of this strategy.

In formulating a semantic map or web, it is useful first to display a completed map on the chalkboard or a transparency using the important vocabulary terms from a content assignment or narrative trade book that your students are going to read in the near future. At the primary-grade level, the map (web) obviously should be a simple one. Illustrate to students how the map shows the relationship among the important vocabulary terms. Then place a partially completed map on the chalkboard or a transparency either before or after the students read a portion of the material. Then they can complete it *with your help* if necessary.

Only after students have had considerable experience with completing semantic maps or webs should they be asked to construct one independently or even with a partner. In many cases it is a good idea to have them construct a web with one or more partner(s). The partially completed map or web can be duplicated for each student to complete independently or with a partner(s). If semantic mapping is not presented carefully with much preparation, a student can experience frustration and never wish to use this strategy again. It also is important that semantic mapping be used as a strategy fairly often instead of just once or twice if it is eventually to be used independently.

QUESTIONING STRATEGIES, QARS, AND RECIPROCAL QUESTIONING (THE REQUEST PROCEDURE)

Questioning strategies for question–answer relationships (QARs) can be used both as an assessment strategy and a teaching strategy for comprehension. In several research studies, Raphael (1982) taught students three kinds of QARs or questioning strategies. QAR instruction encourages students to consider both their prior knowledge and the reading material when answering questions. The relationship for questions with answers directly stated in the material in one sentence is called "right there." Students should look for appropriate words in the questions and then read the sentence containing the answer.

The relationship between questions and their answers in the material that required information from a number of sentences or paragraphs is called "think and search." The relationship between questions for which the answer has to come from the student's own prior knowledge is called "on my own."

It is important that teachers ask all students, including those with learning and reading disabilities, mainly "think and search" (interpretive or critical) and "on my own" (creative) questions if they are to be able to respond at higher levels of comprehension rather than at the literal or factual level. For example, in a research study Guszak (1967) found that teachers asked mainly literal or lower-level questions. Although this study is not recent, the results undoubtedly would be about the same today because lower-level questions are easy for the teacher to both formulate and to evaluate. If students have not been asked many "think and search" and "on my own" questions about the material that they have heard read aloud to them or read for themselves, it is not logical to assume that they ever will become competent in answering these important types of questions. Even young children and those with special needs can make a beginning in answering questions that evaluate higher levels of comprehension.

In the research studies about QARs, researchers found that *modeling the decision* about the kind of QAR that questions constituted was an important part of teaching the students about the concept of QARs. *Supervised practice* following a teacher's modeling also was important. It is interesting to note that average and below-average students made the greatest improvement after training in the use of QARs.

Raphael (1986) modified QAR interaction to include four categories, clustered under two different headings. In the modified plan the "on my own" category is divided into questions that involve both the reader's prior knowledge ("author and you") and the text information and those that can be discovered from the reader's experience without any information from the material ("on my own"). Here is a diagram designed by Raphael that illustrates the recent and useful QARs.

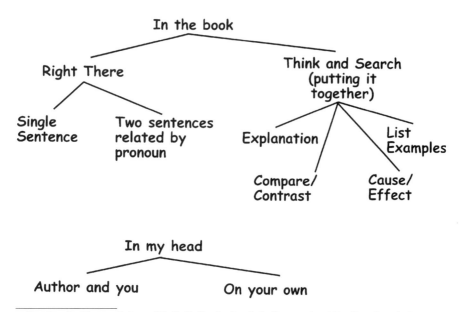

Reprinted with permission of Taffy E. Raphael and the International Reading Association.

Reciprocal questioning (the ReQuest procedure) is a useful strategy for helping students in third grade and beyond to become active questioners at the interpretive level of comprehension. The original ReQuest procedure was developed by Manzo (1969) and has been used and revised by many different reading specialists. It is one of the most useful strategies for improving interpretive and critical comprehension skills. My teacher-trainees have used it successfully in many different teaching and tutoring settings for many years.

Here are the main steps in this strategy:

1. The teacher tells the students to ask several higher-level questions about each sentence in a selection they think the teacher might ask.

2. The teacher then answers each question as fairly and completely as possible and tells the students they must subsequently do the same.

3. Then the teacher and the students both silently read the first sentence.

4. The teacher closes the book, and a student asks questions about that sentence that the teacher is to answer.

5. Next the student closes the book, and the teacher asks questions about the material. The teacher should provide an excellent model for the student's questions. The questions always should be interpretive, critical, or creative.

6. After a number of additional sentences, the procedure can be modified to use an entire paragraph instead of individual sentences if the students seem able to do so.

THE HERRINGBONE TECHNIQUE

The herringbone technique is very effective in improving reading comprehension ability at the second-grade level and beyond. This strategy helps students to locate important information in either narrative or content material by asking variations of the following six basic comprehension questions: *Who? What? When? Where? How?* and *Why?* Prepare a fish outline or a plain outline and place it on posterboard. If you laminate it, it can be used again and again with different narrative and content materials. **Note:** Younger students like the fish outline while older students may prefer to use the traditional outline. The student writes (dictates) the main idea on the horizontal line and the appropriate details on the slanted lines of the fish outline or traditional outline. These are the details that answer the six questions mentioned earlier (Tierney, Readence, & Dishner, 1990).

To present the herringbone technique, show the fish diagram or simple diagram variation of the strategy on the chalkboard or a transparency. Students should not be asked to use this strategy until it has been thoroughly explained and demonstrated. They also need directed practice with it before they are asked to complete it independently. Even then it may be helpful to have them work with a partner(s) while completing it. Depending on the material, they can complete the herringbone form either as they are reading or when they have finished reading. It often is more effective to have them complete the form during their reading.

After the students have completed this technique, a follow-up large group or small group discussion often is helpful. Students can be helped to notice that the material does not always provide all of the information that is required to complete the herringbone diagram or that some of the information required on the outline is not particularly helpful to the comprehension of the material. If a few students think that some of the missing information is important, they can be encouraged to locate it by using other resources.

A reproducible herringbone diagram in the form of the fish outline and a reproducible copy of the more traditional herringbone diagram are provided. You can duplicate either one and have your students use it.

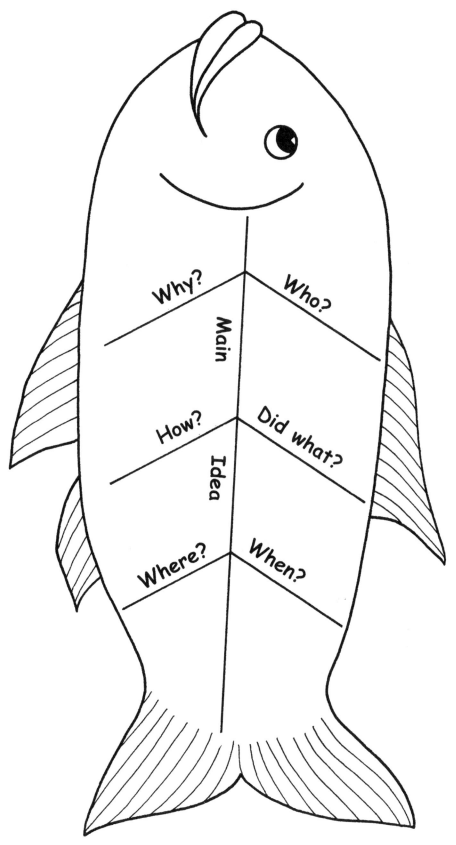

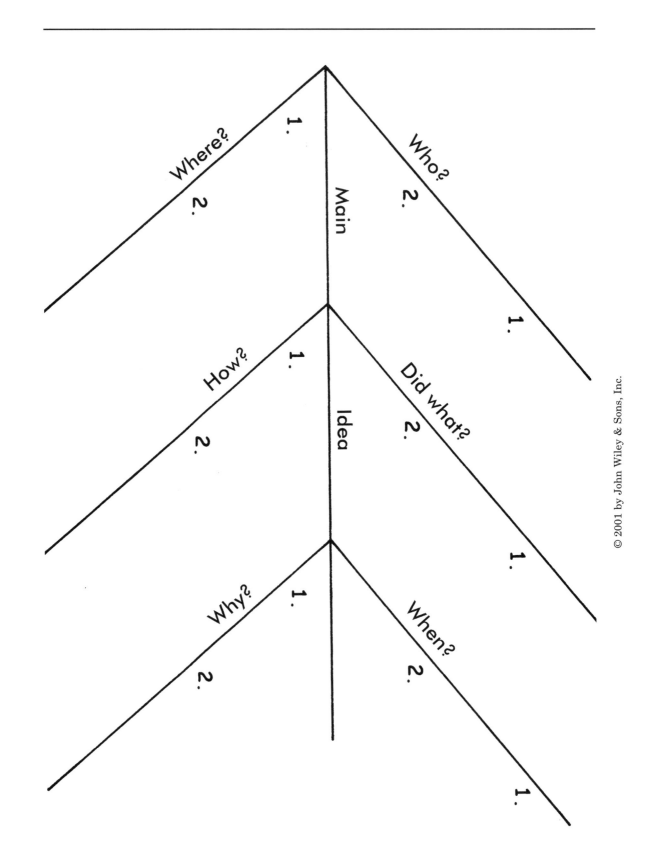

Where? 1. 2.

Who? 1. 2. 1.

Main

How? 1. 2.

Did what? 1. 2. 1.

Idea

Why? 1. 2.

When? 1. 2. 1.

OTHER STRATEGIES

There are a number of other strategies that can be used to improve the various levels of comprehension. Due to space limitations, only a few more are listed here. You are encouraged to consult the professional books in the references at the end of this chapter for suggestions about how to implement these and many other comprehension strategies. Over the years my teacher-trainees have used all of them successfully in teaching and tutoring elementary and junior high school students.

- Observing punctuation marks such as periods, commas, colons, semicolons, and the exclamation point.

- Having students combine sentences by using connective words and subordinate clauses.

- Calling students' attention to such connecting words as *and, however, therefore, neither, either, but, which, that,* and so forth.

- Placing a number of items or later placing words into the correct category (categorization or classification activities).

- Writing an ending to an incomplete story.

- Writing an alternative ending to a story.

- Adjusting the reading rate to the difficulty of the material and the reader's purpose for reading it.

- Allowing students to have think-time to answer comprehension questions, especially higher-type comprehension questions.

- Having older students complete analogies such as *shoe is to foot as glove is to* _____ *(hand)*.

- Having students bring two or three types of articles to class. Then have them distinguish between articles that describe actual events and those that are the writer's ideas.

- Helping students determine an author's purpose by providing them with several types of books and articles. Then have them classify the book and articles as to the reasons they were written.

- Teaching older students various paragraph patterns of organization, such as enumeration, generalization, comparison/contrast, cause/effect, sequential, and question–answer.

- Telling students of the importance of using *text lookbacks*, which are simply looking back in the reading material to find the answer to a specific question. It may involve rereading a sentence, a paragraph, or a section or skimming or scanning the reading material.

- Selecting several paragraphs that describe several events that resulted in a final event. Then ask students what happened to cause the final event.

➡ Giving students a slip of paper on which is written a job title and the characteristics of that job. Help students to determine which characteristics are the most important to success on that job.

➡ Improving students' understanding of mood by giving them large pieces of drawing paper and crayons. Then play an instrumental CD or tape for 3 to 5 minutes, turn off the player, and have students draw anything they like.

➡ Participating in creative dramatics.

➡ Writing in the text for wordless (textless) books.

➡ Reading books that invite writing. Because writing is highly related to reading, it is a powerful tool to integrate what one already knows with reading information as well as to discover what one understands and does not understand. Graves, Juel, and Graves (1998) include a list of books that invite writing (p. 256).

➡ Listening to music that invites writing. Music also can easily be related to reading. Graves, Juel, and Graves (1998) include a list of books that invite musical connections (p. 260). In addition, Jacobi-Karna (1996) gives an extensive list of children's book titles that suggest musical possibilities.

➡ Using the book *Down by the River* (Hallworth, 1996) will help connect children with the artist. This is a collection of African-American rhymes, games, and songs.

GAMES FOR IMPROVING ABILITY IN COMPREHENSION

Games are not the best way to improve comprehension. However, the following games should be interesting and useful to students. In addition, other helpful games can be found in various teacher resource books, including those contained in the references for this chapter.

Story Puzzles

TO CONSTRUCT THE GAME

Locate an interlocking puzzle with no more than 100 pieces. On the back of the puzzle write your own story or copy a story from a basal reader or some other type of material with a marker.

TO PLAY THE GAME

Have the student find a flat surface where he or she can play the game independently or with a partner. Have the student(s) put the puzzle together, matching the picture segments.

Making Matches

TO CONSTRUCT THE GAME

This game provides practice in various elements of comprehension. You need a piece of half-inch-thick plywood the same size as a sheet of 8" × 11" paper. You also need to have some shoelaces.

Drill two columns of holes 1" apart down the center of the piece of plywood, as shown in the illustration. Make holes the entire length of the board, spacing them the same vertical distance as four linespaces on a computer. The holes should be just big enough to allow the shoelaces to pass through them easily. Attach shoelaces through the holes in the left column. Tie a knot on the back side so they will not be pulled through. Make sure each string in the left column is long enough to thread through any hole in the right column.

Construct different activities, such as completing sentences, sentence opposites, sentences with the same meanings, and so forth. Space each set of activities four vertical computer linespaces apart so that they will correspond with the holes on the board. Use clear tape or a tack at the top and bottom of each column of questions and answers to hold the dittoed material in place.

TO PLAY THE GAME

Have a student, individually or with a partner, use the board to practice those comprehension skills that this game stresses. Students should enjoy working with the matching boards.

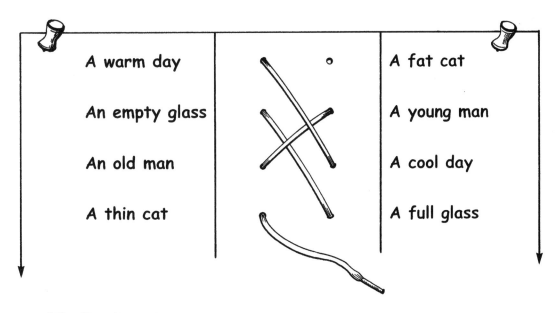

The Reading Wizard

TO CONSTRUCT THE GAME

This game provides practice in reading to answer specific comprehension questions that are found in the material. You should select a basal reader or literature selection for each student.

TO PLAY THE GAME

Choose one student to be the "Reading Wizard." The selected student asks a comprehension question relating to the reading lesson and calls on a classmate to answer. If the student answers correctly, he or she is the "Wizard," and that student makes up the next question. Those students who do not answer a question correctly have another chance to be the "Wizard" with continued play.

Classifying Words Game

TO CONSTRUCT THE GAME

This game provides practice in the ability to classify related words. You need a pocket chart to construct the game. You also need to make some small word cards from posterboard. In addition, each student who is going to play this game needs to have his or her own brown envelope.

Divide the pocket chart into four columns. In the first three columns in each row, place three related word cards. Leave the fourth column blank.

TO PLAY THE GAME

Have the students select a word card from their envelopes that belongs in the same category as the other three words in that row. Here are some examples of words that could be written on cards and put in the pocket chart.

pizza	hamburger	taco	_____
poodle	bloodhound	beagle	_____
skip	run	walk	_____
television	radio	videotape	_____
coat	dress	shirt	_____
kitchen	bedroom	bathroom	_____
dish	fork	spoon	_____
duck	goose	chicken	_____

For a variation, instead of giving a word to complete a category, use four words in which one word does not fit in the category illustrated by the other three words. Have students find and remove the incorrect word.

Read and Follow the Directions

TO CONSTRUCT THE GAME

This game is designed to improve sentence comprehension and the ability to follow directions. Construct sentence cards out of posterboard that require students to perform certain actions.

TO PLAY THE GAME

As the cards are flashed before the entire class, a small group of students (or an individual student) calls on a specific student to read and follow the directions written on the card. Examples of directions that can be written on the sentence cards are as follows:

➡ Walk to the classroom door and open it. Then walk back to your desk.

➡ Stand up behind your desk and turn around two times.

➡ Draw a large circle on the chalkboard. Then draw a smaller circle inside the large circle.

➡ Write your first and last names on the chalkboard in large letters.

Positive Word or Negative Word?

TO CONSTRUCT THE GAME

This game provides practice in critical or evaluative reading, in particular the author's purpose in writing the material. You need written or tape-recorded actual or made-up advertisements.

TO PLAY THE GAME

Have students in the intermediate grades locate and circle or make a list of words that they can classify as either "positive" or "negative" words. Discuss how the use of these words influences our thinking about a certain product. You also can discuss characters in books about whom the author wants to give a positive or negative impression.

Here are some "positive" words:

democracy	excellent	stunning	economical
safety	freedom	fresh	wonderful
spectacular	lovely	dazzling	beautiful
young	talented	wealthy	brilliant

Here are some "negative" words:

illness	cheat	steal	worn out
breaks	fraud	corrupt	over-priced
injuries	unattractive	disease	break down
unhealthy	starve	inedible	peels

REPRODUCIBLES FOR IMPROVING ABILITY IN COMPREHENSION

This section includes several reproducible activity sheets that you can use as is or modify to improve various elements of comprehension.

ACTIVITY SHEET FOR DISCRIMINATING BETWEEN FACT AND OPINION
Third-Grade Level

Read each of these sentences to yourself. Some sentences are *statements of true facts*, some sentences are *statements of false facts*, and some sentences are *statements of opinion*. In the blank before each sentence write the letters *TF* if it is a statement of a *true fact*, write the letters *FF* if the sentence is a statement of a *false fact*, or write the letter *O* if the sentence is a statement of an *opinion*. Then try to write a place or person on the line that you could use to check your answer such as a science textbook, a library book, a computer program, an encyclopedia on CD-ROM, a person, your teacher, or the zoo. You can work with a partner(s) if you want to.

_____ 1. A gila monster is a reptile that can live in the Sonoran Desert in southern Arizona.

_____

_____ 2. A kangaroo is a marsupial that lives in Australia.

_____

_____ 3. A baby duck is called a gosling.

_____

_____ 4. A cat is a better pet for a girl than a dog.

_____

_____ 5. Ostrich meat tastes better than either beef or pork.

_____

_____ 6. A skunk has no effective means of defense.

_____

_____ 7. A deer can make a snorting type of noise.

_____

_____ 8. Walt Disney World is the most fun place for a child to visit.

_____

_____ 9. Black bears hibernate in the winter.

_____

_____10. A white rhinoceros is not an endangered species.

_____

_____11. A boa constrictor makes an interesting pet.

_____

_____12. An opossum can hang from a tree branch by its rat-like tail.

_____

_____13. A baby horse is called a colt.

_____

_____14. An ostrich lays very large eggs.

_____

_____15. A turtle can live without its shell.

_____

Answer key: TF, TF, FF, O, O, FF, TF, FF, O, TF, TF, FF

ACTIVITY SHEET FOR PROVERBS
Fifth-Grade Level

Read each of these proverbs silently. Then write your explanation of each proverb on the lines under it. You can work with a partner(s) if you want to.

1. Don't count your chickens until they're hatched.

   _____
   _____
   _____

2. You can't have your cake and eat it too.

   _____
   _____
   _____

3. A fool and his money are soon parted.

   _____
   _____
   _____

4. The grass always looks greener on the other side.

   _____
   _____
   _____

5. Look before you leap.

   _____
   _____
   _____

6. Haste makes waste.

   _____
   _____
   _____

7. Strike while the iron is hot.

_____

_____

_____

8. You can lead a horse to water but you can't make him drink.

_____

_____

_____

9. You can't teach an old dog new tricks.

_____

_____

_____

10. Make hay while the sun shines.

_____

_____

_____

11. It never rains but it pours.

_____

_____

_____

12. Every cloud has a silver lining.

_____

_____

_____

13. If the shoe fits wear it.

_____

_____

_____

14. Where there's smoke there's fire.

_____

_____

_____

15. Birds of a feather flock together.

_____

_____

_____

16. Curiosity killed the cat.

_____

_____

_____

17. A bird in the hand is worth two in the bush.

_____

_____

_____

18. Out of the frying pan and into the fire.

_____

_____

_____

19. Two heads are better than one.

_____

_____

_____

20. The grass always looks greener on the other side.

_____

_____

_____

RELIABILITY OF INFORMATION ACTIVITY SHEET
Sixth-Grade Level

Read each of the following statements to yourself or with a partner. Then check the source that you believe is the *most reliable* of the three that are included for each of these statements.

1. The disease of acquired immune deficiency syndrome (AIDS) is at epidemic levels in such countries of southern Africa as South Africa, Zimbabwe, and Botswana.
   _____ a. Jeffrey Henricks, a researcher with the World Health Organization
   _____ b. Sue Keeran, a sixth-grade health teacher
   _____ c. Frank Muhammad, an orderly at the Woodruff Medical Center

2. It is imperative that young adults abstain from smoking.
   _____ a. Dr. Matt Franken, a therapist at a mental health center
   _____ b. Dr. Larry Dustman, an orthopedic surgeon
   _____ c. Dr. Salli Washington, a physician with the American Lung Association

3. Driving a snowmobile in the winter can be very dangerous unless the person is very careful.
   _____ a. Joan Carlson of the American Safety Council
   _____ b. Barbara Bull of the Manitowish Waters Sno-Bunnies Snowmobile Club
   _____ c. Ed St. Germain of the Lac du Flambeau Chamber of Commerce

4. A prospective buyer of a golden retriever puppy should be certain that its parents have been screened for hip displasia.
   _____ a. Tony Grigalunas, an owner of a golden retriever
   _____ b. Blanca Lopez of the Golden Retriever Association of America
   _____ c. Sandy Foster, an amateur breeder of golden retrievers

RELIABILITY OF INFORMATION ACTIVITY SHEET *(Cont'd)*

5. It is important to change the oil and oil filter in an automobile on a regular basis.
   _____ a. Susan Robb, the owner of a classic Thunderbird
   _____ b. Bert Terraro, an auto mechanic at Jackson's West Side Garage
   _____ c. Sam Mungo, a university professor of mathematics

6. Pablo Picasso was an artist who greatly influenced modern abstract art.
   _____ a. Frank Mills, a university professor of art education
   _____ b. Joan Everson, a physical education teacher at North Lakeland Elementary School
   _____ c. Anne Harding, a curator at the Museum of Natural History

7. It is important for anyone with diabetes to have regular eye examinations.
   _____ a. Dr. Betty Endicott, an obstetrician/gynecologist at Bloomington Medical Center
   _____ b. Dr. Dennis Goldberg, an internist at Bloomington Medical Center
   _____ c. Dr. Robert Lee at the Midwest Eye Clinic

8. Everyone should exercise on a regular basis to greatly benefit their health and well-being.
   _____ a. David Stoneman, a specialist in sports medicine
   _____ b. Barry Slotky, an insurance actuary
   _____ c. Latasha Johnson, a third-grade physical education teacher

9. Although the Internet is an excellent source of information, it is not infallible.
   _____ a. Susan Ichniowski, a kindergarten teacher
   _____ b. John Gray, a computer expert with Gray's Computer Corner
   _____ c. Mike Flynn, a sixth-grade student

10. Regular exercise and diet may reduce a woman's risk of breast cancer.
    _____ a. Maribeth Halliday, a middle school science teacher
    _____ b. Doris Poirez, an executive secretary
    _____ c. Dr. Everett Reynolds of the American Cancer Society

11. The McAllen, Texas, area is one of the fastest growing areas in the United States.

    _____ a. Dan Brady, the lieutenant governor of Texas

    _____ b. Rosa Gomez, a resident of McAllen, Texas

    _____ c. Dan Rodriguez of the United States Census Bureau

12. It is important for elderly people to have their hearing tested regularly.

    _____ a. Deb Pitcher, an audiologist at the Champaign Audiology Center

    _____ b. Rose Schade, the administrator of Bellflower Nursing Home

    _____ c. Juliana Novak, a nurse at the Community Cancer Center

13. It is very dangerous to drink alcohol and drive an automobile.

    _____ a. Mark Pitner, an emergency room nurse

    _____ b. Sam McGinnis, a used car salesman

    _____ c. Eve Di Nardi of Mothers Against Drunk Driving (MADD)

14. It may be dangerous for middle-age and elderly men to shovel their own snow.

    _____ a. Dr. Scott Robbins, a plastic surgeon at Novak Medical Associates

    _____ b. Dr. Holly Thiel, a cardiologist at Novak Medical Associates

    _____ c. Rae Ann Ajo, a nurse at Novak Medical Associates

15. The majority of African-American voters vote Democratic in national elections.

    _____ a. Dr. Andrew Jackson, African-American physician

    _____ b. Kevin McCarty, a strategist for the Democratic party

    _____ c. Ella Woodson, an African-American fifth-grade teacher

16. All dogs should be vaccinated against distemper and parvovirus.

    _____ a. Dr. David Bodine, a veterinarian at the Kruger Animal Hospital

    _____ b. Sharon Callans, a dog breeder

    _____ c. Rich Enzenbacher of the Vilas County Humane Society

17. Parents should read to their very young children on a regular basis.
    _____ a. Pam Eschenbauch, a kindergarten teacher at Winchester Elementary School
    _____ b. Ryan Sutherland, a high school biology teacher
    _____ c. Eric Palmquist, the principal of Oak Creek Middle School

18. All children should learn to swim so that they will always be safe in the water.
    _____ a. Joe Merna of the American Red Cross
    _____ b. Susie Barta, a lifeguard at Ash Park pool
    _____ c. Betti Smiley, a second-grade teacher at Mackinaw Elementary School

19. Australia is an extremely interesting country to visit.
    _____ a. Dennis Taylor, a travel consultant
    _____ b. Donna Workman, a homemaker who visited Australia in 2000
    _____ c. Steve Barger, an airline pilot for American Airlines

20. The cheetah is the fastest animal in the world.
    _____ a. Dianne Wildcat, Assistant Director of Miller Park Zoo
    _____ b. Dr. Gary Hauken, a veterinarian at Northeastern Animal Hospital
    _____ c. Ethel Jacobi, a high school science teacher

Answer key: a, c, a, b, b, a, c, c, a, c, a, b, a, b, a, c, a

Name _____ Grade _____

ANTICIPATION/REACTION GUIDE
Sixth-Grade Level

As you read the story (found later on this activity sheet) about Geronimo, an Apache Native American, you will find out a number of facts about his life and the way that the Apache Native Americans lived during the latter part of the nineteenth century.

Before you read this story, write *Yes*, *No*, or *Sometimes* on the line under the word *Before* to show what you believe to be true at this time. After you have read the story, write *Yes*, *No*, or *Sometimes* on the line under the word *After* to show what you now believe to be true.

Before   **After**

_____   _____   1. Geronimo was born in what now is the state of New Mexico.

_____   _____   2. Geronimo was an Apache Native American chief.

_____   _____   3. Geronimo was said to possess supernatural powers and was a medicine man and spiritual leader.

_____   _____   4. Geronimo was a rather passive unemotional man.

_____   _____   5. The Lac du Flambeau band of Native Americans were members of the Apache tribe.

_____   _____   6. Raids against neighboring tribes were a common occurrence among the Chiricahua Apache Native Americans.

_____   _____   7. Geronimo's life changed radically after his family was murdered by Spanish troops from Mexico.

_____   _____   8. Geronimo violently hated all whites after the murder of his family.

_____   _____   9. Geronimo and the other Chiricahuas were treated well on the San Carlos Reservation.

_____   _____   10. Geronimo escaped from the San Carlos Reservation three times.

ANTICIPATION/REACTION GUIDE *(Cont'd)*

Before   **After**

_____   _____ 11. Geronimo escaped to Mexico in 1876, only to be recaptured almost immediately.

_____   _____ 12. Amazingly, it required 8,000 soldiers and 500 scouts to track down Geronimo and his band of Chiricahuas in Mexico.

_____   _____ 13. All of the scouts who tracked Geronimo were Mexican mercenaries.

_____   _____ 14. Geronimo became an Apache silversmith for a time in the early 1880s.

_____   _____ 15. The United States government always honored its treaties with Geronimo and the Apache Native Americans.

_____   _____ 16. Geronimo's final surrender in 1886 was the last Native American action in the United States.

_____   _____ 17. Geronimo was buried in his birthplace in the Southwest.

_____   _____ 18. Geronimo's story illustrates the unfair way that Native Americans were treated by the United States government.

GERONIMO

Geronimo (jur-ähn'-ĭ-mōh) or *Goyathlay* ("one who yawns") was born in 1829 in what is today western New Mexico. However, at that time it was still Mexican territory. He was a Bedonkohe Apache Native American who was a leader of the Chiricahua Apache band.

He was given the name Geronimo by Mexican soldiers, although the reason for this is not known. As leader of the Apaches he had unparalleled raiding success that some attributed to supernatural powers. Geronimo was never an Apache chief but rather was a medicine man, a seer, and a spiritual and intellectual leader both in and out of battle. The Apache chiefs depended on his wisdom.

To the Apaches Geronimo demonstrated the Apache values of aggressiveness and courage in the face of difficulty. These qualities inspired great fear in the settlers of the area. The Chiricahua band of Apaches had a migratory life, following the seasons hunting and fishing. When food was scarce, it was the custom to raid neighboring tribes. Raids and vengeance were an honorable way of life among the tribes of this region.

Geronimo's life changed in 1858 when he arrived home from a trading trip to Mexico to find that his wife, his mother, and his three children had all been murdered by Spanish troops from Mexico. This caused Geronimo to hate whites so much that he apparently vowed to kill all of them that he could. After that time he constantly terrorized Mexican settlements.

Although all the Apaches west of the Rio Grande River were ordered to the San Carlos Reservation, an arid part of eastern Arizona, Geronimo escaped from the reservation three times. When the United States Army tried to move the Chiricahuas to a reservation in 1876, Geronimo fled to

GERONIMO *(Cont'd)*

Mexico, managing to avoid being captured for over a decade. Although press reports exaggerated Geronimo's activities, it required over 5,000 United States soldiers, one quarter of the entire army, 500 scouts, and 3,000 Mexican soldiers to track down Geronimo and his band.

In May 1882 Apache scouts who were working for the United States Army surprised Geronimo in his mountain sanctuary, and he agreed to return with his people to the reservation. After a year of farming, the sudden arrest and imprisonment of another Apache warrior along with rumors of trials and hangings prompted Geronimo to leave with 35 warriors and 109 women and children. Later Geronimo surrendered to the army. Unfortunately, the United States government broke its agreement and took Geronimo and 450 Apache men, women, and children to Florida to be confined. Later they were moved to Fort Sill, Oklahoma. In later life Geronimo became a rancher and sold Geronimo souvenirs.

Geronimo's final surrender in 1886 was the last Native American guerrilla action in the United States. At the end his group consisted of only 16 warriors, 12 women, and 6 children. In confinement many of the Apaches died of various diseases, including tuberculosis. Geronimo died on February 17, 1909, a prisoner of war unable to return to his homeland. He is buried at Fort Sill, Oklahoma, where he died far from his homeland in the Southwest.

Geronimo's life story is another example of the tragic way in which the United States government treated many of the Native Americans. His is a story of broken promises, exile, and unhappiness.

FOR ADDITIONAL READING

Burns, P., Roe, B., & Ross, E. (1996). *Teaching reading in today's elementary schools* (pp. 161–309). Boston: Houghton Mifflin.

Cheek, E., Flippo, R., & Lindsey, J. (1997). *Reading for success in elementary schools* (pp. 95–176). Madison, WI: Brown & Benchmark.

Gipe, J. (1998). *Multiple paths to literacy* (pp. 207–240). Columbus, OH: Merrill/Prentice Hall.

Graves, M., Juel, C., & Graves, B. (1998). *Teaching reading in the 21st century* (pp. 184–289). Needham Heights, MA: Allyn & Bacon.

Hall, K. (1997). *Reading stories for comprehension success.* West Nyack, NY: The Center for Applied Research in Education.

Harris, A., & Sipay, E. (1990). *How to increase reading ability* (pp. 510–631). NY: Longman.

Heilman, A., Blair, T., & Rupley, W. (1998). *Principles and practices of teaching reading* (pp. 202–296). Upper Saddle River, NJ: Prentice Hall.

May, F. (1998). *Reading as communication* (pp. 205–267). Upper Saddle River, NJ: Prentice Hall.

Miller, W. (1990). *Reading comprehension activities kit.* West Nyack, NY: The Center for Applied Research in Education.

———. (1999). *Ready-to-use activities and materials for improving content reading skills* (pp. 188–292). West Nyack, NY: The Center for Applied Research in Education.

———. (2000). *Strategies for developing emergent literacy* (pp. 177–216). Boston: McGraw-Hill.

Rubin, D. (1991). *Diagnosis & correction in reading instruction* (pp. 322–381). Needham Heights, MA: Allyn & Bacon.

Savage, J. (1998). *Teaching reading and writing: Combining skills, strategies, and literature* (pp. 157–248). Boston: McGraw-Hill/Prentice Hall.

Shanker, J., & Ekwall, E. (late). (1998). *Locating and correcting reading difficulties* (pp. 141–183). Columbus, OH: Merrill.

Vacca, J., Vacca, R., & Gove, M. (1995). *Reading and learning to read* (pp. 184–260). NY: HarperCollins Publishers.

Walker, B. (1996). *Diagnostic teaching of reading* (pp. 192–322). Columbus, OH: Merrill/Prentice Hall.

WORKS CITED IN CHAPTER 6

Adams, M. (1991). *Beginning to read: Thinking about learning about print.* Urbana-Champaign, IL: Center for the Study of Reading.

Anderson, R., Wilson, P., & Fielding, L. (December 1985). A New Focus on Free Reading. Paper presented at the National Reading Conference, San Diego, CA.

————. (1988). Growth in reading and how children spend their time outside of school. *Reading Research Quarterly, 23*, 285–303.

Chall, J. (1987). Two vocabularies for recognition and meaning. In M. G. McKeown and M. E. Curtis (Eds.), *The nature of vocabulary acquisition* (pp. 7–17). Hillsdale, NJ: Lawrence Erlbaum.

Dale, E. (1969). *Audio-visual methods in teaching.* NY: Holt, Rinehart & Winston.

————. (1965). Vocabulary measurement: Techniques and major findings. *Elementary English, 42*, 895–901.

Dale, E., & O'Rourke, J. (1971). *Techniques of teaching reading.* Chicago: Field.

Davis, F. (1944). Fundamental factors in comprehension in reading. *Psychometrika, 9*, 185–197.

Gale, D. (1982). Why word play? *The Reading Teacher, 36*, 220–222.

Gambrell, L., & Javitz, P. (1993). Mental imaging text, illustrations, and children's story comprehension. *The Reading Teacher, 28*, 264–276.

Graves, M. (1987). Roles of instruction in vocabulary development. In M. G. McKeown & M. E. Curtis (Eds.), *The nature of vocabulary acquisition* (pp. 165–184). Hillsdale, NJ: Lawrence Erlbaum.

Graves, M., Juel, C., & Graves, B. (1998). *Teaching reading in the 21st century* (pp. 184–289). Needham Heights, MA: Allyn & Bacon.

Greaney, V. (1980). Factors related to amount and types of leisure reading. *Reading Research Quarterly, 15*, 337–357.

Guszak, F. (1967). Teaching questioning and reading. *The Reading Teacher, 21*, 227–234.

Hallworth, G. (1996). *Down by the river.* NY: Scholastic Cartwheel.

Hartman, D. (1994). The intertextual links of reading using multiple passages: A postmodern (semiotic) cognitive view of meaning making. In R. B. Ruddell, M. R. Ruddell, & H. Singer, (Eds.), *Theoretical models and processes of reading.* Newark, DE: International Reading Association.

Jacobi-Karna, K. (1996). Music and children's books. *The Reading Teacher, 49*, 56–64.

Koos, K. (1986). Puppet plays. *First Teacher, 7.5*, 56–64.

Manzo, A. (1969). The ReQuest Procedure. *Journal of Reading, 13*, 123–126.

McGinley, W., & Denner, P. (1987). Story impressions: A prereading/writing strategy. *Journal of Reading, 31*, 248–253.

Miller, W. (1999). *Ready-to-use activities & materials for improving content reading skills* (pp. 188–191). West Nyack, NY: The Center for Applied Research in Education.

Nagy, W., & Herman, P. (1987). Breadth and depth of vocabulary knowledge. In M. G. McKeown and M. E. Curtis (Eds.), *The nature of vocabulary acquisition* (pp. 19–35). Hillsdale, NJ: Lawrence Erlbaum.

Ogle, D. (1986). K-W-L: A teaching model that develops active reading of expository text. *The Reading Teacher, 39*, 564–570.

———. (1989). The know, want to know, learn strategy. In D. Muth (Ed.), *Children's comprehension of text* (pp. 205–223). Newark, DE: International Reading Association.

Raphael, T. (1982). Question-answering strategies for children. *The Reading Teacher, 36*, 186–190.

———. (1986). Teaching question-answer relationships, revisited. *The Reading Teacher, 39*, 516–522.

Readence, J., Bean, T., & Baldwin, R. (1981, 1992). *Content area reading: An integrated approach*. Dubuque, IA: Kendall/Hunt.

Ruddiman, J. (1993). The vocab game: Empowering students through word awareness. *Journal of Reading, 36*, 400–401.

Rumelhart, D. (1980). Schemata: The building blocks of cognition. In R. J. Spira, B. C. Bruce, & W. F. Bruner (Eds.), *Theoretical issues for reading comprehension* (pp. 33–58). Hillsdale, NJ: Lawrence Erlbaum.

Schwartz, R., & Raphael, T. (1985). Concept of definition: A key to improving students' vocabulary. *The Reading Teacher, 39*, 198–205.

Searfoss, L., & Readence, J. (1994). *Helping children learn to read*. Boston: Allyn & Bacon.

Shanklin, N., & Rhodes, L. (1989). Comprehension instruction as sharing and extending. *The Reading Teacher, 42*, 496–500.

Shibles, E. (1959). Vocabulary of first-grade children. *Elementary School Journal, 30*, 216–221.

Stauffer, R. (1975). *Directing the reading-thinking process*. NY: Harper & Row.

———. (1980). *The language experience approach to the teaching of reading*. NY: Harper & Row.

Taylor, T., Frye, B., & Marayama, M. (1990). Time spent on reading and reading growth. *American Educational Research Journal, 27*, 351–362.

Tierney, R., Readence, J., & Dishner, E. (1990). *Reading strategies and practices: A compendium* (pp. 312–316). Needham Heights, MA: Allyn & Bacon.

Tyson, E., & Mountain, L. (1982). A riddle or pun makes learning words fun. *The Reading Teacher, 36*, 17–173.

Chapter 7

TEACHING READING TO STUDENTS WITH SPECIAL NEEDS

Do you think North American schools have been effective in teaching reading to students who have special needs of various types? Because such students represent a large part of the school population today and are expected to make up an even larger portion in the future, it is important that their reading needs be met effectively (Coballes-Vega 1992). With the advent of *inclusion* in most elementary schools, it is crucial that classroom reading teachers and tutors have easy access to information that will help them effectively teach and reinforce reading skills. Most of these teachers simply do not have the expertise and materials to teach reading to students with various kinds of special needs.

Of course, the ideal is for each classroom reading teacher and tutor to have sufficient support from special educators. Even if this happens, the reading teacher or tutor often must provide some of the instruction and practice. This chapter is designed to provide classroom reading teachers and tutors with concise, easy-to-understand descriptions of students who have various types of special needs. In addition, it suggests guidelines, strategies, and materials to implement reading instruction with such students.

INTRODUCTION

It is important to remember that the students who are labeled "at-risk" are actually—like all students—*students of promise*. In some ways it does them a disservice to call them "at-risk." To verify that they indeed are students of promise, reading teachers and tutors must have a deep belief in the worth of each student, have an accepting attitude toward them and their unique characteristics, and give them unqualified support. Any teacher or tutor must celebrate their uniqueness and their culture. Most of the students who are labeled as having special needs can succeed with appropriate instruction and proper support. Many years ago my doctoral adviser told me that *almost all students can learn to read*, no matter what environmental, emotional, or physical limitations they face. After working with thousands of students over many years, I agree that this is true.

Savage (1994) has coined an interesting acronym for teachers and tutors of the twenty-first century: *AHANA* which is an acronym for African-American, Hispanic,

Asian, and Native American. He prefers to use it because this term does not have the negative connotations that often surround the word *minority*. Bill Cosby wrote, "The word *minority* has connotations of weaknesses, lesser value, self-doubt, tentativeness, and powerlessness" (1990, p. 61). AHANA pupils bring prior knowledge to schools that is not usually well reflected in the curriculum. Such children need to see their own world reflected in trade books and other reading materials. In the words of a white middle-class mother who has adopted a young Asian child, "I would like my child to read books that have children that look like him." Often this does not happen.

North American schools today have an increasing tendency to label children who have special needs. Some of the labels are as follows:

children with learning disabilities

children who have attention deficit disorders (ADD)

children who have attention deficit/hyperactivity disorders (ADHD)

educable mentally handicapped

children with mild disabilities

children who speak English as a second language (ESL)

children with limited English proficiency (LEP)

bilingual children

children who are culturally or linguistically diverse

children with visual impairments

children with hearing impairments

children with speech and language disorders

Using such labels for students has both advantages and disadvantages. However, the disadvantages may outweigh the advantages as least in some cases. Here are the major strengths of using such labels:

➡ Students who are identified as having some kind of special need may receive the specially trained teachers and the special materials they need to expedite their learning as much as possible.

➡ Such students may be grouped—at least for part of the school day—with students who have similar reading abilities and needs.

➡ Such students should receive the individually prescribed instruction that can enable them to achieve at as high a level as possible.

➡ Without the use of a label, some teachers might not be aware of the special needs of a certain child.

➡ These children may experience more success than otherwise would be the case if their unique needs had not been identified and theoretically met.

However, labeling a student also has several limitations of which a reading teacher or tutor should be aware:

➡ There may be a self-fulfilling prophecy both for the teacher and the student. This is a concept that states a student performs in about the same way in which his or her teacher expects the pupil to perform. For example, the self-fulfilling prophecy is the main reason why students in the inner city often achieve significantly below their potential level. Some teachers teach in inner-city schools without being willing or properly trained to do so. They then may expect limited achievement from their so-called "at-risk" pupils and receive equally little in return. One of my teacher-trainees tutored an African-American sixth-grade boy several years ago who had just moved to central Illinois from inner-city Chicago. He was reading on the third-grade level. However, because he was both intelligent and motivated, when he received appropriate instruction, he was able to read up to grade level in a short time. I feel sure that Tyrone was the victim of the self-fulfilling prophecy.

➡ The use of a label may be detrimental to a student's self-esteem. For example, how would you feel if you were said to be learning disabled, mildly disabled, attention deficit disordered, or attention deficit/hyperactivity disordered? Wouldn't you view yourself in a different way than if you were called a good student or even a fairly good student?

➡ Some of the labels currently being used in schools are difficult to define precisely, so a student may be incorrectly labeled. For example, a student who is said to be LD, ADD, or ADHD may not be labeled correctly. Some of the children who are labeled as LD, ADD, or ADHD simply may have behavior problems with which the teacher cannot easily deal. In some cases it may be easier to give a student a label and provide him or her with a behavior-altering drug such as Ritalin® than to have a disruptive student in the classroom. In one Midwestern city the school board publicly stated that this was happening in its school system. Of course, the teachers in that school system were upset about this statement, and they asked for a retraction from the board. Both sides eventually compromised, and the matter was settled. However, it is probable that there was at least some truth in the board's statement.

➡ Unfortunately, not all teachers enjoy teaching a class made up of children with special needs or even one child who has special needs. As stated before, only teachers who are prepared to and who desire to teach special needs children should do so.

In summary, before a special needs student is labeled in any way, the teacher or tutor should be absolutely certain that the label is correct and that its use will significantly help the student to receive more effective instruction.

TYPES OF STUDENTS WITH SPECIAL NEEDS

This section provides some of the characteristics of students with special needs. The material contained in this section is general, and there are significant differences among students who are given any of these labels.

Pellicano defined "at-risk" pupils as "uncommitted to deferred gratification and to school training that correlates with competition, and its reward, achieved status" (1987, p. 47). In general, the following is a brief comparison of expected and exhibited school behaviors of some students with special needs, especially those who have learning disabilities, attention deficit disorders, attention deficit/hyperactivity disorders, or are culturally or linguistically diverse. Of course, not all students with a specific type of special needs have any of the exhibited behaviors mentioned here.

Expected Behavior	Exhibited Behavior
good listeners	inattentive listeners
good readers	reading below grade level
good writers	disinterested in writing and often exhibiting poor writing mechanics
self-controlled	impulsive
initiators	unmotivated
independent	dependent or disinterested
organized	disorganized
high self-esteem	low self-esteem
able to delay immediate gratification for long-term rewards	desires immediate gratification
good social skills	poor social skills

STUDENTS WITH LEARNING DISABILITIES (LD)

The term *learning disability (LD)* was first used by Kirk (1963) to refer to students who—despite apparently average or above average intelligence—have great difficulty with school learning. The most common definitions of learning disability include the following features:

➡ A significant gap between expected achievement levels based on intelligence test scores and actual performance in at least one area (reading [most common], mathematics, spelling, writing, etc.)

➡ An uneven profile in achievement, with achievement in some areas being very high and in others, very low

➡ Poor achievement not due to low intelligence or emotional maladjustment

➡ Poor achievement apparently not due to environmental factors

The federal government's definition of learning disability states the following:

"Specific learning disability" means a disorder in one or more of the basic psychological processes involved in understanding or in using language, spoken or written, which may manifest itself in an imperfect ability to listen, speak, read, write, or spell or do mathematical calculations (*Federal Register*, p. 1, 1977).

In addition, a learning disabled student *may* exhibit some or many of the following behavioral characteristics, which may be used in making the identification: hyperactivity to a moderate degree, distractibility to a moderate degree, perceptual problems, attention problems of a mild nature, and ineffective learning or problem-solving strategies. Not all of the children who have learning disabilities are identified in kindergarten, first grade, or even second grade. Thus, they go undiagnosed until most of the basic reading skills are presented, almost ensuring that they will have reading problems later on.

STUDENTS WITH ATTENTION DEFICIT DISORDERS (ADD) OR ATTENTION DEFICIT/HYPERACTIVITY DISORDERS (ADHD)

The number of children who are identified as attention deficit disordered (ADD) and attention deficit/hyperactivity disordered (ADHD) has increased significantly. Shaywitz and Shaywitz (1992) stated that "attention deficit disorder (ADD) currently represents one of the most frequently diagnosed neurobehavioral disorders in childhood, affecting perhaps as much as *20 percent* of the school-aged population" (p. vii). Although the 20% figure probably is much too high, millions of students have been identified as ADD and represent one of the three subgroups: ADD without hyperactivity, ADD with hyperactivity, and ADD with aggression. According to the American Psychiatric Association's (APA's) *Diagnostic and Statistical Manual of Mental Disorders (DSM-IV)* (American Psychiatric Association, 1994), attention deficit/hyperactivity disorder (ADHD) is the diagnostic classification the APA uses and defines as "a persistent pattern of inattention and/or hyperactivity that is more frequent and severe than is typically observed in individuals at a comparable level of development" (p. 78). According to this manual, children with ADHD represent about 3 to 5% of the school-aged children, and they can be classified as one of three subtypes: ADHD predominantly inattentive, ADHD predominantly hyperactive/impulsive, and ADHD combined inattentive and hyperactive/impulsive. The American Psychiatric Association stated that ADHD in its severe form is very impairing and affects social, familial, and scholastic achievement.

Children with ADHD often exhibit inattention, hyperactivity, and/or impulsivity. These children usually tend to exhibit normal sensory acuity, and intellectual, perceptual, and social-emotional abilities ranging from average to above average Such children's reading, spelling, and arithmetic achievement often is significantly below that of their classmates. About 50% of children with ADHD have difficulty in reading (Dykman & Ackerman, 1992).

In addition, the American Psychiatric Association (1994) has stated that in order for a child to be diagnosed with ADHD, he or she must display for six months or more at least eight of the following fourteen characteristics before the age of seven:

1. Fidgets, squirms, or seems restless
2. Has difficulty remaining seated
3. Is easily distracted
4. Has difficulty waiting his or her turn
5. Blurts out answers
6. Has difficulty following instruction
7. Has difficulty sustaining attention
8. Shifts from one unfinished task to another
9. Has difficulty playing quietly
10. Talks excessively
11. Interrupts or intrudes on others
12. Does not seem to listen
13. Often loses things necessary for tasks
14. Frequently engages in dangerous activities

These students often are treated with prescription medication, the most common of which are Ritalin®, Cylert®, and Dexedrine®. All of these medications are amphetamines that apparently curtail an ADHD student's inattention and disruptive behavior. Ritalin can be very effective with some students, enabling them to concentrate better so that they can learn to read. The theory behind the use of medication is that as children mature, they will eventually outgrow the ADHD and thus their need for the medication. This may or may not happen.

ESL, LEP, or Bilingual Students

ESL pupils are those children who speak English as a second language. They make up the most rapidly expanding population in North American schools. Students who are labeled *bilingual* are very different in their language and literacy abilities. Some of them may be fluent orally in their home language only but not able to read and write it. A few may have had a strong background of knowledge and skills in their home country. Other students may have had few educational opportunities in their home, where English is not spoken. Others may have a fair mastery of oral English but will continue to have serious difficulties in written English. Therefore, there are great differences among students who have the designation *bilingual*, a term that must be defined more precisely to be useful. Students who are acquiring English as a second language may possess strong potential for fluency and literacy in two languages. However, the extent to which this potential may be realized depends on their educational opportunities at home, in their community, and, perhaps most important, in school.

It is important to understand that more than 6% of the children in the public and private schools in the United States now are classified as limited English proficient (LEP) (Scarcella, 1990). According to data collected by the National Clearinghouse on Bilingual Education (1995), 66% of these children are in the elementary grades, 18% are in middle school, and 14% are in high school. The vast majority of these children—75% of them—speak Spanish at home. However, the rest of them speak other languages, such as Japanese, Hmong, Vietnamese, Korean, Cambodian, Cantonese, and others. Research also shows that it takes nonnative speakers of English between six and eight years to reach the oral skill level of their English-speaking classmates (Collier, 1987). This indicates that it is not an easy task for such students to become proficient in English, and reading teachers and tutors should be aware of this.

Within the category of bilingual children, the following four main categories sometimes are recognized:

➠ *English-dominant pupils with a home language other than English.* These pupils may need to improve their academic achievement in English-speaking schools while continuing to develop the home language skills and cultural ties that their parents want them to maintain.

➠ *Bilingual, bicultural pupils who are generally fluent in both languages.* Bilingual education enhances these students' academic experiences while reinforcing the cultural and linguistic identity of their families.

➠ *Limited English proficient (LEP).* These children probably are the most typical of those receiving bilingual and ESL instruction. They do not have sufficient English language skills to achieve in the regular classroom and need specific instruction for developing linguistic and academic skills.

➠ *English-speaking monolingual pupils with no minority language background.* Because the law requires classes to be integrated, English-speaking pupils who have no knowledge of other languages also may be in bilingual classes. This may help to socialize minority pupils and also help them to benefit from exposure to a second language, such as Spanish.

Note: As of summer 1998, all classes in the state of California must be totally conducted in English because it is the official state language. This is not in keeping with the principles of bilingual instruction. This mandate also may be implemented in other states in the future.

You can easily identify ESL or LEP pupils by listening to them speak. However, you must make this evaluation over a period of time because a student simply may be reserved or shy and not want to talk much at first.

CULTURALLY OR LINGUISTICALLY DIVERSE STUDENTS

Almost every major language has a number of different dialects. Dialects are alternative language forms often used by regional, social, or cultural groups. Although dialects are usually understandable by speakers of the same main language group, they are different in several ways: sounds (*chump* for *jump*), vocabulary (*señor* for *Mr.*), and syntax (*Is hot now* for *It is hot now*). All dialects are equally logical, precise, and are all governed by rules.

However, usually one dialect is considered the standard language form in a society because it is used by the educationally, socially, and economically advantaged members of that society. In the United States the standard language is called *Standard American English (SAE)*. It usually is thought to be the form of English spoken by newscasters in most parts of the country. It normally is the goal of schools to teach standard English to all students because they must compete in a society that recognizes this as the standard form of speech. However, each student's diverse dialect always should be respected while attempting to add standard English on a gradual, tactful, supportive basis.

A common nonstandard dialect in the United States is *black English*. However, people in Appalachia, the Northeast, and the South also each have a clearly definable dialect. Although the speakers of each of these dialects share certain language conventions, there may be some degree of variation within the dialect. Here are the more common characteristics of black English.

Language Element	Standard American English	Black English
	Phonological Differences	
Initial Sounds*		
/th/—/t/	*thick*	*tick*
/th/—/d/	*those*	*dose*
/str/—/skr/	*stream*	*scream*
/thr/—/tr/	*throw*	*trow*
Final		
/r/—no sound	*floor*	*floe*
/l/—no sound	*pool*	*poo*
/sk/—/ks/	*ask*	*aks*
General		
Simplify final consonant blends	*walked*	*walk*
	jumps	*jump*
	rest	*ress*
/i/—/e/ before nasals	*pin*	*pen*

*The phoneme on the left is the sound in Standard American English, while the phoneme on the right is the sound in black English.

Language Element	Standard American English	Black English
	Syntactic Differences	
Dropping *to be* verbs	*Shaundra is running.*	*Shaundra running.*
Using *be* for extended time	*Tamara is happy today.*	*Tamara be happy today.*
Subject-predicate agreement		
to be verbs	*I am studying.*	*I is studying.*
	There were five puppies in the litter.	*There was five puppies in the litter.*
Third-person singular verbs	*Yetti goes to work.*	*Yetti go to work.*
Irregular verbs	*Eddie flew to Chicago.*	*Eddie flied to Chicago.*
Double negatives	*My father doesn't want pizza.*	*My father don't want no pizza.*
Omission of indefinite article	*Please give me a piece of cake.*	*Please give me piece of cake.*
Use of more for comparatives	*Sam's brother is older than he.*	*Sam's brother older than he.*

Here are the major differences between Standard American English and Spanish.

Language Trait	Standard American English	Spanish
	Phonological Differences	
/a/—/e/*	rat	ret
/a/—/e/	hate	hete
/i/—/e/	pig	peeg

---

*The phoneme on the left is the sound in Standard American English, while the phoneme on the right is the sound in Spanish.

Language Trait	Standard American English	Spanish
	Phonological Differences *(Cont'd)*	
/b/—/p/	*bat*	*pat*
/z/—/s/	*fuzz*	*fus*
/j/—/ch/ or /y/	*jam*	*cham* or *yam*
/th/—/d/	*thump*	*dump*
/th/—/s/	*those*	*sose*
	Syntactic Differences	
Negatives	*Guillermo is not at work.*	*Guillermo is no at work.*
	The children don't go to school.	*Children no go to school.*
	Please don't spill the milk.	*Please no spill the milk.*
Tense	*The doctor will see you now.*	*The doctor see you now.*
	Luci played the piano yesterday.	*Luci play piano yesterday.*
Use of *be*	*My mother is forty.*	*My mother has forty years.*
	Caesar is thirsty.	*Caesar has thirst.*
Omission of determiner	*My grandfather is a dentist.*	*My grandfather is dentist.*
Omission of pronoun		
in questions	*Is it six o'clock?*	*Is six o'clock?*
in statements	*It is a beautiful day.*	*Is beautiful day.*

Culturally or linguistically diverse pupils are children who belong to an ethnic or minority group that differs from that of Caucasian Anglo-Saxon Americans. In addition to African American (black) and Latino children, Native Americans and Asian-Americans, among others, are considered to be culturally or linguistically diverse. In addition to having a dialect that is different from that of Standard American English, some students may differ in their values and orientation toward and interest in school.

The term *multicultural education* refers to developing an understanding and appreciation of various racial and ethnic groups. This awareness should permeate the entire curriculum, and pupils should be taught with consideration for their cultural heritage, their language preferences, and their individual lifestyles.

MILDLY MENTALLY HANDICAPPED STUDENTS

The American Association on Mental Deficiency (AAMD) has defined *mental retardation* in the following way:

> Mental retardation refers to significantly subaverage general intellectual functioning existing concurrently with deficits in adaptive behavior and manifested during the developmental period (Grossman, 1973).

According to this definition, two elements must be present for a student to be categorized as mentally retarded, mentally handicapped, or mildly mentally disabled: intellectual functioning that is significantly below average *and* inadequate adaptive behavior. According to the AAMD, "subaverage general intellectual functioning" indicates that a student must have an IQ score on the Wechsler Intelligence Scale for Children-Revised (WISC-R) of 69 or below. Children who have IQs between 70 and 85 are sometimes called *slow learners*, and reading instruction also must be adapted for them. However, they normally are not called mentally retarded or handicapped. In evaluating adaptive behavior, the AAMD indicates that the educator must consider the age of the student in making this judgment.

Usually both mentally handicapped students and slow learners possess some of the same learning characteristics to a greater or lesser degree. Although they normally progress through the same developmental stages as do all other students, they usually do so at a slower rate. These students may have difficulty in perceiving, thinking, learning, socializing, and handling emotions. This is especially true in the academic tasks of literacy, such as reading, writing, and spelling. Such students usually also have the following characteristics, which should be considered when planning a reading program for them:

- ➡ Delayed language development with a higher frequency of speech and language problems

- ➡ Short attention span with possible distractibility

- ➡ Inadequate short-term memory especially in words, ideas, and numbers

- ➡ Difficulty in grasping abstract concepts but less difficulty in grasping concrete ideas

- ➡ Deficiency in oral and silent reading, locating main ideas and significant details, using context clues, and interpretive comprehension

- ➡ Ability to learn sight words and phonics with appropriate instruction that has sufficient meaningful repetition

VISUALLY IMPAIRED STUDENTS

Visually impaired students include the legally blind and partially sighted. A person who is considered legally blind has visual acuity that is less than 20/200. This means that with the better eye, a legally blind person can see at least 20 feet (or less) what a normally sighted person can see at 200 feet, even with the best possible correction. A partially sighted person has visual acuity that is between 20/200 and 20/70 with his or her better eye.

Legally blind persons are not necessarily entirely blind. Eighty-two percent of the legally blind have sufficient vision to be able to read print with the assistance of large-print books or magnifying glasses. Twenty-one percent of the legally blind use only Braille for reading. Over one-half (52%) use large- or regular-print books for most or all of their reading. About one-tenth of 1% of school-aged students in the United States are believed to be visually impaired (*Federal Register*, 1984).

Visual impairment usually does not greatly alter a student's language development as hearing impairment often does. The intelligence (IQ) scores of students with visual impairment are not significantly different from those of their normally sighted classmates. It appears that visual impairment has little direct influence on either linguistic or cognitive functioning (Hallahan & Kauffman, 1982).

Visually impaired students may compensate for their limitations by improved listening skills, greater attention, and more acute tactile sensations. Teachers should be able to recognize behaviors that may indicate a student's possible visual problems. Although visual screening takes places in most, if not all, elementary schools, occasionally undetected vision problems may occur. This happens occasionally with children who are being tutored for reading problems. The following symptoms may indicate a child who needs additional visual testing by an ophthalmologist or optometrist:

- Squinting
- Rubbing eyes often
- Holding reading materials very close or very far away from the eyes
- Having red or watery eyes
- Covering one eye while reading
- Having crusty material around eyes and lashes

With proper instruction and instructional modifications, the majority of visually impaired students can make good progress in reading.

HEARING IMPAIRED STUDENTS

Hearing impaired students have reduced sensitivity to sounds in their environment because of genetic factors, illness, or some type of trauma. Usually hearing impaired students are not sensitive to sounds softer than about 26 decibels (dB, a unit of measure for the relative loudness of sounds). A classification system used by the Conference of Executives for American Schools for the Deaf defines degree of hearing impairment as follows:

Category of Hearing Impairment	Amount of Hearing Loss
Mild	26–54 dB
Moderate	55–69 dB
Severe	70–89 dB
Profound	More than 90 dB

Persons with hearing losses greater than 90 dB usually are considered deaf, while those with less severe hearing losses usually are said to be hard of hearing.

In addition to knowing the degree of hearing loss, it also is helpful to know when the hearing loss took place. It is obvious that the earlier the hearing loss occurred, the less likely the student will have adequately developed language ability. The student with a hearing loss that occurred at an early age may experience considerable difficulty with reading comprehension, perhaps especially with interpretive comprehension. This may be especially true if the hearing loss has gone undetected for a long period of time. About two-tenths of 1% of school-aged students are thought to be deaf and hard of hearing (*Federal Register*, 1984).

Some students with a hearing impairment compensate by using amplifying devices, speechreading (lip reading), sign language, finger spelling, or some combination of these. Some students with hearing impairments receive an oral communication program dependent on amplification and speechreading, while others receive a manual communication program dependent on sign language and finger spelling.

Students with hearing impairments have begun to receive a total communication program that incorporates both oral and manual aspects. Such students are dependent on the visual information in a classroom for obtaining information including the reading teacher's or tutor's facial expression and lip movements and written information in the classroom.

Although most, if not all, schools today screen students for hearing impairments, some students with mild or moderate hearing losses may go undetected.

You may request additional auditory testing using an audiometer for any student who has the following symptoms:

→ Has frequent earaches, head colds, or sinus infections

→ Has difficulty following oral directions

→ Often asks to have directions and explanations repeated

→ Is easily distracted by external noises

→ Has poor oral language development

→ Mispronounces words

→ May have great difficulty with phonics

➡ Gets tired easily during listening tasks

➡ May be learning disabled, mentally handicapped, or emotionally disturbed

STUDENTS WITH SPEECH AND LANGUAGE DISORDERS

Students who have speech disorders produce oral language abnormally in terms of *how* it is said, not in what is said. There are several classifications of speech disorders:

➡ Phonological disorders (e.g., substituting *w* for *r*)

➡ Voice disorders (unusual pitch, loudness, or voice quality)

➡ Disorders associated with abnormalities of the mouth and nose (e.g., an orofacial cleft)

➡ Disorders of speech flow (stuttering)

➡ Disorders associated with the muscles used for speech production

However, students who have language disorders have difficulty expressing their ideas in oral language or have difficulty understanding the ideas expressed by other people. Students who have language disorders may not have developed verbal language, may use words in abnormal ways (such as echoing words spoken to them), may have delayed language development, or may have interrupted language development.

According to the *Federal Register* (1975), about 3% of school-aged students have speech disorders and about one-half of 1% have language disorders. Some students with speech disorders may do fairly well in reading, while students with language disorders may have a difficult time developing proficiency in reading comprehension because such reading success is dependent on adequate language proficiency.

You may want to consider the following elements before referring a student to a speech pathologist:

➡ Substantially less mature oral language than that of his or her peers

➡ Inability to tell a story with all its elements

➡ Making substitutions or omissions of sounds such as /w/ for /r/ or /l/, /b/ for /v/, /f/ for voiceless /th/, /t/ for /k/, voiceless th/ for /s/, /d/ for voiced /th/, and voiced /th/ for /z/

➡ Pitch, loudness, and quality very different from those of other students

➡ Difficulty being understood by other students

➡ Speaking much more rapidly than other students, thus causing difficulty in being understood

➡ Particular difficulty in understanding and following directions

THE PHILOSOPHY OF INCLUSION

Inclusion means that students with special needs are assigned to regular classrooms for the entire instructional day and are allowed to participate in all school activities and functions. This type of inclusive system obviously requires very good support systems. Classrooms must be made physically accessible to accommodate the needs of all students. In addition to the physical setting, provisions must be made for additional well-trained personnel, staff development, and technical assistance. This may mean that in addition to the regular classroom teacher, a special education teacher will be made available to co-teach the entire class. It is important that the special education teacher be involved in the instruction of the entire class so that the other students do not become overly aware of the students who have special needs (Friend & Cook, 1992).

In most elementary schools, inclusion has replaced mainstreaming as the way of organizing instruction for students with special needs. Inclusion is the ultimate result of The Education for All Handicapped Children Act, or Public Law 94-142. The most important part of PL 94-142 states that

> in order to receive funds under the Act every school system in the nation must make provision for a free, appropriate public education for every child . . . regardless of how, or how seriously, he may be handicapped.

In addition to requiring schools to provide a free public education for all students with special needs, two other provisions of this legislation affect the reading teacher or tutor: *individual educational plans* (*IEPs*) and the concept of the *least restrictive environment*.

INDIVIDUAL EDUCATIONAL PLANS

Public Law 94-142 mandates that a multidisciplinary team consisting of trained educational specialists evaluate each student who has special needs. This team then submits a report at a case conference meeting at which a representative of the schools, the student's teacher, the parent(s), and other appropriate people responsible for developing an IEP for the student are present. According to federal guidelines (United States Government Printing Office, 1975, p. 3), an IEP must include these elements:

→ A statement of the present levels of performance

→ A statement of the annual goals, including short-term instructional objectives

→ A statement of the specific educational services to be performed

→ The extent to which each student will be able to participate in regular educational programs

→ The projected date for the beginning and anticipated duration of the services

→ Appropriate objective evaluation procedures

→ A schedule for determining at least annually whether or not the instructional objectives are being achieved

THE LEAST RESTRICTIVE ENVIRONMENT

One of the most important decisions made at the group conference, in addition to whether or not to place the student in any type of special education program, concerns the recommended instructional environment. The IEP must state the extent to which the student will be placed in the regular classroom.

The inclusion philosophy states that as much as possible the student's learning be done in a regular classroom setting with his or her own teacher doing much of the teaching. Any special education teacher usually then becomes a consultant to the regular classroom teacher, providing him or her with appropriate instructional strategies and materials. In addition, the special education teacher may come into the student's classroom and work with him or her on an individual basis or even teach a group of students or the entire class. The concept behind inclusion is to avoid singling out a student with any type of special needs. Inclusion also assumes that the student's own teacher can best present much of the required material to him or her with the unqualified support of the special educator without a pull-out program. Unfortunately, according to research, pull-out programs often have not resulted in long-term gains for students.

The following are some of the main advantages of inclusion:

→ It enables students to participate in the regular classroom and school activities as much as possible.

→ It may avoid stigmatizing students because they are separated from their classmates in a pull-out program.

→ The regular classroom teacher and the special education teacher work cooperatively in planning each student's program, so the student should have the best learning experiences possible.

→ Inclusion should teach all students to be tolerant of others who are different from them.

The following are the main limitations of inclusion:

→ Regular classroom teachers must receive true support from special educators if inclusion is to be successful. Regular classroom teachers cannot be expected to know how to teach all types of students with special needs without appropriate, long-term support from special education teachers.

→ Students with special needs must be actively welcomed into a regular classroom by both the reading teacher and the rest of the students so that they do not feel stigmatized or different. This may not always happen unless the teacher makes a concerted effort to ensure that this is the case.

→ The educational opportunities for the other students in the classroom must not be neglected by the need to help students with special needs. All students need to be provided with the best possible appropriate educational experiences.

→ The parents of students with special needs must have the inclusion philosophy explained to them in detail before the school begins to implement it.

STRATEGIES FOR TEACHING READING TO STUDENTS WITH SPECIAL NEEDS

GENERAL GUIDELINES FOR TEACHING READING SKILLS

Here are some basic guidelines, adapted from Mohr (1995), that you can think about when teaching reading skills to students with special needs.

➡ Observe the student in authentic settings. Assess his or her learning styles, strengths, and differences and the conditions of any disability or difference that may interfere with learning.

➡ Teach to a student's strengths while correcting weaknesses and developing compensation skills.

➡ Provide both oral and written directions in the classroom and give both visual and auditory cues for directions and instructions.

➡ Modify a reading task when a student cannot master it. Change the way in which it is presented or change the method of response.

➡ Be aware of auditory and visual distractions in the classroom. Even minor ones can be very distracting to some students, such as a pencil being sharpened or being seated near a window or door.

➡ Assess a student's understanding of the material or directions by following up with a specific question. *Don't* ask, "Are you sure you understand?"

➡ Repeat or rephrase what is being said in the classroom by changing the vocabulary and mode of presentation or method of instruction.

➡ Provide help through peer tutoring or the "buddy system." Provide reinforcement for newly learned or previously learned reading skills by allowing a student with special needs to become a peer tutor to another student who is just beginning to learn a skill.

➡ Match a student's learning style with an appropriate selection of methods and materials. Use the learning styles (visual, auditory, kinesthetic, combination) and unique strengths of all learners in the classroom as tools for planning instruction.

➡ Include all students in classroom activities and projects. Maximize the similarities and minimize the differences of class members during classroom participation.

➡ Evaluate students on their individual performances *without lowering the standards for the class.* Use alternative evaluation devices that ensure success, not failure.

➡ Manage a student's behavior positively, consistently, and assertively. Set limits, structure consequences, and follow through. The use of behavior modification techniques, contingency contracting, praise, encouragement, and positive recognition will help ensure success for all students. Some students with disabilities and learning differences may need different types of discipline.

GUIDELINES FOR TEACHING READING SKILLS TO ESL, LEP, AND BILINGUAL STUDENTS

A number of strategies have been suggested to help teachers or tutors promote both multicultural awareness and linguistic diversity. Some of these strategies are equally valuable with other types of students who have special needs. Here are the most common instructional approaches for limited English-speaking students:

→ *Immersion Approaches*—These approaches make no special provisions for LEP students. As teachers or tutors instruct all students in oral and written skills in English, limited English-speaking students are expected to pick up as much as they can from being immersed in English. This has been the traditional form of instruction for LEP students in the United States although it has not necessarily been the most effective.

→ *ESL Approaches*—These approaches teach limited English-speaking students oral English skills first before any reading instruction begins. Usually ESL approaches require that students leave the classroom for this instruction. Special ESL teachers work with students in structured oral drills to develop fluency in oral English. After they have begun to establish fluency in oral English, reading instruction is then started.

→ *Bilingual Approaches*—These approaches promote the development of reading and writing skills in the student's native language along with either formal or informal instruction in English. After students have learned to read and write in their own language and acquired proficiency in oral English, reading instruction in English begins. Bilingual approaches require special teachers who are fluent in the native language of the students with whom they work.

Here are some general guidelines for teaching culturally diverse children:

→ Study their culture.

→ Participate in their community.

→ Value their unique contributions.

→ Share your ideas with other teachers.

→ Discuss common concerns.

→ Provide a supportive, accepting classroom environment.

→ Develop the students' prior knowledge.

→ Use *multicultural literature* as much as possible.

Here are several other effective suggestions for working with limited English-speaking (LEP) students:

→ Speak more slowly and distinctly than normal but not in an artificial manner.

→ Use shorter sentences and few long words, and simplify concepts as much as possible.

➡ Seat the child near the front of the classroom so that he or she can see and hear better and have less distractions.

➡ Use manipulative materials and concrete demonstrations as much as possible, especially in science and mathematics.

➡ Use visual materials, such as pictures, videotapes, appropriate interactive computer software, diagrams, dioramas, etc., as often as possible.

➡ Allow students to answer with only one or two words if necessary.

➡ Do not correct errors of vocabulary, comprehension, accent, or structure.

➡ Assign a compatible "buddy" to work with the student whenever it is required.

➡ Provide a supportive classroom environment.

➡ Do not expect perfection in English in too short a time period.

GUIDELINES FOR TEACHING READING TO STUDENTS WHO ARE ECONOMICALLY IMPOVERISHED

Delpit (1995) has presented ten principles for teaching students who are economically impoverished. While some students who do not speak English as a native language are both urban and economically disadvantaged, a number are not. However, most of what Delpit wrote also applies to students who are learning English as a second language. All of these principles apply equally well to all students with or without special needs.

➡ Do not just teach content, but recognize students' unique strengths and try to teach more, not less, than the regular curriculum.

➡ Provide students with the basic skills, conventions, and strategies necessary for success in education in the United States.

➡ Empower students to challenge racist views of their abilities and worth.

➡ Whatever reading strategies or materials you use, expect critical thinking from the students.

➡ Always build on a student's strengths while correcting his or her weaknesses.

➡ Use experiences from the student's own culture.

➡ Assess a student's needs and then address them with many diverse strategies and materials.

➡ Honor and respect each student's culture.

➡ Create a sense of family and caring.

➡ Foster a sense of students' connection to community—to something greater than themselves.

Beaty (1997) provided the following suggestions that teachers or tutors can use for any student with special needs. They also are useful with all students. Beaty wrote that in order for students to know they are accepted, you must show them they are accepted by the way you look at them, talk with them, and interact with them. She provided the following points for developing a student's self-esteem as a worthy person:

1. Accept yourself as a worthy person.

2. Accept each student as a worthy person.

3. Show your acceptance by

   ➡ Allowing students to answer with only one or two words if necessary

   ➡ Not correcting errors of vocabulary, comprehension, accent, or sentence structure

   ➡ Not expecting perfection in English in too short a time period

   ➡ Encouraging a compatible "buddy" to work with the student whenever it is required

   ➡ Providing a supportive classroom environment

TRADE BOOKS FOR DIVERSE LEARNERS

This section includes a sampling of the trade books for diverse learners that you can use with elementary school students. These books all can be used as springboards to activities about students from different cultures or with other special needs. Trade books for students with special needs were fairly uncommon in the past. However, recently many such trade books have come on the market. Many of these books have been popular because of the quality of the writing by new authors in the field. A number of these authors are multicultural writers whose books come from their own prior knowledge. In addition, technology breakthroughs in reproducing book art have encouraged outstanding artists to enter the field of illustrating children's trade books. The children featured in such trade books can be important in students' lives. You can introduce students to book heroes from every culture and with every type of disability and then follow up the reading with valuable extension activities.

The importance of books to students' awareness of people from different cultures or with special needs cannot be overstated. For example, Ramsey (1991) wrote that

> children's books are a primary vehicle for this kind of teaching. By engaging children in stories, we enable our young readers and listeners to empathize with different experiences and points of view and experience a wide range of social dilemmas. . . . When children role play situations and characters in a book, they learn how to perceive situations from a variety of perspectives and literally be "in another person's shoes." (pp. 168–169)

Here are some trade books that you may want to use with your students to help create a culturally diverse, inclusive atmosphere.

African-American Literature

Aardema, V. (1989). *Rabbit makes a monkey of lion: A Swahili tale*. NY: Dial. (I*: P–7)

———. (1977). *Who's in rabbit's house? A Masai tale*. NY: Dial. (I: P–8)

Adoff, A. (1982). *All the colors of the race*. NY: Lothrop, Lee & Shepard. (I: 8–11)

———. (Ed.). (1994). *My black me: A beginning book of Black poetry*. NY: Dutton. (I: 9–YA)

Brenner, B. (1978). *Wagon wheels*. NY: Harper & Row. (I: P–7)

Bryan, A. (1980). *Beat the story drum, pum-pum*. NY: Atheneum. (I: 7–10)

Caines, J. (1988). *I need a lunch box*. NY: HarperCollins Publishers. (I: P–7)

Clifton, L. (1970). *Some of the days of Everett Anderson*. NY: Holt. (I: P–7)

Cooper, F. (1994). *Coming home: From the life of Langston Hughes*. NY: Philomel. (I: 7–10)

Curtis, C. (1995). *The Watsons go to Birmingham—1963*. NY: Delacorte. (I: 10–YA)

Feelings, T. (1995). *The middle passage*. NY: Dial. (I: 10–YA)

Greenfield, E. (1977). *Africa dreams*. NY: Harper. (I: P–8)

———. (1973). *Rosa Parks*. NY: Harper. (I: P–8)

———. (1974). *Sister*. NY: Crowell. (I: 9–11)

Hamilton, V. (1992). *Drylongso*. San Diego: Harcourt. (I: 9–11)

———. (1968). *The house of Dies Drear*. NY: Simon & Schuster. (I: 10–YA)

Haskins, J. (1993). *Get on board: The story of the underground railroad*. NY: Scholastic. (I: 10–12)

Hopkinson, I. (1993). *Sweet Clara and the freedom quilt*. NY: Alfred A. Knopf. (I: 8–11)

Johnson, A. (1990). *When I am old with you*. NY: Orchard. (I: P–8)

Lester, J. (1993). *Long journey home: Stories from Black history*. NY: Dial. (I: 11–YA)

Maddern, E. (1993). *The five children: A West African creation tale*. NY: Dial. (I: 9–12)

Mathis, S. (1995). *The hundred penny box*. NY: The Viking Press. (I: 8–10)

Mendez, P. (1989). *The black snowman*. NY: Scholastic. (I: P–7)

Myers, W. (1993). *Malcom X: By any means necessary*. NY: Scholastic. (I: 9–11)

Naidoo, B. (1986). *Journey to Jo'burg: A South African story*. NY: Harper. (I: 9–11)

Pinkney, A. (1994). *Dear Benjamin Banneker*. San Diego: Harcourt. (I: 7–0)

———. (1993). *Seven candles for Kwanzaa*. NY: Dial. (I: 6–9)

Ringgold, F. (1991). *Tar beach*. NY: Crown. (I: 6–9)

Schroeder, A. (1996). *Minty: A story of young Harriet Tubman*. NY: Dial. (I: 7–9)

---

*Indicates interest level by age.

Sisulu, E. (1996). *The day Gogo went to vote: South Africa.* Boston: Little, Brown & Company. (I: 7–10)

Taylor, M. (1987). *The friendship.* NY: Dial. (I: 8–11)

———. (1987). *The gold Cadillac.* NY: Dial. (I: 8–11)

Towle, W. (1993). *The real McCoy: The life of an African-American inventor.* NY: Scholastic. (I: 7–9)

Walter, M. (1990). *Mariah keeps cool.* NY: Macmillan. (I: 8–11)

Wisniewski, D. (1992). *Sundiata: Lion king of Mali.* NY: Clarion. (I: 8–11)

Woodson, J. (1992). *Last summer with Maizon.* NY: Delacorte. (I: 11–YA)

———. (1992). *Maizon at Blue Hill.* NY: Delacorte. (I: 11–YA)

Latin American Literature

Ancona, G. (1993). *Pablo remembers: The fiesta of the Day of the Dead.* NY: Lothrop, Lee & Shepard. (I: 6–9)

———. (1994). *The piñata maker/El piñatero.* San Diego: Harcourt. (I: 6–9)

Cisneros, S. (1989). *The house on Mango Street.* Houston: Arte Publico. (I: 12–YA)

Cowley, J. (1996). *Gracias, the Thanksgiving turkey.* NY: Scholastic. (I: 5–8)

Czernecki, S., & Rhodes, T. (1994). *The hummingbird gift.* NY: Hyperion. (I: 6–9)

Delacre, L. (1989). *Arroz con leche: Popular songs and rhymes from Latin America.* NY: Scholastic. (I: P–8)

———. (1996). *Golden tales: Myths, legends and folktales from Latin America.* NY: Scholastic. (I: 9–12)

Emberly, R. (1990). *My house/Mi casa: Book in two languages.* Boston: Little, Brown & Company. (I: P–7)

Faucher, R. (1988). *Cesar Chavez.* NY: Harper & Row. (I: 8–10)

Garza, C. (1996). *Family pictures/Cuadros de familia.* San Francisco: Children's Book Press. (I: 6–10)

Hurwitz, J. (1993). *New shoes for Silvia.* NY: Morrow. (I: P–7)

Markun, P. (1993). *The painter of Sabana Grande.* NY: Bradbury. (I: 6–9)

Martinez, A. (1991). *The woman who outshone the sun/La mujer que brillaba aun mas que el sol.* San Francisco: Children's Book Press. (I: 7–10)

Mohr, L. (1979). *Felita.* NY: Bantam. (I: 9–12)

Mora, P. (1994). *The desert is my mother/El desierto es mi madre.* Houston: Arte Publico/Piñata. (I: P–6)

Soto, G. (1990). *Baseball in April and other stories.* NY: Harcourt. (I: 9–12)

———. (1995). *Chato's kitchen.* NY: Putnam. (I: 7–9)

———. (1992). *Neighborhood odes.* NY: Harcourt. (I: 9–YA)

———. (1991). *Taking sides.* NY: Harcourt. (I: 10–12)

———. (1993). *Too many tamales.* NY: Putnam. (I: 6–9)

Native American Literature

Bruchac, J. (1996). *Between earth and sky: Legends of Native American sacred places.* San Diego: Harcourt. (I: 10–13)

———. (1995). *The boy who lived with bears and other Iroquois stories.* NY: HarperCollins Publishers. (I: 8–11)

———. (1993). *The first strawberries: A Cherokee story.* NY: Dial. (I: P–8)

Bunting, E. (1995). *Cheyenne again.* NY: Clarion. (I: 6–9)

Caduto, M., & Bruchac, J. (1992). *Keepers of all the animals: Native American stories and wildlife activities for children.* Golden, CO: Fulcrum. (I: 6–12)

Cohen, C. (1988). *The mud pony.* NY: Scholastic. (I: 6–9)

Dorris, M. (1994). *Guests.* NY: Hyperion. (I: 8–10)

Esbensen, B. (1988). *The star maiden: An Ojibway tale.* Boston: Little, Brown & Company. (I: 8–10)

Goble, P. (1978). *The girl who loved wild horses.* Scarsdale, NY: Bradbury. (I: 6–8)

Martin, R. (1993). *The boy who lived with the seals.* NY: Putnam. (I: 6–9)

Miles, M. (1971). *Annie and the old one.* Boston: Little, Brown & Company. (I: 8–11)

Osofsky, A. (1992). *Dreamcatcher.* NY: Orchard. (I: 6–9)

Ross, G. (1995). *How the turtle's back was cracked.* NY: Dial. (I: 6–9)

Sneve, V. (1995) *The Hopis.* NY: Holiday House. (I: 7–10)

Speare, E. (1983). *Sign of the beaver.* Boston: Houghton Mifflin. (I: 10–12)

Steptoe, J. (1984). *The story of jumping mouse.* NY: Lothrop, Lee & Shepard. (I: 9–13)

Wheeler, B. (1986). *Where did you get your moccasins?* St. Paul, MN: Pemmican Publications. (I: 5–7).

Asian-American Literature

Breckler, R. (1992). *Hoang breaks the lucky pot.* Boston: Houghton Mifflin. (I: 6–9)

Buck, P. (1986). *The big wave.* NY: Harper & Row. (I: 9–11)

Coerr, E. (1977). *Sadako and the thousand paper cranes.* NY: Dell. (I: 9–11)

Demi. (1991). *The empty pot.* NY: Holt. (I: P–7)

Hong, L. (1993). *Two of everything: A Chinese folktale.* Morton Grove, IL: Albert Whitman. (I: 6–9)

Huyunh, Q. (1982). *The land I lost: Adventures of a boy in Vietnam.* NY: Harper & Row. (I: 10–12)

Lewis, J. (1980). *The Chinese word for horse and other stories.* NY: Schocken Books. (I: 9–11)

Lord, B. (1984). *In the year of the boar and Jackie Robinson.* NY: Harper & Row. (I: 9–11)

Mochizuki, K. (1993). *Baseball saved us.* NY: Lee & Low. (I: 6–9)

Morris, W. (1987). *The magic leaf.* NY: Atheneum. (I: P–7)

Paek, M. (1988). *Aekyung's dream.* San Francisco: Children's Book Press. (I: 7–9)

Say, A. (1993). *Grandfather's journey.* Boston: Houghton Mifflin. (I: 5–8)

Yashima, T. (1969). *Crow Boy.* NY: The Viking Press. (I: P–7)

Yep, L. (1985). *Dragonwings.* NY: Harper & Row. (I: 9–11)

Young, E. (1990). *Lon Po Po: A Red-Riding Hood Story from China.* NY: Philomel. (I: 5–9)

Literature about Other Cultures

Burgie, I. (1992). *Caribbean carnival: Songs of the West Indies.* NY: Morrow/Tambourine. (I: All ages)

Climo, S. (1996). *The Irish cinderlad.* NY: HarperCollins Publishers. (I: 5–9)

Herriot, J. (1997). *James Herriot's animal stories.* NY: St. Martin's Press. (I: P–8)

Joseph, L. (1991). *A wave in her pocket: Stories from Trinidad.* NY: Clarion. (I: 8–12)

Lewis, J. (1994). *The Christmas of riddle moon.* NY: Penguin Press. (I: 4–8)

Lowry, L. (1989). *Number the stars.* Boston: Houghton Mifflin. (I: 10–13)

Nye, N. (1994). *Sitti's secret.* NY: Four Winds. (I: 10–13) (Trade book about Palestine)

Polacco, P. (1988). *The keeping quilt.* NY: Simon & Schuster. (I: 7–10) (Trade book about Russian people)

———. 1992). *Mrs. Katz and Tush.* NY: Bantam. (I: 6–9)

SanSouci, R. (1995). *The faithful friend.* NY: Simon & Schuster. (I: 7–10)

Literature about Gender Issues

Cole, J. (1986). *The magic school bus at the waterworks.* NY: Scholastic. (I: 6–9)

Hoffman, M. (1991). *Amazing Grace.* NY: Dial. (I: 6–8)

Lasky, K. (1983). *Beyond the divide.* NY: Macmillan. (I: 11–YA)

Merrill, J. (1992). *The girl who loved caterpillars.* NY: Philomel. (I: 7–10)

Paterson, K. (1991). *Lyddie.* NY: Penguin/Lodestar. (I: 11–YA)

Zolotow, C. (1992). *William's doll.* NY: Harper & Row. (I: P–8)

Literature about Exceptional Learners

Barrett, M. (1994). *Sing to the stars.* Boston: Little, Brown & Company. (I: 8–10) (Trade book about a visual impairment)

Booth, B. (1991). *Mandy.* NY: Lothrop, Lee & Shepard. (I: 6–8) (Trade book about a hearing impairment)

Brown, T. (1982). *Someone special just like you.* NY: Holt. (I: P–6) (Trade book about children with various disabilities)

Byars, B. (1970). *Summer of the swans.* NY: The Viking Press. (I: 10–13) (Trade book about a child who is developmentally disabled)

Cohen, M. (1983). *See you tomorrow, Charles.* NY: Greenwillow Books. (I: 5–7) (Trade book about a visual impairment)

Fanshawe, E. (1975). *Rachel.* NY: Bradbury. (I: P–8) (Trade book about a child in a wheelchair)

Fleming, V. (1993). *Be good to Eddie Lee.* NY: Philomel. (I: 7–9) (Trade book about a child with Down's syndrome)

Litchfield, A. (1977). *A cane for her hand.* Morton Grove, IL: Albert Whitman. (I: 8–11) (Trade book about a child with a visual impairment)

Little, J. (1987). *Little by little: A writer's education.* NY: The Viking Press. (I: 12–YA) (Trade book about a child with a visual impairment)

Miller, M., & Ancona, G. (1991). *Handtalk school.* NY: Four Winds. (I: All ages) (Trade book about hearing loss and American Sign Language)

Philbrick, R. (1993). *Freak the mighty.* NY: Blue Sky Press/Scholastic. (I: 10–14) (Trade book about a boy who is very large and a boy who is very bright)

Rosenberg, M. (1988). *Finding a way: Living with exceptional brothers and sisters.* NY: Lothrop, Lee & Shepard. (I: 7–9) (Trade book about children with diabetes, severe asthma, and spina bifida)

Slote, A. (1973). *Hang tough, Paul Mather.* Philadelphia: Lippincott. (I: 9–11) (Trade book about a boy with leukemia)

Spense, E. (1976). *October child.* London: Oxford University Press. (I: 9–11) (Trade book about an autistic child)

Taylor, T. (1989). *The cay.* Boston: Houghton Mifflin. (Trade book about a visual impairment)

MULTICULTURAL LIBRARY

The following are special collections of children's storybooks that explore life in a variety of different cultures, from Inuit to Chinese to Mexican-American and Native American. They are all available from Simon & Schuster Children's Books.

Multicultural Library PreK–3

Nessa's Fish by Nancy Luenn

Sitti's Secrets by Naomi Shihab Nye

Not So Fast Songolo by Niki Daly

Love Flute by Paul Goble

Tutankhamen's Gift by Robert Sabuda

Very Last First Time by Jan Andrews

Abiyoyo by Pete Seeger

A Birthday Basket for Tia by Pat Mora

Con Mi Hermano/With My Brother by Eileen Roe

The Girl Who Loved Wild Horses by Paul Goble

The Moon Lady by Amy Tan

Multicultural Library 4–6

Brothers of the Heart by Joan Blos

The Best Bad Thing by Yoshiko Uchida

The Eternal Spring of Mr. Ito by Sheila Garrigue

Doctor Coyote: A Native American Aesop's Fables retold by John Bierhorst

A Jar of Dreams by Yoshiko Uchida

Kai: A Mission for Her Village by Dawn Gill Thomas

People of the Breaking Day by Marcia Sewell

This Same Sky: A Collection of Poems from Around the World selected by Naomi Nye

Crossing the Starlight Bridge by Alice Mead

African-American Library PreK–3

Now Let Me Fly: The Story of a Slave Family by Dolores Johnson

Uncle Jed's Barbershop by Margaree King Mitchell

Masai and I by Virginia Kroll

Nettie's Trip South by Ann Turner

Apt. 3 by Ezra Jack Keats

The Boy and the Ghost by Robert D. SanSouci

Sukey and the Mermaid by Robert D. SanSouci

Clean Your Room, Harvey Moon by Pat Cummings

Half a Moon and One Whole Star by Crescent Dragonwagon

Harriet and the Promised Land by Jacob Lawrence

The Train to Lulu's by Elizabeth Fitzgerald Howard

Wiley and the Hairy Man by Molly Garrett Bang

Africa Brothers and Sisters by Virginia Kroll

African-American Library 4–6

Letters from a Slave Girl by Mary E. Lyons

Zeely by Virginia Hamilton

Stitching Stars: The Story Quilts of Harriet Powers by Mary E. Lyons

Yolanda's Genius by Carol Fenner

Mississippi Chariot by Harriette Gillem Robinet

The Jazz Man by Mary Weik

M. C. Higgins, the Great by Virginia Hamilton

The Planet of Junior Brown by Virginia Hamilton

I Am the Darker Brother: An Anthology of Modern Poems by African Americans edited by Arnold Adoff

From Miss Ida's Porch by Sandra Belton

Evie Peach, St. Louis, 1857 by Kathleen Duey

RESOURCES AND BIBLIOGRAPHIES FOR TEACHING READING TO DIVERSE STUDENTS

Banks, J. (1994). *An introduction to multicultural education.* Needham Heights, MA: Allyn & Bacon.

Bello, Y. (1992). Caribbean children's literature. Harris, V. (Ed.), *Teaching multicultural literature in grades K–8* (pp. 243–265). Norwood, MA: Christopher-Gordon.

Dale, D. (1985). *Bilingual books in Spanish and English for children.* Littleton, CO: Libraries Unlimited.

Friedburg, J., Mullins, J., & Sukiennik, A. (1992). *Portraying persons with disabilities: An annotated bibliography of nonfiction for children and teenagers.* New Providence, NJ: Bowker.

Harris, V. (1990*).* African American children's literature: The first one hundred years. *Journal of Negro Education, 59,* 540–545.

Jenkins, E., & Austin, J. (1987). *Literature for children about Asians and Asian Americans: Analysis and annotated bibliography with additional readings for adults.* Westport, CT: Greenwood.

Kruse, G., & Horning, K. (1991). *Multicultural literature for children and young adults: A selected listing of books 1980–1990 by and about people of color.* Madison, WI: Cooperative Children's Book Center.

MacCann, D. (1992). Native Americans in books for the young. Harris, V. (Ed.), *Teaching multicultural literature in grades K–8.* Norwood, MA: Christopher-Gordon.

New York Public Library. (1989). *The black experience in children's books.* NY: New York Public Library.

Robertson, D. (1992). *Portraying persons with disabilities: An annotated bibliography of fiction for children and teenagers.* New Providence, NJ: Bowker.

Schon, J. (1986). *Basic collection of children's books in Spanish.* Metuchen, NJ: Scarecrow Press.

———. (1988). *A Hispanic heritage: A guide to juvenile books about Hispanic people and culture.* Metuchen, NJ: Scarecrow Press.

———. (1983, 1985, 1987). *Books in Spanish for children and young adults, Series II, III, IV.* Metuchen, NJ: Scarecrow Press.

Sims, R. (1982). *Shadow and substance: Afro-American experience in contemporary children's fiction.* Chicago: National Council of Teachers of English/American Library Association.

Slapin, B., & Seale, D. (1988). *Books without bias: Through Indian eyes.* Berkeley, CA: Oyate.

Stensland, A. (1979). *Literature by and about the American Indian.* Urbana, IL: National Council of Teachers of English.

Yokota, J. (1993). Asian and Asian American literature for children: Implications for classroom teachers and librarians. Miller, S., & McCaskill, B. (Eds.), *Multicultural literature and literacies: Making space for difference* (pp. 229–246). Albany, NY: State University of New York Press.

Sources for Multicultural Teaching Aids

The following are two good sources for multicultural dolls and puppets:

Multicultural Family Puppets
Learning Resources
380 N. Fairway Drive
Vernon Hills, IL 60061
1-800-222-3909

Realistically detailed puppet families are available:

Asian Family Puppets
Hispanic Family Puppets
White Family Puppets
Black Family Puppets
Asian Indian Family Puppets

Each set sells for $19.95.

Constructive Playthings
1227 East 119th Street
Grandview, MO 64030

Here is a good source for multicultural speaking and music tapes:

Claudia's Caravan
Multicultural/Multilingual Materials
P.O. Box 1582
Alameda, CA 94501

This is a good source for Asian and Hispanic cooking sets:

Childcraft
20 Kilmer Road
P.O. Box 3081
Edison, NJ 08818

RESOURCE BOOKS FOR TEACHING STUDENTS WITH VARIOUS SPECIAL NEEDS

Here is a sampling of the professional resource books that teachers and tutors of students with various kinds of special needs may find helpful. They can be ordered from

Prentice Hall/The Center for Applied Research in Education
P.O. Box 11071
Des Moines, IA 50336
Telephone 1-800-288-4745
Fax 515-284-2607

Barnes, D., & Barnes, C. (1989). *Special educator's survival guide.*

Bernstein, R. (1993). *Ready-to-use phonic activities for special children.*

Claire, E. (1998). *ESL teacher's activities kit.*

———. (1990). *ESL teacher's holiday activities kit.*

Elman, N. (1984). *The special educator's almanac.*

Flick, G. (1998). *ADD/ADHD behavior-change resource kit.*

Fry, E., Kress, J., & Fountoukidis, D. (2000). *The reading teacher's book of lists*, fourth edition.

Grevious, S. (1993). *Ready-to-use multicultural activities for primary children.*

Harwell, J. (1987). *Complete learning disabilities handbook.*

———. (1996). *Complete learning disabilities resource library: Ready-to-use information & materials for assessing specific learning disabilities* (volume I); *Ready-to-use tools & materials for remediating specific learning disabilities* (volume II).

———. (1989). *Ready-to-use learning diasabilities activities kit.*

Josel, C. (1999). *Ready-to-use ESL activities for every month of the school year.*

Kreplin, E., & Smith, B. (1996). *Ready-to-use flannel board stories, figures and activities for ESL children.*

Kreplin, E. (1996). *Sound & articulation activities for children with speech and language problems.*

Kress, J. (1993). *The ESL teacher's book of lists.*

Mannix, D. (1995). *Life skills activities for secondary students with special needs.*

———. (1992). *Life skills activities for special children.*

Mauer, R. (1994). *Special educator's discipline handbook.*

Pierangelo, R. (1995). *The special education teacher's book of lists.*

———. (1994). *A survival kit for the special education teacher.*

Pierangelo, R., & Giuliani, G. (1999). *Special educator's guide to 109 diagnostic tests.*

Stowe, C. (2000). *How to reach & teach students with dyslexia.*

———. (1999). *Let's write: A ready-to-use activities program for learners with special needs.*

Rief, S. (1998). *The ADD/ADHD checklist.*

———. (1993). *How to reach & teach ADD/ADHD children.*

———. (1996). *How to reach & teach all students in the inclusive classroom.*

Stull, E. (1994). *Multicultural discovery activities for the elementary grades.*

Waring, C. (1995). *Developing independent readers: Strategy-oriented reading activities for learners with special needs.*

———. (1999). *Developing letter-sound connections: A strategy-oriented alphabet activities program for beginning readers and writers.*

STRATEGIES FOR TEACHING READING TO CULTURALLY OR LINGUISTICALLY DIVERSE STUDENTS

This section discusses several strategies you can use to teach reading to culturally or linguistically diverse students. All of these strategies must be somewhat modified to be appropriate for the different students whom you are teaching. Some of these strategies have been discussed in detail in other chapters of this book, so they are only mentioned briefly here.

➠ *Whole language programs*—This type of reading program is especially useful with students who are culturally or linguistically diverse because each student reads and writes on his or her own level. The themes of the units also can be selected to reflect the unique prior knowledge and experiences of the students with whom you are working. In addition, multicultural literature of various types (see the preceding section of this chapter) can be used in whole language units. Whole language is very effective with diverse students because it builds on a student's natural language base and uses materials that are based on different cultures.

➠ *The language-experience approach*—This approach may be the single most useful approach for teaching beginning reading skills to students who are culturally or linguistically diverse. In addition, it is highly motivational and allows diverse students to experience immediate success. LEA is effective with students who are culturally or linguistically diverse because it uses each student's own unique experiences and language patterns in the dictated or child-written experience books, stories, and charts.

➠ *Predictable (patterned) trade books*—Using predictable (patterned) trade books for early reading experiences is highly effective because they enable students to become immediately involved in successful reading experiences and the patterned language is easy for them to read. In addition to the predictable books that are listed in Chapter 3, you may want to use the book entitled *Wishes, Lies, and Dreams: Teaching Children to Write Poetry* by Kenneth Koch (NY: Perennial Library, 1970). This book contains many sentence patterns written by Koch's multicultural students—patterns that will inspire any culturally or linguistically diverse student.

➠ *Wordless picture books*—According to Early (1991, p. 249), the wordless picture book *The Angel and the Soldier Boy* (NY: Alfred A. Knopf, 1987) motivated a group of second language learners to generate rough drafts or dictations related to their imaginations of what was happening in this wordless book. Following each child's writing or dictating of the rough draft, the teacher helped the second language learners merge their material and edit a composite together.

Here is the summary of this wordless picture book:

> As a little girl falls asleep, her angel and soldier dolls come to life. Suddenly some pirates rob her piggy bank and kidnap the soldier doll. The angel doll finally frees the soldier doll, and they get back from their great adventure before the little girl wakes up.

Wordless picture books are helpful for second language learners because they use their own language patterns; they use their imaginations; they make tape recordings to go with the books, thus enhancing their oral language development; they dramatize the book, which provides them practice in oral English; and they can reread their own writing or dictations or read the class-compiled experience booklet.

➠ *Learning centers*—Well-organized and well-equipped learning centers make it possible for students who are culturally or linguistically diverse to learn a great deal on their own through playful interaction with materials while teachers provide attention to individuals or small groups.

➠ *Modeling and scaffolding*—Modeling and scaffolding strategies are especially helpful to students with all kinds of diverse backgrounds. Modeling enables students to see the type of behavior they are supposed to emulate, while scaffolded instruction allows teachers to mediate learning experiences for students. A teacher who mediates serves as an intermediary in helping diverse learners to negotiate meaning. The most important element in scaffolding is providing support to the student.

➠ *Cooperative learning groups*—When using cooperative learning groups, the teacher usually gives heterogeneous groups of several (three to six) students a topic to research and later report back on to the entire group. This type of group is most useful at the upper primary- and intermediate-grade levels. It is especially useful with second language learners because it allows them to work on their own reading level with native English-speaking students.

➡ *Rosetta Stone technique*—The Rosetta Stone is an ancient stone that contains the same text in Egyptian hieroglyphics, Egyptian demotic script, and several ancient Greek languages. The discovery of the Rosetta Stone allowed linguists to decipher Egyptian hieroglyphics, which they did not know how to read, based on their knowledge of ancient Greek, which they could read.

A valuable vocabulary technique for working with a class or a group of students who have different language backgrounds is based on this concept. If you make a chart of common English words in one column, students who speak other languages can provide the equivalent words from each of their languages in the other columns. As an alternative, nonnative students might bring in a word from their native language, write it on the chart, and ask the equivalent English words and words from other languages that are represented in the class. You also can use words from content reading assignments as entries in the "Rosetta" chart and have students add the words from their languages.

Whatever the source of words you place on the chart, be sure to practice pronouncing both non-English and English words with the nonnative speakers as well as with the rest of the class or group. In this way all students will be able to do well at some parts of the task.

➡ *Media approaches*—Using videotapes, films, filmstrips, pictures, experiments, demonstrations, concrete objects, dioramas, and story boards may be especially useful with students who are culturally or linguistically diverse. All of these media approaches enable students to understand more clearly the concepts that are being presented.

➡ *Choral reading*—Norton (1995) wrote that books that include repetitive language are excellent for oral reading. The teacher reads the book to the class or group, and then the teacher (tutor) and students chorally read it in unison. In this approach the teacher selects individual words and phrases and emphasizes choral reading (with all or several students reading in unison). Choral reading can lead to greater enjoyment of reading, a faster reading rate, a better use of phrasing, a better comprehension of text, and a decrease in oral reading miscues (McCauley & McCauley, 1992).

➡ *The participation of family members and friends*—It is very important to involve the family and friends of students who are culturally and linguistically diverse as much as possible in the reading program. To do so greatly enhances the chances that the student will be successful in school. Some of the ways in which you can involve the family and friends of students who are nonnative English speakers are as follows: paid or volunteer reading tutors, lunchroom and playground supervisors, and classroom visitors who share elements of their cultural heritage. Teachers can give workshops for family members and friends about how reading skills currently are taught and can provide packets of materials that family members and friends can use at home with students to promote reading skills (trade books, children's magazines and newspapers, appropriate reading games, and simple meaningful activity sheets).

➡ *Provide authentic experiences*—Here are several of the authentic experiences that can be used for culturally or linguistically diverse students:

➡ Give students a choice as to what language they will answer in.

➡ Allow students to read books in their primary language (an earlier section of this chapter provided several sources for children's trade books in Spanish).

➡ Have students listen to audiotapes that accompany appropriate trade books. Make your own read-along because the commercially available audiotapes often are read too rapidly for students who are linguistically diverse.

➡ Have the students compile bilingual dictionaries.

➡ Have students make books about their home or family supplemented with illustrations or photographs and captioned in both English and the home language.

➡ Give a class party and invite culturally or linguistically diverse adults.

➡ Provide direct experiences, such as school trips or classroom visitors.

➡ Provide second-hand experiences, such as videotapes, films, puppets, and pictures, to enable students to learn English in meaningful ways.

➡ *Arts and crafts activities*—All types of arts and crafts activities can be adapted to encourage students to tap into their cultural heritage. If you wish, family members and friends also can be involved in these activities, providing their own unique contributions.

➡ *Additional suggestions:*

➡ Make frequent checks on new English vocabulary and meaningful application of new English vocabulary.

➡ Question students about their reading and have them elaborate on their own experiences.

➡ Use consistent language and do not use synonyms or idioms.

➡ Use scaffolded instruction, teacher coaching, and teacher modeling.

➡ Use approaches that involve high levels of student involvement and interaction.

STRATEGIES FOR TEACHING READING TO STUDENTS WITH OTHER SPECIAL NEEDS

This section contains several strategies for teaching reading to students with other special needs, such as learning disabilities or physical disabilities. Each of these strategies should be modified depending on the needs and abilities of your students. They are explained briefly, so you are encouraged to read more about any of them that seem relevant for your students.

→ *The language-experience approach*—This approach is extremely useful for teaching beginning reading skills to students with learning disabilities, attention deficit disorders, attention deficit/hyperactivity disorders, mental handicaps, and hearing impairments.

→ *Mnemonic devices*—These devices are designed to improve a student's memory. When used cautiously, a mnemonic device can be helpful in enabling a student with learning disabilities, attention deficit disorders, or attention deficit/hyperactivity disorders to remember important material. Mnemonic devices that may be useful in the upper primary or intermediate grades include acronyms, acronymic sentences, rhymes, or abbreviations.

→ *Behavior management*—Behavior management strategies may be useful with students who do not respond to traditional management procedures or who are unable to control their behaviors with self-monitoring methods. Behavior modification strategies such as counseling, modeling, reality therapy, and having the student and teacher construct a contract outlining acceptable behavior (the teacher and student both sign the contract) also can be effective.

→ *Multisensory approaches*—This concept is based on two premises: Students learn through their senses, and the more senses tapped during the teaching–learning process, the greater are the chances that learning will take place. Having students use more than one sense at a time in a lesson (for example, having them see, hear, and touch a goat) is thought to be more effective than having them use one or both of the traditional senses used in school (seeing and/or hearing a goat). Here is a brief description of some multisensory approaches for students who have special needs. You are encouraged to read more about any of them that may be useful with your students.

   → *Gillingham and Stillman's VAK Strategy* (1970)—Using the Visual-Auditory-Kinesthetic (VAK) procedure, students associate and learn eight VAK links. The VAK strategy and corresponding links can be used to teach students with special needs how to read words, phrases, and sentences.

   → *Fernald's Visual-Auditory-Kinesthetic-Tactile (VAKT) Strategy* (1943)—This is the most well-known and powerful strategy that you can use with students who have special needs. Although the strategy has four stages, its basic premise involves the students seeing, hearing, tracing, and writing what they are to learn. This strategy can be used to develop synthetic and analytic phonics, sight vocabulary, and phrase reading.

   → *Dwyer and Flippo's Multisensory Spelling and Sight Word Strategy* (1983)—This strategy is primarily based on Fernald's VAKT strategy and uses the following steps:

   1. Look at the word carefully.
   2. Talk about the word to determine its meaning and pronunciation.

3. Close your eyes, visualize the word, and write it in the air.

4. Write the word on paper without looking at it.

5. Check its spelling and write it again from memory.

6. Write the word in a sentence.

Dwyer and Flippo suggest additional steps if students need more reinforcement. They state that although seeing the word, "feeling" it, and hearing it is time-consuming, the multisensory procedure helps to strengthen memory. They also state that review is necessary for long-term retention of difficult words, so they recommend that each student keep a word bank.

➡ *Analytical-Tutorial Word Identification Strategy*—Lindsey, Beck, and Bursor (1981) proposed a strategy for developing and reinforcing students' vocabulary and sight word learning. You begin the process by using a modification of LEA, which also includes using the Fernald VAKT strategy and having students develop a vocabulary-and-story file. After a student has shown that he or she can read the story and knows the high-frequency vocabulary, you can work with a teacher of a lower grade level to develop a cross-grade tutorial program.

➡ *Technology*—A variety of technological devices have been designed to help students with various kinds of disabilities. For example, overhead transparency projectors may be replaced by a video camera called an *ELMO*. This device displays text material, graphics, and almost any image that is placed on its glass top on a video monitor. It is more adaptable than the overhead projector when presenting visual images. Many devices that are based on closed captioning will help hearing impaired students. A machine known as an *Optacon* translates images to tactile Braille-like print or synthesized speech. Print-to-speech translators are being refined, and a variety of them will eventually be available. The *Kurweil Reading Machine* reads aloud printed material placed on a glass desk. A student can pause it; rewind to hear a word; and control volume, pitch, and speech rate.

THE CARBO APPROACH TO READING

Marie Carbo (1987) is well identified with teaching reading to students with special needs. She wrote that "many poor readers are predominantly global, tactile, and kinesthetic learners" (p. 198). By *global* Carbo meant that these students often learn better when they can progress from the whole to the part—just the opposite direction from most phonics programs. Carbo recommends the following teaching strategies:

➡ Use whole text selections with "unequal learners" that inspire high interest and high emotional involvement.

➡ Have them join the reading teacher or tutor and others in choral reading.

➡ Write or dictate stories.

➡ Listen to story tapes.

➡ Combine the *repeated reading technique*, in which a student reads a story or trade book, with the *fluency level* with story tapes.

Carbo recommends the following for emphasizing the tactile and kinesthetic learning modes of students with special needs: computers, typewriters, active games, drawing, writing, pantomime, verbal drama, puppets, and following written directions for making things. In summary, Carbo states that good teaching of the type that all students need is most useful with students who have special needs.

READING RECOVERY STRATEGIES

Although a teacher must have extensive training and supervision before he or she can become a Reading Recovery teacher, any reading teacher or tutor can use some or all of the Reading Recovery strategies with beginning readers who are having difficulty in learning the basic reading skills.

The Reading Recovery Program™ was developed by Marie Clay in New Zealand in the 1980s and has been researched extensively by Pinnel & Estice (1990) researchers from Ohio State University. It is effective with at-risk first graders primarily because the teachers who use it are trained reading observers and teachers; the phonic skills are usually taught in a meaningful way; and reading and writing skills are integrated.

A typical Reading Recovery lesson follows this pattern:

1. The child builds fluency by rereading some of his or her previously read books (many of which have patterned language and are short and easy to read).

2. The child then rereads yesterday's new book while the teacher observes his or her miscues. Therefore, assessment and instruction are integrated.

3. If the child still needs work on letters, he or she identifies movable plastic letters on a magnetic board. The child also can manipulate the letters to form new words such as changing *mat* to *cat*, to *rat*, to *sat*, to *hat*, to *bat*, to *that*, and so forth.

4. The child writes his or her own sentence or story, getting help on letter–sound relationships if necessary.

5. The child then edits the story.

6. The child then reads a new trade book guided by the teacher/tutor's emphasis on meaning, confirmation, and self-correction.

7. The child reads the new book independently.

The entire Reading Recovery lesson usually lasts about thirty minutes.

STRATEGIES FOR STUDENTS WITH DYSLEXIA

Students with dyslexia who are having difficulty in learning to read can benefit from many of the strategies that were discussed in this chapter. However, the following also may be helpful:

➠ Integrate the three cueing systems (meaning, grammar, and sight/phonic) as much as possible. Students can do the following:

  ➠ Listen to the teacher or tutor read a trade book. The teacher should have previewed the book; the student can make predictions about the book's content; and the teacher can help the student look at new vocabulary.

  ➠ Suggest what word(s) can fit in each of the blanks in oral cloze exercises.

  ➠ Point to individual words as he or she reads, if necessary, and use meaning clues first, grammar clues next, and phonic clues last.

➠ Have students read independently by suggesting trade books that they will enjoy reading. Here are some resources parents and teachers can use to help students locate appropriate trade books:

Holdren, J., & Hirsch, E., Jr. (Eds.). (1996). *Books to build on: A grade-by-grade resource guide for parents and teachers.* NY: Delta.

Lipson, E. (1991). *The New York Times parent's guide to the best books for children.* NY: Times Books.

Wilson, E. (1987). *Books children love: A guide to the best children's literature.* NY: Crossway Books.

➠ Cynthia Stowe has written a helpful teacher's resource book entitled *How to Reach and Teach Students with Dyslexia* (West Nyack, NY: The Center for Applied Research in Education, 2000). Here are several of the suggestions from this book that seem especially useful:

  ➠ Present *phonemic awareness*, which is a child's ability to discriminate between various consonant and vowel sounds.

  ➠ Help students become familiar with the physical structure of books.

  ➠ Help students to learn the names and the sounds of letters by using a source such as Cynthia Waring's *Developing Letter-Sound Connections: A Strategy-Oriented Alphabet Activities Program for Beginning Readers and Writers* (West Nyack, NY: The Center for Applied Research in Education, 1999).

  ➠ Use multisensory instruction, in which the student sees, hears, says, and feels the information.

  ➠ Connect the letter name or sound with a tangible object.

  ➠ First present the consonant sounds and then present the vowel sounds.

  ➠ Use the *Wilson Reading System* with adolescents and adults who are dyslexic. This system first presents a few consonants and then all five short vowel sounds. To obtain specific information about this system, contact

Wilson Reading System
Wilson Language Training Corporation
Milbury, MA 01527-1943
Telephone 508-865-5699

SPECIFIC SUGGESTIONS FOR TEACHING ADHD OR DYSLEXIC STUDENTS

Heilman, Blair, and Rupley (1998) have presented some teaching suggestions for working with ADHD students that are equally helpful for working with dyslexic students.

⟶ Seat the student near the teacher's desk.

⟶ Place the student at the front of the classroom with his or her back to the rest of the class.

⟶ Surround the student with good role models and encourage peer tutoring and cooperative–collaborative learning.

⟶ Avoid seating the student near distracting stimuli such as air conditioners, doors, and windows.

⟶ Avoid changes in schedules and disruptions. Such students usually do not handle change well.

⟶ Encourage family members to set up a good study space and good study routines at home.

CLASSROOM ACCOMMODATIONS FOR VISUALLY AND HEARING IMPAIRED STUDENTS

Savage (1998) suggested classroom accommodations for visually and hearing impaired students. He wrote that students with visual problems should have preferential seating, enhanced computer screens, a class buddy, time adjustments for assignments, and large-print books. Students with hearing impairments should be fitted with effective hearing aids, have a classroom buddy, have visual reinforcement of class learning, learn some phonics, and read natural language in good literature. Both visually impaired and hearing impaired students should use a computer word-processing program for their writing. Savage (1998) stated that all students with special needs always should be treated as part of the class.

FOR ADDITIONAL READING

Cox, C., & Boyd-Batstone, P. (1997). *Crossroads: Literature and language in culturally and linguistically diverse classrooms.* Columbus, OH: Merrill/Prentice Hall.

Gipe, J. (1998). *Multiple paths to literacy* (pp. 340–378). Upper Saddle River, NJ: Prentice Hall.

Gunning, T. (1996). *Creating reading instruction for all children* (pp. 448–485). Boston: Allyn & Bacon.

Heilman, A., Blair, T., & Rupley, W. (1998). *Principles and practices of teaching reading* (pp. 532–568). Upper Saddle River, NJ: Prentice Hall.

Juel, M., Juel, C., & Graves, B. (1998). *Teaching reading in the 21st century* (pp. 432–475). Needham Heights, MA: Allyn & Bacon.

May, F. (1998). *Reading as communication* (pp. 429–461). Upper Saddle River, NJ: Prentice Hall.

Sampson, M., Sampson, M., & Allen, R. (1995). *Pathways to literacy* (pp. 476–508). Orlando, FL: Harcourt Brace and Company.

Savage, J. (1998). *Teaching reading & writing: Combining skills, strategies, and literature.* Boston: McGraw-Hill.

———. (1994). *Teaching reading using literature.* Madison, WI: Brown & Benchmark.

Stowe, C. (2000). *How to reach & teach students with dyslexia.* West Nyack, NY: The Center for Applied Research in Education.

Temple, C., Martinez, M., Yokota, J., & Naylor, A. (1998). *Children's books in children's hands* (pp. 81–133). Needham Heights, MA: Allyn & Bacon.

Vacca, J., Vacca, R., & Gove, M. (1995). *Reading and learning to read* (pp. 512–535). NY: HarperCollins College Publishers.

WORKS CITED IN CHAPTER 7

American Psychiatric Association. (1994). *Diagnostic and statistical manual of mental disorders.* Washington, DC: American Psychiatric Association.

Beaty, J. (1997). *Building bridges with multicultural literature.* Upper Saddle River, NJ: Prentice Hall.

Carbo, M. (1987). Deprogramming reading failure: Giving unequal learners an equal chance. *Phi Delta Kappan, 69,* 197–202.

Coballes-Vega, C. (1992). *Considerations in teaching culturally diverse children.* Report No. ED0-SP-90-2. Washington, DC: Office of Educational Research and Improvement.

Collier, V. (1987). Age and rate of acquisition of second language for academic purposes. *TESOL Quarterly, 21,* 617–641.

Cosby, B. (1990). 45 years from today. *Ebony, 46,* 61.

Delpit, L. (1995). *Other people's children.* Paper presented to the National Reading Conference, New Orleans.

Dwyer, E., & Flippo, R. (1983). Multisensory approach for teaching spelling. *Journal of Reading, 27,* 171–172.

Dykman, R., & Ackerman, P. (1992). Attention deficit disorder and specific reading disability: Separate but often overlapping. In S. Shaywitz & B. Shaywitz (Eds.), *Attention deficit disorder comes of age: Toward the end of the twenty-first century* (pp. 165–183). Austin, TX: Pro-ED.

Early, M. (1991). Using wordless picture books to promote second language learning. *ELT Journal, 45,* 245–251.

Fernald, G. (1943). *Remedial techniques in high school.* NY: McGraw-Hill.

Friend, M., & Cook, L. (1992). The new mainstreaming. *Instructor, 101,* 30–34.

Gillingham, A., & Stillman, B. (1970). *Remedial training for children with specific disability in reading, spelling, and penmanship.* Cambridge, MA: Educators Publishing Service.

Grossman, J. (Ed.) (1973). *Manual on terminology and classification in mental retardation, 1973 revision.* Washington, DC: American Association of Mental Deficiency.

Hallahan, D., & Kauffman, J. (1982). *Exceptional children.* Englewood Cliffs, NJ: Prentice Hall.

Heilman, A., Blair, T., & Rupley, W. (1998). *Principles and practices of teaching reading.* Upper Saddle River, NJ: Prentice Hall.

Kirk, S. (1963). *Educating exceptional children.* Needham Heights, MA: Allyn & Bacon.

Lindsey, J., Beck, F., & Bursor, D. (1981). An analytical-tutorial method for developing adolescents' sight vocabulary. *Journal of Reading, 24,* 591–594.

McCauley, J., & McCauley, D. (1992). Using choral reading to promote language learning for ESL students. *The Reading Teacher, 45,* 526–533.

Mohr, L. (1995). *Teaching diverse learners in inclusive settings: Steps for adapting instruction.* Paper presented at the Council for Exceptional Children Annual Conference. Indianapolis.

National Clearinghouse for Bilingual Education. (1995). *Ask NCBE.* January 20.

Norton, D. (1995). *Through the eyes of a child: An introduction to children's literature.* Columbus, OH: Merrill/Prentice Hall.

Pellicano, R. (1987). At risk: A view of social advantage. *Educational Leadership, 44,* 47–50.

Pinnell, G., Fried, M., & Estice, R. (1990). Reading Recovery: Learning how to make a difference. *The Reading Teacher, 43,* 282–295.

Ramsey, P. (1991). *Making friends in school: Promoting play relationships.* NY: Teachers College Press.

Savage, J. (1998). *Teaching reading & writing: Combining skills, strategy, & literature.* Boston: McGraw-Hill.

———. (1994). *Teaching reading using literature* (pp. 324–380). Madison, WI: Brown & Benchmark.

Scarcella, R. (1990). *Teaching language minority students in the regular classroom.* Englewood Cliffs, NJ: Prentice Hall.

Shaywitz, S., & Shaywitz, B. (Eds.). (1992). *Attention deficit disorder comes of age: Toward the end of the twenty-first century.* Austin, TX: Pro-ED.

United States Government Printing Office. (1975, 1977, 1984). *Federal Register, 40, 42, & 49.*

Chapter 8

THE SUPPORT OF FAMILY MEMBERS AND FRIENDS WITH READING

When I was a young child, my parents were afraid to help me with beginning reading skills. Elementary school administrators and teachers of that time repeatedly warned family members that teaching children reading skills was the sole job of the education professional and that any attempt by family members to teach reading could result in irreparable harm. Thus, although I probably was linguistically adept, I entered first grade not knowing a single letter name, letter sound, or sight word.

Today, of course, it is very different. Educators now encourage family members to teach beginning reading skills for which young children seem ready. In addition, family members are encouraged to support and supplement the student's reading program throughout elementary school. This represents a positive change for students, family members, and schools.

This final chapter briefly explains the importance of having the support of family members and friends in a student's reading program. It then suggests a number of practical classroom-tested strategies and materials that can be used to support a student's reading program. They are valuable whether that program is presented by a classroom teacher, special reading teacher, learning disabilities teacher, or reading tutor. Included are some activities that the reading teacher or tutor can use to help family members and friends participate in the reading program. The chapter concludes with several reproducible pages and some reading games.

THE IMPORTANCE OF HAVING THE SUPPORT OF FAMILY MEMBERS AND FRIENDS IN THE READING PROGRAM

As stated previously family members providing reading help either before school entrance or while a child was attending school was discouraged. In the 1940s and 1950s it was believed that parents did not know the proper methods to use in helping their children with reading and, therefore, could do harm if they tried. By the 1960s and 1970s it became more popular to teach and reinforce reading skills in the home. In the 1990s and early 2000s family members have lost some confidence in the schools and have taken much more initiative both in presenting and reviewing reading skills. The continued popularity of home schooling, for example, illustrates decreasing confidence in reading instruction, especially in public schools.

In addition, the prevelance of reading problems in schools have motivated both reading teachers and tutors to ask family members for help. The classic book *A Nation at Risk* (1984, U.S.A. Research, Inc.) discussed the pervasiveness of reading problems and motivated teachers to enlist the aid of family members. The federal Title I program also has motivated family involvement in schools. Teachers and tutors are generally making a concerted effort to make family members and friends feel comfortable at school, especially in the case of children from homes in which the adults often felt uncomfortable at school or were unsuccessful in school. Without making a real effort, teachers may be viewed as "outsiders" by family members.

Theoretically, there is said to be more family involvement in schools all the time, but busy families in which both parents work or single-parent families often make such involvement in the reading program more difficult than it was in the past. Families have significant demands placed upon them today. Therefore, it is important to involve the elderly population, such as grandparents and other senior citizens, in supporting the school reading program. There also are nearly twelve million children who live in poverty today that compounds the problem.

Reading teachers and tutors must meet family members "where they are" and provide as many opportunities for school involvement as possible. To involve family members in their children's reading program may be difficult and require patience, tact, and time. Teachers and tutors must believe that family members want the best for their children and proceed from that point on. However, when this relationship is initiated by the school without true support from family members, individuals will not be committed or truly involved in the process. An activity that is *not* enjoyable for family members is assigned workbook pages that must be completed as "homework." A more effective type of "homework" may be having the child read aloud at home to a family member or friend, or having a family member or friend read aloud to the child.

How Family Members and Friends Can Support the Reading Program

There are a multitude of ways in which family members and friends can support either a classroom reading program or special reading program. Here is a brief description of some of them.

Read to the Young Child Regularly

Countless research studies conducted over a period of many years have found that *reading to the young child is the single most significant factor that influences their reading achievement in the primary grades.* Reading aloud to a child is valuable because it shows him or her that reading is an important activity, provides a good reading model, increases prior knowledge, and motivates the child to want to learn to read.

When reading to a very young child, use "feel and touch" books that are durable and often made of cardboard. Preschoolers and beginning readers enjoy predictable books. Have the child join in the refrain or act out a verse of the book. When family members or friends read a book aloud to a young child, he or she can ask the child to predict the book content from the title and to make predictions while the book is being read. The reader should pause at various points and ask the child questions such as these: *"What do you think will happen next?"* . . . *"What do you want to happen next?"* . . . *"What would you like to have happen next?"* When the book is finished, the child can be asked several questions about the book's content. These questions should be both lower- and higher-level questions that will motivate the child to think. Instead of questions, sometimes the child can be asked to retell the content of the book.

There are a number of additional activities that can be used when reading aloud to children. Here are a few of them:

➡ Have the child point to the pictures and try to describe what is happening in them.

➡ Emphasize the various *concepts of print*—knowing what a letter or word is, knowing that reading begins at the left and goes to the right of a line, knowing that reading begins at the top of a page and goes to the bottom, knowing that pictures are different from print, and understanding word boundaries.

➡ Sometimes have the child turn the pages while he or she is being read to. It will motivate him or her to follow along and pay attention.

Here are some resources that are primarily for family members, but reading teachers and tutors can use them as well. Many of the books include excellent children's book lists, while two (marked with an asterisk) are good anthologies.

Butler, Dorothy. (1998). *Babies need books: Sharing the joy of books with your child from birth to six.* NY: Atheneum.

Cullinan, Bernice. (1992). *Read to me: Raising kids who love to read.* NY: Scholastic.

*Fadiman, Clifton. (Ed.). (1990). *The world treasury of children's literature.* Boston: Little, Brown & Company.

Graves, R. (Ed.). (1988). *The RIF (Reading Is Fundamental) guide to encouraging young readers.* NY: Doubleday.

Hearne, B. (1999). *Choosing books for children: A commonsense guide.* NY: Delacorte Press.

Kimmel, M. (1991). *For reading out loud: A guide to sharing books with children.* NY: Dell Publishing Company.

Larrick, N. (1975). *A parent's guide to children's reading.* NY: Bantam Books.

*Russell, William. (Ed.). (1992). *Classics to read aloud to your children.* NY: Crown.

Sader, M. (1990). *Reference books for young readers: Authoritative evaluations of encyclopedias, atlases, and dictionaries.* NY: Bowker.

Trelease, J. (1989). *The new read-aloud handbook.* NY: Penguin.

The Library of Congress–Children's Literature Center prepares an annual list of more than 100 of the best children's books recently published for preschool through junior high school age. To order *Books for Children, #8* write to the Consumer Information Center, 101Z, Pueblo, CO 81009.

The organizations below also publish lists of children's books and other helpful brochures that are available free of charge or at a nominal cost as well as books for parents on helping children learn to read. You can request titles and ordering information directly from:

American Library Association
Publications Order Department
50 East Huron Street
Chicago, IL 60611

International Reading Association
800 Barksdale Road
PO Box 8139
Newark, DE 19714

Reading Is Fundamental, Inc.
Publications Department
Smithsonian Institute
600 Maryland Avenue, SW, Suite 500
Washington, DC 20024

Encourage Reading for Pleasure and Information on a Regular Basis

Since reading is a skill that improves with motivated practice just like any other skill—such as golf or tennis—it is important for the child to read material on his or her independent or low instructional level on a regular basis. Good readers find reading a rewarding activity, so they are motivated to read both for pleasure and information. However, those with reading or learning difficulties do not find it easy or rewarding, and often are reluctant to read any type of material unless they are required to do so. This is one main reason why good readers usually become better readers, while individuals with reading problems do not improve.

It also is more difficult for family members to motivate children to read for pleasure or information because there are so many competing activities than there were in the past. Television, the Internet, computer games, and organized children's sports programs are just some of the activities that compete for a child's reading time.

There are many ways to motivate children to read both for information or pleasure. Ask the children's librarian at your local public library to suggest award-winning books that would motivate children. Encourage the child to put aside a book that is too difficult or that does not really appeal to him or her. As an adult you can do this—why shouldn't a child be able to do it? Have the child "try out a book for difficulty" by turning to the middle of the book and selecting a passage of about *100 words*. Then have him or her "put down a finger" for every word in this *100-word passage* that cannot be immediately identified. If the child has put down more than *5 fingers*, the book probably is too difficult and should not be selected.

Paired reading has been used successfully with readers of various ages in a number of countries. When paired reading is first used, the family member and child must focus on "doing it right." Some of the things that should be stressed are synchronizing the pace of reading, ensuring that genuine praise is given and criticism is not, supplying the words that are needed, conversing calmly rather than trying to teach directly, and deciding what comments to record. In paired reading the family member or friend should try to read together with the child at least five days a week for 10-15 minutes. Find a place that is quiet and away from the television, radio, telephone, and other distractions. Sit comfortably side-by-side looking at the book together. When the child gets a word wrong or can't identify a word, say what the word is and have the child repeat it. Praise the child for getting a word correct, getting all the words in a sentence correct, and for self-correcting. You also can encourage the child to talk about the reading, ask what might happen next, and what the child thinks about what was just read and what it reminds him or her of. The family member or friend also should keep a log or diary of what was read. The advantages of paired reading are that it is easy, risk-free, puts the child in control, and models key elements of good reading, such as reading fluency and good expression.

Every child from about the age of four should have his or her own library card. Encourage the child to go to the library regularly and select books to read at home. These books should be as varied as possible and should be both narrative and informational. If possible, help the child start a home library. Many of the books in this home library can be fairly inexpensive paperbacks. As much as possible, the home environment should stress books and stress reading as a free-time activity. It will help if family members and friends model reading for information and pleasure, and give books as gifts at least some of the time.

Children can read all types of materials at home: narrative and informational books, children's magazines and newspapers, the local newspaper, acceptable comic books and comic strips, cartoons, riddles, acceptable jokes, reference books, and material on the Internet all can be motivating for students. The important thing is that students are reading—no matter what they are reading—as long as their family members consider it acceptable.

School work and homework also should be monitored by family members. Family members should talk to the child about his or her school day and look at the work that was brought home. In turn, teachers should monitor the work that is sent home to be completed. Homework always must be meaningful and not just busy work that takes up time. It should be clear and challenging. Sharing a book with a family member or friend may be the most effective type of homework for many elementary-school children, especially those in the primary grades, although even older students can benefit greatly from it.

An interesting trend in the United States involves the *Reading Olympics Program*. These programs vary from school system to school system and from one class to another. Here is how one such program worked in the middle part of the year in a first-grade class. There was a contest in which children were challenged to read as many books as they could, and to read these books aloud to one of their family members. After they finished reading the book aloud, the family member asked them questions about the story or had them retell it. The student in this particular first-grade class who won the Read-Aloud Olympics contest read *120 books* aloud to his parents (Rubin, 1991).

Many of the resource books listed in the earlier section are equally applicable for helping family members and friends locate appropriate material for their children to read at home.

Here are addresses of some agencies, associations, and organizations that deal with family literacy. They can be contacted for suggestions on how to work with children on reading.

Barbara Bush Foundation
1002 Wisconsin Avenue, NW
Washington, DC 20007

Even Start Compensatory Education Programs
U.S. Department of Education
400 Maryland Avenue, SW
Room 2043
Washington, DC 20202

International Reading Association
800 Barksdale Road
P.O. Box 8139
Newark, DE 19714

National Center for Family Literacy
Waterfront Plaza
325 West Main Street
Suite 200
Louisville, KY 40202

Reading Is Fundamental (RIF)
600 Maryland Avenue, SW
Suite 500
Washington, DC 20024

In addition, the following sources may be useful for family members if their child has a *reading problem or learning disability:*

ERIC Clearinghouse on Disabilities and Gifted Children
The Council for Exceptional Children
1920 Reston Drive
Reston, VA 21091

National Information Center for Children and Youth with Disabilities
P.O. Box 1492
Washington, DC 20013

National Institute of Child Health and Development
U.S. Department of Health and Human Services
9000 Rockville Pike, Bldg. 31
Bethesda, MD 20892

The National Library Service for the Blind and Physically Handicapped
Library of Congress
Washington, DC 20542

Office of Special Education and Rehabilitative Services
U.S. Department of Education
Washington, DC 20202

In addition to the publication *Helping Your Child to Read*, the U.S. Department of Education publishes a number of books on related subjects. To find out what is available and how to order, request the Consumer Information Catalog that lists nearly 200 federal publications. The catalog is free from the Consumer Information Center, Pueblo, Colorado.

The following list of children's magazines are helpful for families and friends who want to support their children's reading.

General Interest Magazines for Ages 2–12

> *Cricket, the Magazine for Children.* P.O. Box 52961, Boulder, CO 80322.

> *Highlights for Children.* 2300 West Fifth Avenue, Columbus, OH 43272.

Story Magazines for Ages 4–9

> *Chickadee.* Young Naturalist Foundation, P.O. Box 11314, Des Moines, IA 50340.

> *Ladybug.* Cricket Country Lane, Box 50284, Boulder, CO 80321.

> *Sesame Street Magazine.* Children's Television Workshop, One Lincoln Plaza, New York, NY 10023.

Science, Nature, Sports, Math & History for Ages 7–12

> *Cobblestone: The History Magazine for Young People.* Cobblestone Publishing, Inc., 30 Grove Street, Peterborough, NH 03458.

> *DynaMaths.* Scholastic, Inc., 730 Broadway, New York, NY 10003.

> *National Geographic World.* National Geographic Society, 17th and M Streets, NW, Washington, DC 20036.

> *Odyssey.* Kalmbach Publishing Company, P.O. Box 1612, Waukesha, WI 53187.

> *Ranger Rick.* National Wildlife Federation, 1400 16th Street, NW, Washington, DC 20036.

> *Sports Illustrated for Kids.* Time Inc., Time & Life Building, Rockefeller Center, New York, NY 10020.

> *3-2-1 Contact.* Children's Television Workshop, One Lincoln Plaza, New York, NY 10023.

> *U*S*Kids.* Field Publications, 245 Long Hill Road, Middletown, CT 06457.

> *Zillions.* Consumers Union, 101 Truman Avenue, Yonkers, NY 10703.

The Language-Experience Approach

Language-experience activities can be used very effectively both with beginning readers and older disabled readers. The language-experience approach (LEA) is successful because it uses the child's own experiences and language patterns in the dictated story and is highly motivational.

To use LEA the family member or friend should participate in some type of motivating activity with the child. This can be a family excursion, a cooking or baking activity, an art activity, a construction activity, or an activity involving a family pet. There also are many other opportunities to involve the child in dictating an experience story.

When the activity has been participated in, the family member or friend can follow this procedure in using LEA:

- Have an interesting preliminary discussion about the experience.
- Have the child dictate an account of the experience. Try to motivate him or her to use complete sentences and dictate the account of the experience in correct order.
- Have the family member or friend transcribe what the child says by using block print on an experience chart or an $8\frac{1}{2}" \times 11"$ sheet of paper.
- Have the child read the dictated experience story aloud, with the family member or friend providing support when needed.
- Have the child underline selected sight words from the story that later are printed on individual $3" \times 5"$ word cards to be placed in a *Word Bank* (a large brown envelope or shoe box) and reviewed periodically.
- Beginning phonics and word structure also can be presented from the dictated experience stories.
- The experience stories that the child has dictated can be placed into an experience booklet, bound, and then illustrated by him or her. The child then should read them again and again to review sight words and the other reading skills that were presented.

Activities that Family Members and Friends Can Do in the Classroom

If family members and friends cannot participate regularly in the classroom reading program, they still can be involved by devoting several hours, a morning, an afternoon, or a day to the class once in a while. Such volunteers could read to the class or a small group, share a skill at which they are proficient, go along on school trips, or participate in special events such as birthday or holiday celebrations. If individuals can only volunteer occasionally, they should be involved in activities that are worthwhile and helpful. Some of the reading tasks that such volunteers can do are the following:

- Read to and with individual children.
- Read to and with small groups.

➠ Listen to children read.

➠ Transcribe or type dictated language-experience stories.

➠ Take students to the school library.

➠ Do activities such as bookbinding of language-experience booklets, helping to plan and put up a bulletin board, woodworking, and so on.

➠ Supervise art activities.

➠ Talk to and with children about topics of interest.

➠ Share their skills in special short-term projects.

➠ Judge classroom contests.

However, if individuals are going to participate on a regular basis in a child's reading program, with proper training and supervision they can become real partners in the learning process by serving as aides, tutors, or resource persons. Teachers who want to have volunteers participate on a regular basis must be willing to spend time nurturing, encouraging, and training these volunteers. Expecting too much too soon is probably the biggest mistake teachers can make in working with volunteers.

With training from the teacher, family members and friends can do the following:

➠ Provide remedial reading or reading enrichment work to children.

➠ Conduct small-group instruction on a regular basis.

➠ Lead "author's chair" or literary conversation groups.

The individual schedules, talents, and interests of family members and friends, along with the characteristics and needs of individual children and classrooms, should dictate the extent to which they can play active roles in their children's education in school.

Seven Steps to Creating a Literate Home Environment

Here are seven steps to consider in providing a literate home environment for children. These steps summarize points that were made earlier in the chapter.

1. Talk with your child regularly and try to answer his or her questions.

2. Listen to your child and elaborate on what he or she has said.

3. Read aloud to (with) your child every day. The *"lap method"* in which a young child sits in a family member or friend's lap is especially effective.

4. Praise your child when he or she has performed a reading activity well.

5. Be a reader yourself. Have family time for reading in the evening. Sustained silent reading can be used at this time. In this activity each family member reads self-selected material for a specific period of time such as *15 or 20 minutes*.

6. Write to or with your child as often as possible.

7. Limit television watching and emphasize watching educational shows such as *Sesame Street, Reading Rainbow*, and *Mister Roger's Neighborhood.*

What Can the Reading Teacher or Tutor Do to Help Family Members and Friends Participate in the Reading Program?

There are several activities that a reading teacher or tutor can provide to help family members or friends participate in any reading program.

Family Literacy Programs

The reading teacher or tutor can conduct family literacy programs. A good family literacy program contains the following elements:

➡ It must show respect for and understanding of the diversity of families.

➡ It always should build on the literacy behaviors already present in families.

➡ It should be cognizant and respectful of the home language of each child.

➡ It should never take a "fix the family" attitude.

➡ When family members, friends, or children attend a family literacy meeting, child care and refreshments always should be provided.

➡ It always should follow sound educational practices, such as developing letter–sound connections, the language-experience approach, reading games, and more.

➡ The program can be for family members alone, children alone, or family members and children together.

➡ It should improve interactions between family members and children.

➡ It should provide family members with practical ideas and ready-to-use materials to use at home.

➡ It should provide functional literacy learning activities such as community life programs, filling in job applications, using the library for pleasure and information, and so forth.

Present Reading Workshops for Family Members and Friends

Either the reading teacher or tutor (or both) can present practical reading workshops for family members or friends that tell them about the school reading program and how they can best support it.

A reading workshop for family members or friends can have one or more of the following elements:

➡ *Newsletters* that are sent home at the beginning of the year explaining the reading program. Subsequent newsletters can be sent periodically and can include suggestions that family members or friends can use to support the reading program, directions for constructing home-made reading games, lists of books for informational or recreational reading at home, description of instructional units that the teacher is planning and lists of materials that can be used at home to support them, and so forth. A sample newsletter is included in the next part of this chapter.

➡ Instructional packets that are made at school and then used at home. These packets can contain directions for making language-experience booklets, directions for constructing reading games, lists of reading materials of various types, and directions for constructing reading aids such as an "animal tachistoscope," among many others. The reading teacher or tutor can supervise the making of each of the reading games or reading aids, explaining how they can be used at home to support the child's reading program.

➡ Send checklists home that family members can use to assess family behaviors that may support a child's reading program. On the next page are several sample questions from such a checklist for preschool and early primary grades. The next section of this chapter contains several *reproducible checklists* at various reading levels that address family members and their role in their child's reading program.

➡ The reading program used in any classroom or special reading program must be thoroughly explained to family members and interested family friends. This should be done at the beginning of a school year or the tutoring sessions, and on a regular basis during the reading program. These explanations may be made on a whole-class, small-group, or an individual basis. To encourage family members or friends to attend such informal workshops, concrete motivation should be given such as refreshments, child care, transportation, and so forth.

Parent–Teacher Conferences

Parent–teacher conferences can be useful if the family member and reading teacher or tutor exchange information about the child and if the meeting is kept positive. Families or friends must be told exactly how to help the child in reading, and should be given easy-to-use activities and materials that take very little preparation time.

The teacher must stress that adults can do the following, especially with a child who has dyslexia or learning disabilities:

➡ Observe one area of the child's performance at a time and first emphasize that area of reading with which the child needs the most help.

➡ Observe the child's focus and concentration while reading and his or her areas of interest.

➡ Notice when the child gets tired of reading or learning reading skills. There is no point pushing the child beyond the point. It can do him or her harm.

➡ Notice how well the child relates to his or her classmates—*the social factor.*

➡ Observe the child's expressive (oral) and receptive (listening) skills.

➡ Notice what methods of reinforcement seem to be the most effective with the child—*concrete rewards* like a small present or something to eat *or praise* like, "I really like how you read that chapter without stopping for 15 minutes."

➡ Try to evaluate the child's reading strengths and weaknesses.

Recommended Books on Dyslexia or Severe Reading Disability

Here are the titles of some books that the reading teacher or tutor can recommend to individuals whose children have dyslexia, reading disabilities, or learning disabilities.

Anderson, W., Chitwood, S., & Hayden, D. (1997). *Negotiating the special education maze: A guide for parents and teachers.* Bethesda, MD: Woodbine House.

Flick, G. (1994). *Power parenting for children with ADD/ADHD: A practical parent's guide for managing difficult behaviors.* West Nyack, NY: The Center for Applied Research in Education.

Greene, L. (1998). *Finding help when your child is struggling in school: From kindergarten through junior high school.* NY: Golden Books.

Hall, S., & Moats, L. (1999). *Straight talk about reading; How parents can make a difference during the early years.* Lincolnwood, IL: NTC Publishing Group.

Rief, S. (1998). *The ADD/ADHD checklist: An easy reference for parents and teachers.* Paramus, NJ: Prentice Hall.

Shore, K. (1994). *The parents' public school handbook: How to make the most of your child's education, from kindergarten through middle school.* Columbus, OH: Fireside Books.

———. (1998). *Special kids problem solver: Ready-to-use interventions for helping all students with academic, behavioral, and physical problems.* West Nyack, NY: The Center for Applied Research in Education.

Stevens, S. (1996). *The LD child and the ADHD child: Ways parents and professionals can help.* Winston-Salem, NC: John F. Blain Publisher.

Stowe, C. (2000). *How to reach & teach students with dyslexia.* West Nyack, NY: The Center for Applied Research in Education.

Teacher-Made Brochure

Either a teacher or an entire elementary school can construct a brochure to give to family members about how to support their child's reading program. The purpose of the brochure is to give family members and friends a brief overview of what their children are learning in reading and how to help them at home. *Such a brochure always should be short, colorful, well illustrated, and written in easy-to-understand language that is free of educational jargon.*

Such a brochure can contain the following:

➡ *Introduction*—State goals for children's work in reading and expectations of what will be accomplished.

➡ *Role of family members and friends*—Stress the importance of the *home–school connection*.

➥ *Steps family members and friends can take*—Briefly but clearly suggest reading activities in which family members or friends and children can participate. Suggest routines (such as for doing homework) that should be established.

➥ *Materials*—Provide lists of the kinds of books and materials that family members or friends should try to provide in the home for the child.

➥ *Other readings*—Either provide or suggest other sources of information about the home–school connection and reading and writing growth.

How to Establish a Home–School Library Exchange

The following materials are needed for such an exchange:

➥ Books to be distributed to students (at least 100 in various genres)

➥ Plastic bags

➥ Record-keeping forms

Here are the procedures that can be used in a home–school exchange:

➥ Make a list of all the books that are to be exchanged and stamp all the books with the name of the class.

➥ Make sign-out cards for all the books. Place the sign-out cards in pockets in the books.

➥ Send a letter home informing family members that books will be sent home and ask them to read the books aloud to their child or supervise their child's own reading. They then should fill out a very brief response form. Let family members know how long the books may be kept and how often students will be bringing books home.

➥ Tell children about the procedures for taking books home, reading the books at home, sharing them with their family, and then bringing them back.

➥ Construct home report forms with space for students' names, book titles, dates read, and brief notes from family members or friends about the experience, such as *"Did your child enjoy the book? What was his or her favorite part of the book? How did he or she react to the book? How well did the child read the book on his or her own?"*

➥ Allow enough time on the first book distribution day for children to select a book and complete the sign-out card (with help if necessary). Place each book and a home report form in a plastic bag to protect the book.

➥ Tell the children the return date for the book—one day, several days, or a week.

➥ On a specified day shortly after the book was sent home and read, have children share their experiences about reading the book. Encourage children to talk about the books that they have read and make recommendations to their classmates.

➡ Keep good records on books as they are returned and on the home report sheets. Keep track of students' responses to the book as a guide for choosing books to add to the classroom library.

➡ After a specified period of time, such as a month of successful home–school library exchange, give students a classroom party as a reward for their reading and taking care of the books.

Homework Help Hot Line

A reading teacher or an elementary school can set up an after-school hot line for family members or friends to call for help with their children's homework. If teachers are going to staff the hot line, they should receive compensation for doing so.

A less expensive alternative might be to have paid teacher's aides or volunteers who are former educators, such as retired teachers, staff the hot line on a rotating basis. In any case, each person who staffs the hot line will have to coordinate his or her help with the child's teacher to be sure that appropriate homework help is given.

Intergenerational Literacy Initiatives

Intergenerational literacy initiatives are designed to improve the literacy development of both adults and children. Such programs view family members and children as co-learners and are characterized by systematic instruction for both adults and children. Instruction may take place when family members and children work in either collaborative or parallel settings. The instruction with adults is intended to improve their reading skills and at the same time teach them how to work with their children in reading.

As one example, *Parents and Children Together* is a nationwide intergenerational literacy program established by the National Council for Family Literacy (NCFL) in Louisville, Kentucky. Caregivers who do not have a high school diploma and their three- and four-year-old children attend school together from three to five days a week. An early childhood program is provided for the children while the family members attend an adult education program to learn reading, math, and parenting skills.

In the adult education part of the program, family members work on improving their reading and math skills and are taught to set goals and work with other parents in the program. "Parent Time" is a part of the program during which the adults discuss a variety of topics ranging from discipline to self-esteem. The last part of the program is "Parent and Child Together" time. During this hour families play together, with the activities being led by the children. Family members discover that they can learn both with and from their children. Early childhood teaching strategies are taught to family members.

REPRODUCIBLES THAT CAN BE USED TO SUPPORT THE HOME–SCHOOL CONNECTION

The next part of this chapter contains several reproducibles that can be used to support the home–school connection. You are encouraged to duplicate and use any of them in their present form or modify them in any way you wish.

CHECKLIST FOR FAMILY
MEMBERS OF YOUNG CHILDREN

	Yes	Not so Often as I Should
1. I read aloud to my child every day.	❏	❏
2. I listen to my child and try to answer his or her questions.	❏	❏
3. I explain things to my child as much as I can.	❏	❏
4. I watch special TV shows with my child.	❏	❏
5. My child and I discuss special TV shows.	❏	❏
6. I limit the amount of time that my child watches television.	❏	❏
7. I spend quality time with my child.	❏	❏
8. I ask my child to read simple picture books to me.	❏	❏
9. I ask my child appropriate questions about his or her reading.	❏	❏
10. I praise my child when he or she has earned it.	❏	❏
11. I am patient with my child.	❏	❏
12. I take my child to interesting places and talk with my child about what he or she has seen.	❏	❏
13. I do not pressure my child about his or her reading.	❏	❏
14. I read and write in the presence of my child.	❏	❏
15. I try to be a good role model in reading activities with my child.	❏	❏

READING CHECKLIST FOR
FAMILY MEMBERS AND FRIENDS
Preschool Children

	YES	SOMETIMES	NO
1. I read children's books to my child at least once a day.	❑	❑	❑
2. Before reading a book to my child, I ask him or her to predict its content from the title.	❑	❑	❑
3. I encourage my child's active participation in the book while I am reading it to him or her.	❑	❑	❑
4. I read predictable books with repeated words and phrases to my child, and encourage him or her to read along with me.	❑	❑	❑
5. If my child likes it, I read his or her favorite books over and over again.	❑	❑	❑
6. I encourage my child to act out favorite books that he or she has heard.	❑	❑	❑
7. My child owns some of his or her own books.	❑	❑	❑
8. I take my child to the library and help him or her select books to read.	❑	❑	❑
9. My child has his or her own library card.	❑	❑	❑
10. I show my child that I value reading by reading myself for information and pleasure.	❑	❑	❑
11. I answer my child's questions about letters, words, and numbers.	❑	❑	❑
12. My child can identify the capital and lower-case letter names.	❑	❑	❑
13. My child can identify a few simple words by sight such as *STOP*, *cat*, *dog*, *mother*, or *father*.	❑	❑	❑
14. I encourage my child to rhyme words including non-sense words, such as those found in Dr. Seuss books.	❑	❑	❑
15. I try to teach my child *concepts about print* such as:	❑	❑	❑

➥ the difference between words and pictures
➥ the difference between letters and words
➥ reading from top to bottom and left to right
➥ word boundaries (the white spaces between words)

READING CHECKLIST FOR
FAMILY MEMBERS AND FRIENDS *(Cont'd)*
Preschool Children

	YES	SOMETIMES	NO
16. I limit the amount of television that my child watches.	❏	❏	❏
17. I encourage my child to watch educational television shows such as *Sesame Street, Mister Roger's Neighborhood*, animal or nature shows, and similar programs.	❏	❏	❏
18. I provide writing materials in the home for my child, such as pencils, markers, chalk, crayons, and unlined paper.	❏	❏	❏
19. There is a chalkboard in the home for my child to use.	❏	❏	❏
20. I take my child to interesting places, such as a zoo, wildlife preserve, museum, planetarium, grain farm, dairy farm, county fair, or dog show.	❏	❏	❏
21. Before and after a trip outside the home, I encourage conversation about it.	❏	❏	❏
22. I have the child dictate language-experience stories about various activities. Then I write them, and the child and I read them aloud together. We select important sight words to put in a *word bank*.	❏	❏	❏
23. I use standard English and interesting vocabulary while talking with my child.	❏	❏	❏
24. I answer my child's questions as completely as I can.	❏	❏	❏
25. I tell my child interesting stories about special occasions in my own childhood.	❏	❏	❏
26. I provide "sorting activities" such as sorting socks on laundry day.	❏	❏	❏
27. I listen to what my child says and try to spend quality educational time with him or her.	❏	❏	❏
28. I encourage my child to do all kinds of writing such as *scribbling, letter strings*, and *invented spelling*.	❏	❏	❏
29. I help my child to print the various capital and lower-case letter names.	❏	❏	❏

READING CHECKLIST FOR
FAMILY MEMBERS AND FRIENDS *(Cont'd)*
Preschool Children

	YES	SOMETIMES	NO
30. I have taught my child to print his or her own first name correctly.	❏	❏	❏
31. I encourage my child to "make words" with magnetic letters.	❏	❏	❏
32. I encourage my child to write for real purposes such as grocery lists, birthday cards, and thank-you notes.	❏	❏	❏
33. I provide manipulative materials in the home for my child such as drawing paper, construction paper, markers, crayons, colored pencils, and glue.	❏	❏	❏
34. My child and I cook and bake using simple recipes with rebuses (pictures).	❏	❏	❏

NOTES:

_____

_____

_____

_____

_____

_____

_____

_____

_____

_____

_____

_____

_____

READING CHECKLIST FOR FAMILY MEMBERS AND FRIENDS
Primary-Grade Children (K–3)

	YES	SOMETIMES	NO
1. I encourage my child to read silently at home for information or pleasure on a regular, if not daily, basis.	❏	❏	❏
2. I have my child read narrative (story) or informational (factual) books aloud to me on a regular basis.	❏	❏	❏
3. I read materials aloud to my child that are too difficult for him or her to read independently, but are interesting.	❏	❏	❏
4. When my child meets a word that he or she can't identify while reading, I encourage him or her to first guess its meaning from the rest of the sentence and then sound it out.	❏	❏	❏
5. My child understands and can apply letter–sound relationships (phonics) to identify unknown words.	❏	❏	❏
6. My child seems to understand what he or she reads.	❏	❏	❏
7. I encourage my child to creatively dramatize/act out books and stories that he or she has read.	❏	❏	❏
8. My child has a place to store his or her own books.	❏	❏	❏
9. My child has "space" at home where he or she can read silently.	❏	❏	❏
10. My child sees me reading for pleasure and information (modeling).	❏	❏	❏
11. Our family has a quiet time in the evening or on weekends in which each of us reads our own material.	❏	❏	❏
12. I encourage my child to "play school" with siblings or other children.	❏	❏	❏
13. My child owns some of his or her own books.	❏	❏	❏
14. My child has a library card and goes to the library regularly and checks out books to read at home.	❏	❏	❏

READING CHECKLIST FOR
FAMILY MEMBERS AND FRIENDS *(Cont'd)*
Primary-Grade Children (K–3)

	YES	SOMETIMES	NO
15. My child plays reading games at home such as Sight Word Bingo, Phonics Bingo, or Memory either with me or other children.	❑	❑	❑
16. My child plays reading-related games on the computer.	❑	❑	❑
17. My child has writing materials at home such as pencils, markers, and lined paper.	❑	❑	❑
18. My child has a chalkboard at home.	❑	❑	❑
19. My child writes for practical purposes such as birthday cards, thank-you notes, grocery lists, or pen pal letters.	❑	❑	❑
20. I encourage my child to use either invented spelling or traditional spelling when writing.	❑	❑	❑
21. I encourage my child to write creative prose or poetry if he or she expresses an interest in this.	❑	❑	❑
22. My child can write and then read a story about a personal experience, such as a family trip.	❑	❑	❑
23. My child can use a word-processing program on our home computer.	❑	❑	❑
24. Our family goes on educational outings to such places as the zoo, museum, planetarium, wildlife preserve, and so forth.	❑	❑	❑
25. I encourage my child to be persistent, responsible, and independent in doing his or her chores at home.	❑	❑	❑
26. I help my child with his or her homework if it is necessary, but I make sure he or she takes responsibility for doing it.	❑	❑	❑
27. I try to spend quality educational time with my child.	❑	❑	❑
28. I try to answer my child's questions honestly and completely.	❑	❑	❑

READING CHECKLIST FOR
FAMILY MEMBERS AND FRIENDS *(Cont'd)*
Primary-Grade Children (K–3)

	YES	SOMETIMES	NO
29. I monitor my child's television viewing and encourage him or her to watch educational programs.	❏	❏	❏
30. I attend parent–teacher conferences and other school events, such as open houses and parent–teacher association meetings.	❏	❏	❏
31. I try to support my child's teacher and school if possible.	❏	❏	❏
32. I am an unpaid or paid volunteer at my child's school.	❏	❏	❏
33. I volunteer to share my expertise with my child's class, such as culture, work experiences, travel, hobbies, and so forth.	❏	❏	❏
34. I serve on school committees if I am qualified and given the opportunity.	❏	❏	❏

NOTES:

_____

_____

_____

_____

_____

_____

_____

_____

_____

_____

READING CHECKLIST FOR FAMILY MEMBERS AND FRIENDS
Intermediate-Grade Students (4–6)

	YES	SOMETIMES	NO
1. I encourage my child to read silently at home for information or pleasure on a regular, if not daily, basis.	❏	❏	❏
2. I read materials aloud to my child that are too difficult for him or her to read independently, but are interesting.	❏	❏	❏
3. When my child meets a word he or she can't identify while reading, I encourage him or her to first guess its meaning from the sentence and then divide it into syllables (parts of a word) and sound it out.	❏	❏	❏
4. My child understands and can apply word structure and letter–sound relationships (phonics) to identify unknown words that cannot be identified by context.	❏	❏	❏
5. My child seems to understand the narrative (story) and informational (factual) books that he or she reads.	❏	❏	❏
6. I encourage my child to share his or her reading with me.	❏	❏	❏
7. My child has a place to store his or her own books.	❏	❏	❏
8. My child has "space" where he or she can read or do homework without interruptions.	❏	❏	❏
9. My child is able to understand and study such content reading as social studies and science.	❏	❏	❏
10. I encourage my child to work collaboratively with other students in content reading assignments.	❏	❏	❏
11. My child sees me reading for pleasure and information.	❏	❏	❏
12. Our family has a quiet time in the evening or on weekends in which each of us reads our own material.	❏	❏	❏
13. My child owns some of his or her own books.	❏	❏	❏

READING CHECKLIST FOR
FAMILY MEMBERS AND FRIENDS *(Cont'd)*
Intermediate-Grade Students (4–6)

	YES	SOMETIMES	NO
14. My child has a library card and goes to the library regularly and checks out books to read at home.	❏	❏	❏
15. My child uses the Internet to research topics of interest both for school assignments and for personal use.	❏	❏	❏
16. My child reads relevant educational software on the computer.	❏	❏	❏
17. My child has writing materials at home such as pencils, ball-point pens, and lined (notebook) paper.	❏	❏	❏
18. I encourage my child to use correct spelling at home and at school.	❏	❏	❏
19. My child writes creative prose and poetry.	❏	❏	❏
20. My child does practical writing at home, such as expository or persuasive compositions.	❏	❏	❏
21. My child can use a word-processing program on the computer.	❏	❏	❏
22. Our family goes on educational outings to such places as the zoo, museum, planetarium, wildlife preserve, and so forth.	❏	❏	❏
23. I encourage my child to be independent and responsible.	❏	❏	❏
24. I try to spend quality educational time with my child.	❏	❏	❏
25. I try to answer my child's questions honestly and completely.	❏	❏	❏
26. I monitor my child's homework, helping him or her if necessary, but requiring that he or she is responsible for completing it.	❏	❏	❏
27. I encourage my child to do as well as possible in school, and I monitor his or her school performance.	❏	❏	❏

READING CHECKLIST FOR
FAMILY MEMBERS AND FRIENDS *(Cont'd)*
Intermediate-Grade Students (4–6)

	YES	SOMETIMES	NO
28. I attend parent–teacher conferences and other school events such as open houses and parent–teacher association meetings.	❑	❑	❑
29. I try to support my child's teacher and school if possible.	❑	❑	❑
30. I am an unpaid or paid volunteer at my child's school.	❑	❑	❑
31. I volunteer to share my expertise with my child's class, such as culture, work experiences, travel, hobbies, special interests, and so forth.	❑	❑	❑
32. I serve on school committees if I am qualified and given the opportunity.	❑	❑	❑
33. I monitor my child's television watching.	❑	❑	❑
34. I monitor my child's use of the Internet.	❑	❑	❑

NOTES:

SAMPLE NEWSLETTER FOR
FAMILY MEMBERS AND FRIENDS

Dear family and friends,

Many of the family members and friends of my students have asked me for suggestions about *how to support the school reading program at home.*

Although there are many good ways of doing this, I have found the following to be especially helpful. You are encouraged to adapt these suggestions to best meet the needs and interests of your own children.

Supporting the School Reading Program at Home

1. Encourage your child to read silently at home for information or pleasure on a regular basis.

2. Read materials aloud to your child that are too difficult for him or her to read independently, but are interesting.

3. When your child meets a word that he or she can't easily identify while reading, encourage him or her to first guess its meaning from the rest of the sentence and then break it apart and sound it out.

4. Emphasize that the child should try to understand what he or she is reading.

5. Purchase as many books as you can for your child's home library. Many of these can be inexpensive paperback books.

6. Provide a place at home for your child to store his or her books.

7. Provide a place at home in which your child has his or her own "space" where reading and studying can be done without interruptions.

8. Read for pleasure and information yourself so that your child has a good reading model.

9. Have a quiet time in the evening or on weekends in which each family member reads his or her own self-selected material.

10. Encourage your child to get a library card, and go to the library regularly and check out books to read at home.

11. Have your child share his or her reading at home with you.

12. Encourage your child to play reading games at home.

13. Provide writing materials in the home such as pencils, markers, and lined and unlined paper.

14. Encourage your child to write for practical purposes, such as grocery lists or thank-you notes, using the form of writing of which he or she is capable—scribbling, letter strings, invented spelling, or conventional spelling.

15. Encourage your child to write creative prose or poetry using the form of writing of which he or she is capable—scribbling, letter strings, invented spelling, or conventional spelling.

16. If a home computer is available, encourage the use of a word processing program.

17. Take your child on educational outings to such places as a museum, planetarium, wildlife preserve, or an exhibit.

18. Help your child with his or her homework if it is necessary, but be sure he or she takes responsibility for it. Do not complete homework for your child.

19. Monitor your child's television viewing and use of the Internet.

20. Monitor your child's school performance, providing positive feedback when it is earned and support when it is needed.

21. Encourage your child to be persistent, responsible, and independent while doing jobs at home.

22. Try to spend as much quality educational time as possible with your child.

23. Attend parent–teacher conferences and school events such as open houses and parent–teacher association meetings.

24. Try to support the child's teacher and school even if you don't completely agree with what is happening. However, express any real concerns first to the child's teacher and later to the school administration so that concerns can be addressed.

25. If there is an opportunity, volunteer at the child's school.

26. Volunteer to share your expertise with your child's class. This can be about your culture, unique experiences, travel, hobbies, or special interests.

27. Serve on school committees if you are qualified, have the time, and are interested.

Thank you very much for supporting your child's reading program! I know your support will benefit your child very much.

Sincerely yours,

READING GAMES FOR PRIMARY-GRADE CHILDREN

Here are four games that family members and friends can use to review sight words and phonic skills that are taught at the primary grades.

Memory

TO CONSTRUCT THE GAME

Make target sight words out of posterboard. Make two sets of identical word cards. Then place the cards face down on a flat surface such as a table or desk.

TO PLAY THE GAME

Shuffle the two sets of cards and place them separately on the table or large desk. Then have a player turn up a card on one set and try to find the card that matches it in the other set. When he or she has made a match, have the child pronounce the word and, if correct, keep the card. Then the other player has a turn. The winner is the player who has made more matches and pronounced the words correctly.

Fishing for Sight Words

TO CONSTRUCT THE GAME

Print the target sight words with a dark marker on individual fish about 1" × 2". (See the fish pattern below.) Attach a paper clip to the head of each fish. Construct a "fishing pole" by using a ruler or stick with a string attached to it. Tie a small magnet to the end of the string.

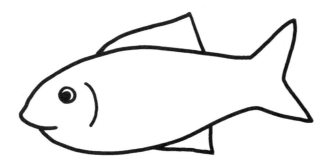

TO PLAY THE GAME

Place all of the "fish" containing the sight words into a container such as a decorated shoe box or a fish bowl without water. Then have the child fish for each sight word using the fishing pole. As the child is able to "land" a fish, he or she must identify the sight word. If the child can do so, he or she keeps the fish. If the child cannot identify the sight word written on the fish, he or she must "throw" it back into the container. If you wish, two or more children can take turns fishing for sight words, and the child who has caught the most fish after a specified time period is the winner.

Phonic Bingo

TO CONSTRUCT THE GAME

Make cards that look like Bingo cards out of cardboard. (See the illustration.) Print initial consonants (*f*, *s*, *b*, etc.), consonant blends (*bl*, *dr*, *sp*, etc.), and consonant digraphs (*ch*, *sh*, *th*, etc.) on the cards in random order. Have children make tokens out of small squares of colored construction paper or any other appropriate materials.

s	f	ch	br
g	sl	th	v
d	dr	w	tr
r	h	j	sh

TO PLAY THE GAME

Pronounce a word beginning with one of the consonants, consonant blends, or consonant digraphs. Tell the children to look at their cards for the letter or letter combination that represents that word's initial sound. Tell those children who have a word beginning with that letter or letter combination to cover it up with a token of some kind. Continue to pronounce words until one child has covered his or her entire card. The first child who does this is the winner, or the game may continue until all the cards are covered if you do not want one child to be declared the only winner.

Going to the Grocery Store

TO CONSTRUCT THE GAME

You need five large shopping bags labeled *a, e, i, o,* and *u* and many empty containers (boxes, cartons, or cans) of food whose names include the target vowel sounds.

TO PLAY THE GAME

Have the children playing this game sort the food items into the correct shopping bag. Tell them whether they are to listen for and then sort by long vowel sounds (*key words are* **ate, each, ice, oat, use**) or short vowel sounds (*key words are* **apple, egg, igloo, ostrich, umbrella**). Here are some suggested foods that can be used for this game.

Long Vowels

tomatoes	pie	beans	grapes
peaches	raisins	cheese	cake
Coke®	rice	prunes	ice cream
tomato juice	grape juice	potato	tea

Short Vowels

catsup	apple	jam	eggs
fish	pickles	olives	ham
chips	muffins	nuts	milk
chicken	pumpkin	salad	figs

FOR ADDITIONAL READING

Morrow, L. (1997). *Literacy development in the early years* (pp. 52-85). Needham Heights, MA: Allyn & Bacon.

Rasinski, T. (Ed.). (1995). *Parents and teachers: Helping children learn to read and write.* Fort Worth, TX: Harcourt Brace College.

Rubin, D. (1991). *Diagnosis & correction in reading instruction* (pp. 429-453). Needham Heights, MA: Allyn & Bacon.

Salinger, T. (1996). *Literacy for young children* (pp. 67-86). Columbus, OH: Merrill/Prentice Hall.

Stowe, C. (2000). *How to reach & teach students with dyslexia* (pp. 301-310). West Nyack, NY: The Center for Applied Research in Education.

United States Department of Education. Office of Educational Research and Improvement. (1998). *Helping your child learn to read.* Washington, DC: http://www.interlog.com/~klima/ed/helpr.html

WORKS CITED IN CHAPTER 8

Rubin, D. (1991). *Diagnosis & correction in reading instruction* (p. 436). Needham Heights, MA: Allyn & Bacon.

USA Research. (1984). *A nation at risk: The full account.* Washington, DC: U.S.A. Research Incorporated.

INDEX

Page numbers appearing in italics refer to tables and figures.